Modality

OXFORD **PHILOSOPHICAL** CONCEPTS

OXFORD PHILOSOPHICAL CONCEPTS

Christia Mercer, Columbia University
Series Editor

PUBLISHED IN THE OXFORD PHILOSOPHICAL CONCEPTS SERIES

Efficient Causation
Edited by Tad Schmaltz

Sympathy
Edited by Eric Schliesser

The Faculties
Edited by Dominik Perler

Memory
Edited by Dmitri Nikulin

Moral Motivation
Edited by Iakovos Vasiliou

Eternity
Edited by Yitzhak Y. Melamed

Self-Knowledge
Edited by Ursula Renz

Embodiment
Edited by Justin E. H. Smith

Dignity
Edited by Remy Debes

Animals
Edited by G. Fay Edwards and Peter Adamson

Pleasure
Edited by Lisa Shapiro

Health
Edited by Peter Adamson

Evil
Edited by Andrew Chignell

Persons
Edited by Antonia LoLordo

Space
Edited by Andrew Janiak

Teleology
Edited by Jeffrey K. McDonough

The World Soul
Edited by James Wilberding

Powers
Edited by Julia Jorati

The Self
Edited by Patricia Kitcher

Human
Edited by Karolina Hubner

Love
Edited by Ryan Hanley

Modality
Edited by Yitzhak Y. Melamed and Samuel Newlands

FORTHCOMING IN THE OXFORD PHILOSOPHICAL CONCEPTS SERIES

The Principle of Sufficient Reason
Edited by Fatema Amijee and Michael Della Rocca

{ OXFORD PHILOSOPHICAL CONCEPTS }

Modality

A HISTORY

Edited by Yitzhak Y. Melamed and Samuel Newlands

OXFORD
UNIVERSITY PRESS

Oxford University Press is a department of the University of Oxford. It furthers the University's objective of excellence in research, scholarship, and education by publishing worldwide. Oxford is a registered trade mark of Oxford University Press in the UK and certain other countries.

Published in the United States of America by Oxford University Press
198 Madison Avenue, New York, NY 10016, United States of America.

© Oxford University Press 2024

All rights reserved. No part of this publication may be reproduced, stored in a retrieval system, or transmitted, in any form or by any means, without the prior permission in writing of Oxford University Press, or as expressly permitted by law, by license, or under terms agreed with the appropriate reproduction rights organization. Inquiries concerning reproduction outside the scope of the above should be sent to the Rights Department, Oxford University Press, at the address above.

You must not circulate this work in any other form
and you must impose this same condition on any acquirer.

Library of Congress Cataloging-in-Publication Data
Names: Melamed, Yitzhak, Y. 1968– editor. | Newlands, Samuel, editor.
Title: Modality : a history / edited by Yitzhak Y. Melamed and Samuel Newlands.
Other titles: Modality (Oxford University Press)
Description: New York, NY : Oxford University Press, [2024] |
Series: Oxford philosophical concepts |
Includes bibliographical references and index.
Identifiers: LCCN 2023043233 (print) | LCCN 2023043234 (ebook) |
ISBN 9780190089863 (paperback) | ISBN 9780190089856 (hardback) |
ISBN 9780190089887 (epub)
Subjects: LCSH: Modality (Theory of knowledge)—History.
Classification: LCC BD218.5.M63 2024 (print) | LCC BD218.5 (ebook) |
DDC 121—dc23/eng/20231031
LC record available at https://lccn.loc.gov/2023043233
LC ebook record available at https://lccn.loc.gov/2023043234

DOI: 10.1093/oso/9780190089856.001.0001

Paperback printed by Marquis Book Printing, Canada
Hardback printed by Bridgeport National Bindery, Inc., United States of America

In memory of Simo Knuuttila

Contents

SERIES EDITOR'S FOREWORD ix

ACKNOWLEDGMENTS xi

LIST OF CONTRIBUTORS xiii

INTRODUCTION xvii
YITZHAK Y. MELAMED AND SAMUEL NEWLANDS

1 Aristotle on Modality 1
   MARKO MALINK

2 Modality in Medieval Latin Philosophy 31
   SIMO KNUUTTILA

Reflection: Necessity in the Cosmology of Tommaso Campanella 55
   EMANUELE COSTA

3 Modality and Essence in Early Modern Philosophy: Descartes, Malebranche, and Locke 61
   ANAT SCHECHTMAN

4 Crescas and Spinoza on Modality 85
   YITZHAK Y. MELAMED

5   Leibniz on Modality   118
SAMUEL NEWLANDS

Reflection: The Infinity of Worlds in Modern Kabbalah   144
JONATHAN GARB

6   Hume on Modal Discourse   148
THOMAS HOLDEN

7   Modality in Kant and Hegel   171
NICHOLAS F. STANG

Reflection: Music and Modality   207
DOMENICA G. ROMAGNI

8   Modality in 20th-Century Philosophy   221
KRIS MCDANIEL

Reflection: Vacuism and the Strangeness of Impossibility   252
ROHAN FRENCH

9   Modality and Essence in Contemporary Metaphysics   263
KATHRIN KOSLICKI

Reflection: Clarice Lispector—Writing of Necessity   294
PAULA MARCHESINI

BIBLIOGRAPHY 303

INDEX 327

Series Editor's Foreword

Oxford Philosophical Concepts (OPC) offers an innovative approach to philosophy's past and its relation to other disciplines. As a series, it is unique in exploring the transformations of central philosophical concepts from their ancient sources to their modern use.

OPC has several goals: to make it easier for historians to contextualize key concepts in the history of philosophy, to render that history accessible to a wide audience, and to enliven contemporary discussions by displaying the rich and varied sources of philosophical concepts still in use today. The means to these goals are simple enough: eminent scholars come together to rethink a central concept in philosophy's past. The point of this rethinking is not to offer a broad overview, but to identify problems the concept was originally supposed to solve and investigate how approaches to them shifted over time, sometimes radically. Recent scholarship has made evident the benefits of reexamining the standard narratives about western philosophy. OPC's editors look beyond the canon and explore their concepts over a wide philosophical landscape. Each volume traces a notion from its inception as a solution to specific problems through its historical transformations to its modern use, all the while acknowledging its historical context. Each OPC volume is a history of its concept in that it tells a story about changing solutions to its well-defined problem. Many editors have found it appropriate to include long-ignored writings drawn from the

Islamic and Jewish traditions and the philosophical contributions of women. Volumes also explore ideas drawn from Buddhist, Chinese, Indian, and other philosophical cultures when doing so adds an especially helpful new perspective. By combining scholarly innovation with focused and astute analysis, OPC encourages a deeper understanding of our philosophical past and present.

One of the most innovative features of OPC is its recognition that philosophy bears a rich relation to art, music, literature, religion, science, and other cultural practices. The series speaks to the need for informed interdisciplinary exchanges. Its editors assume that the most difficult and profound philosophical ideas can be made comprehensible to a large audience and that materials not strictly philosophical often bear a significant relevance to philosophy. To this end, each OPC volume includes Reflections. These are short stand-alone essays written by specialists in art, music, literature, theology, science, or cultural studies that *reflect on* the concept from their own disciplinary perspectives. The goal of these essays is to enliven, enrich, and exemplify the volume's concept and reconsider the boundary between philosophical and extraphilosophical materials. OPC's Reflections display the benefits of using philosophical concepts and distinctions in areas that are not strictly philosophical, and encourage philosophers to move beyond the borders of their discipline as presently conceived.

The volumes of OPC arrive at an auspicious moment. Many philosophers are keen to invigorate the discipline. OPC aims to provoke philosophical imaginations by uncovering the brilliant twists and unforeseen turns of philosophy's past.

Christia Mercer
Gustave M. Berne Professor of Philosophy
Columbia University in the City of New York

Acknowledgments

We would like to thank the copyeditor, Judith Hoover, and the indexer, Jonas Zhaojun Zhai for their outstanding work on this volume. Lucy Randall, Peter Ohlin, and Christia Mercer provided very valuable advice in the course of preparing the volume.

Contributors

EMANUELE COSTA is an assistant professor of philosophy at Vanderbilt University. He focuses on the history of philosophy and metaphysics, especially on the Early Modern period and on figures such as Spinoza, Elizabeth of Bohemia, Leibniz, and Anne Conway. In metaphysics, he is particularly interested in mereology and theory of relations.

ROHAN FRENCH is an associate professor of philosophy at the University of California, Davis. He works primarily on philosophical and technical issues in modal and substructural logics.

JONATHAN GARB is the Gershom Scholem Professor of Kabbalah in the Department of Jewish Thought at the Hebrew University of Jerusalem. In 2014, he received the Israel Academy of Sciences and Humanities' Gershom Scholem Prize for Kabbalah Research. His latest book is *A History of Kabbalah: From the Early Modern Period to the Present Day* (Cambridge University Press, 2020).

THOMAS HOLDEN is a professor at the University of California, Santa Barbara. He is the author of *The Architecture of Matter: Galileo to Kant* (Oxford University Press, 2004), *Spectres of False Divinity: Hume's Moral Atheism* (Oxford University Press, 2010), and *Hobbes's Philosophy of Religion* (Oxford University Press, 2023). He has also published papers on the metaphysics of Hobbes, Bayle, Berkeley, Hume, and Shelley.

SIMO KNUUTTILA was professor of theological ethics and the philosophy of religion at the University of Helsinki. His books include *Modalities in Medieval*

Philosophy (Routledge, 1993) and *Emotions in Ancient and Medieval Philosophy* (Oxford University Press, 2004), and he published widely on many topics in ancient, medieval, and modern philosophy.

KATHRIN KOSLICKI is a professor of theoretical philosophy at the University of Neuchâtel. Koslicki's research interests in philosophy lie mainly in metaphysics, the philosophy of language, and ancient Greek philosophy, particularly Aristotle. In her two books (*The Structure of Objects*, Oxford University Press, 2008; *Form, Matter, Substance*, Oxford University Press, 2018), she defends a neo-Aristotelian analysis of concrete particular objects as compounds of matter (*hulē*) and form (*morphē*).

MARKO MALINK is Professor of Philosophy and Classics at New York University University. He is the author of *Aristotle's Modal Syllogistic* (Harvard University Press, 2013), and various articles on Aristotle's logic and metaphysics as well as on the history of logic.

PAULA MARCHESINI is a Brazilian American philosopher and musical artist and currently a postdoctoral fellow at Johns Hopkins University. Her work focuses on the concepts of time and eternity and how they inspire human creation in western philosophy, cosmology, and art.

KRIS MCDANIEL is the William J. and Dorothy K. O'Neill Professor of Philosophy at the University of Notre Dame. He is the author of *The Fragmentation of Being* and *This Is Metaphysics*, and has published on a variety of topics in metaphysics and the history of philosophy.

YITZHAK Y. MELAMED is the Charlotte Bloomberg Professor of Philosophy at Johns Hopkins University. He works on Early Modern philosophy, German Idealism, medieval philosophy, and some issues in contemporary metaphysics (time, mereology, and trope theory), and is the author of *Spinoza's Metaphysics: Substance and Thought* (Oxford University Press, 2013), and *Spinoza's Labyrinths* (Oxford University Press, forthcoming). Currently, he is completing a book on Spinoza and German Idealism, and an intellectual biography of Spinoza.

SAMUEL NEWLANDS is Carl E. Koch Professor of Philosophy at the University of Notre Dame. He is the author of *Reconceiving Spinoza* (Oxford University Press, 2018) and dozens of articles in early modern studies. He is the co-editor of *Metaphysics and the Good* (Oxford University Press, 2009) and *New Essays on Leibniz's Theodicy* (Oxford University Press, 2014).

DOMENICA G. ROMAGNI is an assistant professor at Colorado State University. She specializes in Early Modern philosophy, philosophy of music, and history and philosophy of science. She received her Ph.D. from Princeton University, a BA with concentration in philosophy from Johns Hopkins University, and a BM in cello performance from the Peabody Conservatory.

ANAT SCHECHTMAN is an associate professor of philosophy at the University of Texas at Austin. She has written on Descartes, Spinoza, Leibniz, and Locke, publishing in *Mind*, *Philosophical Review*, *Journal of the History of Philosophy*, and elsewhere. She is currently writing a monograph about Early Modern notions of infinity.

NICHOLAS F. STANG is an associate professor of philosophy and Canada Research Chair (Tier II) in metaphysics and its history at the University of Toronto. He is the author of *Kant's Modal Metaphysics* (Oxford University Press, 2016) and the co-editor (with Karl Schafer) of *The Sensible and Intelligible Worlds: New Essays on Kant's Metaphysics and Epistemology* (Oxford University Press, 2022). His work focuses on the intersection of German Idealism and analytic philosophy, primarily in the areas of logic, metaphysics, and epistemology.

Introduction

Yitzhak Y. Melamed and Samuel Newlands

1. Modality

Usually, hippos don't fly. But *can* they fly, or *must* they stay strolling on earth? Numbers don't bark, nor *can* they bark. God *cannot* create a stone he *cannot* lift. We *cannot* change the past, but is our future *necessary*?—Our language is saturated with modal verbs and notions, and we can hardly think without employing the notions of necessity and possibility. But what *are* necessity and possibility? What do we really mean when we pronounce these magical words: 'possible,' 'necessary,' 'necessarily,' 'impossible,' 'can,' 'must,' and their like?

Contemporary philosophers are quite familiar with the claim that a proposition is necessarily true just in case it is true in all *possible* worlds, and possibly true just in case it is true in at least one *possible* world. But even so, we cannot explain *possibility* itself solely by appealing to *possible* worlds, on a pain of obvious circularity. Think for a moment of a highly intelligent creature who has no modal notions whatsoever:

what would she learn if you told her that a proposition is possibly true just in case it is true in some possible world?

Another familiar mantra is that conceivability is a guide to possibility, but it would be bizarre to try to *explain* possibility through conceivability. Think again about our highly intelligent creature who is not familiar with modal terms: what would she learn if we told her that to be possible is to be conceiv-*able*? This would be like someone explaining what is it to be *hroch* by saying that 'to be *hroch* is to be conceiv-*ahroch*.')[1]

Providing a non-circular explanation of the notions of possibility and necessity is a non-trivial task, and we might hope that philosophy would be of help here. Well, perhaps. The nine chapters comprising this book attempt to unpack the history of such modal concepts, as they have developed over the last two and a half millennia of western philosophy. Philosophical reflections on modality has been quite vigorous and prolific over most periods of this history, and with this volume, we invite you to join us in exploring some of humanity's most basic and ubiquitous concepts.

Being fully aware of the challenge and difficulty of the task, we devised an additional measure to display the wide-ranging meaning and significance of modality. Scattered among the main historical-philosophical chapters, there are small-scale studies, or *Reflections*, on the role of modality in other endeavors of the human spirit: cosmology, religion, music, literature, and logic. These *Reflections* will partly complement, partly challenge, and partly suggest an alternative to the narrative of the main chapters.

2. A History of Modality

Modal concepts like necessity and possibility were used by some of the earliest Greek philosophers, but Aristotle was arguably the first to

---

[1] *Hroch* is "hippo" in Czech.

develop a full-blown theory of modality and to explore connections between modality and many other philosophical topics. Indeed, as many of the chapters in this volume illustrate, Aristotle largely set the framework for modal theorizing for centuries, and even later innovations were often made in response to Aristotelian accounts. And as the final chapter makes clear, certain aspects of Aristotle's modal metaphysics are once again front and center in contemporary discussions of modality.

In the first half of "Aristotle on Modality," Marko Malink presents Aristotle's rich account of necessity, possibility, and contingency. Aristotle distinguished various kinds of necessity and possibility, distinctions that he embedded in his logic, semantics, theory of truth, and accounts of powers and agency. Some of these embeddings proved more controversial than others, and Malink outlines some of the main criticisms of Aristotle's theories that Aristotle's own students raised, as well as criticisms made by later Stoic philosophers. One perennial topic of discussion among ancient Greek philosophers concerns the distribution of necessity and the threat of fatalism. Many of the debates about the nature and source of contingency and the general relation of modality to time would be repeated in later centuries.

Aristotle's influence on theories of modality continued well into the medieval period, as Simo Knuuttila discusses in "Modality in Medieval Latin Philosophy." Knuuttila focuses on the complex relation between temporal and modal notions in the Latin and Arabic Aristotelian traditions. Following Aristotle, medievals tended to interpret modal notions like necessity and possibility in terms of time and change. On this so-called "statistical model," for example, necessary truths are truths that are *always* true, and possible truths are at least *sometimes* true. This interlacing of modality and temporality had wide-ranging implications for medieval accounts of logic, metaphysics, and natural sciences. One important point of disagreement between some Latin and Arabic medievals concerned how to treat non-temporal divine possibilities, disagreements that ultimately led to more general challenges to the statistical model itself. As Knuuttila discusses, Duns Scotus developed an alternative framework for analyzing modal concepts in terms of *consistency* rather than temporality, an approach that had far-reaching consequences for late medieval discussions in theology, metaphysics, and modal logic.

While the 17th century marks a significant shift in the history of western philosophy, there remained important points of continuity between early modern discussions of modality and this Aristotelian heritage. In "Modality and Essence in Early Modern Philosophy," Anat Schechtman draws attention to one such important point of continuity: the roles of *essences* in grounding modal facts. This connection between essences and modality held even as some early moderns became more skeptical about the role of essences in metaphysics, leading to a corresponding skepticism about some modal claims. Schechtman traces this interplay across Descartes, Malebranche, and Locke, revealing how many of their most well-known contributions in metaphysics—on substance, causation, and natural kinds, respectively—hinges on their diverging views about the status of essences.

Among early moderns, Spinoza's views on modality came to be especially well-known, though mostly as an example of modal theorizing gone awry. Spinoza was widely seen as endorsing necessitarianism, the view that all things exist necessarily and all truths are necessarily true, a view that seems to leave no place at all for contingency. In "Crescas and Spinoza on Modality," Yitzhak Y. Melamed traces some of the roots of Spinoza's modal conclusions to medieval Jewish philosophers, especially Hasdai Crescas, a bold and original anti-Aristotelian. Like Crescas, Spinoza seems to distinguish two notions of contingency, which affords us a richer understanding of his apparent necessitarianism. Melamed also contends that some of the textual evidence against reading Spinoza as a necessitarianism has been misunderstood and that there is a straightforward sense in which Spinoza did indeed adopt a form of strict necessitarianism, a modal conclusion that Spinoza's fellow early moderns roundly rejected.

One of Spinoza's early readers saw necessitarianism as especially threatening: Leibniz. Leibniz worried not only about the practical consequences of affirming necessitarianism. He was also concerned that some of his own theological and metaphysical positions led straightforwardly to necessitarianism. In "Leibniz on Modality," Samuel Newlands traces some of Leibniz's career-spanning efforts to block that path to necessitarianism, many of which were rooted in Leibniz's different analyses of modal concepts. Those efforts have faced steep criticism by Leibniz's later readers, some of which turn on deeper disagreements about the very structure of modality. Newlands also explores Leibniz's efforts to ground possibilities in the divine mind, a view that distinguished Leibniz from both Descartes' and Spinoza's nearby grounding accounts and placed him much closer to medieval scholastics like Duns Scotus.

One commitment shared by most of the philosophers discussed up to this point is a kind of realism about modality: necessity and contingency are mind-independent properties of their bearers, be they objects or propositions. In "Hume on Modal Discourse," Tom Holden argues that Hume rejects this widespread commitment and endorses an account of modal concepts as expressions of human mental states, such as our habits to make certain inferences and our inability to conceive of certain propositions. Put more succinctly, Hume grounds modality wholly within the human mind. Holden shows how Hume's expressivist treatment of modal discourse is rooted in his philosophy of language and his more general views about the science of human nature.

Hume was not the last to provide an alternative, human-centric account of the domain of modal concepts. In "Modality in Kant and Hegel," Nick Stang discusses Kant's version of the thesis that modal concepts do not describe the properties of objects and instead express the relation of our concepts to our cognitive capacities. Kant draws an important distinction between *logical* modality and *real* modality based on his distinction between the two basic faculties of human cognition, namely sensibility and understanding. Stang then turns to Hegel's rejection of Kant's account and Hegel's return to treating modal categories as determinations of objects. But as usual, Hegel does not merely reject the alternative. Instead, he tries to undermine what had seemed like a choice point between object-oriented accounts and cognition-oriented accounts of modality by showing how modal notions like necessity express *both* determinations of objects *and* the relation between thinking and its objects as different structural moments in the unfolding of what Hegel calls "the Absolute."

Kant's account of modality also profoundly shaped early 20th-century work on modal concepts, as Kris McDaniel shows in "Modality in 20th-Century Philosophy." McDaniel first traces how Kant's views became a foil for both the phenomenological tradition in Husserl and Heidegger and the analytic tradition in Russell and Quine. He then turns to the resurgence of modal theorizing in the second half of the 20th century, most especially through the contributions of Barcan Marcus in modal logic, Kripke in modal semantics, and David Lewis in modal metaphysics.

In the final chapter, "Modality and Essence in Contemporary Metaphysics," Kathrin Koslicki highlights another important aspect of the recent modal revival. As previous chapters have highlighted, there has been a long-standing agreement that some modal facts are importantly connected to facts about so-called *Aristotelian essences*. (Even modal skeptics like Quine endorsed this connection; his skepticism about such essences fueled his corresponding skepticism about object-oriented modal theories.) Koslicki focuses on the fraught relationship between essences and modality in contemporary metaphysics. After summarizing Kit Fine's non-modal account of essences and his important challenges to modal accounts of essences, Koslicki responds to recent attempts to meet those challenges. This debate is not only philosophically rich; as Koslicki concludes, it also reveals some of the theoretical roles ascribed to essences by all sides of the dispute.

On the one hand, this 21st-century return to broadly Aristotelean concepts of essences and modality reminds us how philosophical debates and conceptual developments often draw on and even echo earlier historical traditions, sometimes in surprising epicycles. (That the leading, largely deflationary views of modality in the mid-20th century would be followed immediately by a roaring comeback of Aristoteliean essentialism would have been hard to foresee at the time!) On the other hand, Koslicki's chapter provides ample evidence of how much more philosophically sophisticated reflections on modality have become over the centuries, an enriching of modal concepts and modal theories due in no small part to the contributions of the historical figures discussed in this volume.

3. Problems of Modality

The philosophy of modality is a field replete with problems, puzzles, and quandaries, many of which readers will encounter in the nine chapters and five reflections of this volume these. As an appetizer, let us survey some of the more perennial and general philosophical questions involving modal concepts.

Which things or events are necessary, possible, or contingent (i.e., neither necessary nor impossible)? This question is frequently tagged as a question about modal *distribution*. Is there anything by virtue of which things or events have the modal status they have? This question is commonly tagged as a question about the *grounding* of modality. What are the *vehicles*, or bearers, of modal status—are they propositions (*de dicto* modalities), or things and their qualities (*de re* modalities)? What is the relation between *de dicto* and *de re* modalities? Are there compelling philosophical reasons to pursue the study of modality in terms of *de re* rather than *de dicto* modalities, or the other way around?

We can also ask about the relationship between modality and other philosophical issues. What is the relation between the modal status of things and their *essences*? Are all modal features of a thing grounded in its essence? Are there things which exist (or don't exist) just by virtue of their essence? Can we make sense of nested modalities? Is *possibly-possible* a predicate that is any different from *possible*, simpliciter? Can we make sense and use of the notion of an *impossible* world? Is necessitarianism—the view that all things happen necessarily—true? Is there any place for morality if necessitarianism is true? How is determinism related to necessitarianism?

The study of the history of the philosophy of modality raises some pressing questions of its own. Over the past half-century or so, the standard account of modality appealed to the elegant conceptual machinery of possible worlds. It has become a bit of modal orthodoxy to claim that necessary truths are true in *all* possible worlds, possible truths are true in *some* possible worlds, and actual truths are true in *this* possible world. The development of possible worlds is commonly attributed to G. W. Leibniz (1646–1716), and in the 20th century, the corresponding semantics of possible worlds is mostly associated with the work of the young Saul Kripke (1940–2022). Obviously, philosophers have been employing modal concepts before the arrivals of Leibniz and Kripke. As the chapters of this volume will show, there are clear medieval anticipations of the notion of possible worlds, which allow for the conception of *simultaneously* alternative possibilities.

But it is also noteworthy that in ancient, medieval, and early modern periods, many philosophers deployed a very different framework for modality. This alternative understands modal notions in terms of *times* rather than possible worlds. According to this so-called "Statistical" conception of modality (and keeping with the focus of modal *truths*), to be necessarily true is to be at *all* times, to be possibly true is to be true at *some* time, and to be actually true is to be true *now*. (To make historical matters even more complex, in both medieval and early modern philosophy, such temporal conceptions of modality were used alongside both early possible-worlds modalities *and* a third framework of modality centered on concepts of *potentiality* and *actuality*.) As one might expect, there is a rich history of the mingling of these distinct conceptions of modality together, and unpacking this complex history requires careful attention and scholarly scrutiny. And given the long history of interaction among all these different basic modal frameworks, subtle fusions and confusions among distinct strands of modal concepts are likely to persist in our current philosophical discourse.

The work of Professor Simo Knuuttila, the author of the chapter on modality in medieval philosophy in this volume, contributed immensely to the reconstruction of the history of the Statistical model of modality and of the history of the philosophy of modality in general. As we were wrapping up the work on this volume, we learned the bitter news of his untimely death. Apart from being a towering figure in the study of the history of modality, Professor Knuuttila was also an extremely generous and kind philosophical conversant, as we witnessed repeatedly during the workshop on this volume, which turned out to be Simo's last trip to the US. We dedicate this volume to his blessed memory.

CHAPTER 1

Aristotle on Modality

Marko Malink

1. Introduction

Ever since the beginnings of philosophical thought in Greek antiquity, philosophers have made use of modalities such as necessity and possibility. In particular, the concepts of necessity and 'what must be' played an important role in Pre-Socratic thought.[1] For example, Anaximander maintained that things perish into that from which they came to be "in accordance with what must be" (*kata to chreôn*).[2] Heraclitus held that "everything comes about in accordance with strife and what must be" (*kat' erin kai chreôn*).[3] In his poem, Parmenides

---

1 See, e.g., the entries on necessity in Aëtius I 25–26. Cf. J. Mansfeld and D. T. Runia, *Aëtiana V: An Edition of the Reconstructed Text of the Placita with a Commentary and a Collection of Related Texts* (Leiden: Brill), 655–671 and 2085–2086.
2 DK 12 B1.
3 DK 22 B80; see also DK 22 A8. Cf. G. S. Kirk, *Heraclitus: The Cosmic Fragments* (Cambridge: Cambridge University Press, 1962), 238–244.

asserts that what is (*to eon*) is entirely still and changeless because "powerful Necessity [*Anagkē*] holds it in the bonds of a limit, which encloses it all around."[4] Among the atomists, Democritus identified necessity with a whirl of atoms, holding that "everything comes about in accordance with necessity, inasmuch as the whirl—which he calls necessity—is the cause of the coming about of all things."[5] Finally, Plato in the *Timaeus* describes the creation of the cosmos as the result of the interplay between divine demiurgic Intelligence and natural Necessity.[6]

While necessity figures centrally in the cosmologies presented by Plato and the Pre-Socratics, we do not have any evidence that these thinkers provided an account of the nature of necessity in general. The first philosopher known to have provided such an account is Aristotle. In his logical and metaphysical works, Aristotle develops a systematic theory of necessity and related modalities such as possibility and impossibility.

2. ARISTOTLE
2.1. *Kinds of Necessity and Possibility*

Aristotle had a keen interest in modalities. Not only did he put them to wide-ranging use throughout his works, he made them the subject of philosophical study in their own right. In *Metaphysics* Δ, he distinguishes various uses of modal terms. For example, the term 'necessary' (*anagkaion*) may be applied to things without which one cannot live, such as nourishment (Δ 5 1015a20–22). Since the Greek word for

---

4 DK 28 B8 30–1. For Parmenides on necessity, see also DK 28 A37.
5 Diogenes Laërtius 9.45. More specifically, Democritus took necessity to consist in 'the resistance, motion, and impact' of atoms (Aëtius I 26.2). Leucippus held that everything comes about 'from reason and by necessity' (Aëtius I 25.4).
6 *Tim.* 47e3–48b3. For Necessity in the *Timaeus*, see F. M. Cornford, *Plato's Cosmology: The Timaeus of Plato* (London: Routledge, 1935), 159–177.

'necessity' (*anagkê*) originally means 'force', what is brought about by force and violence may also be called 'necessary' (1015a26–33). Aristotle argues that these and other uses of 'necessary' can be reduced to a more abstract notion of necessity, which he characterizes as "that which cannot be otherwise" (1015a33–b6). In Aristotle's logical works, necessity figures prominently in the discussion of syllogisms (*syllogismoi*). The conclusion of a syllogism follows by necessity (*ex anagkês*) from the premises.[7] Aristotle does not undertake to define this kind of deductive necessity in terms of more fundamental concepts, but treats it as primitive.[8] He distinguishes deductive necessity (*necessitas consequentiae*) from the absolute necessity of the conclusion deduced (*necessitas consequentis*). For Aristotle, the latter kind of necessity obtains when the conclusion is true by necessity or when it is a modalized proposition such as "A necessarily belongs to all B." Aristotle emphasizes that a proposition may follow with deductive necessity from certain premises without being absolutely necessary.[9]

In his discussion of final causes, Aristotle appeals to what he calls 'hypothetical necessity' (*anagkê ex hypotheseôs*).[10] Something is hypothetically necessary if it is needed for the realization of a certain end. For example, if a saw is to be able to fulfill its function, it needs to be made from iron or another suitable material. Thus, there is a hypothetical necessity to the effect that, if there is to be a saw, it must be made from iron or another suitable material. Aristotle likens hypothetical necessity to deductive necessity (*necessitas consequentiae*): just as it is necessary for the conclusion of a syllogism to obtain if the premises

---

7 *APr.* 1.1 24b18–20, *Top.* 1.1 100a25–27, *Rhet.* 1.2 1356b16–18, *SE* 1 164b27–165a2.
8 See J. Lear, *Aristotle and Logical Theory* (Cambridge: Cambridge University Press, 1980), 2–14.
9 *APr.* 1.10 30b31–40, *APost.* 1.6 75a22–27.
10 *Phys.* 2.9 200a11–30, *PA* 1.1 639b21–640a6. For this type of necessity, see J. Cooper, "Hypothetical Necessity and Natural Teleology," in *Philosophical Issues in Aristotle's Biology*, ed. A. Gotthelf and J. G. Lennox (Cambridge: Cambridge University Press, 1987), 243–274.

obtain, so it is also necessary for that which is hypothetically necessary to obtain if the relevant end is to obtain.[11]

In addition to necessity, Aristotle studies the modalities of possibility and impossibility. The Greek terms for 'impossible' (*adynaton*) and 'possible' (*dynaton*) are closely related to the term for 'capacity' (*dynamis*). Thus, when applied to objects, these terms can be used to express the possession or lack of a capacity. For example, they may be used to express that a man is capable (*dynatos*) or incapable (*adynatos*) of begetting children (*Metaphysics* Δ 12 1019a32–b22). In another use, however, these terms are applicable not to objects but to propositions. A proposition is impossible if its contradictory opposite is true by necessity, and a proposition is possible if its contradictory opposite is not necessarily false (Δ 12 1019b22–32).

The latter description of possibility is characteristic of what is known as one-sided possibility rather than two-sided possibility (or, contingency). Two-sided possible is that which is neither necessary nor impossible. By contrast, one-sided possible is that which is not impossible. Thus, two-sided possibility is as it were bounded on two sides by what is necessary and by what is impossible, whereas one-sided possibility is only bounded on one side by what is impossible. For example, the Pythagorean theorem is necessary, hence one-sided possible, but not two-sided possible. The proposition "Socrates is sitting," on the other hand, is not necessary, and hence both one- and two-sided possible. While modern modal logic focuses on one-sided possibility, Aristotle studies both kinds of possibility. In the *Prior Analytics*, two-sided possibility is introduced as the primary kind of possibility, while one-sided possibility is regarded as secondary and due to a homonymy of the term 'possible' (1.13 32a18–21). The former is more in keeping with Aristotle's notion of capacity (*dynamis*), which is essentially two-sided: according to Aristotle, anything that

---

11 *Phys.* 2.9 200a15–27, 2.7 198b7–8.

has the capacity to φ also has the capacity not to φ (*Metaphysics* Θ 8 1050b8–16).

In *De interpretatione* 13, Aristotle discusses the following square of modal expressions and their negations (22a14–31):

possible	not possible
not impossible	impossible
not necessary	necessary not

possible not	not possible not
not impossible not	impossible not
not necessary not	necessary

Aristotle asserts that the first expression in each quadrant of the square implies the second and third expressions (22a14–23). For example, in the upper left-hand quadrant, 'possible' implies both 'not impossible' and 'not necessary'. This implication requires that 'possible' be understood as expressing not one-sided but two-sided possibility. In the right-hand column, by contrast, 'not possible' is taken to imply 'necessary not', and 'not possible not' is taken to imply 'necessary'. These implications require that the occurrences of 'possible' in these expressions be understood as expressing not two-sided but one-sided possibility. For if 'possible' is understood in the two-sided sense, then 'not possible' does not imply 'necessary not' but only the disjunction of 'necessary' and 'necessary not'. Thus, the above square of modal expressions is incoherent in that 'possible' expresses two-sided possibility in the left-hand column, but one-sided possibility in the right-hand column.

Aristotle proceeds, in *De interpretatione* 13, to eliminate this incoherence by revising the initial square of modal expressions. To this end, he provides an argument showing that 'necessary' implies 'possible' (22b11–14). He argues that, by the law of excluded middle, whatever is necessary is either possible or not possible. If it is not possible, something would be both necessary and impossible, which is absurd.

Hence, whatever is necessary is possible. In this way, Aristotle shows that 'necessary' is not incompatible with 'possible', and thus establishes the one-sided use of 'possible'. Based on this, Aristotle revises the original square by transposing 'not necessary' and 'not necessary not' in the left-hand column, as follows (22b10–28):[12]

possible   not possible
not impossible   impossible
not necessary not   necessary not

possible not   not possible not
not impossible not   impossible not
not necessary   necessary

In this revised square, 'possible' is not used ambiguously but expresses one-sided possibility in all occurrences.[13]

2.2. The Possibility Rule

In *Metaphysics* Θ, Aristotle develops a theory of capacity (*dynamis*) and actuality (*energeia*). He argues against the Megaric view that something is capable of φ-ing only at those times at which it is actually φ-ing (Θ 3). Aristotle does not explain on what grounds the Megarics held this view, but it may be related to the temporal account of possibility adopted by Diodorus Cronus (on which see below).[14] In the course of

---

[12] See H. Weidemann, *Aristoteles: Peri Hermeneias*, 3rd ed. (Berlin: de Gruyter, 2014), 437–446.

[13] A similar argument establishing the one-sided use of 'possible' appears in *Prior Analytics* 1.13 (32a21–29). This argument starts from the assumption that the modal expressions 'not possible', 'impossible', and 'necessary not' are equivalent. From this Aristotle infers that their contradictory opposites—'possible', 'not impossible', and 'not necessary not'—are equivalent. See M. Malink, "Aristotle on One-Sided Possibility," in *Logical Modalities from Aristotle to Carnap: The Story of Necessity*, ed. M. Cresswell, E. Mares, and A. Rini (New York: Cambridge University Press, 2016), 29–39.

[14] See S. Bobzien, "Chrysippus' Modal Logic and Its Relation to Philo and Diodorus," in *Dialektiker und Stoiker: Zur Logik der Stoa und ihrer Vorläufer*, ed. K. Döring and T. Ebert (Stuttgart: Franz Steiner Verlag, 1993), 70–73.

rejecting the Megaric position, Aristotle puts forward his own characterization of capacity:

> Something is capable (of φ-ing) if nothing impossible will obtain if the actuality of that of which it is said to have the capacity belongs to it. (*Metaphysics* Θ 3, 1047a24–26)

According to Aristotle, this characterization of capacity avoids the Megaric view. For example, it implies that Socrates is capable of walking even when he is not walking, given that nothing impossible follows from the supposition that he is walking. Aristotle gives a similar characterization of two-sided possibility in the *Prior Analytics*:

> By 'being possible' and 'the possible' I mean that which is not necessary but through which nothing impossible will result if it is put as being the case. (*Prior Analytics* 1.13 32a18–20)

Based on this characterization of possibility, Aristotle puts forward a rule of inference concerning the deductive consequences of hypotheses that are not impossible:

> It is clear that if something false but not impossible is hypothesized, what follows because of the hypothesis will be false but not impossible. For example, if A is false but not impossible, and if when A is B is, then B will also be false but not impossible. (*Prior Analytics* 1.15 34a25–29; see also Θ 4 1047b9–11)

The rule stated by Aristotle in this passage can be formulated as follows:

POSSIBILITY RULE: Given the premise that A is possible, and given a valid deduction of B from A, you may infer that B is possible.

This possibility rule is valid if B is deduced from A alone. Problems may arise, however, if B is deduced from A with the help of a further premise, C. In this case, B is not guaranteed to be possible whenever A is possible. (To see this, let A be the possible proposition "Socrates is walking," C the proposition "Socrates is sitting," and B the impossible proposition "Socrates is both walking and sitting.")

The possibility rule plays an important role in Aristotle's writings. Aristotle applies it not only in his modal logic, in *Prior Analytics* 1.15, but also in physical and metaphysical contexts, in works such as the *Physics*, *De caelo*, *De generatione et corruptione*, and the *Metaphysics*.[15] For example, in *Metaphysics* Θ 4 Aristotle uses the possibility rule to refute an opponent who claims of an event which is manifestly impossible that it is possible. Specifically, the opponent claims that it is possible to measure the diagonal of a square by a magnitude which also measures the side of the square, even though such a measuring will never occur. Aristotle refutes this opponent by *reductio* as follows (Θ 4 1047b3–14):

1. It is possible that the diagonal has been measured   (assumption for *reductio*)
2. The diagonal has been measured   (assumption for possibility rule)
3. The diagonal is measured   (from 2)
4. Odd numbers are equal to even numbers   (from 3; see *APr.* 1.23 41a26–27)
5. It is possible that odd numbers are equal to even numbers   (possibility rule: 1, 2–4)
6. It is not possible that odd numbers are equal to even numbers   (premise)

---

15 See Jacob Rosen and Marko Malink, "A Method of Modal Proof in Aristotle," *Oxford Studies in Ancient Philosophy* 42 (2012): 179–261; M. Malink and J. Rosen, "Proof by Assumption of the Possible in *Prior Analytics* 1.15," *Mind* 122 (2013): 953–986.

7. It is not possible that the diagonal has   (*reductio*: 1–5, 6)
   been measured

Aristotle goes on, in *Metaphysics* Θ 4, to use the possibility rule to establish a law of propositional modal logic to the effect that, if B follows necessarily from A, then the possibility of B follows necessarily from the possibility of A (1047b14–26).[16] Moreover, Aristotle endorses the converse of this law, that if the possibility of B follows necessarily from the possibility of A, then B follows necessarily from A (1047b26–30). However, it is not clear on what grounds Aristotle takes himself to be justified in asserting the latter law. Unlike the former law, the latter is problematic and has been the subject of dispute among commentators.[17]

In *De caelo* 1.12, Aristotle applies the possibility rule in order to show that whatever is eternal is imperishable:

> If something that exists for an infinite time is perishable, it would have a capacity for not existing. If, then, it exists for an infinite time, let that of which it is capable obtain. Then it will actually exist and not exist simultaneously. Now something false would follow because something false was posited. But if the hypothesis were not impossible, then what follows would not be impossible as well. Therefore, everything that always exists is imperishable without qualification. (*De caelo* 1.12 281b20–25)

Aristotle's argument in this passage can be reconstructed as follows:

1. X is eternal and perishable   (assumption for *reductio*)
2. X exists for all time   (from 1)

---

16 See Kit Fine, "Aristotle's Megarian Manoeuvres," *Mind* 120 (2011): 1023–1028; Rosen and Malink, "A Method of Modal Proof in Aristotle," 234–242. For another statement of this principle, see *APr.* 1.15 34a5–7.
17 See Fine, "Aristotle's Megarian Manoeuvres," 993–1023.

3. | It is possible that X does not exist for some time (from 1)
4. | | X does not exist for some time (assumption for possibility rule)
5. | | X exists for all time (iterated from 2)
6. | | X exists and does not exist simultaneously for some time (from 4, 5)
7. | It is possible that X exists and does not exist simultaneously for some time (possibility rule: 3, 4–6)
8. It is not possible that X exists and does not exist simultaneously for some time (premise: principle of non-contradiction)
9. It is not the case that X is eternal and perishable (*reductio*: 1–7, 8)
10. Nothing is both eternal and perishable (generalization: 9)

The main problem with this proof is that the statement in line 6 is deduced not from the assumption in line 4 alone, but from this assumption together with the iterated statement in line 5. As we have seen, this means that the possibility of the statement in line 4 does not suffice to guarantee the possibility of that in line 6. Consequently, it is not clear whether the step performed in line 7 is warranted. It may be warranted if the iterated statement in line 5 is guaranteed to be necessary, for whatever is deduced from something possible in conjunction with something necessary is possible. However, Aristotle does not provide any explanation of why the statement in line 5 should be regarded as necessary. In the absence of such an explanation, the natural conclusion to draw is that Aristotle's argument in the passage just quoted is invalid.[18]

---

18 See Rosen and Malink, "A Method of Modal Proof in Aristotle," 195–204.

2.3. Modality and Time

In *De caelo* 1.12, Aristotle argues that whatever is eternal is imperishable. Hence, whatever is perishable is not eternal. This means that whatever has the capacity not to exist fails to exist at some point of time. In view of this, some commentators attribute to Aristotle a principle of plenitude to the effect that every possibility is realized at some time.[19] However, it is disputed whether Aristotle accepted such a principle of plenitude. It is clear that he does not accept it in its full generality. For example, he maintains that it is possible for a particular cloak to be cut up even if the cloak never will be cut up (*De interpretatione* 9 19a12–18). Thus, while Aristotle may endorse a principle of plenitude for the domain of eternal beings, he does not accept it unqualifiedly for the domain of sublunary, non-eternal beings.[20]

Chapter 9 of the *De interpretatione* contains a celebrated discussion of future contingent propositions such as "There will be a sea-battle tomorrow." Aristotle's aim in this chapter is to refute an argument for fatalism. The argument starts from a principle of bivalence to the effect that, for any proposition *p* and any time *t*, either *p* is true at *t* or *p* is false at *t*. The argument for fatalism assumes that this principle of bivalence applies to future contingent propositions. Thus, for example, if there will be a sea-battle tomorrow, the proposition "There will be a sea-battle tomorrow" is already true today. In Aristotle's view, this has the consequence that "it was always true to say of anything that has happened that it would be so" (18b10–11). Given this, Aristotle reasons as follows:

> But if it was always true to say that it was so, or would be so, it could not not be so, or not be going to be so. But if something cannot

---

19 For example, see J. Hintikka, *Time and Necessity: Studies in Aristotle's Theory of Modality* (Oxford: Oxford University Press, 1973), 93–113; S. Waterlow, *Passage and Possibility: A Study of Aristotle's Modal Concepts* (Oxford: Oxford University Press, 1982), 2.
20 See R. Sorabji, *Necessity, Cause and Blame: Perspectives on Aristotle's Theory* (London: Duckworth, 1980), 128–135.

not happen it is impossible for it not to happen; and if it is impossible for something not to happen it is necessary for it to happen. Everything that will be, therefore, happens necessarily. So nothing will come about as chance has it or by chance; for if by chance, not by necessity. (*De interpretatione* 9 18b11–16)

According to Aristotle, the necessity of the future described in this passage entails fatalism. If the future is necessary in the sense that everything that will be happens by necessity, then "there would be no need to deliberate or to take trouble, thinking that if we do this, this will happen, but if we do not, it will not" (18b31–33). In this way, the assumption that the principle of bivalence holds for future contingent propositions leads to fatalism. But Aristotle rejects fatalism and the necessity of the future. He writes:

> We see that what will be has an origin both in deliberation and in action, and that, in general, in things that are not always actual there is the possibility of being and of not being; here both possibilities are open, both being and not being, and consequently, both coming to be and not coming to be. Many things are obviously like this. For example, it is possible for this cloak to be cut up, and yet it will not be cut up but will wear out first. (*De interpretatione* 9 19a7–14)

Thus, Aristotle rejects the argument for fatalism presented in *De interpretatione* 9. It is a subject of debate how exactly he intends to reject it. According to a prominent interpretation, Aristotle does so by denying that the principle of bivalence applies to future contingent propositions.[21] On this account, Aristotle holds that these propositions

---

21 See P. Crivelli, *Aristotle on Truth* (Cambridge: Cambridge University Press, 2004), 198–233; Weidemann, *Aristoteles: Peri Hermeneias*, 223–328; cf. also R. Gaskin, *The Sea Battle and the Master Argument* (Berlin: de Gruyter, 1995), 1–184.

are neither true nor false at the time of their utterance. For example, today it is neither true nor false to say that there will be a sea-battle tomorrow.

2.4. The Modal Syllogistic

In the initial chapters of the *Prior Analytics*, Aristotle presents his theory of assertoric, non-modal syllogisms (chapters 1.1–2 and 1.4–7). As is well known, this theory deals with the following four kinds of categorical proposition:

AaB	A belongs to all B	(Every B is A)
AeB	A belongs to no B	(No B is A)
AiB	A belongs to some B	(Some B is A)
AoB	A does not belong to some B	(Not every B is A)

Aristotle goes on to develop a theory of modal syllogisms in *Prior Analytics* 1.3 and 1.8–22. This deals with categorical propositions which contain modal qualifiers such as 'necessarily' and 'possibly', as in "A necessarily belongs to all B" and "A possibly does not belong to some B." As before, Aristotle focuses on four kinds of modalized propositions containing the qualifier 'necessarily':

Aa_NB	A necessarily belongs to all B
Ae_NB	A necessarily belongs to no B
Ai_NB	A necessarily belongs to some B
Ao_NB	A necessarily does not belong to some B

These necessity-propositions are categorical propositions consisting of a predicate term, a subject term, and a copula. For example, in the proposition Aa_NB, A is the predicate term, B the subject term, and 'a_N' indicates a modally qualified copula expressed by phrases such as 'necessarily belongs to all'.

Aristotle does not discuss the semantics of the modal propositions studied in the modal syllogistic. He does not provide an account of their meaning or truth-conditions. Instead, he lays down a number of syllogistic moods and conversion rules determining the logical properties of these propositions. With regard to N-propositions, Aristotle posits the following three conversion rules (*Prior Analytics* 1.3):

e_N-conversion: Ae_NB, therefore Be_NA
i_N-conversion: Ai_NB, therefore Bi_NA
a_N-conversion: Aa_NB, therefore Bi_NA

Moreover, Aristotle posits four perfect syllogistic moods consisting of N-propositions in the first figure (*Prior Analytics* 1.8):

Barbara NNN: Aa_NB, Ba_NC, therefore Aa_NC
Celarent NNN: Ae_NB, Ba_NC, therefore Ae_NC
Darii NNN: Aa_NB, Bi_NC, therefore Ai_NC
Ferio NNN: Ae_NB, Bi_NC, therefore Ao_NC

These perfect moods and conversion rules suffice to derive all valid moods of the form NNN endorsed by Aristotle, with the sole exception of Baroco NNN and Bocardo NNN. The last two moods are derived by means of the method of ecthesis applied to o_N-propositions (1.8 30a7–14).

In *Prior Analytics* 1.9–11, Aristotle discusses syllogistic moods which have a mixed premise pair consisting of an N-proposition and an assertoric proposition. He identifies four perfect moods deriving an N-conclusion from such mixed premise pairs in the first figure (*Prior Analytics* 1.9):

Barbara NXN: Aa_NB, BaC, therefore Aa_NC
Celarent NXN: Ae_NB, BaC, therefore Ae_NC
Darii NXN: Aa_NB, BiC, therefore Ai_NC
Ferio NXN: Ae_NB, BiC, therefore Ao_NC

In these moods, the major premise and the conclusion are N-propositions while the minor premise is an assertoric proposition (indicated by the letter 'X'). By contrast, Aristotle rejects the corresponding first-figure moods of the form XNN, in which the major premise is assertoric and the minor premise is an N-proposition (*Prior Analytics* 1.9). For example, he argues that AaB and Ba_NC do not yield the conclusion Aa_NC (30a23–32).

In *Prior Analytics* 1.10–11, Aristotle uses the above conversion rules and perfect moods to derive moods of the form NXN and XNN in the second and third figures. An example is the mood Camestres XNN (BaA, Be_NC, therefore Ae_NC). Aristotle derives this mood by means of a direct deduction as follows (1.10 30b14–18):

1. BaA (premise)
2. Be_NC (premise)
3. Ce_NB (from 2 by e_N-conversion)
4. Ce_NA (from 1 and 3 by Celarent NXN)
5. Ae_NC (from 4 by e_N-conversion)

This derivation employs both the mood Celarent NXN and the rule of e_N-conversion. However, it is often thought that Aristotle's commitment to the former is in tension with his commitment to the latter. Specifically, commentators have argued that the validity of Celarent NXN requires a *de re* reading of e_N-propositions, whereas the validity of e_N-conversion requires a *de dicto* reading of these propositions.[22] The two readings offer different accounts of the truth-conditions of e_N-propositions. They are usually formulated by reference to the

---

22 A. Becker, *Die Aristotelische Theorie der Möglichkeitsschlüsse* (Berlin: Junker und Dünnhaupt, 1933), 42; W. Kneale and M. Kneale, *The Development of Logic* (Oxford: Clarendon Press, 1962), 89–91; Hintikka, *Time and Necessity*, 139–140; Sorabji, *Necessity, Cause and Blame*, 202; G. Striker, *Aristotle's Prior Analytics: Book 1* (Oxford: Clarendon Press, 2009), xvi–xvii, 115; similarly, R. Patterson, *Aristotle's Modal Logic: Essence and Entailment in the Organon* (Cambridge: Cambridge University Press, 1995), 41–87.

individuals that fall under the subject and predicate terms. On the *de re* reading, an e_N-proposition Ae_NB is taken to be true just in case every individual that falls under B is such that it is necessary for it not to fall under A. On this reading, Celarent NXN is valid but e_N-conversion is not valid. To see that e_N-conversion is not valid, suppose that no moving thing is an animal (as Aristotle does at 1.9 30a28–33, 30b5–6). In this case, every individual that falls under 'moving' is such that it is necessary for it not to fall under 'animal' (given that any individual that is not an animal is such that it is impossible for it to be an animal). Hence 'animal' is e_N-predicated of 'moving' on the *de re* reading. But not every individual that falls under 'animal' is such that it is necessary for it not to fall under 'moving'. Hence, 'moving' is not e_N-predicated of 'animal' and the rule of e_N-conversion is invalid on the *de re* reading.

On the *de dicto* reading, Ae_NB is taken to be true just in case it is necessary that no individual falls under both A and B. On this reading, e_N-conversion is valid but Celarent NXN is not valid. To see that Celarent NXN is not valid, consider the terms 'healthy' and 'ill'. It is necessary that no individual falls under both of them. Hence 'ill' is e_N-predicated of 'healthy' on the *de dicto* reading. Moreover, we may suppose that every human is healthy (as Aristotle does at 1.18 37b35–38). But it is not necessary that no individual falls under both 'man' and 'ill'. Hence, 'ill' is not e_N-predicated of 'man' and Celarent NXN is invalid on the *de dicto* reading.

In sum, the *de dicto* reading validates e_N-conversion and the *de re* reading validates Celarent NXN, but neither reading validates both. Consequently, some commentators hold that e_N-propositions are used ambiguously in the modal syllogistic: when Aristotle employs Celarent NXN, he tacitly relies on the *de re* reading, and when he employs e_N-conversion, he relies on the *de dicto* reading. On this view, Aristotle's modal syllogistic is incoherent. For, as we have seen, Aristotle employs both Celarent NXN and e_N-conversion in one and the same proof. It is important to note, however, that Aristotle does not formulate either the *de re* or the *de dicto* reading in the *Prior Analytics*. It is not clear that he had in mind either reading when he developed the modal syllogistic. At any rate, alternative interpretations of e_N-propositions are available which validate both Celarent NXN and e_N-conversion. For example, an e_N-proposition Ae_NB may be taken to be true just in case for any individual concept that falls under A and any individual concept that falls under B, it is necessary that these two individual concepts do not designate the same individual.[23] Alternatively, the truth-conditions of e_N-propositions may be formulated by reference, not to the individuals that fall under the subject and predicate terms, but to the predicative relations in which these terms stand.[24] On such alternative interpretations, Aristotle's treatment of N-propositions in *Prior Analytics* 1.8–11 can be viewed as a coherent system of modal logic without assuming any ambiguity in his use of e_N-propositions.

2.5. Truth and Necessity

Aristotle takes the adjectives 'necessary' and 'true' to signify attributes of the same type. In particular, as we have seen, both signify attributes of propositions that can serve as premises and conclusions of deductive arguments. Thus, Aristotle writes in the *Posterior Analytics*:

> Now when the conclusion is from necessity, nothing prevents the middle term through which it was proved from not being necessary; for one can deduce something necessary from things that are not necessary, just as one can deduce something true from things that are not true. But when the middle term is from necessity, the

---

[23] See H. Brenner, "Eine vollständige Formalisierung der aristotelischen Notwendigkeitssyllogistik," in *Beiträge zum Satz vom Widerspruch und zur Aristotelischen Prädikationstheorie*, ed. N. Öffenberger and M. Skarica (Hildesheim: Olms, 2000), 336.

[24] See M. Malink, *Aristotle's Modal Syllogistic* (Cambridge, MA: Harvard University Press, 2013), 114–176.

conclusion too is from necessity, just as from true things it is always true. (Aristotle, *Posterior Analytics* 1.6 75a1–6)

Consider a valid deductive argument in which a conclusion φ has been deduced from premises ψ and χ. Aristotle claims that, if both ψ and χ are true, it follows that φ is true, but not vice versa.[25] Moreover, he claims that, if both ψ and χ are necessary, it follows that φ is necessary, but not vice versa.[26]

For Aristotle, the premises and conclusions of deductive arguments are linguistic expressions endowed with signification.[27] He maintains that the truth of these linguistic expressions has its ground (*aition*) in the being of a non-linguistic object:

> Among things which convert as to implication of being, what is in some way the ground [*aition*] of the being of the other might reasonably be called prior in nature. . . . That man is converts as to implication of being with the true sentence about it. For if man is, the sentence whereby we say that man is is true; and this converts, for if the sentence whereby we say that man is is true, then man is. But the true sentence is in no way the ground of the being of the object, while the object seems somehow the ground of the sentence's being true; for it is because the object is or is not that a sentence is called true or false. (Aristotle, *Categories* 12 14b11–22)

In this passage, Aristotle considers items which "convert as to implication of being." By this he means pairs of items such that the being of the one entails the being of the other and vice versa. The being of one of these items is the ground of the being of the other. The former item is thus prior in nature to the latter. In Aristotle's example, the latter

---

[25] Similarly, *APr.* 2.2 53b11–16.
[26] Similarly, *APr.* 1.15 34a19–24.
[27] *APr.* 1.1 24a16–17 and *De int.* 4–5.

item is the truth of a sentence and the former item is a certain object.[28] If the sentence in question is an existential sentence such as "Man is" (or "Man exists"), the corresponding object can be taken to be the object that is asserted to exist by the sentence, e.g., the human species.[29] Thus, the being (or existence) of the human species is the ground of the sentence's "Man is" being true, but not vice versa. Aristotle does not explain what the requisite object is if the sentence in question is not an existential sentence but a predicative sentence, such as "Socrates is pale." Commentators have argued that, in this case, the object is a state of affairs.[30] On this account, the object corresponding to the sentence "Socrates is pale" is the state of affairs of Socrates' being pale, and the being (or obtaining) of this state of affairs is the ground of the sentence's being true, but not vice versa.

According to Aristotle, a state of affairs involves two constituents: the subject and the predicate. Each of these may be either an individual or a universal. The being (obtaining) or non-being (non-obtaining) of a state of affairs is a matter of the combination or separation of these two constituents:[31]

> Being true or false, on the side of objects, consists in being combined or being divided. Thus, when we think of what is divided that it is divided and of what is combined that it is combined, we think truly, but when we are in a state contrary to that of the objects, we think falsely.... For it is not because we have the true thought that you

---

28 Similarly, *Cat.* 5 4b8–10.
29 See Crivelli, *Aristotle on Truth*, 104–105.
30 D. W. Hamlyn, "The Correspondence Theory of Truth," *Philosophical Quarterly* 12 (1962): 193–205 at 194; Gabriel Nuchelmans, *Theories of the Proposition: Ancient and Medieval Conceptions of the Bearers of Truth and Falsity* (Amsterdam: North-Holland, 1973), 33–34; Peter Simons, "Aristotle's Concept of State of Affairs," in *Antike Rechts- und Sozialphilosophie*, ed. O. Gigon and M. W. Fischer (Frankfurt a. M.: Peter Lang, 1988), 97–112 at 103–106; Crivelli, *Aristotle on Truth*, 104–105.
31 See also *Metaph.* E 4 1027b18–23.

are pale that you are pale; instead, it is because you are pale that we who say so speak the truth. (Aristotle *Metaphysics* Θ 10, 1051b1–13)

In this passage, Aristotle takes the sentence "You are pale" to express the being (or obtaining) of the state of affairs of your being pale.[32] Thus, for example, the sentence "Socrates is pale" is true because the state of affairs of Socrates being pale obtains, i.e., because a certain relation of combination obtains between the individual Socrates and the universal pallor.

A similar account applies in the case of necessity. For example, the sentence "All triangles have 2R" is necessary because a special relation of combination obtains between the universal triangle and the universal 2R. Thus, Deborah Modrak writes, "Like truth, Aristotle construes necessity (also possibility) as a predicate that belongs to a statement in virtue of the character of the corresponding state of affairs.... Thus if a statement expresses a necessary truth, it does so in virtue of the real relation between the entities that the subject and the predicate represent. The crucial relation, from this perspective, is the one between an ontological subject and something that is necessarily predicated of it."[33]

What is the special kind of relation that underwrites the necessity of a sentence? In the case of assertoric universal affirmative sentences of the form "A belongs to all B" (AaB), Aristotle makes it clear in the *Posterior Analytics* that AaB is necessary just in case A is predicated per se of B.[34] Moreover, Aristotle characterizes the notion of per se predication by reference to the essence, or definition, of A and B.[35] Thus, as Jonathan Barnes points out, in the case of assertoric universal

---

[32] Crivelli, *Aristotle on Truth*, 57; P. Crivelli, "Truth in *Metaphysics* E 4," *Oxford Studies in Ancient Philosophy* 48 (2015): 204.

[33] D. K. W. Modrak, *Aristotle's Theory of Language and Meaning* (Cambridge: Cambridge University Press, 2001), 66, 72.

[34] *APost.* 1.6 74b5–10, 75a28–37. See H. Lorenz, "Understanding, Knowledge, and Inquiry in Aristotle," in *The Routledge Companion to Ancient Philosophy*, ed. J. Warren and F. Sheffield (New York: Routledge, 2014), 290–303 at 295–300.

[35] *APost* 1.4 73a34–b2.

affirmative propositions, Aristotle maintains that their "necessity is ultimately grounded in essential or definitional connections."[36] If 'N(φ)' is used to express the statement that the proposition φ is necessary, Aristotle endorses the following principle:

If N(AaB), then N(AaB) because A is predicated per se of B.

However, this account of the necessity of a-propositions does not carry over straightforwardly to the other kinds of assertoric proposition considered in the *Analytics*. Aristotle does not provide an account of what grounds the necessity of necessary e-, i-, and o-propositions. It is not clear that the relation of per se predication can in fact provide an account of their necessity. Instead, such an account can be provided by the necessity-propositions theorized by Aristotle in the modal syllogistic, such as $Ae_N B$. Recall that, in these propositions, 'e_N' indicates a modally qualified copula expressed by phrases such as 'necessarily belongs to no'. Thus, whereas 'N(AeB)' asserts the necessity of a negative non-modal proposition, '$Ae_N B$' asserts that a certain modal relation obtains between the terms A and B, namely, the modal relation denoted by the copula 'e_N'. Thus, if the assertoric proposition AeB is necessary, its necessity can be taken to be grounded in the fact that the modal relation denoted by 'e_N' obtains between the terms A and B. Thus, we have:

If N(AaB), then N(AaB) because $Aa_N B$
If N(AeB), then N(AeB) because $Ae_N B$
If N(AiB), then N(AiB) because $Ai_N B$
If N(AoB), then N(AoB) because $Ao_N B$

---

36 J. Barnes, *Aristotle's Posterior Analytics*, 2nd ed. (Oxford: Clarendon Press, 1993), 120. Similarly, R. D. McKirahan, *Principles and Proofs: Aristotle's Theory of Demonstrative Science* (Princeton, NJ: Princeton University Press, 1992), 84 maintains that, for Aristotle, "scientific necessity is grounded in per se relations."

3. Theophrastus, Eudemus, and Later Peripatetics

Aristotle's modal syllogistic has been the subject of criticism since antiquity. Theophrastus and Eudemus, both pupils of Aristotle, rejected one of the central assumptions of the modal syllogistic: they denied the validity of Aristotle's perfect moods of the form NXN.[37] Theophrastus and Eudemus gave a number of counterexamples to show that Barbara NXN is invalid. Two of them are as follows:[38]

> Every human being necessarily is an animal.
> Every moving thing is a human being.
> But it is not the case that every moving thing necessarily is an animal.

> Every walking thing necessarily is walking by means of legs.
> Every human being is walking.
> But it is not the case that every human being necessarily is moving by means of legs.

In addition to these counterexamples, Theophrastus and Eudemus argued that a mixed premise pair consisting of an N-proposition and an assertoric proposition cannot entail an N-conclusion, on the grounds that the conclusion cannot have stronger modal force than the weaker premise.[39] Moreover, they gave the following argument against the validity of Barbara NXN:

> If B belongs to all C but not by necessity, it is possible that B be disjoined from C at some time (*pote*). But when B has been disjoined from C, then (*tote*) A will also be disjoined from it. And if this is so,

---

[37] For an overview of Theophrastus' work on modal logic, see W. W. Fortenbaugh, P. M. Huby, R. W. Sharples, and D. Gutas, *Theophrastus of Eresus: Sources for His Life, Writings, Thought and Influence: Part One* (Leiden: Brill, 1992), 173–231.
[38] Alexander *in APr.* 124.24–30; see also Philoponus *in APr.* 124.24–28.
[39] Alexander *in APr.* 124.8–17.

A will not belong to C by necessity.[40] (Alexander of Aphrodisias *in APr.* 124.18–21)

In this argument, Theophrastus and Eudemus appeal to the notion of a term being disjoined from another term at some time. Thus, they seem to adopt a temporal interpretation of modal propositions. In doing so they depart from Aristotle, who does not give a temporal interpretation of modal propositions in his modal syllogistic.

Theophrastus' and Eudemus' rejection of Barbara NXN was widely influential in antiquity, and was embraced by Neo-Platonists such as Themistius, Syrianus, and Proclus.[41] On the other hand, some Peripatetics, including Alexander of Aphrodisias and two of his teachers, Sosigenes and Herminus, undertook to defend Aristotle against these objections.[42] The arguments put forward on both sides of the debate were discussed by Alexander in a lost treatise entitled *On the Difference between Aristotle and His Associates concerning Mixtures of Premises*.

4. The Megarics

The nature of modalities was an important topic of discussion among the philosophers of the Dialectical, or 'Megaric', school. In particular, Diodorus Cronus and Philo made contributions to modal logic and the theory of modality. Philo considered a modal system involving the modalities of possibility, impossibility, necessity, and non-necessity. According to Boethius, he defined them as follows:

> Philo says that possible is that which is capable of being true by the statement's own nature. . . . In the same way, Philo defines what is

---

40 See also Philoponus *in APr.* 124.11–16.
41 See Pseudo-Ammonius *in APr.* 38.38–39.2, Philoponus *in APr.* 123.15–17.
42 For Alexander, see Pseudo-Ammonius *in APr.* 39.1. For Sosigenes, see Pseudo-Ammonius *in APr.* 39.24–26 and Philoponus *in APr.* 126.20–23. For Herminus, see Pseudo-Ammonius *in APr.* 39.31–34 and Alexander *in APr.* 125.3–29.

necessary as that which is true and which, as far as it is in itself, is not capable of being a falsehood. Non-necessary is that which, as far as it is in itself, is capable of being false, and impossible is that which by its own nature is not capable of being true. (Boethius *in De interpretatione* 234.10–21)

Philo characterized the modality of a proposition by reference to its intrinsic capacity of being true or false. For example, the proposition "This piece of wood is burning" is possible on the grounds that it is intrinsically capable of being true. The proposition is possible even if the piece of wood referred to in it is prevented by external circumstances from burning, e.g., because it is lying at the bottom of the sea.[43]

In Philo's definitions, modalities are not reduced to non-modal notions, but are characterized in terms of a proposition's intrinsic capacity of being true or false. By contrast, Diodorus Cronus characterized the modality of a proposition in non-modal terms by reducing it to temporal notions, as follows:

Diodorus determines that possible is that which either is or will be, impossible is that which is false and will not be true, necessary is that which is true and will not be false, and non-necessary is that which either already is or will be false. (Boethius *in De interpretatione* 234.22–26)

This definition of modalities is based on the assumption, shared by most logicians in antiquity, that propositions can change their truth-value over time. A proposition may be true now and false at a later time, and vice versa. According to Diodorus, a proposition is possible just in case it either is true now or will be true at some time in the future. Thus, unlike Philo, Diodorus does not take the proposition

---

43 See Alexander *in APr.* 184.6–10.

"This piece of wood is burning" to be possible if the piece of wood is lying at the bottom of the sea and will never emerge from this position. Diodorus' definition of possibility is rejected not only by Philo but also by Plato and Aristotle. Plato takes the view, in the *Timaeus* (41a–b), that the cosmos was created and that it is possible for it to perish, but that it will never perish, being maintained by god. Aristotle, as we have seen, holds that it is possible for a cloak to be cut up even if it never will be cut up.

In order to defend his temporal definition of possibility, Diodorus put forward a celebrated argument which is known as the Master Argument.[44] While the argument itself has not been transmitted, Epictetus describes its import as follows:

> The Master Argument seems to have been developed from the following starting points. There is a general conflict between the following three statements: every past true proposition is necessary, the impossible does not follow from the possible, and something is possible which neither is true nor will be true. Being aware of this conflict, Diodorus used the plausibility of the first two statements in order to show that nothing is possible that neither is nor will be true. (Epictetus *Dissertationes* 2 19.1)

Diodorus argued that the following three claims are incompatible:

C1 Every true proposition about the past is necessary.
C2 If a proposition is possible, then no impossible proposition follows from it.
C3 There is a proposition which is possible but which neither is nor will be true.

---

44 See Alexander *in APr.* 183.34–184.6.

Diodorus accepted C1 and C2, and thus concluded that C3 is false. C2 is a principle of modal propositional logic that is endorsed by Aristotle in *Metaphysics* Θ 4 and *Prior Analytics* 1.15. C1 relies on the intuition that the past is unalterable and, in this sense, necessary. Accordingly, true propositions about the past cannot change their truth-value, and hence are necessary in the sense of being ineluctible. Aristotle seems to accept a version of C1 when he states that "what has come to be cannot not have come to be" (*EN* 6.2 1139b8–9), and that "what has come to be has necessity" (*Rhetoric* 3.17 1418a5). Cicero formulates C1 as follows:

> All truths concerning the past are necessary . . . since they are unalterable and since past truths cannot change from true to false. (Cicero *De fato* 14)

Commentators have offered various accounts of how Diodorus established the incompatibility of C1–C3 in his Master Argument. According to one prominent account, the argument can be reconstructed as follows:[45]

1. Proposition p is not true and will never be true. (hypothesis)
2. At some past time, it was the case that p will never be true. (from 1)
3. It is necessary that, at some past time, it was the case that p will never be true. (from 2; by C1)

---

[45] For this reconstruction of the Master Argument, see A. N. Prior, "Diodoran Modalities," *Philosophical Quarterly* 5 (1955): 205–213; H. Weidemann, "Das sogenannte Meisterargument des Diodoros Kronos und der Aristotelische Möglichkeitsbegriff," *Archiv für Geschichte der Philosophie* 69 (1987): 37–48; similarly, S. Bobzien, "Logic: The 'Megarics' and the Stoics," in The Cambridge History of Hellenistic Philosophy, ed. K. Algra, J. Barnes, J. Maansfeld, and M. Schofield (Cambridge: Cambridge University Press, 1999), 88–92. For an overview of several alternative reconstructions, see Gaskin, *The Sea Battle*, 217–296.

4. It is not possible that, at no past time, it (from 3)
   was the case that p will never be true.
5. If p, it follows that, at no past time, it was (premise)
   the case that p will never be true.
6. It is not possible that p. (from 4, 5; by C2)

This argument employs C1 and C2 to establish that, if a proposition is not true and will never be true (line 1), then this proposition is not possible (line 6). By contraposition, this means that every proposition which is possible either is true or will be true at some time. This is the negation of C3.

In addition to C1 and C2, the above reconstruction relies on two substantive assumptions. First, it assumes that the inference from line 1 to line 2 is valid. Second, it assumes that the premise in line 5 is justified. While neither of these assumptions appears in Epictetus' summary of the Master Argument, each of them has some plausibility. If the two assumptions are granted, the above reconstruction provides a compelling argument that C1 and C2 are incompatible with C3.

5. The Stoics

According to Diodorus, any proposition that neither is nor will be true is impossible. For example, if the proposition "Fabius dies on land" neither is nor will be true, then it is impossible. Hence, if Fabius in fact will die at sea, Diodorus' definition precludes the counterfactual possibility of him dying at land and, in this way, raises the threat of fatalism. The Stoics sought to avoid the fatalistic consequences of Diodorus' definition of possibility.[46] In particular, Chrysippus rejected this definition and the Master Argument that Diodorus gave in support of it.

---

46 See S. Bobzien, *Determinism and Freedom in Stoic Philosophy* (Oxford: Oxford University Press, 1998), 102–108, 116–119.

Chrysippus refuted the Master Argument by denying one of its basic assumptions, namely, C2, the claim that nothing impossible follows from something possible. He argued against C2 as follows:

> Chrysippus says that nothing precludes something impossible following from something possible.... For he says that in the conditional 'If Dio is dead, this one is dead', which is true when Dio is pointed at, the antecedent 'Dio is dead' is possible, since it can at some time become true that Dio is dead. But 'This one is dead' is impossible; for once Dio has died, the assertible 'This one is dead' is destroyed, since the object of the pointing [*deixis*] no longer exists. For the pointing is of a living being and with respect to a living being. So if when Dio is dead the phrase 'this one' is no longer admissible, and if Dio does not come into existence again so that it is possible to say of him 'This one is dead', then 'This one is dead' is impossible. (Alexander *in APr.* 177.25–178.1)

Chrysippus maintains that the conditional 'If Dio is dead, this one is dead' is true when Dio is pointed at. Accordingly, Chrysippus maintains that the consequent, 'This one is dead', follows from the antecedent, 'Dio is dead'. The antecedent is possible, since it will be true at some time. The consequent, however, is impossible, on the grounds that it is false as long as Dio lives and is destroyed when Dio has died. According to Chrysippus, when Dio is dead, the assertible 'This one is dead' ceases to subsist because the object of the *deixis* expressed by the phrase 'this one', i.e. Dio, no longer exists. Given this, something impossible, 'This one is dead', follows from something possible, 'Dio is dead'.

Having rejected one of the assumptions of the Master Argument, Chrysippus was free to reject Diodorus' temporal definition of modality. Instead, he adopted a definition of possibility that resembles Philo's characterization of a possible proposition as one which is intrinsically capable of being true, but strengthens it by the additional requirement that the proposition not be hindered from being true by any external circumstances:[47]

> A proposition is possible if it is capable of being true, and not hindered from being true by external circumstances. . . . A proposition is necessary if it is not capable of being false, or is capable of being false, but is hindered by external circumstances from being false. (Diogenes Laërtius 7.75)

Thus, unlike Diodorus, Chrysippus regards the proposition "Fabius dies at land" as possible even if Fabius will in fact die at sea, provided that the proposition is intrinsically capable of being true and that no external circumstances prevent it from being true. In this way, Chrysippus avoids the fatalistic consequnces of Diodorus' definition. On the other hand, unlike Philo, Chrysippus does not regard a proposition such as "This piece of wood is burning" as possible when the piece of wood is lying at the bottom of the sea. For, even if the proposition is intrinsically capable of being true, there are external circumstances which prevent it from being true (viz., the quantities of water surrounding the piece of wood at the bottom of the sea). In this way, Chrysippus' characterization of possibility establishes a middle ground between Philo's and Diodorus' accounts of possibility, allowing for a wider class of possible propositions than the latter while being more restrictive than the former.

Philo, Diodorus, and Chrysippus took necessity and possibility, just like truth and falsehood, to be properties of propositions.[48] As such, necessity and possibility are not represented by any object-language modal operators in Stoic propositional logic. As Susanne Bobzien has

---

47 See Bobzien, *Determinism and Freedom*, 112–116. For a discussion of the relation between the accounts of possibility given by Philo, Diodorus, and Chrysippus, see 97–122; Bobzien, "Chrysippus' Modal Logic."

48 Bobzien, "Chrysippus' Modal Logic," 66; Bobzien, *Determinism and Freedom*, 101–102; Bobzien, "Logic," 117.

pointed out, "Stoic modal logic is not a logic of modal propositions, e.g. propositions of the type 'It is possible that it is day' or 'It is possibly true that it is day', formed with modal operators which qualify states of affairs, or propositions. Instead, their modal theory was about non-modalized propositions like 'It is day', insofar as they are possible, necessary and so on."[49]

---

[49] Bobzien, "Logic," 117.

CHAPTER 2

Modality in Medieval Latin Philosophy

Simo Knuuttila

Until the late 13th century, Latin modal philosophy was inclined to follow the ancient extensional interpretation of modality in terms of time and change, except that divine non-temporal possibilities were treated separately. Arabic thinkers mostly did not make this division, excluding al-Ghazali's theological theory. In the 12th century, some Latin authors put forward philosophical criticism of the principles of extensional interpretation such as the necessity of the present and the necessity of natural invariances. Duns Scotus developed this approach into a systematic theory of modality as alternativeness that influenced late medieval modal logic and modal thinking in general.

1. Modal Propositions in Early Medieval Textbooks

Early medieval logic owed a great debt to Boethius's sixth-century translations of Aristotle's *Categories* and *De interpretatione* (*Peri hermeneias*) and Porphyry's introductory work (*Isagoge*). Boethius' two commentaries on *De interpretatione* provided discussions about modal terms and modal propositions based on late ancient modal theories. Following this tradition, Peter Abelard (1179–1142) wrote several treatises on logic incorporating new systematic ideas on the semantics of terms and the nature of consequence. There were other masters of logic at the time of Abelard, and the impact of this interest is shown in numerous later 12th- and early 13th-century works on logic contributing to the teaching of dialectic.[1] One of these treatises was the anonymous *Dialectica Monacensis*, so called by its editor, which involved an analysis of the fine-structure of modal propositions; a similar approach was found in many other medieval logic texts. In discussing the quantity (universal, particular, singular) and quality (affirmative, negative) of the modals, the author states that modal terms may be adverbial or nominal. The modal adverb qualifies the copula "is," the structure of adverbial modal propositions without negation being:

(1) quantity/subject/modalized copula/predicate (e.g., Every A is-necessarily B).

The negation may be located in different places, either

(2) quantity/subject/copula, negated mode/predicate (e.g., Every A is-not-necessarily B)

---

[1] More than twenty anonymous late 12th- and early 13th-century works on logic are edited in L. M. De Rijk, *Logica Modernorum I–II* (Assen: Van Gorcum, 1962–1967).

or

(3) quantity/subject/modalized negative copula/predicate (e.g., Every A is-necessarily-not B).

In (2), the mode is denied; in (3) the modal adverb qualifies the negative copula. Modal propositions with the structure of (1)–(3) were sometimes called *de re* modalities but more usually called divided modalities because the modal term divided the proposition and did not pertain to it as a whole. Modal propositions with nominal modes could be taken to mean that what was expressed by a non-modalized proposition was necessary, possible, or impossible, their standard form being

(4) subject/copula/mode (e.g., That every A is B is necessary).

Modal propositions with this structure could be called modalities *de dicto* or, more usually, compound modalities.[2] It was said in the above text that the compound modalities were addressed in Aristotle's *De interpretatione* and the divided ones in his *Prior Analytics*.[3] In the 12th century, some logicians applied the grammatical distinction between categorematic and syncategorematic terms to modal notions. Categorematic terms of a proposition were taken to be the subjects and the predicates and syncategorematic terms to have meaning in combination with the categorematic terms. Modal terms had a categorematic meaning in the compound readings and a syncategorematic meaning in the divided readings of propositions.[4] These distinctions were often mentioned in discussing the compound-divided ambiguity in fallacious reasoning in Aristotle's *On sophistical refutations* (166a23–30).[5]

---

2   De Rijk, *Logica Modernorum*, II.2, 479–480, 570.
3   De Rijk, *Logica Modernorum*, II.2, 480.
4   See Joke Spruit, "Thirteenth-Century Discussions on Modal Terms," *Vivarium* 32 (1994): 196–226.
5   For medieval discussions, see note 18.

As for the logic of unanalyzed modal propositions, Aristotle mentioned its basic inferences without a further development in *Prior Analytics* I.15. They were studied in later ancient discussions and applied in medieval logic as follows: if the antecedent of a good consequence is necessary/possible, the consequent is necessary/possible.[6] These rules of inference, together with the inter-relational definitions of modal terms, embodied a virtually exhaustive insight into the basic propositional modal logic, but the main theoretical interest was in the modal syllogistic, the logic of which was more complicated.[7]

Modifying Boethius' systematization of Aristotle's remarks on modalities in *De interpretatione* 12 and 13, 12th- and 13th-century logicians often presented the equivalent combinations of various modal terms and negations and the inferential relations between modal propositions with the help of a diagram about contradictories, contraries, subcontraries, and subalternatives. The terms "possible" and "contingent" were used synonymously in these diagrams; later the nominal definition of "possibility" was usually "not impossible," as in Aristotle's *De interpretatione*, and that of "contingency" was "neither necessary nor impossible," corresponding to the notion of possibility in the modal syllogistic in Aristotle's *Prior Analytics*. The relations of the diagram were usually applied to compound modals and to singular divided modals.[8] Peter Abelard's misguided remarks on universal and particular divided modals in this context show that the questions of the relations between modal operations, quantifiers, and negation were far from clear.[9] This topic was systematically analyzed

---

6 See, e.g., Peter Abelard, *Dialectica*, ed. L. M. de Rijk (Assen: Van Gorcum, 1956), 202.6–8, 209.5; Peter Abelard, *Glossae super Perihermeneias*, ed. Klaus Jacobi and Christian Strub (Turnhout: Brepols, 2010), IX, 531–532, 553–554.
7 See Henrik Lagerlund, *Modal Syllogistics in the Middle Ages* (Leiden: Brill, 2000).
8 De Rijk, *Logica Modernorum*, II.2, 431.19–26; see also Simo Knuuttila, *Modalities in Medieval Philosophy* (London: Routledge, 1993), 106–108.
9 Abelard, *Glossae super Peri hermeneias* XII, 454–544.

in John Buridan's famous modal octagon which was copied in many early printed books.[10] Aristotle's theory of modal syllogistic in the *Prior Analytics* was discussed in various ways by Avicenna, Averroes, and other Arabic authors.[11] The first Latin commentary on this work was an anonymous treatise from the second half of the 12th century with explanations often derived from various ancient notes.[12] This was not an influential work, but Robert Kilwardby's Parisian commentary (c. 1240) exercised considerable influence on numerous 13th-century commentaries.[13] Kilwardby held that Aristotle's logic involved a true theory of reality and, consequently, interpreting Aristotle's modal syllogistic demanded extensive metaphysical considerations, such as restricting the necessity premises to those involving essential terms and distinguishing between various kinds of minor assertoric and contingency premises, depending on the nature of the major premise that "appropriated" a certain kind of minor premise.[14]

2. THE NECESSITY OF THE PRESENT AND OF WHAT ALWAYS IS IN LOGICAL TREATISES

A remarkable feature of many ancient and medieval texts on modality is their tendency to treat modal terms extensionally by referring to

---

10 See George E. Hughes, "The Modal Logic of John Buridan," in *Atti del Convegno internazionale di storia della logica: Le teorie delle modalità*, ed. Giovanna Corsi, Corrado Mangione, and Massimo Mugnai (Bologna: CLUEB, 1989), 93–111; Elizabeth Karger, "John Buridan's Theory of the Logical Relations between General Modal Formulae," in *Aristotle's* Peri Hermeneias *in the Latin Middle Ages*, ed. Henk Braakhuis and C. Kneepkens (Haren: Ingenium, 2003), 429–444.

11 See Paul Thom, *Medieval Modal Systems: Problems and Concepts* (Aldershot: Ashgate, 2003); Tony Street and Nadja Germann, "Arabic and Islamic Philosophy of Language and Logic," in *The Stanford Encyclopedia of Philosophy*, ed. Edward N. Zalta, spring 2021 edition, https://plato.stanford.edu.

12 Anonymus Aurelianensis, *"Anonymus Aurelianensis III" in Aristotelis* Analytica *priora*, ed. Christina Thomsen-Törnqvist (Leiden: Brill, 2015).

13 Robert Kilwardby, *Notule libri Priorum*, 2 vols., ed. Paul Thom and John Scott, Auctores Britannici Medii Aevi 23 (Oxford: Oxford University Press, 2016).

14 Metaphysical principles in Kilwardby's modal syllogistic are discussed in Paul Thom, *Logic and Ontology in the Syllogistic of Robert Kilwardby* (Leiden: Brill, 2007). For modality in 13th-century

the real history as the scope of their application. Some background assumptions of this habit of thought can be discerned in those 12th- and 13th-century works on logic in which temporally indefinite utterance token propositions are necessary if they are always true when uttered and impossible if always false when uttered.[15] This is in accordance with what is called a statistical model for modality in which possibility is typically assumed to be at some time actual.[16]

Let us take a look at the widely accepted and related thesis of the necessity of the present in these treatises. The historical starting point was Aristotle's remark in *De interpretatione* 9 (19a23–26) that what is actual is necessary when it is, though not necessary without qualification. Boethius explained that Socrates necessarily sits when he sits because his non-sitting, say standing, is not possible with respect to that time, but is not simply necessary because his standing is possible at another time if he is not always sitting.[17] The sentence "A seated man can be standing" was often analyzed in terms of a temporal composition-division distinction: a seated man cannot stand while seated, this

---

logic, see also Lagerlund, *Modal Syllogistics*, 19–52; Sarah Uckelman, "Modalities in Medieval Logic" (PhD diss., University of Amsterdam, 2009).

15 See Aristotle, *Metaphysics* IX.10, 1051b9–17; for necessity as unchanging truth, impossibility as unchanging falsity, and contingency as changing truth, see Boethius, *Commentarii in librum Aristotelis* Peri hermeneias *I–II*, ed. Carl Meiser (Leipzig: Teubner, 1877–1880), vol. I, 124.30–125.14. For some similar later formulations, cf. De Rijk, *Logica Modernorum*, II.2, 481.22–482.9; Raina Kirchhoff, *Die Syncategoremata des Wilhelm von Sherwood: Kommentierung und historische Einordnung* (Leiden: Brill, 2008), 474–475. Aquinas writes in *In duodecim libros Aristotelis Metaphysicorum expositio*, ed. Marie-Raymond Cathala and Raymundo M. Spiazzi (Turin: Marietti, 1971), IX, 11.1900: "In things that can be compounded and divided, the same statement is sometimes true and sometimes false; for example, 'Socrates is seated' is true when he is seated and false when he is standing. But in things which cannot be otherwise, namely, in those that are always compounded or divided, it is not possible that the same statement is sometimes true and sometimes false, but that which is true is always true and that which is false is always false."

16 According to Boethius, what always is, is necessary, what never is, is impossible, and what is possible, is at least sometimes actual (*In Periherm.* I, 125.2–5, 200.19–201.3; II, 237.1–5, 241.5–7); a property that belongs to all members of a group is necessary with respect to that group and a possible property belongs to some members (I, 120.24–121.16). For further medieval examples, see Simo Knuuttila, "Medieval Modal Theories and Modal Logic," in *Handbook of the History of Logic 2: Mediaeval and Renaissance Logic*, ed. Dov M. Gabbay and John Woods (Amsterdam: Elsevier, 2008), 509–512.

17 Boethius, *In Periherm.* I, 121.25–122.18; II.242.24–243.4.

corresponding to the false compound reading, but the proposition was true in the divided sense explicated by phrases like "at another time."[18] In Boethius, the necessity of the present prevented the acceptance of

(5) p (now) & it is possible that not-p (now).

Boethius argued that "it is not possible that somebody could be sitting and not sitting at the same time; therefore, no one who is sitting can be non-sitting at the time when he is sitting."[19] In regarding (5) as false, Boethius and his followers did not consider counterfactual alternatives, but instead thought that if an allegedly unactualized present possibility is treated as actualized, something impossible follows. If a temporally impossible proposition is not simply necessarily false, it has a changing truth value and may be true in the future.[20]

While this was one of Aristotle's ideas for qualifying the necessity of the present, he also argued that the necessity of an event at a certain time did not imply that it would have been antecedently necessary. Aristotle held that there are genuine singular possibilities with respect to a future point of time, which may be realized or remain unrealized.[21]

This idea of diachronic modalities was further developed by the Stoics and then applied by Boethius: if the possibility that p and the possibility that non-p refer to a definite future time, say t, these propositions may be diachronically possible now; if non-p will be true at t, the

---

18 De Rijk, *Logica Modernorum*, I, 210.10–17, 311.8–15, 316.1–7; II.2, 687.21–688.1; William of Sherwood, *Introductiones in logicam*, ed. Hartmut Brandt and Christoph Kann (Hamburg: Meiner, 1995), 178–180; Peter of Spain, *Tractatus called afterwards Summule logicales*, ed. L. M. de Rijk (Assen: Van Gorcum, 1972), VII, 70–71; Lambert of Auxerre (?), *Logica*, ed. F. Alessio (Florence: La Nuova Italia Editrice, 1971), 158; Richard Sophista, *Abstractiones*, ed. Mary Sirridge and Sten Ebbesen with E. J. Ashworth, Auctores Britannici Medii Aevi 25 (Oxford: Oxford University Press for the British Academy, 2016), 325. William of Sherwood uses as a premise the statement that what is possible will be true (*Introductiones*, 178); see also the editors' note 237.

19 Boethius, *In Periherm.* II, 241.10–12, Boethius assumes that the impossibility of "p at t and non-p at t" implies the denial of "p at t and it is possible at t that non-p at t," this being equivalent to how Boethius understood the necessity of the present: "if p at t then it is necessary that p at t."

20 Boethius, *In Periherm.* I, 121.25–122.4; II.241.29–242.5.

21 Aristotle, *De interpretatione* 9, 19a12–17; *Nicomachean Ethics* III.5, 1114a17–19; *Metaphysics* VI.3.

antecedent possibility that p will disappear before *t* does not remain a simultaneous alternative.[22] Diachronic prospective alternatives are options of which the non-actualized ones are rendered impossible by the actualized alternatives.

The same view of the necessity of the present was used in early obligations logic. Logical treatises on obligations (*De obligationibus*) dealt with rules for disputations in which various propositions were put forward by an opponent and evaluated by a respondent. In a standard model, a false and contingent proposition was first put forward and the consistency of new propositions was then evaluated with respect to the initial position and other previously evaluated propositions.[23] An anonymous 13th-century treatise, putatively attributed to William of Sherwood, included the following rule about accepting an initial position:

(6) When a contingently false statement referring to a present instant is posited, one has to deny that it is [now].[24]

When this false but not impossible statement was "You are in Rome," treating it as true demanded one deny that the time at which the statement was assumed to be true was the present time. The time rule (6), which was based on the principle of the necessity of the present, was also included in other 13th-century obligations treatises.[25] In the putative Sherwood treatise, rule (6) is proved with an argument that is more simply described and criticized by Robert Grosseteste in his *De*

---

22 Boethius, *In Periherm.* II, 190.14–191.2.
23 For medieval obligations logic, see Mikko Yrjönsuuri, "Duties, Rules and Interpretations in Obligational Disputations," in *Medieval Formal Logic: Obligations, Insolubles and Consequences*, ed. Mikko Yrjönsuuri (Dordrecht: Kluwer, 2001), 3–34.
24 Anonymous, *De obligationibus*, ed. Romuald Green, in "The Logical Treatise 'De obligationibus': An Introduction with Critical Texts of William of Sherwood (?) and Walter Burley" (PhD diss., University of Louvain, 1963), 8.32–33.
25 L. M. de Rijk, "Some Thirteenth Century Tracts on the Game of Obligation I–II," *Vivarium* 12 (1974): 112–113; 13 (1975): 32.

libero arbitrio (c. 1230).²⁶ The necessity of the present is here defended by arguing that the hypothesis of an unrealized possibility with respect to the actual instant is impossible because the assumption of its actuality leads to contradiction. This is what Aristotle maintained in *De caelo* I.12, 281b15-25, a text not mentioned here but later often associated with the proposed view that there are no unrealized possibilities. Aristotle held that nothing is in vain in nature (e.g., *De caelo* I.4, 271a34). Boethius applied this often repeated principle to unrealized possibilities in the same way as the argument criticized by Grosseteste.²⁷

In addition to the thesis of the necessity of the present, there was another popular doctrine about the behavior of the truth of propositions that was called "the matter of propositions." It was associated with the logical theory of the square of oppositions which defined the relations of contradiction and contrariety between universal and particular affirmative and negative propositions and divided the types of such propositions into three classes depending on how the propositions were true or false. Aquinas writes:

> In necessary matter all affirmative propositions are determinately true; this holds for propositions in the future tense as well as in the past and present tenses; negative propositions are false. In impossible matter the contrary is the case. In contingent matter, however, universal propositions are false and particular propositions are true. This holds for the future tense propositions as well as those in the past and present tenses. In indefinite propositions, both are at once true in the future tense propositions as well as in the past and present tense propositions.²⁸

---

26 Robert Grosseteste, *De libero arbitrio* in Neil Lewis, "The First Recension of Robert Grosseteste's *De libero arbitrio,*" *Mediaeval Studies* 53 (1991): 53.
27 Boethius, *In Periherm.* II, 236.11-18.
28 Thomas Aquinas, *In Aristotelis libros Peri hermeneias et Posteriorum analyticorum expositio*, ed. Raymundo M. Spiazzi (Turin: Marietti, 1964), I.13, 168; for the same view of contingency, see De Rijk, *Logica Modernorum*, II.2, 138.24-26 and Albert the Great, *Liber I Perihermeneias*, vol. 1 of

Aquinas explains that modalities in necessary matter are founded on per se predication and those in impossible matter on per se repugnance.[29] Contingent propositions are addressed in terms of an extensional interpretation, contrary universal propositions of contingent matter being false, particular propositions true, and contrary indefinite propositions true. Actualization in some cases or at some time, albeit not in all or always, is the hallmark of contingency. Propositions are apparently treated as temporally unqualified type-propositions because otherwise it would be impossible that propositions like "All horses are sleeping" are ever true.[30]

What about propositions which are universally and always true without being based on a per se inclusion such as those about inseparable accidents? Aquinas says that they may be called necessary and consequently always true because they include a non-formal per se predication based on the matter of things.[31] There was another answer in Averroes. In discussing Aristotle's modal syllogistic, Averroes refers to a distinction between essential and accidental modalities. The syllogistic necessity premises correspond to essentially necessary relations between things referred to by "necessary terms" which immutably stand for the things they signify. Statements of this kind are necessary per se and always true. If an affirmative statement is always true when the non-necessary subject term is actual, it is necessary *per accidens*, such as inseparable accidents.[32] Averroes also writes that there

---

Opera omnia, ed. August Borgnet (Paris: Vivès, 1890), 5.6, 422. The doctrine of the matter of propositions was developed in late ancient times and was known to Latin authors through Boethius. It was often used in Arabic philosophy as well. For the history, see Knuuttila, "Medieval Modal Theories," 507–509.

29 Boethius, *In Periherm.* I.13, 166.

30 Cf. note 15.

31 Aquinas, *In Aristotelis libros Peri hermeneias et Posteriorum analyticorum expositione*, I, 14.121; see also Jeroen van Rijen, *Aspects of Aristotle's Logic of Modalities* (Dordrecht: Kluwer, 1989), 144.

32 Averroes, *Quaesita octo in librum Priorum*, in *Aristotelis Opera cum Averrois commentariis* I.2b (Venice, 1562), IV.3.83–84; cf. Thom, *Medieval Modal Systems*, 81–85. A similar distinction between essential and accidental necessity was applied in Kilwardby's discussion of modal conversion rules. They are said to apply only to essential necessity proposition and not to accidental

are statements which are impossible *per accidens* and possible per se. These are always false, although their falsity is not based on essential incompatibility between the terms. While Averroes held that there are no eternally unrealized generic possibilities in nature, the per se possibilities corresponding to accidental impossibilities seem to be an exception. However, Averroes characterizes these as possibilities which are not even meant to be realizable. They are conceptual assumptions which as such are in disagreement with the necessary order of things but possible in an abstract way, such as a body greater than the universe, all bodies being at rest, or a motion faster than the diurnal motion. Averroes deals with these counter-possible possibilities in explaining Aristotle's indirect proofs in the *Physics*.[33] Making use of this argument, Aquinas operates with the levels of the Porphyrian tree; for example, something is possible for a member of a species because there are examples of it in other species of the genus. Flying is not possible for humans *qua* humans but is possible for humans *qua* animals, because there are flying animals.[34]

The notions of accidental necessity and impossibility were more commonly applied to temporally indefinite propositions which are always truly or falsely uttered after having once changed their truth-value; for example, "I have walked," "I have not walked," and other past tense singular statements.[35]

---

necessities such as "All literate beings are necessarily humans" (*Notule libri Priorum*, 8.133–142; 40.162–174). See also Roger Bacon, *Summulae dialectics*, ed. Alain de Libera, *Archives de l'histoire doctrinale et littéraire du moyen âge* 54 (1987): 198. For Averroes' views in Gersonides, an early 14th-century Jewish philosopher, see *The Logic of Gersonides: A Translation of Sefer ha-Heqqesh ha-Yashar The Book of the Correct Syllogism*, trans. Charles H. Manekin (Dordrecht: Kluwer, 1992).

33   Averroes, *Questions in* Physics, trans. Helen T. Goldstein (Dordrecht: Kluwer, 1991), 31–32, 138–141; *Paraphrasis in quatuor libros De caelo* in *Aristotelis Opera cum Averrois commentariis* (1562), V, 315.

34   Thomas Aquinas, *In octo libros Physicorum Aristotelis exposition*, ed. Mariani Maggiòlo (Turin: Marietti, 1965), VII.2, 896. See Simo Knuuttila and Taneli Kukkonen, "Thought Experiment and Indirect Proof in Averroes, Aquinas, and Buridan," in *Thought Experiments: Methodological and Historical Perspectives*, ed. Katerina Ierodiakonou and Sophie Roux (Leiden: Brill, 2011), 83–99.

35   See William of Sherwood, *Introductiones in logicam*, 34.435–443; De Rijk, *Logica modernorum*, II.2, 429.1–10, 481.22–482.14; Bacon, *Summulae dialecticae*, 261; Sophista, *Abstractiones*, 326–328.

3. Extensional Modalities in Metaphysics and Natural Philosophy

Writers using modal terms extensionally in logic and other branches of philosophy usually did not define them in this way, thinking that modalities had a metaphysical foundation. Nevertheless, things were classified as necessary or contingent from the point of view of their occurrence in the historical sequence of events without an idea of alternative domains. While this one-world model was an influential part of the ancient intellectual heritage, it was not applied to divine possibilities by Christian authors and, moreover, some 12th-century thinkers became skeptical of its suitability for modal semantics, preferring the view of modality as alternativeness (see Section 4). This approach was left in the background in 13th-century Aristotelianism, but it was revived in late medieval thought by the works of John Duns Scotus and became dominant after him. In this section I shall deal with various forms of extensional modalities in medieval philosophy, beginning with Averroes and his Latin followers, who systematized modal terms in accordance with the statistical paradigm.

John of Jandun, an early 14th-century Parisian Averroist, writes in his questions commentary on Aristotle's *Metaphysics*:

> If something that never exists is assumed to be possible, an impossibility follows in the sense that something simultaneously is and is not, for as far as it is always non-existent, it is non-existent at any instant of time, and as far as it is possible, it will exist and have being, for when possible is assumed to be actual etc., and so it will simultaneously be and not be. Therefore no thing that is always non-existent is possible, and conversely, no possible thing is always non-actual, so that all possibilities are sometimes actual. This argument can be formulated in another way with the same result. If something is possible in the future but will be never actual, then the same can simultaneously be and not-be, combining "simultaneity"

with being, but this is impossible.... This is confirmed as follows. If something, say b, is possible in the future, say at the instant a, then b can be at a, but it will not be at a because it never is. Therefore it can simultaneously be and not be; consequently it will simultaneously be and not be at a.[36]

In Jandun's modal semantics, "possibility" refers to actuality at some time; "necessity" refers to what is always actual, whether without qualification or during a certain period, and "impossibility" to what is immutably non-actual. He first discusses possibilities with respect to the history of the universe and then with respect to the future. Many of his formulations are found in Averroes, whose philosophical views Jandun often follows and to whom he refers as the source of the present argument.[37]

Averroes and his followers thought that the statistical interpretation is an Aristotelian theory. In writing in the above text "when possible is assumed to be actual etc.," Jandun refers to Aristotle's definition of possibility in *Metaphysics* IX.3 (1047b30) and *Prior Analytics* I.13 (32a18–20) that if something is possible, it can be assumed to be actual without anything impossible following from this assumption. Aristotle himself refers to this definition in *De caelo* I.12 where he argues that if an omnitemporal thing is maintained to be possibly non-existent, this leads to contradiction because assuming the possibility as actual does so. Jandun also explains this indirect proof for the view that all genuine possibilities are sometimes actualized. Aristotle's reduction argument

---

[36] John of Jandun, *Quaestiones in duodecim libros Metaphysicae* (Venice, 1525), IX.5 (114va–b); for Jandun's commentary, see Roberto Lambertini, "Jandun's Question-Commentary on Aristotle's Metaphysics," in *A Companion to the Latin Medieval Commentaries on Aristotle's* Metaphysics, ed. Fabrizio Amerini and Gabrielle Galluzzo (Leiden: Brill, 2014), 385–411. See also Jandun's *In libros Aristotelis De caelo et mundo quae extant quaestiones* (Venice, 1552), I.34, 21vb.

[37] In his comments of *Metaphysics* IX in *Aristotelis Opera cum Averrois commentariis*, Averroes defends the view that all possibilities will be realized (1562), vol. VIII, 232va. For Averroes's equating temporal and modal terms and a statistical account of modality, see his commentaries on Aristotle's *De caelo* (1562), vol. V, 84r–v, and on *De generatione et corruptione* (Venice, 1562), vol. V, 383v–384r.

was of central systematic significance for the extensional interpretation in Averroist Aristotelianism.[38] While Jandun defended the view that there are no unrealized singular possibilities, Aquinas and many Latin authors thought that some singular possibilities may remain unrealized, such as "This cloak may be cut in the future." Such future singular possibilities were treated as vanishing diachronic possibilities in a Boethian manner.[39]

Extensional modalities were often treated in the more limited context of potencies and causal power. Following Aristotle's division in *Metaphysics* V.12, 13th-century Aristotelians distinguished between modalities based on the definition of possibility as consequential consistency and modalities based on the notion of potency. In his commentary on *Metaphysics* IX, Aquinas states that generic potencies in nature are, qua potencies, intrinsically necessary features of the order of being. They consist of passive potencies as dispositions and active potencies as activators, both determined by the nature or essence of the subjects. Natural potencies are necessarily activated when the agent and the patient meet and the active potency acts and the passive potency is acted on.[40] Active and passive potencies could be separately referred to as non-actualized partial possibilities. This allowed one to speak about unrealized natural possibilities, but these were not full possibilities because not all requirements were fulfilled—it was a problem of the Aristotelian theory that all full natural possibilities were immediately activated so that the difference between potentiality and actuality tended to disappear, although this was just what Aristotle meant to criticize in the Megarians in *Metaphysics* IX. Aquinas thought that all types of natural possibilities were sometimes

---

38 Averroes combines the three texts just mentioned in his discussion of *Metaphysics* IX (233rb). For logical problems in Aristotle's indirect proofs, see Jacob Rosen and Marko Malink, "A Method of Modal Proof in Aristotle," *Oxford Studies in Ancient Philosophy* 42 (2012): 179–261.
39 Aquinas, *In Metaph.* IX.3, 1808; Boethius, *In Periherm.* I.14, 182; I.15, 21; cf. note 22.
40 Aquinas, *In Metaph.* IX.1, 1781–1782; 4, 1818, 1821.

actualized; nothing was in vain in nature such as eternally unrealized potency types.[41]

Medieval Aristotelians treated active potencies as efficient causes and divided them into necessary and contingent ones. Following Avicenna, many authors held that the natural effects were necessary with respect to their actual causes and also followed Averroes' classification of the active causes: necessary causes were always effective when they were in contact with passive powers, contingent causes produced their effect in most cases (*in pluribus*), being prevented by chance in few cases, or were not determined more to acting than not-acting (*ad utrumlibet*). Singular caused events, while necessary as caused effects, were considered statistically necessary or contingent, depending on how the causal factors of the same kind behaved in other situations.[42] Boethius argued against Stoic causal determinism by referring to chance events in nature, *ad utrumlibet* contingencies, and human acts of free choice in Aristotle, but in his *Consolatio philosophiae* he held that divine providence is in fact the ultimate cause of all things.[43] Aquinas' strategy was to refer to the statistical contingency of proximate causes, thinking that it is compatible with the ultimate providential necessity.[44]

Siger of Brabant, Aquinas' Aristotelian contemporary in Paris, wrote that the notions of necessary, impossible to be otherwise, immovable,

---

[41] See, e.g., Aquinas, *In Aristotelis libros De caelo et mundo exposition* I.8, 91; cf. I.26, 258. Aquinas held that if something can be destroyed, it will be destroyed: *Summa theologiae*, ed. Pietro Caramello (Turin: Marietti, 1948–1950). I.2.3. See also Moses Maimonides, *Guide of the Perplexed*, 2 vols., trans. Shlomo Pines (Chicago: University of Chicago Press, 1974), II, 247, 249.

[42] See Anneliese Maier, *Die Vorläufer Galileis im 14. Jahrhundert* (Rome: Edizioni di Storia e Letteratura, 1949), 219–250.

[43] Boethius, *In Periherm.* II, 190.1–5; in *Consolatio philosophiae*, ed. Ludwig Bieler (Turnhout: Brepols, 1957), IV, prose 6; V, prose 6, Boethius states that God's eternal and non-temporal knowledge of things does not make them necessary. This was later interpreted in terms of the distinction between the necessity of the consequence (Nec.(Kp→p)) and the necessity of the consequent (Kp→nec.p); see, for example, Thomas Aquinas, *Summa contra gentiles*, ed. Ceslas Pera, Pietro Marc, and Pietro Caramello (Turin: Marietti, 1961–1967), I, 67. It remains a problem how to combine freedom of the will and the necessity of providential causation.

[44] Aquinas, *Summa contra gentiles* I.67; Aquinas, *Summa theologiae* I.14.13; I.22.2; Boethius, *In Periherm.* I.14.197.

and eternal are mutually interchangeable. These terms, derived from Aristotle's *Metaphysics* V.5, were primarily applied to the first cause without qualification and secondarily to uniformly moving celestial movers and to natural causes in the lower spheres which produced their effects always or, if they were contingent causes, always when not impeded by accidental coincidences. While the notion of necessity was treated extensionally as expressing various kinds of invariances, it was embedded in the essential order of things that determined the occurrences accountable by extensional modalities.[45] Averroes and Aquinas also thought that "impossible to be otherwise" meant unchanging actuality in the metaphysically fixed order of things.[46] Roughly the same view of natural modalities was formerly defended by Boethius and many 12th-century thinkers who argued that natural necessities represented natural habitudes associated with lower causes and controlled by the higher cause of divine power.[47]

Following Boethius, Aquinas criticized the Megarian account that defined necessity as that which always is as being drawn a posteriori. The better way was to base the definition on the nature of things by stating that necessities are what by their nature are determined to be. He adds in the same place that impossibilities are never actual, and contingencies are sometimes actual and sometimes not because of the nature of things.[48] Similar formulations of the explanatory founding of

---

[45] Siger of Brabant, *Quaestiones in Metaphysicam*, ed. William Dunphy (Louvain-la-Neuve: Éditions de l'Institut Supérieur de Philosophie, 1981), 266–270, 376–378. He argued for providential necessity and local contingency in a way similar to that of Aquinas (379–387); see Mikko Posti, "Divine Providence in Medieval Philosophical Theology 1250–1350" (PhD diss., University of Helsinki, 2017).

[46] Aquinas, *In Metaph*. V.6, 840; Averroes, *In Metaph*. V.5, in *Aristotelis Opera cum Averrois commentariis* (1562), vol. VIII, 109va.

[47] Cf. Boethius, *In Periherm*. II, 236. For the common distinction between natural possibilities determined by the nature of things (inferior cause) and the supranatural possibilities of God (superior cause), see, e.g., Alan of Lille, *Regulae caelestis iuris*, ed. N. M. Häring, *Archives doctrinale et littéraire du moyen âge* 78 (1981): 164–165; this was the background of the later doctrine of God's absolute and ordained power; see Hester Gelber, *It Could Have Been Otherwise: Contingency and Necessity in Dominican Theology at Oxford 1300–1350* (Leiden: Brill 2004), 309–349.

[48] Boethius, *In Periherm*. I.14, 183.

modalities occur in other Aristotelians, whether in terms of essential per se predications defined in Aristotle's *Posterior Analytics* I.4 or his theory of natural potencies.

4. INTENTIONAL MODALS

At the heart of medieval western theology was Augustine's creationist conception of God's freedom and power that disagreed with extensionally interpreted philosophical modalities; for Augustine, God has freely chosen the actual world and its providential plan from alternatives which he could have realized but did not will to do. God's eternal ideas of finite things define how the highest being can be imitated in creation, the possibilities thus having an ontological foundation in God's simple essence.[49]

The discrepancy between the Catholic doctrine of God's freedom and power and the philosophical modal conceptions was brought into the discussion by Peter Damian and Anselm of Canterbury in the 11th century, and the same question continued to be attended to in later theological considerations of God's power and providence and historical contingency.[50] While Augustine's idea of divine alternatives was generally known in 13th-century theology, the conception of modality as alternativeness was not often discussed in philosophical contexts increasingly dominated by Aristotelian modal ideas. Anselm of Canterbury attempted to base his theory of philosophical and theological modalities on the notions of power and potency.[51] This was considered as too narrow a basis for modal semantics; Aquinas remarked that divine omnipotence could not be simply defined by

---

[49] See Simo Knuuttila, "Time and Creation in Augustine," in *The Cambridge Companion to Augustine*, ed. David Vincent Meconi and Eleonore Stump (Cambridge: Cambridge University Press, 2014), 82–83, 86–88.

[50] See Toivo Holopainen, *Dialectic and Theology in the Eleventh Century* (Leiden: Brill, 1996).

[51] Simo Knuuttila, "Anselm on Modality," in *The Cambridge Companion to Anselm*, ed. Brian Davies and Brian Leftow (Cambridge: Cambridge University Press, 2004), 124–127.

referring to power without a notion of possibility as that which is not contradictory; this was called absolute possibility.[52] John of Jandun kept philosophical and theological modalities strictly separate: his extensional and determinist modal metaphysics was what reason taught; faith taught otherwise, virtuously but without reason.[53]

In the first part of the 13th century, Robert Grosseteste put forward a philosophical analysis of Augustine's view of God's unrealized possibilities separated from the approach to modality in terms of change and time. He taught that while things are primarily called necessary or possible "from eternity and without beginning" with respect to God's eternal omniscience, there are relative necessities and impossibilities with a beginning in God's providence which are eternal contingencies in the sense that God could have chosen their opposites.[54] The idea of divine choice between alternatives was absent in Avicenna and Averroes, who did not regard it as part of Islamic orthodoxy, but it was defended by al-Ghazali (c. 1056–1111), who criticized Avicenna's necessitarian metaphysics. According to al-Ghazali, while propositions about natural invariances are always true, they are not necessary as Avicenna took it, but could be different because of divine power.[55]

In addition to theological issues, there were some theoretical considerations of the new modal semantics in the 12th century. Abelard made use of traditional modal concepts associated with the nature of things, but he was also interested in possibilities as simultaneous alternatives. Even though what was actual was no longer avoidable, unrealized counterfactual alternatives could have happened at that time.[56]

---

52 Aquinas, *Summa theologiae* I.25, 3; cf. *In Metaph*.V, 14.971.
53 John of Jandun, *In libros Aristotelis De caelo* I.34, 22rb.
54 Robert Grosseteste, *De libero arbitrio*, 168.26–170.33, 178.24–29.
55 See Taneli Kukkonen, "Possible Worlds in the *Tahâfut al-falâsifa:* Al-Ghazâli on Creation and Contingency," *Journal of the History of Philosophy* 38 (2000): 479–502. For metaphysical determinism in Arabic philosophy, see Catarina Belo, *Chance and Determinism in Avicenna and Averroes* (Leiden: Brill, 2007).
56 See Christopher Martin, "Abaelard on Modality: Some Possibilities and Some Puzzles," in *Potentialität und Possibilität: Modalaussagen in der Geschichte der Metaphysik,* ed. Thomas

In explaining Plato's "Platonitas," Gilbert of Poitiers argued that this included all that Plato was, is, and will be as well as what he could be but never is.[57]

"What is once true is always true" was one of the theses of the 12th-century authors, later called *nominales*. They argued that while tensed statements about temporally definite singular events have a changing truth-value, the corresponding non-tensed propositions are unchangingly true or false, without being necessarily true or false for this reason.[58] This agreed with Abelard's view that future contingent propositions are always true or always false.[59]

The discussion about modality received a new orientation when Duns Scotus systematized former intensional ideas in denying the necessity of the present and the equation between necessity and unchangeability. He defined logical possibility as that which it is not repugnant to be and a temporally definite contingent state of affairs as that which could be the case instead of how things are then. He also distinguished between logical modalities and real necessities and possibilities which were based on the potencies of things in the actual world. This new approach had far-reaching consequences for

---

Buchheim, Corneille Kneepkens, and Kuno Lorenz (Stuttgart-Bad Canstatt: Frommann-Holzboog, 2001), 97–122.

57 Knuuttila, *Modalities*, 75–82.

58 Yokio Iwakuma and Sten Ebbesen, "Logico-Theological Schools from the Second Half of the 12th Century: A List of Sources," *Vivarium* 30 (1992): 173–215.

59 Abelard, *Glossae super Peri hermeneias* IX.520–577; Abelard, *Dialectica* 217.27–219.24; see also Peter of Poitiers, *Sententiae Sententiae I*, ed. Philip S. Moore and Marthe Dulong (Notre Dame, IN: University of Notre Dame Press, 1961), 7.133–43; 12.164–223; 14.328–353. Following Abelard, Peter Lombard wrote that "Things cannot be other than as God foreknows them" is true in the compound sense and false in the divided sense. Peter Lombard, *Sententiae in IV libris distinctae*, I–II (Grottaferrata: Editiones Collegii S. Bonaventurae ad Claras Aquas, 1971), I.38.2. Medieval theologians usually thought that future contingent propositions had a definite truth-value in divine knowledge but also held, barring Abelard and Buridan, that this was not Aristotle's view. Aristotle's approach in *Peri hermeneias* was taken to be correctly explained by Boethius: future contingent propositions are not antecedently true or false, but they can be characterized as true-or-false. See Simo Knuuttila, "Medieval Commentators on Future Contingents in *De interpretatione* 9," *Vivarium* 48 (2010): 75–95.

subsequent discussions in theology and metaphysics as well as early 14th-century modal logic.⁶⁰

Scotus' formulation of the notion of synchronic contingency is as follows:

> I do not call something contingent because it is not always or necessarily the case, but because the opposite of it could be actual at the very moment when it occurs.⁶¹

He first distances himself from the extensional division between necessity and contingency and then explains the meaning of contingency in terms of simultaneous alternatives. Referring to obligations logic mentioned above, Scotus states that the time rule (6) and its proof are false since, even if "You are in Rome" is false now, it can be true now. Because of his interpretation of possibility, Scotus states that Aristotle's principle that nothing impossible will follow if a possibility is assumed to be actual is true, except that in assuming that a counterfactual possibility is actual, an incompossibility with respect to what is actual follows.⁶²

While Aquinas and many others before him described divine omnipotence as being determined by absolute possibilities expressed by statements in which the predicate is not repugnant to the subject, Scotus called this "logical possibility" and combined it with the systematic idea of simultaneous alternative domains. According to Scotus, God's intellect has a non-temporal knowledge of all thinkable things,

---

60 For Scotus' modal theory, see Ludger Honnefelder, *Scientia transcendens: Die formale Bestimmung der Seiendheit und Realität in der Metaphysik des Mittelalters und der Neuzeit* (Hamburg: Meiner, 1990); Simo Knuuttila, "Duns Scotus and the Foundations of Logical Modalities," in *John Duns Scotus: Metaphysics and Ethics,* ed. Ludger Honnefelder, Rega Wood, and Mechthild Dreyer (Leiden: Brill, 1996), 127–143; Calvin Normore, "Duns Scotus's Modal Theory," in *The Cambridge Companion to Duns Scotus,* ed. Thomas Williams (Cambridge: Cambridge University Press, 2003), 129–160.

61 John Duns Scotus, *Ordinatio* I, d. 2, p. 1, q. 1–2, n. 86, in *Opera omnia* 2, ed. Commissio Scotistica (Vatican City: Typis polyglottis, 1950–), 178.

62 John Duns Scotus, *Lectura* I, d. 39, q. 1–5, n. 56, n. 72, in *Opera omnia* 17, 498, 504.

which can be partitioned into groups according to the relation of compossibility. One compossible whole is actualized by divine power, but Scotus does not develop a detailed theory of other possible worlds. Possibilities as the objects of divine knowledge and omnipotence have an ontological status as "intentional" beings in divine mind, *esse intelligibile* and *esse possibile*; without having any kind of being by themselves, they form the preconditions for being and understanding.[63] Scotus often says that possibilities are what they are independently of whether God or anything else exists.[64] Metaphysical possibilities are related to a real power of being; logical possibilities alone do not explain why there is something.[65]

While some followers of Scotus continued to argue for non-ontological possibilities, others held that a reference to divine ideas was necessary for understanding them. This was also stressed by Leibniz who criticized the Scotist idea in this respect.[66] Even the interpretations of contemporary commentators are divided.[67] It might be useful to attend to Scotus' view that divine intellect, independently of whether anything else exists, necessarily thinks about all things that are intelligible. The intentional object of God's understanding consists

---

63 John Duns Scotus, *Ordinatio* I.43, nn. 7, 14, in *Opera omnia* 6, 354, 358–360.

64 John Duns Scotus, *Lectura* I.7, n. 32; 39.1–5, n. 49, in *Opera omnia* 16, 484; *Ordinatio* I.7.1, n. 27, in *Opera omnia* 4, 118–119; John Duns Scotus, *Quaestiones super libros Metaphysicorum Aristotelis VI–IX*, ed. Robert R. Andrews (St. Bonaventure: Franciscan Institute, 1997), 9.1–2, n. 18, 514.

65 See Honnefelder, *Scientia transcendens*, 17–18, 64–70.

66 G. W. Leibniz, *Essais de Théodicée*, vol. 6 of *Die philosophischen Schriften*, ed. C. I. Gerhardt (Berlin, 1885), 184.

67 It is argued that if divine thoughts did not exist, there would be no content of possibilities in Scotus; see Tobias Hoffmann, "Duns Scotus on the Origin of the Possibles in the Divine Intellect," in *Philosophical Debates at Paris in the Early Fourteenth Century*, ed. Stephen Brown, Thomas Dewender, and Theo Kobusch (Leiden: Brill, 2009), 359–379; Fabrizio Mondadori, "The Independence of the Possible according to Duns Scotus," in *Duns Scot à Paris, 1302–2002*, ed. Olivier Boulnois, Elizabeth Karger, Jean-Luc Solère, and Gérard Sondag (Turnhout: Brepols, 2004), 313–374. According to Honnefelder, *Scientia transcendens*, 54 and Knuuttila, "Duns Scotus," possibilities that precede being and thinking do not depend on divine omniscience or omnipotence. For Bradwardine's criticism of Scotus in his *De causa Dei* from 1344, see Gloria Frost, "Thomas Bradwardine on God and the Foundations of Modality," *British Journal for the History of Philosophy* 22 (2014): 655–679.

of an actually infinite plurality of intelligibles.[68] What is intelligible is possible, that is, something to which being is not repugnant.[69] Since God does not construct this infinity, all possibilities of intelligibilities are seemingly included in God's necessary act of understanding but not constituted by it.[70]

Scotus's modal theory influenced 14th-century discussions about the division between logical, metaphysical, and natural necessities and possibilities. If logically necessary attributes are attached to things in all thinkable cases in which they occur, one could ask which of the natural invariances traditionally treated as necessities were necessary in this strong sense, and which of them were conditionally necessary with respect to the contingent assumption of natural uniformity. Ockham and Buridan employed this distinction in their philosophy.[71] Buridan straightforwardly applied the statistical model of modality in natural philosophy with the thesis that all possibilities are at some time realized.[72] The Scotist revision of the rules of obligations logic and some other additions made it a widely used tool for considering how to describe possible states of affairs and their mutual relationships. These discussions influenced the philosophical theory of counterfactual conditionals.[73] In criticizing the theory of abstract counterfactual possibilities in Averroes and Aquinas, Buridan argued that if a counterfactual is possible, it can be coherently imagined as actual. If something

---

68 John Duns Scotus, *Tractatus de primo principio/Abhandlung über das erste Prinzip*, ed. Wolfgang Kluxen (Darmstadt: Wissenschaftliche Buchgesellschaft, 1974), IV.9, 68–69.
69 John Duns Scotus, *Ordinatio* I.43, n. 7, 354 in *Opera omnia* 6.
70 For God's infinite theoretical knowledge as necessary, see John Duns Scotus, *Ordinatio* I.38, n. 9, in *Opera omnia* 6, 306.
71 See Simo Knuuttila, "Necessities in Buridan's Natural Philosophy," in *The Metaphysics and Natural Philosophy of John Buridan,* ed. Johannes Thijssen and Jack Zupko (Leiden: Brill, 2001), 72, 76.
72 Knuuttila, "Necessities in Buridan's Natural Philosophy," 72. In his *Quaestiones super libros* De generatione at corruptione *Aristotelis*, ed. Michael Sreijger, Paul Bakker, and Johannes Thiessen (Leiden: Brill, 2010), Buridan explains natural necessities and possibilities in terms of the statistical theory in a way similar to the Averroist account of John of Jandun quoted above, adding that there are no natural powers which could change these invariances (57).
73 Gelber, *It Could Have Been Otherwise*.

cannot be treated in this way, calling it possible is based on conceptual confusion.[74]

5. LATE MEDIEVAL MODAL LOGIC

The influential 14th-century logicians such as William of Ockham, Buridan, and their followers took the notion of possibility as non-contradictoriness with respect to actual and possible beings as the starting point of their logic of modal consequences and modal syllogistic that largely dropped the essentialist assumptions of Kilwardby and Averroes as well as the ideas of change and time. Possibility did not entail actuality and immutable actuality did not entail necessity. Modal statements were discussed separately with respect to compound and divided senses. Divided modals were partitioned into two groups depending on whether the subject term stood for actual beings or unrestrictedly for possible beings, whether actual or not. It was the task of logicians to analyze the relationships between these types of modal statements and, furthermore, the propositional conversions, syllogisms, and other inferences with respect to these. Against this background, it was thought that reconstructing Aristotle's syllogistic theory as a uniform system without distinguishing between the fine structures of modal premises was not possible.[75]

Ockham and Buridan state that the truth of "A white thing can be black" demands the truth of "This can be black" and that "This can be black" and "'This is black' is possible" mean the same.[76] The latter

---

74 John Buridan, *Quaestiones super octo Physicorum libros Aristotelis* (Paris, 1509), 105rb. For the use of non-extensional metaphysical possibilities in Buridan's questions on the *Physics*, see Edith Sylla, "*Ideo quasi mendicare oportet intellectum humanum*: The Role of Theology in John Buridan's Natural Philosophy," in Thiessen and Zupko, *The Metaphysics and Natural Philosophy of John Buridan*, 221–245. She refers to the increasing use of logically possible examples *secundum imaginationem* with omnipotence in 14th-century physics.

75 Lagerlund, *Modal Syllogistics*, 91–201; Thom, *Medieval Modal Systems*, 141–191; Knuuttila, "Medieval Modal Theories," 551–559.

76 William of Ockham, *Summa logicae*, ed. Philotheus Boehner, Gideon Gál, and Stephen Brown (St. Bonaventure: Franciscan Institute of St. Bonaventure University, 1974), II, c. 10; III-1, c.

statement exemplifies a compound reading and the former a divided reading. In Ockham and Buridan, these are equated at the basic level of propositions having demonstrative pronouns as subjects but are separated in the discussion of quantified universal and particular statements. Ockham discusses divided possibility statements with actual and merely possible subjects, but divided necessity statements with actual subjects only, which makes his theory less systematic than that of Buridan, who took the subject terms of all quantified divided modal statements to stand for possible beings if not explicitly restricted to actual ones.[77] The truth of quantified divided affirmative possibility statements demands the truth of all or some relevant singular statements of the type just mentioned, the demonstrative pronoun then apparently referring to an imaginary possible being.[78]

The new modal logic was a remarkable achievement of medieval logic. Buridan's modal syllogistic was dominant in late medieval times, being more systematic than that of Ockham because of its symmetrical treatment of possibility and necessity. It was embraced by Marsilius of Inghen, Albert of Saxony, Jodocus Trutfetter, and others.[79] The rise of the new modal logic was accompanied by theories of epistemic logic and deontic logic called branches of applied modal logic.[80]

32, III-3, c. 10; John Buridan, *Tractatus de consequentiis*, ed. H. Hubien (Louvain: Publications Universitaires, 1976), II, c. 7, concl. 16; John Buridan, *Treatise on Consequences*, trans. Stephen Read (New York: Fordham University Press, 2015).

77 Lagerlund, *Modal Syllogistics*, 112–115.

78 Ockham, *Summa logicae* I, c. 72; III-3, c. 10; Buridan, *Tractatus de consequentiis* II, c. 6, concl. 5. According to Hughes, "The Modal Logic," one could supply a Kripke-style possible worlds semantics to Buridan's modal system. See also Spencer Johnston, "Essentialism, Nominalism, and Modality: The Modal Theories of Robert Kilwardby and John Buridan" (PhD diss., University of St. Andrews, 2015).

79 Lagerlund, *Modal Syllogistics*, 184–227.

80 For further literature about medieval modalities and their influence, see Simo Knuuttila, "Medieval Theories of Modality," in *The Stanford Encyclopedia of Philosophy*, ed. Edward N. Zalta, summer 2021 edition, https://plato.stanford.edu.

Reflection

NECESSITY IN THE COSMOLOGY OF TOMMASO CAMPANELLA

Emanuele Costa

At the intersection of astrology, heresy, divine providence, and eccentric cosmology lies Tommaso Campanella (1568–1639). A paradigmatic figure of the eclectic philosophical environment that dominated the Renaissance, Campanella was a political prisoner for most of his adult life. This Southern Italian astronomer and theologian develops an extensive, exoteric, and in many ways innovative system.

As a poet, philosopher, and a notably prolific writer, it is difficult to extract a homogeneous treatment of necessity from Campanella's works. His understanding of the philosophy of nature is wedged in between the Aristotelian tradition—which he receives from his Scholastic predecessors, and rejects—and the Neoplatonic emanationist heritage. His efforts are focused on developing a philosophical system capable of doing justice to God's omnipotence and perfection, through a stern refutation of the philosophy of Aristotle (whom he describes as the "tyrant of minds").

Campanella offers a dichotomic understanding of metaphysics and cosmology. In his system, God can only be the cause of "unity and essence." Faithful to Neoplatonic principles, he defines God as the supreme source of pure one-ness and mereological simplicity. By contrast, all "dualities, faults, punishments, and deaths" are generated by the "nothingness" that pervades the creatural realm.[1] Conflict, according to Campanella, does not derive from God— who is One, and simple—but results from Love, which affects created things. When two created things, out of Love, both want to occupy the same material location, contrariety ensues.

Contrariety, however, is not opposed to God's omnipotence. Campanella employs an early version of the principle of plenitude, which demands that all possibility is turned into actuality. Adhering to this principle, the perfect will of the One seeks that "plurality and totality in all things is realized."[2] The plurality of imperfect things that flow from God's will is an eternal cascade of contrariety, a combination of opposites and mereological composition.

However, this flow is not without order. The interconnection of all things is guaranteed by the six forms of causation, which Campanella describes expanding on Aristotle's four. To the notions of formal, material, efficient, and final cause, he adds "ideal" and "perfectional" cause, thus strictly regimenting the order of the creatural world.[3] Through these six causes, God's loving will ("Providence") directs and harmonizes the flow of the universe.

The first of God's creations is matter, which for Campanella, equates to material (and spatial) location. Its role is to guarantee the material cause for each subsequent creation. Within this primal material location, God creates the first two "active instrumental causes": heat and cold. These are the "first two opposites," and they are necessarily dual in number, as "duality must immediately follow

---

[1] Tommaso Campanella, *Natural Faith of the Wise Man*, lines 13–17, in *Selected Philosophical Poems*, trans. Sherry Roush (Chicago: University of Chicago Press, 2011).

[2] Tommaso Campanella, *Physiologiæ Compendium*, Latin text ed. Germana Ernst (Milan: Rusconi, 1999), VII, 10, my translation.

[3] Campanella, *Physiologiæ Compendium*, II, 1.

from unity."⁴ The influence of Neoplatonic metaphysical theories is extremely evident in this central tenet of Campanella's cosmology. From the sempiternal interaction of heat and cold, all the different elements—secondary beings—are generated. Stimulated and directed by heat and cold, they continue their fight to occupy the same material locations. Thus, for example, Campanella derives an eccentric astronomy, eliminating the "mobile spheres" entailed by Aristotelian cosmology. He dismisses "motive intelligences" and intermediate spheres, asserting the unity and uniqueness of heaven (following Telesio and Nur ad-Din al-Bitruji, two of his main references). Heaven comprises the sky, and each of the planets that occupy it; they are created out of fire and differentiated in terms of the different quantities of heat with which each is endowed. In contrast, earth (or at least its first principle) is created out of cold, and each of the bodies that inhabit it result from the compenetrating of heaven and earth, of heat battling cold.

And yet, this apparent chaos is highly regulated, according to Campanella, thanks to God's continuous care for his creatures. The proportioned and measured combination of the elements (their "first conflict") generates an infinite number of entities, which is what we call individuals. Thus, entities are born out of conflict, but harmonized through internal necessity.

How is this possible, according to Campanella? Each of these entities receives a "principle." The principle is nothing but a nuclear endowment of necessity, in which "is sown the being that the things were capable of having, and the power and the art and the love to preserve that being."⁵ In other words, Campanella maintains that the generation and preservation of singular beings is guaranteed by an internal necessary principle, which establishes an autopoietic

---

4 Campanella, *Physiologiæ Compendium*, II, 7; VII, 9.
5 Campanella, *Epilogo Magno*, IX, p. 205, in *Physiologiæ Compendium*, trans. Ernst.

mechanism of harmony. The self-production and self-preservation of singular beings is internally generated through a principle, a "seed" of necessity. Campanella maintains that "Providence ordered the conservation of opposite elements, without bonding them with an external restraint, but with a native necessity of action—so that beings could act, without destroying each other—a wonderful thing to behold!"[6] His wonder toward the perfectly harmonized mechanism of living nature is associated, in these texts, with a reverent gratitude toward God, who is the supreme architect of this ordered universe.

In this mechanistic picture, Campanella inserts his understanding of universal necessity:

*Della Providenza divina, li cui instrumenti sono il fato, armonia et
   necessità.*
*[Il primo Senno] inestò l'armonia e corrispondenza di tutte le
parti et attioni per questa maniera della sua operata arte . . . .*
*Et per tutto si fanno le cose necessarie intese da Dio con
libero consiglio, et fatte da gli elementi con necessità amabile,
poiché quel che per necessità viene è per loro meglio.*

*Of divine Providence, whose instruments are Fate, Harmony, and
   Necessity.*
*[The divine Intellect] implanted harmony and the correspondence of all
Parts and actions, in this way, with its masterful art . . . .*
*Everywhere, necessary things are done in accordance with the free will
   of God;*
*And those things are made by the elements with a kindly necessity,
Since that, which is by necessity, happens because it is for the best.*[7]

---

6 Campanella, *Epilogo Magno*, IX, 205, my translation.
7 Campanella, *Epilogo Magno*, IX–X, pp. 205, 209.

In this passage, Campanella states his belief in a benign notion of "Fate, Harmony, and Necessity." These three components are named "Great Influences" (*Influenze Magne*), and they are tasked with preserving God's order in the creatural realm, despite the sempiternal conflict of the elements.[8] Campanella offers the "Influences" as an answer to the skeptic, who doubts whether "the Sun, the planets, and Earth could ever change their course." The response is quick and unapologetic: "not now, not ever."[9] The combined influence of fate, harmony, and necessity holds the universe, an ordered *cosmos*, to its structure, and it ensures the regularity of astronomical entities and living creatures alike. Thus, it permanently influences the singular objects that compose the cosmological mechanism, from the largest to the smallest.

However, it is crucial to Campanella's understanding of necessitarianism that the three "Great Influences" must be the expression of God's unchanged and providential will. The regimentation of the universe through necessity brings harmony to the enduring conflict of the elements. At the same time, it represents the expression of God's providence. This requirement is an internal consequence of Campanella's system. However, it also denotes a reaction to the many accusations of heresy and blasphemy that he had received throughout his life, which had resulted in his imprisonment and torture. It is probably with these accusations in mind that he adds a *caveat* to his treatment of necessity in the *Epilogo Magno*: "If the name of Fate, or Destiny, shall displease the theologians—even though I have declared that it is the same with the divine will, and the accordance of all agent causes in virtue of the first cause—it can be substituted with the name of coordination."[10] Coordination, the harmony of the universe,

---

8 Campanella, *Natural Faith of the Wise Man*, lines 20–21.
9 Campanella, *Epilogo Magno*, VIII, p. 204.
10 Campanella, *Epilogo Magno*, X, p. 206, note A.

the order of the cosmos, God's will—these are all synonyms to Campanella.

The will of God influences the internal necessity present within all things. It bonds power with necessity, harmony with love, and fate with God's wisdom.[11] Through this notion, Campanella is able to reconcile his emanationist metaphysics with a deeply devoted faith in God's providence. His necessitarianism atypically unifies a strict regimentation of the created universe with the refusal to introduce an external force. The concept of necessity, for Campanella, is universal and all-encompassing, and yet singular and internalized by the individuals that populate God's ordered *cosmos*.

---

11 Campanella, *To the Prime Intellect, First Song,* Madrigal 1, lines 7–10, in *Selected Philosophical Poems.*

CHAPTER 3

Modality and Essence in Early Modern Philosophy

DESCARTES, MALEBRANCHE, AND LOCKE

Anat Schechtman

1. INTRODUCTION

Philosophers in the 17th century engaged in a range of debates about modality, including its *nature* (what it is for something to be necessary, possible, or impossible), *scope* (what is necessary, possible, or impossible), and *knowability* (how, if at all, we can know modal facts). They also debated the explanation or *ground* of modality: that in virtue of which something is necessary, possible, or impossible. My interest in this essay is to explore this latter debate, and to tentatively defend two theses about it.

The first thesis is that for central philosophers in the period, a range of important modal facts are grounded in essences. That is, what explains why something is necessary, possible, or impossible is that some entities have the essences they do—where an entity's essence, as will be discussed further below, is what it is to be that entity. The second thesis is that as the 17th century progresses, we witness growing reluctance to admit that some facts are necessary, due to growing reluctance to admit that certain properties belong to essences, or even that essences exist.[1]

I will explore the relation between modality and essence in the 17th century, seeking support for these two theses through three case studies, arranged in chronological order: Descartes' treatment of substance and mode; Malebranche's treatment of causation; and Locke's treatment of necessary connections among properties. In each of these cases, claims about necessity and possibility take center stage. Substance, according to Descartes, is a being that *can* exist apart from other beings, whereas a mode *cannot* exist without its substance. A true cause, according to Malebranche, is such that there is a *necessary* connection between it and its effect. And a central question in the natural sciences is which pairs of properties are *necessarily* connected. I will argue that in each of these cases, the alleged modal facts are explained by essences of certain entities, as per the first thesis. I will also argue that as we move from Descartes to Malebranche to Locke, concerns about the scope and indeed the very existence of essences, and alongside them of modal facts, grow—as per the second thesis.

I should note that in discussing these cases, I will not aim for a full defense of the interpretive claims I will make, which are discussed in detail elsewhere in the literature. Instead, I will aim to motivate the proposed interpretations, and argue that if these interpretations are

---

[1] Anstey claims that for many philosophers in the period, "the most important of [the] necessary facts about the world are facts about the essential natures of things." Peter Anstey, "Locke and the Problem of Necessity in Early Modern Philosophy," in *Logical Modalities from Aristotle to Carnap: The Story of Necessity*, ed. Max Cresswell, Edwin Mares, and Adriane Rini (Cambridge: Cambridge University Press, 2016), 176. This is close to my first thesis, though it omits the explanatory connection on which I will focus. I also part ways with Anstey when it comes to my second thesis, since Anstey regards the main change of attitude in the period as increasing skepticism about our epistemic access to the modality-essence link.

correct, an interesting pattern emerges about the link between essence and modality, one captured by our two theses.

2. Descartes on Substance and Mode

In a well-known passage from *Principles of Philosophy* (1644), Descartes characterizes substance in terms of independence, and modes (his term for accidents or properties) in terms of dependence:

> By *substance* we can understand nothing other than a thing which exists in such a way as to depend on no other thing for its existence.... In the case of created things, some are of such a nature that they cannot exist without other things, while some need only the ordinary concurrence of God in order to exist. We make this distinction by calling the latter 'substances' and the former 'qualities' or 'attributes' of those substances. (*Principles* I.51, AT VIIIA 24/CSM I 210)[2]

Scholars have disagreed about how to understand Descartes' notion of dependence and, accordingly, how to understand the notions of mode and substance (which are characterized in terms of dependence). One popular interpretation takes its cue from the second sentence of the above passage, where, following the claim that substance is an independent being, Descartes contrasts substance with entities that "cannot exist without" other things. This is taken to imply that the relevant notion of dependence is *modal*, concerning what is and is not possible for the entity in question. Let us call it *the modal interpretation*.

---

[2] Citations from Descartes are from René Descartes, *The Philosophical Writings of Descartes*, trans. John Cottingham, Robert Stoothoff, and Dugald Murdoch, 3 vols. (Cambridge: Cambridge University Press, 1985–1992) (abbreviated as CSM for volumes 1 and 2 and CSMK for volume 3), and are given by volume and page number. The original French or Latin are in René Descartes, *Oeuvres de Descartes*, 12 vols., ed. Charles Adam and Paul Tannery (Paris: J. Vrin, 1996–1976) (abbreviated as AT), also given by volume and page number.

Put formally, the modal interpretation consists of the following three claims:

x **depends on** y just in case $y \neq x$ and necessarily, if x exists then y exists.

x is a **substance** just in case for any $y \neq x$, possibly, x exists and y does not exist.

x is a **mode** just in case there is a $y \neq x$ such that necessarily, if x exists then y exists.[3]

Informally, the proposal is that for Descartes, one entity depends on another (in the relevant sense) just in case it is *necessary* that if the former exists the latter exists as well. A substance is independent in this sense: for any given entity *e*, it is *possible* that a substance exists and *e* does not exist. By contrast, a mode depends on another entity, namely its substance: it is *necessary* that if a mode exists, its substance exists as well.

In addition to the second sentence in the passage from *Principles of Philosophy*, there are other passages in Descartes' corpus that highlight various modal facts about substances and modes—what we might call their "modal profile." And some of these facts cohere with the modal interpretation. For example, Descartes claims that mind and body—both substances—can exist apart; that a body, such as a piece of wax, can exist even when various modes it possesses at one time, such as its color, shape, or scent, cease to exist at another time; and that the mind can exist while modes of thought such as perception or volition come and go.[4] In contrast, modes such as color and shape, or perception and volition, cannot exist without the substances of which they are modes.[5]

---

[3] Gonzalo Rodriguez-Pereyra, "Descartes's Substance Dualism and His Independence Conception of Substance," *Journal of the History of Philosophy* 46, no. 1 (2008): 80.

[4] See the Second Meditation (AT VII 30/CSM II 20); the Sixth Meditation (AT VII 78/CSM II 54); the Second Replies (AT VII 169–170/CSM II 119); and *Principles* I.60 (AT VIIIA 28–29/CSM I 213).

[5] *Principles* I.48 (AT VIIIA 23/CSM I 208–209).

At the same time, the modal profiles of substances and modes encompass certain facts that do not sit as well with the modal interpretation. Although Descartes thinks that the mind and the body can exist apart, he also thinks that a body cannot exist without other bodies surrounding it (if it could, it would be surrounded by empty space, as in a vacuum, which Descartes thinks is impossible).[6] Moreover, a substance cannot exist without some mode or another; e.g., a body cannot exist without having some shape, nor a mind without having some thought.[7] And finally, a body cannot exist without some other body bringing it into existence.[8] But if the modal interpretation were correct, these claims would render minds and bodies dependent, *pace* Descartes' repeated claim that they are substances, and hence independent.[9]

A second problem is that the modal interpretation does not explain *why* substances and modes have the modal profiles they do. My mind, for example, can exist without my body—but why? My belief that I am writing cannot exist without my mind, though it can exist without any other thought—but why? What is it about my mind that explains why it can exist without my body, and what is it about my belief that explains why it cannot exist without my mind, though it can exist without any other thought? It is natural to think that these profiles are not the end of the explanatory road. While perhaps there is no further explanation of them in Descartes' view, it is worth searching for an explanation, in case one exists.

---

6 *Principles* II.18 (AT VIIIA 50/CSM I 230–231).

7 Descartes makes this observation in the *Conversations with Burman*: "But the mind cannot ever be without thought; it can of course be without this or that thought, but it cannot be without some thought. In the same way, the body cannot, even for a moment, be without extension" (AT V 150/CSMK 336).

8 I make this observation in Anat Schechtman, "Substance and Independence in Descartes," *Philosophical Review* 125, no. 2 (2016): 185.

9 Some scholars have responded to these observations by revising the theses above so as to focus on a modal relation to some particular entity (see, e.g., Rodriguez-Pereyra, "Descartes's," 80–81)—what I call a 'strict' rather than 'generic' modal relation. This revision, however does not address the last concern mentioned. Other scholars have responded by denying that finite bodies are Cartesian substances; see, e.g., Alice Sowaal, "Cartesian Bodies," *Canadian Journal of Philosophy* 34, no. 2 (June 2004): 217–240. I argue against this view in Schechtman, "Substance," §2.2.

So let us consider an alternative to the modal interpretation, one that arguably better captures—and explains—the modal profiles of substances and modes. At its core is the idea that the type of dependence Descartes invokes in characterizing substances and modes has to do with the *essences* or *natures* of the entities in question. In general, thinkers in the period regard the essence of an entity as what it is to be that entity—what defines it, or what it is "at its core."[10] Descartes himself emphasizes that the whole essence of mind is thought, whereas the whole essence of body is extension; further, he regards thought and extension as monadic, non-relational properties.[11] To be sure, these (and other) essential properties are necessary properties: whatever holds of the essence of an entity holds of it necessarily, for it could not be what it is without that property. But not all necessary properties or relations are essential. For example, it is arguably necessary for human beings to be capable of learning grammar, even though this is not an essential property of human beings.[12] Early modern thinkers, following their predecessors, distinguish between essential properties and necessary but non-essential properties, which in some cases follow necessarily from essential properties.[13]

We will come back to the connection between essentiality and necessity in a moment. But before we do, let us spell out in more detail the alternative to the modal interpretation we are now considering. First, according to this alternative, the relevant sense of dependence in Descartes' characterization of substance is *essential*: one entity depends on another just when the former's essence or nature involves a relation to the latter. In such a case, the former entity is defined partly in

---

10 This traditional understanding of essence goes back to Aristotle, who writes: "the essence of a thing is what it is said to be in respect of itself" (Aristotle, *Metaphysics* Z 1029b14). The expression 'at its core' is from Martin Glazier, "Essentialist Explanation," *Philosophical Studies* 174 (2017): 2879. I will follow Descartes in using 'nature' and 'essence' interchangeably (see, e.g., the Fifth Meditation, AT VII 64/CSM II 45).

11 See *Principles* I.53 (AT VIIIA 25/CSM I 210).

12 See Aristotle, *Topics* I.5 for this example.

13 Aristotle, *Topics* I.5.

terms of its relation to the latter; so, the former depends on the latter. Second, a substance, according to this interpretation, is independent in this sense: its essence involves no relations to any other entities. In effect, it is "self-contained." Finally, a mode is an entity that is dependent (in the relevant sense): its essence involves the *inhering-in* relation to its substance.[14] Let us call this *the nature-based interpretation*, which advances the following three claims:

x **depends on** y just in case $y \neq x$ and (1) there is some relation R such that xRy, and (2) xRy by x's nature but not by y's nature.

x is a **substance** just in case for no $y \neq x$ is there a relation R such that xRy by x's nature but not by y's nature.

x is a **mode** just in case there is some $y \neq x$ and a relation R such that xRy by x's nature but not by y's nature.[15]

With this interpretation in hand, let us now return to the two concerns raised above about the modal interpretation, and see whether the nature-based interpretation fairs better. They were, first, that the modal interpretation does not accurately capture the modal profiles of substances; and second, that it does not explain why substances and modes have the modal profiles they do.

The nature-based interpretation captures the modal profiles of both substances and modes. Recall that essential properties are necessary, but not all necessary properties and relations are essential. Recall also that the whole essence of mind is thought, and the whole essence of body is extension; additionally, part of what it is to be a mode is to inhere in some substance. Given these facts about the natures of substances and modes, the nature-based interpretation captures the relevant modal facts: substances can exist apart, a substance can exist even

---

14 See *Principles* I.64 (AT VIIIA 31/CSM I 215–216).
15 See more detailed discussion in Schechtman, "Substance," §5.

when changing its modes, and modes cannot exist without the substances in which they inhere.

All this is compatible with the above observation that, on Descartes' view, substances bear necessary connections to other entities. Again, a body cannot exist without other bodies surrounding it, a substance cannot exist without some mode or another, and a body cannot exist without some other body bringing it into existence. On the nature-based interpretation, this trio of modal facts does not render minds and bodies dependent. Not all necessary properties or relations are essential ones, so these necessary connections do not entail any conclusions about dependence. The interpretation preserves the coherence of Descartes' claims about the modal profiles of substances and modes.

The interpretation also explains *why* substances and modes have the modal profiles that they do. A mode cannot exist unless its substance exists *because* it is part of the essence of a mode to stand in the inherence relation to its substance. It is possible for one substance, whether a mind or a body, to exist without another substance or mode *because* the essence of a substance does not include a relation to another substance or mode.

What about the other modal facts mentioned above? It may be that there are explanations for various modal facts about an entity that do not appeal to the essence of that entity. Perhaps some are grounded in God (or God's will). More interesting for our purposes is the prospect of a modal fact about one entity being grounded in the essence of another entity. For example, we have seen that Descartes holds that one body cannot exist without other bodies surrounding it. This is not because a body is related to other bodies by *its* essence. Instead, it is arguably something about the essence of space that explains why a vacuum is impossible, and hence why a body cannot exist without other extended substances. If this is correct, then this component of the modal profile of a body is grounded in essence, just not the essence of body.

To summarize, according to the nature-based interpretation, Descartes' notions of dependence, substance, and mode are to be understood in terms of essences, and not in terms of possibility and necessity. At the same time, this interpretation does not merely accommodate but also explains the modal profiles of substances and modes, in terms of essences. If this interpretation is on the right track, then Descartes' treatment of these notions—which is arguably among the most important and influential in 17th-century philosophy—corroborates the first thesis about the period that I set out to defend in this essay: that the ground or explanation of a range of important modal facts is essence.

This understanding of Descartes' view also paves the way for an assessment of our second thesis, concerning changing of attitudes among 17th-century figures toward modal facts. I will argue that subsequent thinkers in the period—in particular, Malebranche and Locke—are more cautious or skeptical about essences than Descartes, and that this explains why they are also more cautious or skeptical about the modal facts that essences allegedly ground.

3. Malebranche on Causation

Let us turn now to a second well-known treatment of modal claims in the 17th century, in Nicholas Malebranche's discussion of causation in the *Search after Truth*, published in 1675. Malebranche there and elsewhere adopts occasionalism, the thesis that God is the only true causal agent in nature, and that no other entity possesses causal powers. When one billiard ball collides with another, for example, it is not the first ball that causes the second to move, but God who causes it to move *on the occasion* of the collision.[16] Similarly, it is not the case "that fire burns, that the sun illuminates, and that water cools," appearances to the contrary notwithstanding.[17] Rather, it is God who does each

---

16 Nicholas Malebranche, *Search after Truth*, trans. and ed. Thomas Lennon and Paul Olscamp (Cambridge: Cambridge University Press, 1997), 660.

17 Malebranche, *Search*, 660.

of these things, *on the occasion* in which fire, sun, or water are present. The ball, fire, water, and sun are what Malebranche calls "occasional causes": their presence is the occasion on which God acts.

Malebranche presents a series of arguments for occasionalism, one of which turns on the modal profile of causal connections. The "No Necessary Connection" (NNC) argument, as it has come to be known in the literature, is stated in the following passage from *The Search after Truth*:

> A true cause as I understand it is one such that the mind perceives a necessary connection between it and its effect. Now the mind perceives a necessary connection only between the will of an infinitely perfect being and its effects. Therefore, it is only God who is the true cause and who truly has the power to move bodies.[18]

The argument can be reconstructed as follows:

1. There is a necessary connection between God's will and its effects.
2. There is no necessary connection between any created entity (i.e., any being other than God) and its putative effect.
3. Something is a true cause only if there is a necessary connection between it and its effect.
4. Therefore, God's will is the only true cause of any effect.

It follows that created entities are at most merely occasional causes of their putative effects.[19]

---

18 Malebranche, *Search*, 450. The label NNC is introduced in Steven Nadler, "'No Necessary Connection': The Medieval Roots of the Occasionalist Roots of Hume," *The Monist* 79, no. 3 (1996): 450.

19 I am here loosely following the reconstructions offered by Sukjae Lee and Sydney Penner. I agree with both that the argument is concerned with the *existence* (or non-existence) of necessary connections, rather than the *mind's perception* (or non-perception) of such connections. See Sukjae Lee, "Necessary Connections and Continuous Creation: Malebranche's Two Arguments

There has been considerable scholarly debate about the merits of this argument. Some scholars accuse Malebranche of equivocating on its central notions. For example, they have argued that premises 1 and 2 are most plausibly read as invoking *metaphysical necessity*, or truth in all possible worlds, whereas premise 3 is true only when "necessary" is interpreted in terms of *nomological necessity*, or truth in possible worlds with the same laws of nature as our own. For example, in worlds in which our familiar laws of mechanics hold, one billiard ball will cause another billiard ball to move in some way upon collision. But in a world with different laws of mechanics, the first ball might cause the second to move in some different way, or not at all. However, there is no world in which God wills something to happen and the willed effect does not follow.[20] The trouble, according to the critics, is that true causation requires only a nomologically necessary connection between cause and effect, and such a connection may hold between a created entity and an effect. Once we acknowledge the distinction between the two types of necessity, we see that premise 3 is true only if 2 is false, and premise 2 is true only if premise 3 is false. Either way, the critics allege, the argument fails.

In response, other scholars have argued that the premises employ a single notion of necessity, and that Malebranche's contemporaries would have found both premises, interpreted accordingly, quite compelling. These scholars claim is that it is anachronistic to invoke nomological necessity: although this is perhaps the plausible reading of premise 3 nowadays, Malebranche's contemporary readers in the 17th century would not have insisted that premise 3 is true only if it invokes

---

for Occasionalism," *Journal of the History of Philosophy* 46, no. 4 (2008): 542–543; and Sydney Penner, "Suárez (and Malebranche) on Necessary Causes," unpublished manuscript, 2018.

20 See, e.g., Steven Nadler, "Malebranche on Causation," in *The Cambridge Companion to Malebranche*, ed. Steven Nadler (Cambridge: Cambridge University Press, 2000), 113–114. I believe that Lee, too, can be fruitfully understood as accusing Malebranche of equivocating on the notion of a cause, though Lee himself does not frame his criticism of NNC as involving an equivocation. Lee's charge is that premise 3 invokes a *total* cause whereas premise 2 invokes a *partial* cause. See Lee, "Necessary Connections," 549.

nomological rather than metaphysical necessity. The reason, these scholars allege, is that such readers viewed causal relations as holding in virtue of the essences of their relata, and hence as holding with metaphysical necessity. So Malebranche's argument does not equivocate, and premise 3 would have been dialectically effective in the period.[21]

For our purposes, it is not crucial to determine whether Malebranche's argument involves an equivocation. Rather, what is important in the present context is that if the response just discussed is right, then Malebranche's immediate predecessors and contemporaries endorsed the thesis that the necessity of causal relations is grounded in essences.

Among the evidence offered for this claim—I lack the space to consider it all—are passages by the late scholastic author Francisco Suárez (1548–1617). In his magnum opus the *Metaphysical Disputations*, Suárez writes:

> [A]mong created causes there are many that operate necessarily once all the things they require for operating are present.... For the sun illuminates necessarily, and fire produces warmth necessarily, and so on for the others. The reason for this must stem from the intrinsic condition and determination of [the cause's] nature, as we will explain in the next assertion.[22]

Invoking some of the same examples as Malebranche, Suárez asserts that there is a necessary connection between the sun and its effect, illumination; and between fire and its effect, warmth. In general, he

---

21 For this line of argument, see Walter Ott, *Causation and Laws of Nature in Early Modern Philosophy* (Oxford: Oxford University Press, 2009), 21; and A. R. J. Fisher, "Causal and Logical Necessity in Malebranche's Occasionalism," *Canadian Journal of Philosophy* 41, no. 4 (2011): 533–537.

22 Francisco Suárez, *On Efficient Causality: Metaphysical Disputations 17, 18, and 19*, trans. Alfred Freddoso (New Haven, CT: Yale University Press, 1994), 270 (DM 19.1.1). My discussion of Suárez was informed to some extent by Penner, "Suárez (and Malebranche)."

claims, there is a necessary connection between all non-rational (e.g., merely bodily) causes and their effects.[23] Suárez indicates that the ground of this necessity has to do with the cause's nature. In the next "assertion," he specifies what it is in the cause's nature that grounds its necessary connection to its effect:

> [T]he cause [must] have a full and sufficient power to act. This is evident per se, since an action must presuppose a sufficient power. And in order for a cause to act necessarily, it must be assumed to be unqualifiedly and absolutely capable [of acting]; but it cannot be absolutely capable [of acting] without sufficient power.[24]

Suárez's position seems to be the following: the necessity of the causal relation is due to causal powers that belong to the cause's nature or essence. What it is to be fire is (inter alia) to have a power to burn, and what it is to be the sun is (inter alia) to have a power to heat and a power to illuminate. Because essential properties are necessary, as discussed above, it is necessary that fire burns and the sun illuminates. Of course, the sun does not always illuminate (e.g., at night), nor does fire always burn (e.g., in the absence of oxygen, or some flammable material). Rather, it is necessary that the cause brings about its effect whenever the requisite conditions are in place.[25] Moreover, Suárez suggests

---

23 "[O]ne should assert that all causes that operate without the use of reason operate as such with the aforementioned necessity" (Suárez, *On Efficient Causality*, 280 (DM 19.1.12)). Suárez's view is that rational agents are not necessary, and hence, "free," in the sense defined above: it is not the case that they "operate necessarily once all the things they require for operating are present." For example, even when all the conditions required for me to raise my arm are present (e.g., I am not paralyzed or restrained), it is not necessary that I raise my arm; I can simply choose not to. For further discussion, see Sydney Penner, "Free and Rational: Suárez on the Will," *Archiv für Geschichte der Philosophie* 95, no. 1 (2013): 1–35. Malebranche, by contrast, makes no exception for rational causes in the NNC argument. Whether Malebranche can nonetheless preserve some sense in which rational causes are free (and hence morally responsible) is a contested question in the literature. For a recent discussion, see Julie Walsh, "Malebranche, Freedom, and the Divided Mind," in *The Battle of Gods and Giants Redux*, ed. Patricia Easton (Leiden: Brill, 2015), 194–216.

24 Suárez, *On Efficient Causality*, 271 (DM 19.1.2).

25 Or, as Suárez says in the passage quoted above, "once all the things they require for operating are present." Among the requisite conditions Suárez goes on to list are "a susceptible and sufficiently

that this is true for all of the entity's causal powers.²⁶ If this is right, then Suárez accepts necessary connections between cause and effect in the case of bodily causes, whose necessity, moreover, is grounded in the essences of the relata.

Descartes is sometimes presented as another proponent of the view that bodies have causal powers. In his purely mechanistic framework, these are simply powers to move other bodies and to resist being moved by other bodies. Indeed, certain central passages in his writings invoke such powers explicitly. For example:

> [W]hen a moving body collides with another, if its power of continuing in a straight line is less than the resistance of the other body, it is deflected so that, while the quantity of motion is retained, the direction is altered; but if its power of continuing is greater than the resistance of the other body, it carries that body along with it, and loses a quantity of motion equal to that which it imparts to the other body. (*Principles* II.40; AT VIIIA 65/CSM I 242)²⁷

Moreover, scholars have claimed that in the same text, Descartes maintains that these powers hold by the body's nature or essence:

---

close" patient, a suitable medium, and the absence of an impediment or something resisting the causal action (see Suárez, *On Efficient Causality*, DM 19.2–3 for the full list).

26 "[S]ince the substantial form is the principal act of the suppositum and that which principally gives it *esse*, it must also be the principal principle or operation. For the operation follows upon the *esse*" (Suárez, *On Efficient Causality*, 52 (DM 18.2.3)). See also the discussion in Robert Pasnau, *Metaphysical Themes 1274–1671* (Oxford: Oxford University Press, 2011), §24.3–4.

27 For additional passages, see Michael Della Rocca, "If a Body Meets a Body: Descartes on Body-Body Causation," in *New Essays on the Rationalists*, ed. Rocco Gennaro and Charles Huenemann (Oxford: Oxford University Press, 1999), 58ff. Some scholars argue that, appearance to the contrary notwithstanding, Descartes does not posit bodily causal powers, and indeed, that he is an occasionalist, just like Malebranche. For a now-classic statement of this position, see Daniel Garber, "How God Causes Motion: Descartes, Divine Sustenance, and Occasionalism," *Journal of Philosophy* 84 (1987): 567–580. For a helpful overview of the debate about the existence of causal powers in Descartes, see Helen Hattab, "Concurrence or Divergence? Reconciling Descartes's Physics with His Metaphysics," *Journal of the History of Philosophy* 45, no. 1 (2007): 49–78.

[W]e must be careful to note what it is that constitutes the power of any given body to act on, or resist the action of, another body. This power consists simply in the fact that everything tends, in so far as it is in itself [*quantum in se est*], to persist in the same state. (*Principles* II.43; AT VIIIA 66/CSM I 243)

In 17th-century parlance, to say of something that it holds of an entity "in so far as it is in itself" (*quantum in se est*) is the same as saying that it holds in virtue of its nature or essence.[28] So Descartes' claim is that bodies possess powers to move other bodies, and that these powers hold in virtue of their essences.

Returning now to Malebranche's NNC argument, the discussion above suggests that Suárez and Descartes indeed accept premise 3—the claim that there is a necessary connection between cause and effect. Moreover, they accept it because they think that causal powers are essential, and since essential properties are necessary, it is necessary that a cause brings about a certain effect, when the requisite conditions are present. If so, then for both Suárez and Descartes, the necessity of causal relations is grounded in essences.[29] This corroborates our first thesis.

There is nonetheless an important disagreement between Suárez and Descartes, on the one hand, and Malebranche, on the other. Examining it will bring us to our second thesis, concerning a narrowing of the scope of essence in the period. Malebranche, unlike his predecessors, rejects the view that bodies and minds have causal powers—let alone powers that follow from their nature or essence. First, he argues, the

---

28 See Della Rocca, "If a Body," 66–67; and Tad Schmaltz, "From Causes to Laws," in *The Oxford Handbook of Philosophy in Early Modern Europe*, ed. Desmond Clarke and Catherine Wilson (Oxford: Oxford University Press, 2011), 37.

29 Moreover, this suggests that for both Suárez and Descartes, the necessity in question is metaphysical rather than nomological, because it is grounded in essential powers rather than laws of nature. For further discussion of the transition, over the course of the early modern period, from a view of causal relations as underwritten by powers to a view of them as underwritten by laws of nature, see Schmaltz, "From Causes to Laws."

very notion of a causal power involves something divine. But of course, minds and bodies are not divine, and so it is incoherent to ascribe causal powers to them:

> If we next consider attentively our idea of cause or of power to act, we cannot doubt that this idea represents something divine.... We therefore admit something divine in all the bodies around us when we posit forms, faculties, qualities, virtues, or real beings capable of producing certain effects through the force of their nature.[30]

Second, focusing on bodies, Malebranche argues that it is incoherent to ascribe causal powers to them, because their essences are incompatible with such powers. Following Descartes, Malebranche takes the essence of bodies to consist in extension.[31] But unlike Descartes, he argues that causal powers are not something that a merely extended entity can possess; to think otherwise is to assume "that bodies have certain entities distinct from matter [extension] in them."[32] Malebranche concludes that bodies are devoid of powers, or as Malebranche often says, are passive.[33]

Combining the observation that Malebranche rejects created causal powers with the observation that Suárez and Descartes accept them, the following hypothesis suggests itself. Perhaps the NNC argument reveals both a common ground and a deep disagreement between Malebranche and his predecessors. The common ground concerns premise 3 and the link between necessity and essence underwriting it: perhaps Malebranche accepts premise 3 because he holds, like Suárez and Descartes, that whatever causal powers an entity has are essential

---

30 Malebranche, *Search*, 446.
31 Malebranche, *Search*, 243ff.
32 Malebranche, *Search*, 446.
33 See, e.g., Malebranche, *Search*, 660. The reasoning extends to minds as well.

to it, and therefore necessary.³⁴ The disagreement, it was already noted, is that Suárez and Descartes think that bodies have causal powers, and Malebranche does not—hence the latter's inclusion of premise 2 in the NNC argument, a premise which Suárez and Descartes would arguably reject.

If this hypothesis is correct, it explains how Malebranche can mount an argument for a conclusion that neither Suárez nor Descartes would accept, employing a premise that they arguably would. It also helps begin to corroborate our second thesis: Malebranche takes the scope of essences to be narrower than either of these two predecessors did.

4. LOCKE ON NECESSARY CONNECTIONS

A rich and interesting discussion of necessity appears in the course of Locke's analysis of knowledge in his *Essay concerning Human Understanding*, first published in 1690. Locke states that knowledge consists in the perception of "agreement or disagreement" among ideas. He identifies four ways in which ideas can agree or disagree, the third of which is the agreement of "co-existence, or necessary connection"³⁵:

> The third sort of agreement or disagreement to be found in our ideas ... is [necessary] co-existence or non-co-existence in the same subject; Thus when we pronounce concerning gold, that it is fixed [i.e.,

---

34 Alternatively, it might be that Malebranche accepts premise 3 because he is antecedently committed to occasionalism and to God being the only true cause in nature (a cause whose effects follow necessarily, because it is omnipotence; recall the discussion of premise 1 above). I do not have the space to argue against this alternative here, and for this reason, present the alternative discussed above as a mere hypothesis. Let me just note that if this is the case, then the NNC argument is a dialectical tool, employing premises that Malebranche thinks his opponents will accept for different reasons than his own.

35 The other three are identity, relation, and real existence. For discussion of Locke's account of knowledge, see Lex Newman, "Locke on Knowledge," in *The Cambridge Companion to Locke's "Essay concerning Human Understanding,"* ed. Lex Newman (Cambridge: Cambridge University Press, 2007), 313–351.

inflammable], our knowledge of this truth amounts to no more but this, that fixedness, or a power to remain in the fire unconsumed, is an idea that always accompanies and is joined with that particular sort of yellowness, weight, fusibility, malleableness, and solubility in *aqua regia*, which make our complex idea signified by the word gold.[36]

Locke is quick to clarify that when we perceive agreement (or disagreement) between ideas, what we know is not just that our ideas stand in a certain relation to each other. In many cases, we also know that there is an agreement (or disagreement) between the objects of these ideas.[37] Thus if we perceive that there is a necessary connection between the ideas of yellowness, weight, and other ideas that make up our idea of gold, on the one hand, and the idea of inflammability, on the other, we know that necessarily, whatever is gold—i.e., whatever is yellow, heavy, and so on—is inflammable.

Locke takes much scientific inquiry to consist in investigations of necessary connections of this sort. Given his well-documented interest in the natural sciences, it is perhaps surprising to see that Locke is quite pessimistic about our ability to attain such knowledge:

[I]n this our knowledge is very short, though in this consists the greatest and most material part of our knowledge concerning substances. The reason whereof is, that the simple ideas whereof our complex ideas of substances are made up are, for the most part, such as carry with them, in their own nature, no visible necessary

---

36 John Locke, *An Essay concerning Human Understanding*, ed. P. H. Nidditch (Oxford: Clarendon Press, 1975), IV.i.6.

37 This is the case when our knowledge is "real." As Locke writes: "It is evident the mind knows not things immediately, but only by the intervention of the ideas it has of them. Our knowledge, therefore is real only so far as there is a conformity between our ideas and the reality of things" (Locke, *Essay*, IV.iv.2).

connexion or inconsistency with any other simple ideas, whose coexistence with them we would inform ourselves about.[38]

In the rest of this essay, I would like to advance two interpretive claims about Locke's position. First, the reason we are ignorant of necessary connections is that such connections are grounded in what Locke calls "real essences," of which we are also ignorant. If this is correct, then Locke's position further corroborates our first thesis. Second, and a bit more tentatively, I will suggest that the reason we are ignorant of real essences is that they do not exist—if real essences are supposed to be what sorts individuals into kinds. If this (admittedly controversial) interpretation is right, then Locke's position also corroborates our second thesis.

Let us begin with the first interpretative claim. Locke famously distinguishes two types of essences in the *Essay*, one of which he calls "real":

> First, Essence may be taken for the very being of anything, whereby it is what it is. And thus the real internal, but generally (in substances) unknown constitution of things, whereon their discoverable qualities depend, may be called their essence.[39]

The second type, which Locke calls "nominal," are "those abstract complex ideas, to which we have annexed distinct general names."[40] To illustrate, the nominal essence of gold is our complex idea of gold—which, Locke says in the above-cited passage, is composed of the simple ideas of yellowness, weight, fusibility, malleableness, and solubility in *aqua regia*. Its real essence is the collection of mostly insensible

---

38 Locke, *Essay*, IV.iii.10. For discussion of Locke's interest in scientific inquiry, see Peter Anstey, *John Locke on Natural Philosophy* (Oxford: Oxford University Press, 2011).
39 Locke, *Essay*, III.iii.15.
40 Locke, *Essay*, III.iii.17.

qualities of the parcel of matter classified by us as gold—qualities such as the shape, size, and texture of its underlying corpuscles—that gives rise to the sensible qualities, including yellowness, weight, fusibility, malleability, and solubility in *aqua regia*.[41]

Going back to Locke's discussion of knowledge of necessary connections, notice that it is focused on connections between sensible qualities, e.g., between the yellowness and inflammability of gold. For Locke's position on knowledge is, once again, that knowledge consists in perceiving an agreement between ideas. And given Locke's empiricism, he is officially committed to the view that we can only have ideas of things outside our own minds to the extent they are presented to us through the senses.[42]

Putting this point together with the distinction between real and nominal essences, we can now see why our ignorance about necessary connections stems from ignorance about real essences. The real essence is what gives rise to an entity's sensible qualities; e.g., it is what makes gold yellow, heavy, fusible, malleable, and soluble in *aqua regia*. If there is a necessary connection among some of an entity's sensible qualities, it too will arise from the real essence; e.g., if inflammability is necessarily connected to gold's other sensible qualities, it will be because whatever makes gold inflammable is necessarily connected to what makes it yellow. Unfortunately, we do not know if this is the case, because we do not have epistemic access to the insensible qualities that make up the real essence. Locke makes this point clearly when he writes:

---

41 Here I have in mind what David Owen calls "the real essence of an unsorted particular." Locke sometimes also talks of what Owen calls "the real essence of a sorted particular." While the former is a set of insensible qualities that give rise to all the entities' sensible qualities, the latter is the subset of insensible qualities that give rise to the subset of its sensible qualities that are included in the nominal essence. See David Owen, "Locke on Real Essences," *History of Philosophy Quarterly* 8, no. 2 (April 1991): 107.

42 We can have ideas of our own minds via reflection, a kind of inner sense. See Locke's discussion of the origin of our ideas in *Essay* II.i.

The ideas that our complex ones of substances are made up of, and about which our knowledge concerning substances is most employed, are those of their secondary [i.e., sensible] qualities; which depending all (as has been shown) upon the primary qualities of their minute and insensible parts [i.e., upon their real essences] . . . it is impossible we should know which have a necessary union or inconsistency one with another.[43]

In the case of gold, we do not know what insensible qualities give rise to its yellowness and inflammability. Accordingly, we do not know if they are necessarily connected.

What was just said supports our first thesis: Locke, like Descartes and Malebranche, takes essences to ground certain modal facts—in this case, the existence of necessary connections between certain qualities.[44] But it also lends support to our second thesis. For Locke's attitude toward the essence-modality link is different from Descartes' in at least one important respect: unlike Descartes, Locke thinks that we do not have epistemic access to the essences that ground these necessary connections; consequently, "it is impossible we should know" those connections.[45]

Some scholars have argued that this is the extent of the change in Locke's attitude: Locke, like Descartes and Malebranche, believes that essences exist; but unlike them, he thinks that essences are unknowable to us.[46] I want to close our discussion by presenting an alternative interpretation of Locke's position, according to which essences, at least as they are traditionally understood, are not merely unknowable

---

43 Locke, *Essay*, IV.iii.11.
44 Hereafter, I will elide 'real' when speaking of Locke's real essences.
45 It is quite clear that Descartes thinks that we have epistemic access to at least some essences. Indeed, some of the most important results of the *Meditations* are achieved by accessing essences of, e.g., mind, body, and God (see in particular the titles of the Second and Fifth Meditations).
46 For a reading of this sort, see Anstey, "Locke," 186.

but *do not exist*.⁴⁷ If so, the change in attitudes toward essences from Descartes to Locke, via Malebranche, concerns not simply the scope but the very existence of essences.

This "eliminativist" interpretation (as I will call it) begins with the observation that, following a traditional Aristotelian understanding of essence, Locke takes the essence of a thing to be commonly understood as what determines the *kind* of thing it is. Gold is one kind; human being and horse are two others. Essences comprise properties shared by all and only individuals of this kind. Locke sometimes uses the term 'species' in addition to 'kind':

> [T]hose who, using the word essence for they know not what, suppose a certain number of those essences, according to which all natural things are made, and wherein they do exactly every one of them partake, and so become of this or that species.⁴⁸

Essence, so understood, plays two roles. First, it grounds all of an individual thing's properties; it is that "whereon their discoverable qualities depend." Second, essence determines the kind to which the individual belongs.

According to the eliminativist interpretation, the problem, in Locke's view, is that the two roles are in tension, and moreover that the first role seriously deflates the notion of essence. Regarding the tension, consider that if essence is to fulfill the second role, it must be *exclusive*, comprising only those properties that are, or give rise to, those properties by virtue of which the entity belongs to a certain kind. For example, the essence of a human being perhaps includes what makes her possess a particular bodily configuration (e.g., being two-legged).

---

47 This interpretation is drawn from the discussion in Pasnau, *Metaphysical Themes*, §27.7. Versions of it are also proposed in Owen, "Locke," and in Pauline Phemister, "Real Essence in Particular," *Locke Studies* 25 (1990): 27–55.

48 Locke, *Essay*, III.iii.17.

But it does not include what makes her possess a particular skin color. However, in order to fulfill the first role, essence must be *inclusive*, comprising *all* of those properties that are, or give rise to, an entity's sensible qualities—including skin color (to stick with the example just given).

The tension is clear enough. What Locke emphasizes, however, is not this tension per se, but rather that the first role directly undermines the interest and import of essence. He writes:

> For I would ask anyone, what is sufficient to make an essential difference in nature, between any two particular beings, without any regard had to some abstract idea, which is looked upon as the essence and standard of a species? All such patterns and standards, being quite laid aside, particular beings, considered barely in themselves, will be found to have all their qualities equally essential, and everything, in each individual, will be essential to it, or, which is more true, nothing at all.[49]

We might summarize Locke's reasoning in this passage as follows. The essence of a given entity is radically individual. For example, it includes not only what makes a particular parcel of matter yellow, heavy, malleable, fusible, soluble in *aqua regia*, and inflammable, but also what makes it dull (or shiny), smooth (or coarse), reflective (or opaque), etc. Independently of some human-imposed sorting scheme, all of these properties of the entity are "equally essential" to it. But that is tantamount to saying that "nothing at all" is essential to it. It has no essence.

On this interpretation, Locke believes that we do not have epistemic access to essences, and concomitantly, to modal facts that essences ground. But he goes further: he thinks that essences do not exist. And neither do the modal facts that essences supposedly ground. Applied

---

49 Locke, *Essay*, III.vi.5; see also III.vi.4.

to the case of gold, we do not know whether, necessarily, gold is inflammable, not because we do not have access to the essence of gold. Rather, there is no such thing as the essence of gold, at least not independently of our own chosen sorting scheme. While it is perhaps necessary to a particular parcel of matter that it is both yellow and inflammable (say, the last guinea ever coined, or a ring on Locke's finger),[50] it is not its essence that makes it so.

If this is correct, then it supports the stronger reading of our second thesis. We find in Locke reluctance to admit that some properties or facts are necessary. But this is *not* due to a mere narrowing of the scope of essences—something we find in Malebranche, by comparison with the largesse of Suárez and Descartes. Rather, the reluctance to admit various modal facts is traceable to a more basic reluctance to admit that essences exist.[51]

---

50 See Locke, *Essay* III.vi.21 and III.iii.18, respectively, for these ways in which Locke picks out a particular parcel of matter while avoiding sorting it as gold.

51 I have received helpful suggestions from James Messina, and from audience members at Simon Fraser University and at Johns Hopkins University. I am also grateful to John Bengson for his extensive input.

CHAPTER 4

Crescas and Spinoza on Modality

Yitzhak Y. Melamed

1. INTRODUCTION

Spinoza's determinism and necessitarianism[1] earned him few sympathetic readers.[2] For most of his contemporaries, necessitarianism was

---

[1] By necessitarianism, I understand the assertion that the actual world is the only possible world. By determinism, I understand the assertion that every event has a cause and is strictly necessitated by its (total) cause. Arguably, these two views do not imply each other. Non-necessitarian determinism asserts that there are many possible worlds, though all worlds are deterministically ordered. Non-deterministic necessitarianism might assert that there is just one possible world, but at least one event in this world has no cause. I discuss further the distinction between determinism and necessitarianism in Section 3.

[2] Two notable exceptions are Nietzsche and Althusser. For Nietzsche's enthusiastic agreement with Spinoza's critique of free will, see Jason M. Yonover, "Nietzsche and Spinoza," in *Blackwell Companion to Spinoza*, ed. Yitzhak Y. Melamed (Hoboken, NJ: Blackwell, 2011), 529–532. For Althusser's approbation of Spinoza's uncompromising determinism, see Yitzhak Y. Melamed, "Spinoza, Althusser, and the Question of Humanism," in Spinoza issue of *Crisis & Critique* 8 (2021): 170–177. I am deeply indebted to Justin Bledin, Hao Dong, Zach Gartenberg, Zev Harvey, and especially Don Garrett and Sam Newlands for their most astute criticisms and comments on earlier versions of this chapter.

Yitzhak Y. Melamed, *Crescas and Spinoza on Modality* In: *Modality*. Edited by: Yitzhak Y. Melamed and Samuel Newlands, Oxford University Press. © Oxford University Press 2024.
DOI: 10.1093/oso/9780190089856.003.0005

one of the major monstrosities of Spinoza's system, and even among recent readers, many still tend to agree with Jonathan Bennett's verdict that it is hard to do good philosophy if one assumes necessitarianism.[3] Spinoza's assertion that he "places freedom not in free decree, but in a *free necessity*"[4] did not help relieve worried readers. Indeed, what could "free necessity" mean at all? Isn't it a plain oxymoron?

That Spinoza was a strict necessitarian was pretty much taken for granted by almost all of his readers during the first three centuries since his death and the publication of his *Opera Posthuma* (1677). But this state of things has changed somewhat over the past half-century, and a number of leading scholars have suggested that Spinoza's commitment to necessitarianism is much less obvious than one would initially think. A significant part of the current chapter will be dedicated to the recent debate about whether Spinoza was a strict necessitarian.

The first section of the chapter will address the philosophy of modality among Spinoza's medieval Jewish predecessors, and, primarily, in Hasdai Crescas (1340–1410/11), a bold and original, anti-Aristotelian philosopher. This section should both complement the discussion of modality in medieval Christian and Islamic philosophy in the previous chapters of this volume[5] and provide some lesser-known historical background to Spinoza's own engagement with modal philosophy. Following a section on Spinoza's *definitions* of his main modal concepts and his understanding of contingency, I will turn, in the third section, to discuss the extent of Spinoza's commitment to necessitarianism.

---

3 Jonathan Bennett, *A Study of Spinoza's* Ethics (Indianapolis, IN: Hackett, 1984), 114, and Jonathan Bennett, *Learning from Six Philosophers,* 2 vols. (Oxford: Clarendon Press, 2001), 1: 176.

4 Spinoza, Ep. 58 (IV/265/30), italics added. For the list of bibliographical abbreviations used in this chapter, see the end of the chapter. Cf. IV/266/35. Unless otherwise marked, all references to Spinoza's works and letters are to Curley's translation: *The Collected Works of Spinoza,* 2 vols., ed. and trans. Edwin Curley (Princeton, NJ: Princeton University Press, 1985/2016). I have relied on Gebhardt's critical edition, Benedict Spinoza, *Opera,* 4 vols., ed. Carl Gebhardt (Heidelberg: Carl Winter, 1925) for the Latin and Dutch texts of Spinoza.

5 See Chapter 2 in this volume.

The recent debate about whether Spinoza was a strict necessitarian has resulted in quite a few insights about Spinoza's modal philosophy, but it has also detracted attention from some basic questions about Spinoza's modal philosophy, and in the fourth and last section of the chapter, I will attempt to chart the foundational questions that still have been barely explored.

The primary aim of this chapter it to provide a survey and outline of the chief elements of Spinoza's modal philosophy. Still, beyond the mere overview of Spinoza's arguments (and some major scholarly debates), I will also advance two original theses. First, I will show that Spinoza makes a distinction between *two* notions of contingency, and that once this important distinction is observed, Spinoza's various assertions about contingency turn out to be consistent. Second, I will discuss the text (E2a1) which is commonly taken to be the strongest and most stubborn proof against the reading of Spinoza as strict necessitarianism; I will show that the basic meaning of this text has been widely misunderstood, and that E2a1 is perfectly compatible with strict necessitarianism.

2. Crescas on Modality

The shadow of the "Great Eagle" (הנשר הגדול)—Maimonides' (1138–1204) Hebrew sobriquet—was cast over almost all aspects and issues in medieval Jewish philosophy, and the subfield of the philosophy of modality is no exception. But figuring out Maimonides' precise stance on this issue is no trivial task. In several texts, Maimonides brings the conflict between divine foreknowledge and human freedom into sharp relief.[6] In his more popular works, Maimonides seems to support freedom of the will. Yet, in various passages in the *Guide of the*

---

6 See, for example, Moses Maimonides, "Eight Chapters," ch. VIII, in *A Maimonides Reader*, ed. I. Twersky (Springfield, NJ: Behrman House, 1972), 379–386.

Perplexed, a very different view emerges, where human will and choice are completely determined by previous causes.[7] In a recent study, Zev Harvey argued that even some of the popular works—such as *Eight Chapters*— are consistent with strict determinism and necessitarianism, once read closely.[8]

In his own magisterial work, the *Wars of the Lord* (מלחמות השם), Gersonides (1288–1344) opted to secure a place for human free choice by advancing the radical view according to which God does *not* know the future choices of human beings. Gersonides' view invites the critical charge of compromising significantly the divine perfection of omniscience. To counter such criticisms, Gersonides argues:

> The fact that God does not have the knowledge of which possible outcome will be realized does not imply any defect in God. For perfect knowledge of something is the knowledge of what that thing is in reality [לפי מה שהוא עליו]; when the thing is not apprehended as it is, this is error, not knowledge. Hence, God knows all these things in the best manner possible, for He knows them insofar as they are ordered in a determinate and certain way, and He knows in addition that they[9] are contingent [אפשריים] insofar as they fall within the domain of human choice [and as such knows them] truly as contingent.[10]

---

7 See Shlomo Pines, "Notes on Maimonides' Views concerning Human Will," *Scripta Hierosolymitana* 6 (1960): 196–198; Alexander Altmann, "The Religion of the Thinkers," in *Religion in a Religious Age*, ed. S. D. Goitein (Cambridge, MA: Association for Jewish Studies, 1974), 35–45; Warren Zev Harvey, "Maimonides' Interpretation of Genesis 3:22" [Hebrew], *Da'at* 12 (1984): 16–18.

8 Harvey, "Maimonides' Interpretation," 18.

9 I have slightly amended Feldman's translation here in order to better fit the original Hebrew.

10 Gersonides, *Milhamot ha-Shem* (Riva di Trento, 1560) III, 4, 23d; Gersonides, *Wars of the Lord*, 3 vols., trans. Seymour Feldman (Philadelphia, PA: Jewish Publication Society, 1984–1999), 2: 118, translation slightly altered. For a helpful comparison of these claims of Gersonides, and similar claims in Abraham Ibn Daud's *Emunah Ramah*, see Charles Touati, *La pensée philosophique et théologique de gersonide* (Paris: Édition de minuit, 1973), 147.

According to Gersonides, the perfection of divine knowledge requires that God must know all things *as they are*.[11] Since future human choices *are* contingent, God must know them as contingent, i.e., he must *not* know which contingent choice (i.e., action) will be actualized ("which possible outcome will be realized").[12]

Discussing Gersonides' view, and addressing arguments both in favor of and against it, Hasdai Crescas pointed out that if we conjoin Gersonides' assertion that God knows future human choices only as contingent with the view (which Gersonides also maintains) that God cannot acquire new knowledge,[13] it follows that even *after* one of the future choices has been realized, God must remain ignorant of this choice and of all events resulting from it. Thus, Crescas writes:

> Since Jacob's going down to Egypt belongs to the modality of the possible [חומר האפשר] and depends on his choice, it would follow [according to Gersonides] that once Jacob chose to go down— at which point God became ignorant of the choice and knew nothing of it—God also had no way of knowing all that followed from that choice, and a fortiori, all that followed from the many choices that were made from among the possible alternatives.[14]

---

11 Notice that Gersonides allows for contingency in a sense far stronger than the one we find in Avicenna, Ibn Daud, and Crescas where a thing is said to be contingent if its essence does not necessitate either its existence or non-existence. For Gersonides, human choices are contingent in the sense that even given all previous causes and all previous facts—and not just the essences at stake—human choices are still not necessary. In Section 2 we will see that Spinoza calls this stronger sense of contingency 'real contingency' (and I will refer to it as '*tout court* contingency', or TC-Contingency).

12 Were God to know now my future choice *c* tomorrow, *c* would have to obtain, and would thus be necessary, rather than contingent (in the stronger sense of contingency addressed in the previous note).

13 The acquisition of knowledge would require a hylic faculty; both Gersonides and Crescas deny that God has such a faculty.

14 Hasdai Crescas, *Or ha-Shem* ([Hebrew: *Light of the Lord*], ed. Rabbi Shlomo Fisher (Jerusalem: Ramot, 1990), II, 1, iii; Hasdai Crescas, *Light of the Lord,* trans. Roslyn Weiss (Oxford: Oxford University Press, 2018), 132.

Ascribing to God ignorance about most events narrated in the Hebrew Bible (i.e., events resulting from Jacob's choice to go down to Egypt) appeared to Crescas as sheer madness, and this consideration, together with other philosophical arguments against Gersonides' view,[15] led Crescas to reject the latter. Instead, Crescas argued that we can preserve a space for human effort and industriousness (i.e., reject fatalism) even as we embrace necessitarianism, if we observe the crucial distinction between, on the one hand, things which are necessary *per se*, and on the other, things which are *per se* possible, yet necessary by virtue of their causes. He thus provides the following characterization of the possible:

> A possible thing that can exist or not exist [הדבר שאפשר שימצא ושלא ימצא] requires a cause to determine [תכריע] its existence over its nonexistence; otherwise, its nonexistence would persist. Therefore, when something possible exists, it is necessarily the case that it was preceded by a cause that necessitated and determined its existence over its nonexistence, so that the existent that was assumed possible turns out to be necessary. And if we investigate the earlier cause, if it, too, was assumed to be possible, and we posit it as existent, then the necessity that turned out to apply in the case of the first possible that was posited as existent will apply to it as well. This will continue until the series culminates in the first cause and first existent, whose existence is necessary by virtue of His essence [מחוייב המציאות], may He be blessed.[16]

Within this broadly Avicennian picture, all things exist necessarily, but only God's existence is necessary per se ("מחוייב המציאות," i.e., necessary by virtue of its essence). All other existing things—including the

---

15 See Crescas, *Or ha-Shem*, II, 1, iii; Crescas, *Light of the Lord*, 130–131.
16 Crescas, *Or ha-Shem*, II, 5, ii; Crescas, *Light of the Lord*, 191. I have slightly amended Weiss' translation here in order to better fit the original Hebrew.

human will—are possible *per se* and necessitated by their causes (ultimately, they are necessitated by the first cause, i.e., God).[17] Human endeavor, claims Crescas, is not futile in order to realize possibilities that are necessitated by their cause, since this very endeavor *is* "the essential cause for accumulating [the sought] goods,"[18] i.e., human endeavor is a cause required for the attainment of most goods we seek.

Crescas' Avicennian distinction between *per se* necessity and *tout court* necessity was shared by many medieval and early modern philosophers, such as Spinoza (as we shall shortly see) and Leibniz (see Chapter 5 in this volume). However, not all of Crescas' readers were happy with his necessitarian conclusion. Thus, Yitzhak Abarbanel (1437–1508), addressing Crescas' suggested alternative to Gersonides' view, writes:

> And I was alarmed at seeing the Pious Rabbi [i.e., Crescas] escape being burnt by the fire of the commentator's [i.e., Gersonides'] heresy only to have him succumb to it in the end. For what possibility remains for the thing that is necessary in respect of its causes when it is after all necessitated and constrained [והלא באמת הוא מוכרח ומחוייב].[19]

Restricting possibility to per se possibility—which by virtue of its causes is either necessarily actualized, or necessarily non-actualized—leaves no room for genuine freedom of the will, claimed Abarbanel. Still, we can point out at least one reader of Crescas who was clearly sympathetic to his necessitarianism. In his celebrated Letter on the

---

17 Crescas employs the distinction between per se and per-another modalities in numerous other places in *Light of the Lord*. See, for example, I, 1, iii where an effect is characterized as possible per se [אפשרי המציאות בבחינת עצמו] yet necessary by virtue of its cause.
18 Crescas, *Or ha-Shem*, II, 5, iii; Crescas, *Light of the Lord*, 193–194. For a helpful discussion of Crescas' necessitarianism, see Warren Zev Harvey, *Physics and Metaphysics in Hasdai Crescas* (Amsterdam: J. C. Gieben, 1998), 137–149.
19 Yitzhak Abarbanel, *Perush ha-Torah* [Hebrew: *Commentary on the Pentateuch*] (Venice, 1579), 18, 20. translated by Roslyn Weiss in her editorial introduction to Crescas' *Light of the Lord*, 11.

Infinite, Spinoza discusses and endorses a proof for God's existence advanced by Crescas which unmistakably embraces a necessitarian position.[20] We will shortly begin our study of Spinoza by scrutinizing his definitions of the core concepts of modality and his understanding of contingency, but before we turn to Spinoza, let me note that in his *Light of the Lord*, Crescas provides a series of arguments in favor of the possibility of alternative universes, or non-actual, possible worlds.[21] His arguments are terse but precise, and thus require close scrutiny and detailed explication which cannot be carried out here.

3. Spinoza's Definitions of Contingency and Other Modal Notions

The *Cogitata Metaphysica* ("Metaphysical Thoughts") is the appendix to Spinoza's 1663 book in which he attempted to present Parts I and II (as well as the opening segment of Part III) of Descartes' book *Principles of Philosophy* in a geometrical (i.e., axiomatic) manner. This is an intriguing text, though it is not always clear whether the claims stated in this text represent Spinoza's own (early) views, the views of Descartes, or perhaps merely the assertions of some late Scholastic authors. Still, the *Cogitata Metaphysica* is extremely rich in discussions of modal philosophy, and therefore we simply cannot afford to disregard it. We will

---

20 See Spinoza, Ep. 12| IV/62/1–10 and Harvey, *Physics and Metaphysics*, 8–13. For a discussion of this proof, see Yitzhak Y. Melamed, "Hasdai Crescas and Spinoza on Actual Infinity and the Infinity of God's Attributes," in *Spinoza and Jewish Philosophy*, ed. Steven Nadler (Cambridge: Cambridge University Press, 2014), 205–211. For a discussion of Crescas' likely influence on Spinoza's rejection of free will, see Harvey, *Physics and Metaphysics*, 137–57. In his marginal notes on Spinoza's Letter of the Infinite, Leibniz observed that Crescas' argument employed the Principle of Sufficient Reason. G. W. Leibniz, *The Labyrinth of the Continuum: Writings on the Continuum Problem, 1672–1686*, trans. and ed. Richard T. W. Arthur (New Haven, CT: Yale University Press, 2001), 117| G. W. Leibniz, *Sämtliche Schriften und Briefe*, Deutsche Akademie der Wissenschaften, multiple volumes in 7 series (Berlin: Akademie Verlag, 1923–), VI 3, 71.

21 Crescas, *Or ha-Shem*, IV, 2; Crescas, *Light of the Lord*, 334–337. It is worth noting that next to his discussion of alternative universes, Crescas still employs "Statistic" modalities, and thus holds that a possibility must be actualized at some time (see, for example, *Or ha-Shem*, IV, 1; *Light of the Lord*, 332). I discuss Statistic modalities in Sections 3–4.

discuss this text while keeping in mind the question of whether they represent Spinoza's views.

The title of the third chapter of part one of the *Cogitata* reads: "Concerning What Is Necessary, Impossible, Possible, and Contingent." Attempting to elucidate the first two notions, Spinoza writes:

> A thing is said to be necessary or impossible in two ways: either in respect to its essence or in respect to its cause. We know that God exists necessarily in respect to his essence, for his essence cannot be conceived without existence. And it is impossible that a chimaera exists in respect to its essence, which involves a contradiction. [Other] things—e.g., material ones—are called either impossible or necessary in respect to their cause. For if we consider only their essence, we can conceive it clearly and distinctly without existence.[22] Therefore, they can never exist by the power and necessity of their essence, but only by the power of their cause, God, the creator of all things. And so, if it is in the divine decree that some thing exists, it will necessarily exist; but if not, it will be impossible that it should exist.[23]

God and chimeras occupy the two extreme poles in Spinoza's modal ontology.[24] God exists necessarily by virtue of its essence, while a chimera necessarily does not exist (i.e., is impossible) just by virtue of

---

22 Regarding things whose essence we can conceive clearly and distinctly without existence, see Spinoza's claims later in the same chapter: "if we were to conceive the whole order of nature, we should discover that *many things whose nature we perceive clearly and distinctly*, that is, whose essence is necessarily such, can not in any way exist. For we should find the existence of such things in nature to be just as impossible as we now know the passage of a large elephant through the eye of a needle to be, although we perceive the nature of each of them clearly" (CM I 3| I/241/ 30–242/2, italics added). Using the terminology I will introduce shortly, we may say that things whose essence we conceive clearly and distinctly without existence are *Essence*-Contingent, yet *Tout Court*-Impossible.

23 CM I 3| I/240/23–241/3.

24 The metric Spinoza is using here seems to be related to his understanding of power. See E1p11d: "To be able not to exist is to lack power, and conversely, to be able to exist it to have power (as is known through itself)" (II/53/29–31). Presumably, God has more power than the middle category things, which in their turn have more power than chimeras. I am indebted to Justin Bledin for raising this question which requires further study.

its contradictory essence. In between God and the chimera, we have things whose essences neither rule in, nor rule out, their existence. These things in the middle category are still—according to the last sentence in the passage above—all either necessary or impossible, but their necessity or impossibility results from external causes, rather than from their mere essences. It is just with regard to things in this middle category that we apply the notions of *possibility* and *contingency* which Spinoza defines as follows:

> A thing is called *possible*, then, *when we understand its efficient cause*, but do not know whether the cause is determined [*attamen an causa determinate sit, ignoramus*]. So we can regard it as possible, but neither as necessary nor as impossible. If, however, *we attend to the essence of the thing alone*, and not to its cause, we shall call it *contingent*. That is, we shall consider it as midway between God and a chimaera, so to speak, because we find in it, on the part of its essence, neither any necessity of existing (as we do in the divine essence) nor any impossibility or inconsistency (as we do in a chimaera). And if anyone wishes to call *contingent* what I call *possible*, or *possible* what I call *contingent*, I shall not contend with him.[25]

Things in the middle category (i.e., everything apart from God and chimeras) are called contingent when we *attend only* to their essence and find nothing in the essence which would either rule in, or rule out, the existence of the thing. The very same things (of the middle category) are also called possible, if we attend not to their essence, but to their external, efficient, causes; due to the limits of our knowledge of the order of the infinitely many external causes of each thing, we do not know whether these external causes obtained. Notice that contingency *in the epistemic sense defined in the last excerpt* is perfectly

---

[25] CM I 3| I/242/11–22. In his discussion of modality in the early *Treatise on the Emendation of the Intellect* (TdIE §53), Spinoza seems not to distinguish between possibility and contingency.

compatible with necessity: a thing whose essence does not involve existence (or contradiction) will be deemed by us as contingent, and yet, insofar as that thing is necessarily caused by an external cause, it is still necessary.

But in the very same discussion in the CM, Spinoza also uses 'contingent' in a significantly different sense, i.e., as being neither necessary nor impossible, *all things considered*.[26] Obviously, contingency in this second (and non-epistemic) sense is *incompatible* with necessity. Spinoza points out the term 'real contingency [*contingens reale*]'[27] as the common expression for this second (and far stronger) sense of contingency. It is possible, though I cannot prove it at this stage, that this notion of strong, 'real contingency' *in things* (rather than in our conception) is inspired by Gersonides' understanding of what is "contingent in *reality* [לפי מה שהוא עליו]," such as human decisions which, for Gersonides, are not necessary even given all previous facts and causes.[28]

Here it is crucial to observe that *it is with regard to real contingency* that Spinoza asserts that "there is nothing contingent in things"[29] and that contingency is "nothing but a defect in our understanding."[30] To keep clear this important distinction between the two senses of 'contingent,' we will henceforth use the term 'E-Contingent' for things whose *essence* is conceived as neither ruling in, nor ruling out, their existence, whereas things—if there are any—which neither exist necessarily nor are impossible, *tout court*,[31] will be called 'TC-Contingent.'[32]

---

26 Namely, regardless of the source of the necessity or impossibility.
27 CM I 3| I/242/30.
28 I an indebted to Zev Harvey for this suggestion.
29 CM I 3| I/242/29. Cf. E1p29 and E1p33s1.
30 CM I 3| I/242/9 and 26. Cf. E2p31c.
31 Namely, things which are contingent in the strongest sense that neither their causes nor their essences rule in, or rule out, their existence.
32 Martial Gueroult also draws a distinction between "contingente absolutement" and "contingente seulement par rapport à son essence." Martial Gueroult, *Spinoza II: L'âme* (Paris: Aubier-Montaigne, 1974), 31. We could just as well have called the weaker contingency 'per se Contingency'

The latter kind of contingency is presumed to be *in things*, the former is conceptual or epistemic.

Having thus documented and briefly clarified the distinction between the two notions of contingency in the *Cogitata Metaphysica*, we are now ready to approach Spinoza's discussions of contingency in his *magnum opus*, the *Ethics*. Frequently, Spinoza's claims about contingency in the *Ethics* are viewed as inconsistent.[33] Against, this view, I will argue that in the *Ethics*—just as in the CM—Spinoza employs 'contingent' in two distinct senses (i.e., the very same two senses we find in the CM), and that once we observe this crucial distinction, the apparent inconsistencies are dispelled.

After endorsing and proving determinism in E1p28,[34] Spinoza turns to prove the following proposition:

E1p29: *In nature there is nothing contingent, but all things have been determined from the necessity of the divine nature to exist and produce an effect in a certain way.* Dem.: Whatever is, is in God (by E1p15); but God cannot be called a contingent thing [*res contingens*]. For (by E1p11) he exists necessarily, not contingently. Next, the modes of the divine nature have also followed from it necessarily and not contingently (by E1p16) . . . if [the modes] have not been determined by God, then (by E1p26) it is impossible, not contingent, that they should determine themselves. Conversely (by E1p27) if they have

---

rather than 'E-Contingency.' After some hesitation, I decided to employ the latter terminology in order to stress the role of our conception of essences in this distinction.

[33] See, for example, Bennett, *Study*, 111. Like Bennett, Samuel Newlands, *Reconceiving Spinoza* (Oxford: Oxford University Press, 2018), 94, reads Spinoza as using 'contingent' univocally. Newlands adds, however, that the modal status of modes is sensitive to how they are conceived: conceived in one way, modes are contingent, conceived in another, they are not (and both conceptions may be adequate, per Newlands).

[34] E1p28: "*Every singular thing, or any thing which is finite and has a determinate existence, can neither exist nor be determined to produce an effect unless it is determined to exist and produce an effect by another cause, which is also finite and has a determinate existence; and again, this cause also can neither exist nor be determined to produce an effect unless it is determined to exist and produce an effect by another, which is also finite and has a determinate existence, and so on, to infinity.*" Cf. E1a3 and E1pp26–27.

been determined by God, it is not contingent, but impossible, that they should render themselves undetermined. So, all things have been determined from the necessity of the divine nature, not only to exist, but to exist in a certain way, and to produce effects in a certain way. *There is nothing contingent*, q.e.d.

Spinoza begins E1p29d by claiming that God is not contingent. Indeed, in E1p11s, Spinoza proves that God's essence involves existence. Thus, God is clearly not a contingent thing (on *either* understanding of contingency). But in the rest of E1p29d, Spinoza seems to be using 'contingent' as TC-Contingency, i.e., as being neither necessary nor impossible, all things considered. This allows him to argue that *the modes* too do not exist contingently, in spite of the fact that it is precisely the modes which constitute the middle category between God and chimeras, i.e., in spite of the fact the essence of a mode does *not* necessitate either its existence or its non-existence (which will qualify the modes as E-Contingent).[35] Employing this strong sense of 'contingent,' Spinoza can conclude: "There is nothing contingent," but this conclusion is perfectly compatible with the ascription of E-Contingency to all modes.

One reader of the *Ethics* who was critically aware of these two senses of contingency in Spinoza is Leibniz. In his 1678 notes on Spinoza's *Ethics*, Leibniz objects that E1p29d is "obscure and abrupt," and then adds:

> The matter depends on the definition of 'contingent' which he has given nowhere.[36] I use the term 'contingent,' as do others, for that whose essence does not involve existence. In this sense, particular things are contingent according to Spinoza himself, by

---

35 See E1p11d | II/53/7–10. Cf. Ep. 12| IV/54/9–17.
36 It seems at this point in time, Leibniz has not studied yet Part Four of the *Ethics*, and specifically, E4d3.

Proposition 24.[37] But if you take 'contingent' in the sense of some of the Scholastics, a usage unknown to Aristotle, and to common life, as that which happens in such a way that no reason of any kind can be given why it should have happened thus rather than otherwise, and as that whose cause is equally disposed to act and not to act when all the conditions, both internal and external, have been fulfilled, then I think such contingency implies a contradiction.[38]

The assertion ascribed here to "some Scholastics," i.e., that certain things have a cause "equally disposed to act and not to act [even] when all the conditions, both internal and external, have been fulfilled" would just as well fit Gersonides' view. Leibniz (at least the Leibniz of 1678), just like Spinoza, would utterly reject the notion that contingency, in this strong sense, ever obtains.

The weaker and epistemic sense of 'contingent' (i.e., E-Contingent) resurfaces at the beginning of Part Four of the *Ethics*, where Spinoza provides explicit definitions for both contingency and possibility. It is worth noting that these definitions appear very late in the book and after Spinoza has already employed both notions quite significantly. One way to explain this late introduction of the definitions is that the strong sense of 'contingent' (TC-Contingent) reflected what Spinoza considered to be a common use of the term,[39] while in Part Four he introduces his own, more technical, use of the term. Be that as it may, let us scrutinize these definitions:

---

[37] "E1p24: The essence of things produced by God does not involve existence." Notice however that Spinoza does not employ the terminology of contingency in E1p24 and its demonstration. Particular things are indeed contingent according to Spinoza's definition of contingency in E4d3 (to be discussed shortly).

[38] G. W. Leibniz, *Philosophical Papers and Letters,* trans. and ed. Leroy E. Loemker (Dordrecht: Kluwer, 1989), 203–204; G I, 149.

[39] This suggestion is supported by the fact that when Spinoza employs the terminology of contingency in contexts that are more general and not dedicated to the philosophy of modality, he employs 'contingent' in the strong sense (TC-Contingent). See, for example, TTP Ch. 19 (III/236/24): "A harm and evil to the whole Republic which would have been uncertain and contingent, becomes certain and necessary." Cf. Ep. 75| IV/312/14.

E4d3: I call singular things contingent insofar as we find [*invenimus*] nothing, while we attend [*attendimus*] only to their essence, which necessarily posits their existence or which necessarily excludes it.

E4d4: I call the same singular things possible, insofar as, while we attend to the causes from which they must be produced, we do not know whether those causes are determined to produce them.

Spinoza defines 'contingent' and 'possible' in terms of our attention or epistemic access to the things at stake.[40] More importantly we should notice that even God's (adequate) ideas of modes, conceives these modes as having an essence not involving existence. Consider *God's* idea of mode M_1. Insofar as M_1 is a mode and not a substance, its essence does not involve existence, and thus—per E4d3—it is contingent (E-Contingent). Were God to conceive M_1 as not being E-Contingent, he would be making an error, by taking a mode for a substance. On the other hand, God cannot conceive M_1 as TC-Contingent, because God's idea of M_1 *must* involve the causes which necessitate M_1's existence.

We will shortly turn to the question of whether Spinoza was a necessitarian or not, but before we do that, let us complete our discussion of Spinoza's definitions of his basic modal notions. In E1d8, Spinoza presents the following definition of eternity:

By *eternity* [*aeternitas*] I understand existence itself, insofar as it is conceived to follow necessarily from the definition alone of the eternal thing.

---

40 Namely, were we to attend to the essence of a chimera, but, due to the high complexity of this essence, be ignorant of the contradiction lurking in this essence, we would consider the chimera a mode and call it 'contingent' (E-Contingent) "due to a defect of our understanding" (i.e., our failure to diagnose the contradiction). Similarly, were we to imagine the essence of a substance and, be unaware of the fact that existence belongs to its essence, we would consider that substance an E-Contingent mode.

Exp.: For such existence, like the essence of a thing, is conceived as an eternal truth, and on that account cannot be explained by duration or time, even if the duration is conceived to be without beginning or end.

The formulation of E1d8 raises several intriguing questions.[41] In earlier studies, I have shown that in E1d8 Spinoza seems to understand eternity not as a temporal notion (i.e., sempiternity, or existence in all times), but rather as a *modal* concept: as self-necessitated existence, or as existence which is necessitated by virtue of the mere essence (or, what is the same: by virtue of its mere definition) of the thing.[42] Whatever is conceived as eternal is not E-Contingent, and whatever is (chimeras excluded) which is not conceived as E-Contingent, is eternal.

4. Spinoza's Necessitarianism

In the previous section we have studied Spinoza's understanding of contingency, and his definitions of modal terms. Already the texts we have surveyed so far seem to support the ascription of necessitarianism to Spinoza. Thus, for example, we have seen that when Spinoza addresses things which are E-Contingent, he would frequently add that these things are still necessitated by their causes and, ultimately, God.[43] In this section, we will expand and deepen our study of Spinoza's discussion of necessitarianism, and then scrutinize E2a1, the text which is widely perceived as the strongest evidence against the ascription of strict necessitarianism to Spinoza.

---

41 For detailed discussion, see Yitzhak Y. Melamed, "Eternity in Early Modern Philosophy," in *Eternity: A History*, ed. Yitzhak Y. Melamed (Oxford: Oxford University Press, 2016), 152–155.

42 See Yitzhak Y. Melamed, "Spinoza's Deification of Existence," *Oxford Studies in Early Modern Philosophy* 6 (2012): 75–104, and especially, 90–96, and Melamed, "Eternity in Early Modern Philosophy," 149–163.

43 See, for example, CM I 3 (I/241/1). Cf. E1p29d.

The general picture we get from Spinoza's discussions of modality in the *Ethics* is that all things are necessitated into existence (or nonexistence) either by their essence or by their efficient causes. Consider, for example, E1p33s:

> A thing is called necessary either by reason of its essence or by reason of its cause. *For a thing's existence follows necessarily either from its essence and definition or from a given efficient cause.* And a thing is also called impossible from these same causes—viz. either because its essence, or definition, involves a contradiction, or because there is no external cause which has been determined to produce such a thing.[44]

We get the very same picture in E1p11d. Here, in the course of proving God's existence, Spinoza formulates what can be viewed as his own version of the Principle of Sufficient Reason (PSR):

> For each thing there must be assigned a cause, or reason, as much for its existence as for its nonexistence. For example, if a triangle exists, there must be a reason or cause why it exists; but if it does not exist, there must also be a reason or cause which prevents it from existing, or which takes its existence away.[45]

According to Spinoza's variant of the PSR, neither existence nor nonexistence can be brute. Once brute existence facts are ruled out of the picture, the path leading to necessitarianism seems unavoidable:

> But this reason, or cause, must either be contained in the nature of the thing, or be outside it. E.g., the very nature of a square circle

---

44 E1p33s| II/74/6–12, italics added.
45 E1p11d| II/52/30–53/2.

indicates the reason why it does not exist, viz. because it involves a contradiction. On the other hand, the reason why a substance exists also follows from its nature alone, because it involves existence (see E1p7). But the reason why a circle or triangle exists, or why it does not exist, does not follow from the nature of these things, but from the order of the whole of corporeal Nature. *For from this [order] it must follow either that the triangle necessarily exists now [jam] or that it is impossible for it to exist now [jam].*[46]

For our purposes, the crucial claims in this passage appear in the discussion of the existence of the "circle or triangle," i.e., modes, or things whose essence does not involve existence (i.e., E-Contingent things). Addressing the existence of these modes of Extension, Spinoza states unequivocally that *(i)* E-Contingent things *must* have a reason for their existence, *(ii)* the reason for the existence of E-Contingent things lies in the order of corporeal nature, and that *(iii)* given the order of corporeal nature, the existence (or non-existence) of E-Contingent things *follows necessarily* ("must follow").

In light of this textual situation,[47] it is no surprise that, until a half-century ago, it was virtually taken for granted that Spinoza is a strict necessitarian. Then, in his important 1969 book, *Spinoza's Metaphysics*, and later in an article co-authored with Gregory Walski, Edwin Curley argued that while Spinoza is a determinist,[48] his version of necessitarianism is moderate rather than strict. On Curley and Walski's interpretation of Spinoza's "moderate necessitarianism," Spinoza's God exists

---

[46] E1p11d| II/53/3–10, italics added.

[47] There are other paths in *Ethics* which seem to lead to necessitarianism though we cannot discuss them in detail here. One such path begins with Spinoza's assertion that God's nature is necessary (E1p16), and then relying on Spinoza's demonstrations that all things follow necessarily from God's nature (E1p16d and E1p29d), infers that all things exist necessarily.

[48] Edwin Curley, *Spinoza's Metaphysics: An Essay in Interpretation* (Cambridge, MA: Harvard University Press, 1969), 101, 106, and Edwin Curley and Gregory Walski, "Spinoza's Necessitarianism Reconsidered," in *New Essays on the Rationalists*, ed. Rocco Gennaro and Charles Huenemann (New York: Oxford University Press, 1999), 244, 255.

necessarily, yet the complete system of all finite modes is *not* necessitated by God's nature, and there are alternative possible worlds that are compatible with God's necessary nature.[49]

Addressing Curley and Walski's arguments, Don Garrett showed convincingly that it is hard to reconcile Spinoza's texts, as well as his commitment to a strong version of the Principle of Sufficient Reason, with the ascription of mere "moderate necessitarianism" to Spinoza.[50] Still, there is *one* text in Spinoza's works which, at least at first sight, does not sit well with the ascription of strict necessitarianism to Spinoza, and this text appears in quite a central place in the *Ethics*: the first axiom of part two:

> E2a1: The essence of man does not involve necessary existence, i.e., from the order of nature it can happen equally that this or that man does exist, or that he does not exist [*Hominis essentia non involvit necessariam existentiam, hoc est, ex naturae ordine, tam fieri potest, ut hic, et ille homo existat, quam ut non existat*].[51]

E2a1 is divided into two parts by "i.e., [*hoc est*]." The first half seems clear: it states that the essence of man does not involve existence (i.e., human beings are E-Contingent), and from this we can infer that a human being is not a substance, but a mode (see E2p10&c).[52] The second part of E2a1 is much more enigmatic, for at least three reasons. First, it appears to be in conflict with Spinoza's unequivocal statement

---

49 Curley, *Spinoza's Metaphysics*, 104–106, and Curley and Walski, "Spinoza's Necessitarianism Reconsidered," 241.
50 See Don Garrett, *Nature and Necessity in Spinoza's Philosophy* (New York: Oxford University Press, 2018), 125–148. Instead of repeating Garrett's arguments, I invite readers to scrutinize the arguments of Curley and Walski alongside those of Garrett, and then to make their own judgment.
51 In the Vatican manuscript of Spinoza's *Ethics*, E2a1 appears at the beginning of the axiom section of part two but without a number. The significance of this—if there is any—is not clear to me. See Benedict Spinoza, *The Vatican Manuscript of Spinoza's* Ethics, ed. Leen Spruit and Pina Totaro (Leiden: Brill, 2011), 122.
52 This is contrary to Descartes' view of the human mind as a genuine substance.

(in E1p11d) about the reason for the existence of modes—such as a triangle or a circle—according to which from the order of nature "it must follow either that the triangle necessarily exists now or that it is impossible for it to exist now."[53] Second, assuming that Spinoza is using "the order of nature" in his customary way as referring to the system of existing things (which includes finite modes), the second part of E2a1 seems to deny not only necessitarianism but also determinism, whereas Spinoza's endorsement of determinism is both well-documented and undisputed. Third, the two parts of E2a1 seem to make *very different claims*: the first part asserts that human beings are E-Contingent, while the second that human beings are both TC-Contingent and are not subject to causal determinism. But then: how could Spinoza connect the two parts of the axiom by a "*hoc est*"? The use of "*hoc est*" indicates either that the two parts of the axiom are equivalent or that the second part elaborates and restricts the meaning of the first part. But neither of these can be the case if the second part indeed endorses human TC-Contingency and indeterminism.

As one would expect, Curley and Walski present the second half of E2a1 as textual evidence against the ascription of strict necessitarianism to Spinoza. Yet, since this second half seems to reject not only necessitarianism, but also determinism (the latter of which they do ascribe to Spinoza), they suggest that the phrase 'order of nature [*ordo naturare*]' is used in E2a1 not in its regular sense as referring to the system of all things in nature, but rather as denoting the laws of nature alone. Under this reading, the second part of E2a1 merely claims that the laws of nature do not suffice to necessitate the existence of finite things.[54] Regrettably, Curley and Walski provide hardly any evidence

---

[53] The claim that the order of nature necessitates the existence of all things appears in numerous other places in Spinoza's corpus. See, for example, CM II 9| I/266/25–27: "if men understood clearly the whole order of Nature, they would find all things just as necessary as are all those treated in Mathematics." Cf. Ep. 12| IV/55/13–15.

[54] Curley and Walski, "Spinoza's Necessitarianism Reconsidered," 254–256. For Curley and Walski, the existence of finite things follows only from the *combination* of the laws of nature and the

for the claim that '*ordo naturae*' in E2a1 is used in this special sense: they do not point out any element in the formulation of E2a1, or in the applications of this axiom later in the *Ethics* (which we will shortly discuss) that supports their surprising reading, and as far as I can see, there is no such element either in E2a1 or in its applications. They point to one other text in which, they argue, Spinoza "clearly" uses '*ordo naturae*' as referring to the laws of nature, but, as Garrett has pointed out, this text is better read according to Spinoza's regular use of '*ordo naturae*'.[55] Moreover, under Curley and Walski's reading, the two parts of E2a1 make significantly different claims, and it is hard to understand why Spinoza should connect the two parts with '*hoc est*'.

Addressing the formulation of E2a1, Garrett reads the axiom as stating that man's essence leaves open whether this or that man exists, and that it is only the order of nature (which includes the prior order of finite modes) that determines the existence or non-existence of a human being. However, Garrett continues, we have only a very limited knowledge of the order of nature, and thus, from *what we know of the order of nature*, the existence of this or that man does not follow. Thus, on Garrett's reading, the second part of E2a1 should have this crucial *epistemic* sense (which is not stated explicitly in the text). In support of his reading, Garrett points to E1p33s1, where Spinoza stresses that "the order of causes is hidden from us."[56] Indeed, when we look systematically at Spinoza's use of the term 'the order of nature' throughout his

---

infinite series of past events. Since, on their reading, the infinite series of past events itself does not follow necessarily from God's nature (and the laws of nature), there are genuinely alternative possible worlds, though each world is ordered in a strict deterministic manner.

55 See Curley and Walski, "Spinoza's Necessitarianism Reconsidered," 255–256 and Garrett, *Nature and Necessity*, 144. Here is the text at stake: "Then there is the ordinary power of God, and his extraordinary power. The ordinary is that by which he preserves the world *in a certain order*; the extraordinary is exercised when he does something beyond the order of nature, e.g., all miracles, such as the speaking of an ass, the appearance of angels, and the like" (CM I 9| I/267/21–24, italics added). Garrett sensibly points out that if '*ordo naturae*' meant only the laws of nature, the proper formulation of the italicized phrase above should have been "with a certain order" rather than "in a certain order."

56 Garrett, *Nature and Necessity*, 144.

writing, our ignorance about this order seems to be its most salient feature.[57]

Another important observation that could lead us toward reconciling E2a1 with Spinoza's standard backing of necessitarianism is suggested by Olli Koistinen. Comparing the second half of E2a1 with Spinoza's claim in E1p11d that "from [the order of nature] it must follow either that the triangle necessarily exists now [*jam*] or that it is impossible for it to exist now [*iam*]," Koistinen stresses the presence of time specification ("now") in the necessitarian text of E1p11d, and the absence of this time specification in E2a1. According to Koistinen, what the second half of E2a1 is trying to secure is that "it is possible that finite things do not exist and in fact for every finite thing such a possibility is actualized."[58]

E2a1 is a non-trivial and interesting text, and one of the measures the *Ethics* provides us in dealing with problematic texts is the examination of the application of a textual unit in subsequent geometrical derivations. Frequently, the meaning of an axiom, definition, or proposition becomes much clearer once we observe the use and application of that definition or axiom. The case of E2a1 is no exception.

E2a1 is used three times in later derivations in the *Ethics*: E2p10d, E2p11d, and E2p30d.[59] In E2p10d and E2p30s, Spinoza employs E2a1 to prove that the human mind and body are not substances. But something else transpires in E2p11d. In E2p11d, Spinoza investigates the ontological status of the human mind and its object. E2p11 and

---

[57] See, for example, TTP ch. 16 (III/191/6): "For the most part we are ignorant of the order and coherence of the whole of nature"; (III/199/15): "but to the order of nature ... which is unknown to us," and TP ch. 2 (III/283/28): "to the order of nature, which we do not know." Cf. E2p30d.

[58] Olli Koistinen, "Spinoza's Modal Theory," in *Blackwell Companion to Spinoza*, ed. Yitzhak Y. Melamed (Hoboken, NJ: Blackwell, 2021), 229. Notice that Koistinen seems to be using here so-called "Statistic" modality. I will address the role of Statistic modality in Spinoza shortly.

[59] In E2p30d, Spinoza uses 'the common order of nature' as denoting the infinite chain of finite causes of the human body, and not as referring to the laws of nature. If, as Curley and Walski argue, the 'order of nature' in E2a1 (upon which E2p30d relies) refers only to the laws of nature, E2p30d would be a trivial fallacy, resulting from an equivocal use of one of the main terms in the argument.

its demonstration are complex, long, and address non-trivial issues in Spinoza's metaphysics and philosophy of mind. Still, since this text is the climax of my entire chapter, it would be best to have it before our eyes. For our purposes, the crucial argument which employs E2a1 appears in the italicized text, toward the end of the demonstration.

> E2p11: The first thing that constitutes the actual being of a human Mind is nothing but the idea of a singular thing which actually exists.
> Dem.: The essence of man (by E2p10C) is constituted by certain modes of God's attributes, viz. (by E2a2) by modes of thinking, of all of which (by E2a3) the idea is prior in nature.... But not the idea of a thing which does not exist. For then (by E2p8c) the idea itself could not be said to exist. Therefore, it will be the idea of a thing which actually exists. But not of an infinite thing. For an infinite thing (by E1p21 and E1p22) must always [semper] exist necessarily. But (by E2a1) it is absurd. Therefore, the first thing that constitutes the actual being of a human Mind is the idea of a singular thing which actually exists, q.e.d.

Spinoza begins E2p11d by showing that the human mind and its object are modes, and not substances. He then shows that both the mind and its object are modes having duration (and not mere formal essences as per E2p8c). Finally, he argues that the human mind and its object *are finite modes, and not infinite modes.*[60] For our purposes, the last step is the crucial one. Were the object of the human mind an infinite mode, claims Spinoza, then by E1p21, it would have to *"always exist necessarily [debet semper necessario existere].* But (by E2a1) it is absurd" (E2p11, emphases added). Thus, we have here clear and unequivocal evidence that Spinoza understands E2a1 as asserting that human beings

---

[60] For a detailed discussion of Spinoza's notion of infinite modes, see Yitzhak Y. Melamed, *Spinoza's Metaphysics: Substance and Thought* (New York: Oxford University Press, 2013), ch. 4.

do not exist *always* (and are thus not infinite modes). Now, where does Spinoza state that in E2a1? The first half of E2a1—stating that the essence of human being does not involve existence—would not commit Spinoza to the claim that human beings do not exist "always," since the infinite modes (qua modes) do not involve existence (E1p24), yet they *do* exist always. Thus, it must be the second part of E2a1 which states that human beings do not exist always. But how, precisely?

Let's have a second look at the Latin of this clause: "*ex naturae ordine, tam fieri potest, ut hic, et ille homo existat, quam ut non existat.*" Arguably, Spinoza is using here '*potest* [can]' in a sense that was very common in Spinoza's time, but one which we normally tend to disregard or neglect. Let me explain. For many ancient, medieval, and early modern philosophers, the basic modal notions of necessity, possibility, and actuality were defined in *temporal* terms (and not, as we would define them, in terms of possible worlds). Under this so-called "Statistic" understanding of modality,[61] a thing or a property is possible just in case it is instantiated in at least *some* time; necessary just in case it is instantiated in *all* times; impossible just in case it is *not* instantiated *in any* time; and actual just in case it is instantiated *now* (compare this with our understanding of possibility as instantiation in at least *some* possible world, necessity as instantiation in *all* possible worlds, and actuality as instantiation in the *current* possible world). At least prima facie, Statistic modalities and Possible-Worlds modalities are orthogonal (e.g., a property can be possible in terms of Statistic modality and necessary in terms of Possible-Worlds modality, and the other way around).

In the next section, we will encounter other passages in the *Ethics* employing Statistic modality. Here, let us consider what does the

---

[61] For a helpful discussion of Statistic (or temporal) modality in Aristotle, Boethius and Scholasticism, see Simo Knuuttila, "Medieval Modal Theories and Modal Logic," in *Handbook of the History of Logic.* vol. 2: *Medieval and Renaissance Logic,* ed. Dov M. Gabbay and John Woods (Amsterdam: Elsevier, 2008), 509–11, and Simo Knuuttila, "Time and Modality in Scholasticism," in *Reforging the Great Chain of Being: Studies in the History of Modal Ideas,* ed. Simo Knuuttila (Dordrecht: Kluwer, 2010), 163–258. For temporal modality in Diodorus Chronus, see Chapter 1, Section 3 in this volume.

second half of E2a1 say, if the modal verb '*potest*' is used there in the Statistic sense? Under the Statistic reading, the claim that from the order of nature it *can* happen (or become) that this man exists, and it *can* happen that this man does not exist, is just to say that *sometimes* from the order of nature it happens/becomes that this man exists, and *sometimes* that this man does not exist.[62]

What Spinoza is saying in the second clause of E2a1 is that the order of nature *does not always brings about the existence* of a specific human being: sometimes it does, sometimes it doesn't, and this is precisely why in E2p11d Spinoza employs this axiom in order to show that a human being is not an infinite mode. Infinite modes exist *always*, and insofar as they are part of the order of nature, it is incompatible with the order of nature that an infinite mode will not exist at any moment. Human beings—not being infinite modes—are such that sometimes the order of nature necessitates their existence, and sometimes, unfortunately, the order of nature necessitates the end of their existence.

Notice that there is *a* sense in which E2a1 (and consequently, E2p10d) assert that human beings 'do not exist necessarily,' but this is not the sense employed by Curley and Walski. If by 'exists necessarily' one means 'exists in all times' (i.e., if one interprets 'necessarily' according to its Statistic sense) then E2a1—*as interpreted by Spinoza in E2p11d*—clearly states that we do not exist necessarily; but the denial of man's necessary existence in the Statistic sense is perfectly compatible with the strictest necessitarianism, since we formulated necessitarianism in terms of Possible Worlds modality, rather than frequency of existence in times.[63] Being non-necessary

---

62 In fact, the second half of E2a1 is just a statement of the Statistic sense of TC-Contingency: of things/qualities which obtain sometimes, and do not obtain other times, by virtue of their causes. The distinction between TC-Contingency and E-Contingency is *orthogonal* to the distinction between the Possible Worlds and Statistic senses of modality.

63 In other words, the claim that man does not always exist is perfectly compatible with necessitarianism. All that necessitarianism requires is that whenever a person does not exist, she does not exist in all possible worlds, and whenever a person does exist, she exists in all possible worlds.

in the Statistic sense, and being non-necessary in the Possible Worlds sense are completely different qualities, and having features of reality that are Statistically non-necessary is perfectly compatible with strict necessitarianism.

Under the reading of E2a1 suggested here, 'order of nature' is used in its standard sense in Spinoza's writings, and the meaning of E2a1 is dictated by Spinoza's own interpretation of the axiom in E2p11d. Under this reading, the '*hoc est*' is used to specify the meaning of the first half of the axiom. If the first half asserts that human beings are modes, the second half spells out that human beings are *finite* modes.[64] The reading also fits neatly Spinoza's claim in E1p11d that from the order of nature "it must follow either that the triangle necessarily exists now or that it is impossible for it to exist now" as well as the numerous other passages endorsing necessitarianism. Finally, let me note that one cannot disregard the employment of E2a1 in E2p11d as some sort of typo or simple error: the argument employed at the end of E2p11d seems to be quite clear, and it is incumbent upon those who reject the interpretation of E2a1 offered here, to provide an alternative explanation for the employment of E2a1 in E2p11d.

Before we conclude our discussion of Spinoza's necessitarianism, let me address a fascinating and important suggestion made recently by Samuel Newlands. According to Newlands' argument, the modal status of things is sensitive to how they are conceived: when we conceive finite modes only through their essence (what Newlands calls the "narrow conception" of a thing), finite modes are (genuinely!) contingent, whereas when conceived in the broader context of the entire order of nature (Newlands' "broad conception"), finite modes are necessary.[65] I am perfectly happy to endorse this last claim, so long as

---

[64] Such a use of '*hoc est*' (i.e., when the second clause specifies and spells out the meaning of the first clause) is common both in Spinoza and in our common discourse. Consider, for example, "there's always one person stuck with cleaning up the mess, *hoc est/namely,* me."

[65] Newlands, *Reconceiving Spinoza*, 92–95.

we make clear that the contingency of finite modes is only epistemic E-Contingency (and not, in-things, TC-Contingency). But Newlands also argues that "both necessitarianism and its denial are consistently true for Spinoza, relative to different ways of conceiving objects in the world,"[66] and here I beg to differ. Newlands is right to my mind in claiming that (i) for Spinoza modes genuinely have an essence not involving existence, and that (ii) we frequently conceive of finite things as detached from the order of causes, and as such regard them as not necessary. However, unlike Newlands, I would argue that when we conceive finite things as detached from the order of nature, and thus consider them as TC-Contingent, our conception is inadequate, erroneous, and non-rational. The place where Spinoza makes this point most clearly is in E2p44 and its corollary:

> E2p44: It is of the nature of Reason to regard things as necessary, not as contingent.
> Dem.: It is of the nature of reason to perceive things *truly* (by E2p41), viz. (by E1a6) as they are in themselves, i.e. (by E1p29), *not as contingent but as necessary*, q.e.d.
> Cor. 1: From this it follows *that it depends only on the imagination that we regard things as contingent,* both in respect to the past and in respect to the future. (Italics added)

The notion of contingency Spinoza employs here is clearly TC-Contingency, not E-Contingency.[67] The first corollary to E2p44

---

66 Newlands, *Reconceiving Spinoza*, 104. For all I can tell, Newlands' narrow conception of a thing (i.e., a thing conceived only through its essence) is compatible not only with the rejection of necessitarianism, but also with *indeterminism*. In this sense, his view is even more radical than Curley's (and accordingly, it faces even more textual challenges). On one occasion (*Reconceiving Spinoza*, 91), Newlands claims that the narrow conception commits Spinoza only to determinism and not to necessitarianism, but as far I can see, the narrow conception does not commit Spinoza even to determinism.

67 For otherwise, E2p44 would have to be interpreted as arguing that when conceived through reason, finite modes have an essence involving existence, which is clearly absurd.

makes clear that when we regard finite things as TC-Contingent, we are conceiving things through the imagination, which Spinoza considered the lowest kind of cognition, and the only cause of falsity and inadequacy (E2p41).[68] Newlands openly acknowledges E2p44 as "the strongest textual threat" to his interpretation, but suggests that perhaps some ideas of the imagination are true.[69] Still, the demonstration of E2p44 makes clear that conceiving finite modes as TC-Contingent is to conceive of them "not truly." All this being said, I think Newlands is right to point out that in Spinoza's (and Leibniz's) treatment of modality there is more structure than what it is usually expressed in our possible worlds theories.[70]

5. Open Foundational Questions

The recent debate about Spinoza's commitment to necessitarianism has helped elucidate many features of Spinoza's modal philosophy, but it has also drawn attention away from some rather basic questions about Spinoza's understanding of modality. In this section, I would like to briefly present some of these still mostly neglected foundational questions.

(i) *What is Necessity?*—Augustine's famous dictum regarding time—"If no one asks me, I know: if I wish to explain it to one that asketh, I know not"[71]—applies just as well to the notion of possibility and necessity. We use the terminology of modality constantly and abundantly in all forms of discourse. Still, providing a non-circular account of the notions of possibility

---

68 Cf. TdIE §84, where Spinoza also stresses the randomness and the disconnectedness of imaginary ideas.
69 Newlands, *Reconceiving Spinoza*, 110 and note 62.
70 See Newlands' discussion of current "finer-grained [modal] notions" at the end of Section 2.1 of Chapter 5, this volume.
71 Augustine, *Confessions*, trans. E. B. Pusey (Chicago: Henry Regnery, 1948), 194 (§11.14).

and necessity proves to be quite difficult. Spinoza seems to think that a kind of "can" is interdefinable with a corresponding kind of "must" along familiar lines. Still, one may and should wonder whether we can rescue from Spinoza an account explaining modality in terms of more basic notions.[72]

(ii) *Bearers of Modality.*—Recent scholarly literature frequently ascribes to Spinoza definite views about the modal status of *propositions*. Spinoza himself usually applies modal determinations to things, properties, and relations (e.g., "*x* necessarily follows from *y*"), and much less so to propositions.[73] In this sense, we can say that for the most part, Spinoza employs *de re*, rather than *de dicto,* modality.[74] How important is the *de re/de dicto* distinction for Spinoza, and to what extent would he allow for the seamless translation from *de re* to *de dicto* modality (and vice versa) are questions which remain open.

(iii) *Modality and Essence.*—Like many of his contemporaries and predecessors, Spinoza considers modality as closely tied to essences: the modal status of modes is partly determined by their essences, and fully determined by God's essence. Yet, unlike his predecessors and contemporaries, Spinoza seems to understand the essence of a thing to be both necessary *and sufficient* for thing's existence.[75] This apparently introduces a significant change in the concept of essence, and Spinoza

---

72 Newlands is the recent commentator who pays most attention to this issue. According to Newlands, Spinoza understands modality as a "function of conceptual relations" (*Reconceiving Spinoza*, 101).
73 The one group of propositions which Spinoza does characterize in modal terms is the eternal truths. See his definition of eternal truth in TdIE §54, note u.
74 On the distinction between *de re* and *de dicto* modality, see Chapter 2, Section 1, this volume.
75 E2d2: "I say that to the essence of any thing belongs that which, being given, the thing is necessarily posited and which, being taken away, the thing is necessarily taken away; or that without which the thing can neither be nor be conceived, and which can neither be nor be conceived without the thing."

seems to be fully aware of it.[76] We do not currently have a comprehensive account of the significance of this shift in the concept of essence, and specifically, it is not clear what is the impact of this shift on the relation between essence and modality.

(*iv*) *Statistic Modality.*—It is quite common in current scholarly literature to spell out Spinoza's modal philosophy employing the conceptual machinery of possible worlds in spite of the fact that Spinoza died shortly before Leibniz developed his theory of possible worlds,[77] and three centuries before Kripke developed his semantics of possible worlds. Still, this anachronism is not necessarily problematic, since even before Leibniz we have quite a rich philosophical literature addressing *synchronic* alternatives (which are hardly theorizable in terms of Statistic modalities),[78] and one can see Leibniz as simply providing a more systematic and elegant frame for discussions of unrealized possibilities and counterfactuals that predated him.

This being said, we should note that there is good textual evidence that on some occasions Spinoza employed modal terms in their Statistic sense. Thus, for example, when Spinoza writes: "all things,

---

[76] See Spinoza's criticism of his predecessors who maintained that "anything without which a thing can neither be nor be conceived" pertains to the essence of the thing (E2p11s| II/193/25–9 and II/194/5–13).

[77] On the possible influence of the three-sided discussion among Leibniz, Tschirnhaus, and Spinoza of the plurality of worlds on Leibniz's development of his theory of possible worlds, see Mark A. Kulstad, "Leibniz, Spinoza and Tschirnhaus: Metaphysics *à Trois*: 1675–1676," in *Spinoza: Metaphysical Themes*, ed. Olli Koistinen and John Biro (Oxford: Oxford University Press, 2003), 182–209, and Yitzhak Y. Melamed, "Spinoza, Tschirnhaus et Leibniz: Qu'est un monde?," in *Spinoza/Leibniz: Rencontres, controverses, réceptions*, ed. Pierre-François Moreau, Raphaële Andrault, and Mogens Laerke (Paris: Presses universitaires de Paris, 2014), 85–95.

[78] See, for example, Simo Knuutila's discussion of Augustine in Chapter 2, Section 4, this volume, and Kukkonen's discussion of Al-Ghazali in Taneli Kukkonen, "Possible Worlds in the *Tahâfut al-falâsifa*: Al-Ghazâli on Creation and Contingency," *Journal of the History of Philosophy* 38 (2000): 479–502).

have *necessarily* flowed, or *always* follow [*omnia necessario effluxisse, vel semper... sequi*]" (E1p17s| II/62/17. italics added), he seems to take 'necessarily' and 'always' as equivalent. Similarly, in E1p21d, Spinoza seems to move seamlessly from the claim that "Thought exists necessarily" (II/66/6) to the claim that "Thought exists in all times" (II/66/8).[79] We have also seen that in E2p11d Spinoza construes (the second half of) E2a1 in terms of Statistic modality.[80] On the other hand, there are passages where Spinoza is using modal terms in a non-temporalized manner (see, for example, E1d8 and E1p11d|II/53/8–10). This raises at least two non-trivial questions. First, we may wonder to what extent Spinoza was aware of the distinction between the Statistic and non-Statistic understandings of modality. Second, we may ask: how would Spinoza consider the relation, if there is any, between Statistic and non-Statistic modalities?

6. Conclusion

In this chapter we have studied Spinoza's and Crescas' modal philosophy. Arguably, both maintained strict necessitarianism, yet both allowed for a sense of contingency in finite things, if by contingency we mean nothing over and above the fact that we conceive the essence of (non-chimeric) finite things as not necessitating either their existence or their non-existence.

Apart from providing a survey of the main elements of Spinoza's modal philosophy, I have argued for two substantial and innovative theses. First, I have argued that there are two distinct notions of contingency at work in Spinoza, and that once we observe the distinction

---

79 Two other texts where Spinoza is switching between claiming that x is necessary and that x always exists are E4p62d (II/257/9–12) and Ep. 35 (IV/181/21).

80 Namely, he understands the claim that the order of nature *can* cause both the existence and the non-existence of a specific human being as the assertion that *sometimes* the order of nature causes the existence of the person, while at *other times* it causes the non-existence of that person (or, in other words, that the order of nature does not necessitate the existence of that person *in all times*).

between these two notions, Spinoza's various pronouncements about contingency, frequently taken to be confused and inconsistent, turn out to be consistent and mostly clear. It should, however, be noted that Spinoza himself is partly responsible for their confusion, for he himself uses the two senses of the term without always sufficiently distinguishing between them. Second, I have argued that in E2a1, widely seen as the strongest textual evidence against the ascription of necessitarianism to Spinoza, Spinoza employs Statistic modality, and that once this axiom is read in this sense, it completely coheres with Spinoza's numerous necessitarian statements. Notably, my interpretation of E2a1, unlike earlier ones, is dictated by Spinoza's own use of this axiom in E2p11d. Thus, I believe, we have finally found a solution to one, stubborn and significant, Spinozistic riddle (i.e., the meaning of E2a1), but, as it commonly happens, the solution of one problem also exposes the terrain of a new uncharted land: how should we reconstruct Spinoza's modal philosophy in light of the realization that he also employed Statistic modalities?

Abbreviations

Spinoza's Works

CM   *Cogitata Metaphysica* (*Metaphysical Thoughts*). An appendix to Spinoza's 1663 *Renati des Cartes Principiorum Philosophiae Pars I and II* (*Descartes's Principles of Philosophy*). Published in 1663.

E   *Ethica* (*Ethics*). Passages in the *Ethics* are referred to by means of the following abbreviations: a(-xiom), c(-orollary), p(-roposition), s(-cholium), and app(-endix); 'd' stands for either 'definition' (when it appears immediately to the right of the part of the book), or 'demonstration' (in all other cases). Hence, E1d3 is the third definition of part 1 and E1p16d is the demonstration of proposition 16 of part 1.

EP   Spinoza's Letters

TDIE *Tractatus de Intellectus Emendatione* (*Treatise on the Emendation of the Intellect*)
TTP *Tractatus Theologico-Politicus* (*Theological Political Treatise*). Published anonymously in 1670.

References to Gebhardt, *Spinoza Opera*, follow this format: volume number/page number/line number. Hence "II/200/12" stands for volume 2, page 200, line 12.

CHAPTER 5

Leibniz on Modality

Samuel Newlands

Gottfried Leibniz is often depicted as the progenitor of contemporary modal metaphysics, the philosopher who formalized our modal vocabulary and introduced possible worlds to eager metaphysicians. Certainly Leibniz's work on modality has had an outsized influence on contemporary work in analytic philosophy, and rightly so: among pre-20th-century philosophers, Leibniz's modal metaphysics displays exceptionally high levels of care, ingenuity, sophistication, and range.

Nevertheless, Leibniz's own interest in modal concepts stems from broader metaphysical and theological concerns. His career-spanning work on modality was largely devoted to disarming what he took to be a looming threat, one that he came to associate with Spinoza. Admittedly, intellectual pressures can sometimes yield creative insights that transcend their original context, and that is clearly true in Leibniz's case. But given the historical and developmental focus of this volume, I will focus on Leibniz's own path into the modal thicket.

Leibniz contributed to three distinct projects involving modality, all of which were lively points of debate in the 17th century. The first concerns the *distribution* of necessity and contingency. What exists, happens, or is true necessarily? What exists, happens, or is true contingently? The second project concerns the *analysis* of modality. What is the nature and true account of necessity and contingency? We might expect an analysis of modality to provide answers to the distribution question, but for Leibniz, the order of discovery usually went in the other direction. He antecedently wanted to avoid certain distribution answers, and he developed various analyses of modality in order to secure the desired distribution. I will present several of his most prominent efforts, some of which seem more promising than others.

Leibniz was also interested in the *grounds* of modality. Like many early moderns, Leibniz thought that God was the ultimate ground of both modal truths and modal truthmakers. But there was fierce disagreement about exactly how God serves as the ultimate ground of modality. Leibniz defends an intellectualist account of the divine grounds of possibility and he offers pointed criticisms of the main alternatives. After exploring Leibniz's grounding account in Section 3, I will conclude by sketching how Leibniz's different modal projects could work in tandem.

1. Modal Distribution

When Leibniz was twenty-five years old, he offered a simple and stark account of the distribution of modality in a letter to his friend Magnus Wedderkopf.

> However, since God is the most perfect mind, it is impossible that he is not affected by the most perfect harmony and thus must bring

about the best by the very ideality of things ... from this it follows that whatever has happened, is happening, or will happen is the best and, accordingly, is necessary. (CP 3–5)

According to this account, all actual events happen necessarily and no non-actual events could have happened. This is an event-based version of *necessitarianism*, according to which the events that actually happen are the only events that could happen.[1]

Leibniz reaches this conclusion by reasoning in the following way about the existence and nature of a perfect God, which I will call the **Necessitarian Argument (NA)**:

1. God exists necessarily.
2. Necessarily, it follows from God's existence that the best possible world exists.
3. Whatever follows from something necessary is itself necessary.
4. The best possible world exists necessarily [from 1–3].
5. The actual world is the best possible world [4 and nature of actuality].
6. The actual world exists necessarily [4–5].
7. Whatever actually happens follows from God's bringing about the actual world.[2]
8. Therefore, all actual events happen necessarily [3, 6–7].

Leibniz came to associate his youthful distribution answer with Spinoza's necessitarianism, and he spent considerable energy over the

---

1 In different passages, Leibniz discusses the modal status of events, propositions, properties, facts, states of affairs, individuals, substances, worlds, and existence. For ease, I will mostly follow Leibniz's presentations in a given context and move fluidly among these different foci, as Leibniz was not as concerned about the *bearers* of modality as were some of the other philosophers discussed in this volume.

2 This premise follows from bedrock Leibnizian commitments in metaphysics; for one version, see PE 44–46.

next forty-five years trying to avoid necessitarianism without abandoning the metaphysical and theological commitments that pushed him toward it. In particular, Leibniz never wavered in accepting the theism of [1], the bestness of the actual world in [5], and the metaphysics of events, individuals, and worlds that yields [7].

Fifteen years later, Leibniz describes his reconsideration of [8]:

> When I considered that nothing happens by chance... and that no thing exists unless its own particular conditions are present (conditions from whose joint presence it follows, in turn, that the thing exists), I was very close to the view of those who think that everything is absolutely necessary.... But the consideration of the possibles, which are not, were not, and will not be, brought me back from this precipice. (PE 94)[3]

Leibniz claims that he drew back from the precipice of necessitarianism by thinking more about possibility. That is, by investigating the *nature* of modality, Leibniz thinks he discovered how to avoid the *distribution* answer of necessitarianism.

Over the course of his career, Leibniz produced several different analyses of modality that target different premises in the Necessitarian Argument. His earliest theory from the 1670s, his **per se analysis**, challenges [3]. While working on infinity and logic in the 1680s, Leibniz developed his **infinite analysis** account, which tries to block the inference to [6] from [4] and [5]. His **moral necessity** account, which features prominently in late correspondence and his *Theodicy*, targets [2]. Let us explore each of these accounts in turn.

---

3 In this passage, Leibniz also firmly distinguishes *modal* notions from *temporal* notions. Though not original to Leibniz, his rejection of temporal models of modality proved decisive for subsequent modal metaphysics.

2. Modal Analyses
2.1. Per se account

A year after writing his letter to Wedderkopf, Leibniz drafted a lengthy dialogue between a theologian and a philosopher in which the theologian presses a version of the Necessitarian Argument against the philosopher.

> *Th*: What is your response going to be to the argument proposed previously: the existence of God is necessary; the sins included in the series of things follow from this; whatever follows from something necessary is itself necessary. Therefore sins are necessary.

The philosopher replies with what looks like a flat-footed rejection of premise [3] of the Necessitarian Argument.

> *Ph*: I reply that it is false that whatever follows from something necessary is itself necessary... why [can't] something contingent [follow from] something necessary? (CP 55)

This reply looks flat-footed because if one understands "following from" to be equivalent to logical entailment, then the contemporary reader has a ready retort on behalf of the theologian: [3] is true because the distribution axiom $[\Box(p \to q) \to (\Box p \to \Box q)]$ encoded in [3] has robust intuitive support and is true on even our weakest contemporary modal logics. (In contemporary formulations, the box symbol should be read as "necessarily.") And as other chapters in this volume make clear, something like this distribution axiom was accepted by many prominent philosophers throughout history as well.

Leibniz himself became dissatisfied with outright denying [3], and he provided a more sophisticated reply when he revised the dialogue a few years later (the material in < > are the additions):

Ph: I reply that it is false that whatever follows from something necessary <per se> is itself necessary <per se> ... why [can't] something contingent <or necessary ex alterius hypothesi> [follow from] something necessary <per se>? ... <For in this place we call *necessary* only what is necessary per se, namely, that which has the reason for its existence and truth in itself. The truths of geometry are of this sort. But among existing things, only God is of this sort; all the rest, which follow from the series of things presupposed—i.e., from the harmony of things or the existence of God—are *contingent* per se and only hypothetically necessary>.

Leibniz now challenges [3] by first distinguishing between being necessary per se and being necessary ex hypothesi.[4] This implies that [3] and [4] are open to at least two different readings:

3a. Whatever follows from something necessary per se is itself necessary per se.

4a. Therefore, the best possible world exists necessarily per se.

3b. Whatever follows from something necessary per se is itself necessary ex hypothesi.

4b. Therefore, the best possible world exists necessarily ex hypothesi.

Leibniz concedes that [4a] is indeed worrisome and capable of delivering the problematic necessitarian conclusion of [8a]:

8a. All actual events happen necessarily per se.

But, Leibniz argues, [3a] is false, and so the argument to [4a] is unsound.

---

4 As other contributors to this volume have shown, this distinction is hardly original to Leibniz.

At the same time, Leibniz accepts [3b] as a true disambiguation of the original [3], which allows him to endorse a modal distribution axiom in the spirit of the contemporary version mentioned above. But Leibniz thinks [4b] is modally harmless because it leads only to [8b]:

> 8b. All actual events happen necessarily ex hypothesi.

Presumably, [8b] is modally harmless because its truth is consistent with some actual events happening contingently and some non-actual events remaining possible.

This is where Leibniz's underlying per se analysis of modality does real work, as the following quasi-dialogue shows:

> Indeed, even if God does not will something to exist, it is possible for it to exist, since, by its nature [*sua natura*], it could exist if God were to will it to exist. [An imagined objection:] But God cannot will it to exist. [Leibniz replies:] I concede this, yet, such a thing remains possible in its own nature [i.e., per se] even if it is not possible with respect to the divine will, since we have defined 'possible in its nature' as that which, in itself, implies no contradiction, even though its coexistence with God can in some way be said to imply a contradiction. (PE 21)

Leibniz usually analyzes modal terms like necessity and contingency partly in terms of formal consistency, as he does in this passage. Necessary propositions are true propositions whose negation entails a contradiction, and contingent propositions are true propositions whose negation does not entail a contradiction.

However, Leibniz points out that the negation of a necessary truth can be inconsistent with two different groups of propositions. It could be inconsistent with a proposition about the subject matter of the original proposition. Consider, for example, a necessary truth from geometry, such as *triangles have three interior angles*. The negation of that proposition is inconsistent with propositions concerning lines, figures, and angles. Compare that with a different truth, such as *Caesar crosses the Rubicon*. What is the falsity of that proposition inconsistent with? Leibniz claims that it is not inconsistent with truths about Roman dictators or rivers. He concedes in this passage that it is inconsistent with the necessary truth that God wills the best possible world to exist, but that is a proposition primarily about God rather than about Caesar or the Rubicon per se.

Leibniz uses this intuitive distinction to develop corresponding accounts of a world's possibility and necessity. His basic idea is that a world is *possible in itself* just in case its per se properties—those properties having to do only with it—are consistent. However, a world can be possible in itself even if its non–per se properties, such as *being suboptimal* or *being chosen by God*, are inconsistent with a necessary truth about something else. Using Leibniz's language from this passage, a non-actual world "remains possible in itself" even if its actual existence can "in some way be said to imply a contradiction," namely in relation to God's willing the best possible world to exist. Put differently, a world can be possible *in itself* even if is not possible *all things considered*, such as when relations to God's willing are taken into account. This distinction between the modal status something has *in itself* and the modal status it has *all things considered* is the core distinction in Leibniz's per se analysis of modality. (As we will see in Section 3, this distinction is deeply rooted in Leibniz's view that a world's possibility is grounded in God's *intellect* and is prior to and unaffected by God's volitions.)

This distinction preserves contingency only if being contingent is consistent with being necessary all things considered, and this is just what Leibniz claims. "Everything that is contingent is necessary in some way. That which is actual is necessary in some way" (GR 536), namely everything actual is necessary all things considered or, as

Leibniz sometimes puts it, on the hypothesis [*ex hypothesi*] that God wills the best possible world to exist.

One important question for this account concerns the extension of per se properties. Which properties of a thing are per se and which are not? Leibniz often refers to *natures* in this context, which is his way of distinguishing between something like the intrinsic properties of a thing and the properties it has in relation to extrinsic things, such as God's will. But Leibniz's own metaphysics of individuals and worlds makes it hard to draw a sharp, neutral distinction between intrinsic and non-intrinsic properties.[5]

If we focus on Leibniz's efforts to avoid the necessitarianism of [8a] in terms of possible worlds, there are two general classes of properties that might be excluded from a world's per se properties. We could exclude various relations to God, such as *being caused to exist by a perfect being*. Alternatively, we could exclude comparative relations to other possible worlds, such as *being the best of all possible worlds*. Leibniz explores both options, but his overall strategy is the same: exclude from the per se properties of a possible world those that, together with facts like [1], [2], and [5], would entail its existence or its non-existence. Insofar as the main goal is to avoid the necessitarian *distribution* answer, we could even functionally define the per se properties of a possible world as just those properties that are jointly consistent both with its existence and with its non-existence. Leibniz concludes that since all possible worlds have per se properties, the existence or non-existence of every possible world is contingent.

Although rich, this account of modality has not been well-received by Leibniz's interpreters. One major worry is that, at the end of the day, it fails to preserve genuine contingency. As Robert Sleigh puts it, "Leibniz's modal distinctions simply lack relevance [to the problem of

---

5 R. C. Sleigh, *Leibniz and Arnauld* (New Haven, CT: Yale University Press, 1990), 48–80.

necessitarianism]" (CP xxvi). Leibniz's distinction between per se and non–per se properties seems irrelevant because it appears to preserve only a stipulated sense of contingency, whereas the real threat of necessitarianism is realized even if only [8b] is true. The worry is that even if the world's existence does not follow from its per se properties and is only all things considered necessary, that modal status is enough to undermine its genuine contingency.

Leibniz might reply that he is not introducing new, wholly stipulated forms of contingency and necessity. As other contributions to this volume have shown, the distinction between per se and ex hypothesi modalities has a long conceptual history, and Leibniz could argue that our pre-theoretical intuitions about "genuine contingency" are too confused or coarse-grained to be reliable guides (CP 51, 59; T 367).

Alternatively, Leibniz could be using this historically familiar distinction to make a subtler claim about the nature of modality. Let us set aside the thorny question about exactly which properties get classified as per se and non–per se. What makes the difference between these two classes? After all, in the case of individuals, both per se and non–per se properties are genuine properties of the individual substance. Leibniz sometimes claims that a thing's per se properties are only *conceptually* distinguished from the rest of its properties:

> And thus everything that will happen to Peter and Judas, both necessary and free, is contained in the perfect individual notion of Peter or Judas, considered from the perspective of possibility [*sub ratione possibilitatis*] by abstracting the mind from the divine decree to create him and is seen there by God. (PE 32)[6]

---

6 Translation slightly modified; see also *L* 204; for further discussion, see Samuel Newlands, "The Harmony of Spinoza and Leibniz," *Philosophy and Phenomenological Research* 81, no. 1 (2010): 64–104.

In this passage, Leibniz points to two different ways of *considering* an individual, ways that track his per se and non–per se distinction. He explains that this difference in conception results from mentally abstracting away some of a thing's genuine properties, namely by excluding from consideration its non–per se properties. Most important, Leibniz implies that genuine modal differences track these conceptual differences. For example, Peter can be conceived both in relation to God's will and also independently of that relation, and that difference in how Peter is conceived tracks or perhaps even generates a genuine modal difference. Considered more narrowly by including only his per se properties, Peter does not exist necessarily. Considered more inclusively by including all his non–per se properties, Peter does exist necessarily. Insofar as Peter's genuine modal status is tied to such conceptual differences, Peter could consistently exist necessarily *and* non-necessarily, relative to these different ways of being conceived.

The general thesis that modal facts are sensitive to conceptual differences is deeply at odds with contemporary, Kripke-inspired accounts of modality. It more closely resembles a family of views sometimes called "anti-essentialist" and associated with modal skeptics like Quine.[7] But we need not impose Quine's full anti-essentialism to appreciate what Leibniz might be advocating. In Leibniz's terms, Kripkean accounts of modality are capable of tracking only all things considered modal facts because they interpret all necessary truths as propositions that are true in *every* possible world. I suspect this interpretation lies behind the contemporary suspicion that [8b] is not modally harmless, since on Kripkean accounts, being all things considered necessary entails being necessary full stop. At the very least, Leibniz's per se analysis requires finer-grained modal distinctions than contemporary possible-worlds semantics typically allow, and this leads to the charge that Leibniz's

---

7 For a starting point, see W. V. Quine, "Reference and Modality," in *From a Logical Point of View*, 2nd ed. (New York: Harper and Row, 1961), 139–159.

distinctions are irrelevant for blocking the Necessitarian Argument—*on the assumption that the true modal semantics are so coarse-grained.* Happily for Leibnizians, in recent years, metaphysicians have raised a chorus of objections to Kripkean modal orthodoxy, often on grounds that its possible worlds framework is too coarse-grained. They have begun reintroducing finer-grained notions, such as grounding, hyperintentionality, and impossible worlds to more adequately account for this richer structure. For those sympathetic with this contemporary movement in metaphysics, Leibniz's per se account appears ready for a fresh evaluation.

2.2. *Infinite analysis*

During the 1680s, Leibniz developed an alternative analysis of necessity and contingency. He claimed that contingent propositions have an interesting feature: their formal proof structure is infinitely long and cannot be completed in a finite number of steps. He argued that there is a deep connection between the modal status of a proposition and its formal proof structure, one that undermines an important step in the Necessitarian Argument. This account of contingency and necessity has come to be known as Leibniz's "infinite analysis" account.

Here is a representative passage in which Leibniz posits the connection between contingency and proof structure:

> Every true universal affirmative proposition, either necessary or contingent, has some connection between subject and predicate. In identities this connection is self-evident; in other propositions it must appear through the analysis of terms. And with this secret, the distinction between necessary and contingent truths is revealed, something not easily understood unless one has some acquaintance with mathematics. For in necessary propositions, when the analysis is continued indefinitely, it arrives at an equation that is an identity; this is what it is to demonstrate a truth with geometrical rigor.

> But in contingent propositions, one continues the analysis to infinity through reasons for reasons, so that one never has a complete demonstration, though there is always, underneath, a reason for the truth, but the reason is understood completely only by God, who alone traverses the infinite series in one stroke of mind. (PE 28)

Leibniz first gestures at his conceptual containment theory of truth. According to this theory, at least for every true proposition of the form *S is F*, the concept of the predicate is contained in the concept of the subject. Leibniz believed that this containment can be demonstrated via a priori "analysis," a formal procedure in which subject and predicate terms are stepwise replaced using definitions and axioms until a formal identity statement, like *A is A*, is reached.

Leibniz then claims that the demonstrations of necessary truths via such analyses is importantly different from the demonstrations of contingent truths. The demonstrations of necessary truths can be completed in a finite number of steps, whereas the demonstrations of contingent propositions cannot. This can be expressed with the following biconditionals:

> A proposition is necessary iff its a priori demonstration can be completed in a finite number of steps.
> A proposition is contingent iff its a priori demonstration cannot be completed in a finite number of steps.

Leibniz then applies these biconditionals to what I called the Necessitarian Argument in Section 1. He claims that the demonstration of [5] cannot be completed in a finite number of steps, in which case [5] is only contingently true and the argument for [6] is invalid. "So, although one can concede that it is necessary for God to choose the best, or that the best is necessary, it does not follow that what is chosen is necessary, since there is no demonstration [completable in finite steps] that it is the best" (PE 30).

According to Leibniz, the demonstration of [5] is not finitely completable because any demonstration of the actual world's bestness involves comparisons with infinitely many possible worlds. Leibniz sometimes makes this point in epistemic terms. For example, he writes, "Since we cannot know the true formal [i.e., demonstrable] reason for existence in any particular case because it involves a progression to infinity . . ." (PE 29). Similarly, he claims, "one may imagine possible worlds without sin . . . but these same worlds again would be very inferior to ours in goodness. I cannot show you this in detail. For can I know and can I present infinities to you and compare them together?" (T 10). But as we will see, Leibniz's appeals to what we can *know* about such demonstrations, as opposed to facts about the demonstrations themselves, are more distracting than helpful.

Undoubtedly, this is an elegant analysis of modality that draws on many other facets of Leibniz's formal work. But considering it as an independent account of modality, most interpreters have judged Leibniz's infinite analysis account to be an egregious philosophical failure that is subject to numerous counter-examples, something of a modal catastrophe. Summarizing the dismal received view, Jeff McDonough and Zeynep Soysal quip that Leibniz's infinite analysis account "may well seem to lack even the minimal virtue of intelligibility."[8]

One general worry about Leibniz's infinite analysis account is that it again appears to change the subject. Leibniz's frequent appeals to our ignorance about infinities in this context make it sound like he is offering only an *epistemic* account of modality, which does not seem to be relevant to the metaphysical modalities in the Necessitarian Argument. If [5] is necessarily true for an omniscient being like God, that seems bad enough. Notice, however, that the underlying biconditionals are not epistemic or perspectival in any way, and so our own

---

8 Jeffrey K. McDonough and Zeynep Soysal, "Leibniz's Formal Theory of Contingency," *Logical Analysis and History of Philosophy* 21 (2018): 17–43. They also provide a succinct overview of the counter-example (and counter-counter-example) literature.

inability to make infinite comparisons is a red herring. The differences in proof structures, not in our grasp of them, are what Leibniz most wants to associate with necessity and contingency.

Still, it is not clear why we should associate modal concepts with the formal proof structure of propositions in the first place. On McDonough and Soysal's recent account, Leibniz was independently interested in issues of what we would now call formal decidability and computability, and he thought he had discovered a way of marking a modal distinction that tracked his metalogical views concerning formal languages and demonstrations.

But insofar as Leibniz's infinite analysis account is *also* supposed to undercut the Necessitarian Argument (as he certainly thought it did), this additional contextualizing does not blunt the charge of changing the subject. Consider Leibniz's claim in the long passage quoted above that even apart from formal proof structure, there is always a reason for the truth of a contingent proposition, one that God alone grasps. Thus, [5] is true for a reason, and it is hard to see what that reason could be other than a fact about the overall bestness of our world. But that reason, whatever it may be, is not contingent in the robustly intuitive sense that it could have been different. If so, then even if there is not a finitely completable demonstration of [5], [6] still follows from the conjunction of [4], the non-contingent *reason* for the truth of [5], and another application of [3]. Unless Leibniz can show that this other, far more familiar sense of "contingency" is misleading or false (as opposed to showing only that he can construct an alternative formal concept of contingency), then his infinite analysis account fails to avoid the conclusion of the Necessitarian Argument, after all.

2.3. *Metaphysical and moral necessity*

Leibniz's first two analyses of modality focus on finite substances and worlds, either their properties or the proof structures of propositions about them. Leibniz's third analysis focuses more directly on God. Leibniz argues that there is an important distinction among the *sources* of God's actions, one that tracks a modal distinction that undermines the Necessitarian Argument.

Leibniz does not always draw the salient distinction in God in the same way. Sometimes he points to a distinction among God's *attributes*, such as between divine power and divine wisdom. Other times, he distinguishes between kinds of divine *causation*, such as between an efficient and a final cause. Yet other times, he distinguishes among kinds of divine *reasons* for acting, such as between goodness-based reasons and "blind," non-axiological reasons. Although distinct, these carvings all line up neatly, according to Leibniz. On the one hand, there is acting by divine *wisdom* through *final* causation for the sake of *goodness*; on the other, there is acting by absolute divine *power* through *efficient* causation on the basis of *non-axiological* reasons.

Leibniz claims that this distinction among divine actions generates a modal distinction in what follows from God:

> [Notice] how much difference there is between ... *an absolute necessity*, metaphysical or geometrical, which may be called blind and which does not depend upon any but efficient causes [and] *a moral necessity*, which comes from the free choice of wisdom in relation to final causes. (T 349)

Leibniz singles out Spinoza as someone who accounts for God's actions exclusively in terms of non-axiological reasons and absolute power (T 173–174). But Leibniz complains that other early moderns also overlook the distinction between moral and metaphysical necessity. Samuel Clarke "confounds moral necessity, which proceeds from the choice of what is best, with absolute necessity; he confounds the will of God with his power" (L 709). Likewise, Pierre Bayle "confuses what is necessary by moral necessity, that is, according to the principle of Wisdom and Goodness, with what is necessary by metaphysical and brute necessity, which occurs when the contrary implies a contradiction" (T 174).

One way to unpack this distinction is to focus on God's bringing about the actual world. Leibniz claims that God's creative power extends quite widely: God can do anything that is metaphysically possible, which he describes in this last passage in terms of formal consistency. With respect to God's absolute, non-moral power, it is possible for God to bring about sub-optimal worlds. Hence, Leibniz concludes, it is not *metaphysically necessary* for God to bring about the best possible world.

However, in deciding which world to create, God takes into account additional, value-based reasons that are based on God's own goodness and wisdom. In particular, God is a perfectly wise agent, and Leibniz thinks that perfectly wise agents choose the best possible option (T 8). Based on divine goodness and wisdom, God decides to bring about the best possible world. Hence, Leibniz concedes, the existence of the best possible world is *morally necessary*, a modal status it has in virtue of the fact that its existence depends on God's value-based character and wise decision-making. Correspondingly, it is *morally impossible* for God to bring about a sub-optimal world, even though it is metaphysically possible for God to do so. Therefore, the existence of the actual world is morally but not metaphysically necessary.

Most important, Leibniz argues that existing with moral necessity is compatible with existing contingently. "But this [moral] necessity is not opposed to [metaphysical] contingency; it is not of the kind called logical, geometrical or metaphysical, whose opposite implies contradiction" (T 282). In fact, Leibniz claims that morally necessary actions involve a "happy necessity," and that it is a perfect-making feature of rational agents to act with moral necessity. "It is only a moral necessity, and it is always a happy necessity to be bound to act in accordance with the rules of perfect wisdom" (T 345).

This distinction allows Leibniz to disambiguate premise [2] of the Necessitarian Argument:

2a. It follows from God's existence with metaphysical necessity that the best possible world exists.
2b. It follows from God's existence with moral necessity that the best possible world exists.

Assuming that the modal distribution principle in [3] also tracks the metaphysical/moral distinction, [2a] leads to the worrisome [8c]:

8c. All actual events are metaphysically necessary.

But, according to Leibniz, [2a] is false for reasons we have just seen. God's creation of the best is only morally necessary. Thus [2b] is true, but Leibniz claims that it leads only to the modally innocuous [8d]:

8d. All actual events are morally necessary.

That conclusion is modally innocuous because moral necessity is compatible with metaphysical contingency. We saw Leibniz even claim that it is a good-making feature of all actual events that they follow from God's acting with perfect wisdom in choosing the best.

Leibniz explicitly appeals to moral necessity only in his later writings, and he sometimes suggests that these appeals are more ecumenical than genuine and that moral necessity is not really a genuine species of necessity at all:

> But necessity of this kind [i.e., moral necessity], which does not destroy the possibility of the contrary, has the name [of necessity] by analogy only: it becomes effective not through the mere essence of things, but through that which is outside them and above them, that is, through the will of God. This necessity is called moral, because for the wise what is necessary and what is owing are equivalent things; and when it is always followed by its effect, as it indeed is in

the perfectly wise, that is, in God, one can say that it is a happy necessity. (T Obj 8)

Leibniz distinguishes here between the modal status things have in virtue of their essence alone and the modal status they have in virtue of their relation to something "outside and above" them (namely, God's will), a distinction that harkens back to his earlier per se modal analysis. Hence, Leibniz might not have intended to offer a new modal distinction at all and might instead just be co-opting the terminology of "moral necessity" for his own theory. If so, then being morally necessary is just what I described in Section 2.1 as being "all things considered necessary," simply with the added emphasis that "all things" includes relations to God's wisdom and goodness.

Regardless of Leibniz's intent, does this moral necessity account successfully block the Necessitarian Argument? Not obviously, at least from the contemporary vantage point. As with his functionally similar per se modal analysis, Leibniz's moral necessity analysis requires a more fine-grained distinction in modal properties than current modal orthodoxy recognizes. Unless modal distribution principles like [3] are sensitive to differences in the *source* of a thing's modal status, pointing out a source distinction in God's attributes or reasons will be irrelevant for its modal status. One could respond that Leibniz *was* introducing (or co-opting) a distinctive kind of modal concept here. But as we have seen repeatedly, that reply just invites the charge of irrelevance: the original contingency threatened by the Necessitarian Argument is not the kind of contingency that Leibniz's moral necessity analysis preserves.

Leibniz's moral necessity account faces an internal worry as well. Leibniz claims that it is morally necessary for God to choose the best. "It is a moral necessity that the wisest should be bound to choose the best" (T 230). However, God's character is not a metaphysically contingent feature of God, in which case it seems to be metaphysically necessary that God acts with moral necessity. To claim that it is only morally necessary for God to act most wisely would be to claim that God acts most wisely because it is most wise to act the most wisely. But since we are asking *why* God acts wisely in the first place, appealing to more moral necessity will not provide an informative answer. Presumably, God acts wisely because it is essential to God's perfect nature to act wisely (CP 21).

Similarly, it seems to be metaphysically necessary that *if* God acts in the wisest way, God brings about the best possible world. It would again be uninformative to say that this connection is only morally necessary and that it is only according to God's wisdom that if God acts wisely, God brings about the best. Moral necessity applies to the *reason* for God's action, not to the connection between God's reason and whatever satisfies that reason. Hence, it will be *metaphysically* necessary that a perfectly wise agent brings about the best possible outcome.

Therefore, it is not metaphysically contingent that God acts most wisely, nor is it metaphysically contingent that *if* God acts most wisely, then God brings about the best possible world. But if (a) it is metaphysically necessary that God acts most wisely and (b) it is metaphysically necessary that bringing about the best possible world follows from God acting most wisely, then applying [3] here would again generate the worrisome necessitarian conclusion of [8c]. And this follows even if the existence of the best follows only from God's wise and value-laden reasons and actions. A little metaphysical necessity, even just within the divine nature, goes a long way.

3. Theistic Ground of Modality

Many early modern metaphysicians operated with a guiding rule when it comes to God: make as much as dependent on God as possible, without compromising God's nature. As Leibniz expresses this idea, "My opinion is that it must be taken as certain that there is as much dependence of things on God as is possible without infringing divine justice" (MP 102). This applies to modality as well, and 17th-century philosophers developed competing accounts of how modality depends on God.

They were primarily interested in two sorts of questions. First, on what *in* God do modal truths and modal truth-makers depend? For example, Descartes thought that modal truths depend primarily on God's will in such a way that necessary truths are necessary *because* God wills them to be necessary. Second, what is the nature of the dependence *by which* modal truths and modal truth-makers depend on God? Descartes claimed that God *causes* modal truths to be true through efficient causation.[9] Although these questions are distinct, the answers often worked in tandem. For Descartes, God's volitions are the grounds of modal facts, and God executes his volitions through efficient causation.

Descartes' answers were not the only option. Indeed, his was the least popular view on offer, though it remains the most discussed today. A nearby variant of Descartes' volitional account, one that has roots in earlier philosophers like Aquinas, appeals to divine *powers* as the grounds of modal truths and modal truth-makers. God's power or capacity to bring about a state of affairs makes that state of affairs possible. Others, including Spinoza and the early Kant, claimed instead that God's actual attributes are the grounds of modal truths and modal truth-makers. On this account, it is possible for something besides God to think because God actually thinks.

Leibniz rejected all of these options. He objects that the volitional and powers accounts are explanatorily backward. God wills and can do various things *because* it is possible to do them, not the other way around (PE 36). Indeed, it is hard to grasp what a pre-modal power or volition would even be, as possibility seems to be built into the very concept of power or willing.

---

[9] For discussion of Descartes' views, see Dan Kaufman, "Descartes's Creation Doctrine and Modality," *Australasian Journal of Philosophy* 80 (2002): 24–41.

Leibniz did sometimes offer grounding answers similar to Spinoza's, but making God's actual features the ground of *all* possibilities requires either a stark restriction on the range of possibilities or else a worrisome expansion of God's nature. Take the standard early modern example of being spatially extended. If God's actual perfections are the ground of the possibility of something being spatially extended, then either being spatially extended is reducible to some other divine feature (as in, e.g., reductive idealism) or else God too is actually extended.[10]

Spinoza's grounding account also threatens to collapse a distinction that was very important for Leibniz's non-necessitarian distribution answer. Leibniz claims that God is not metaphysically necessitated to create this world because "all the possibles cannot be produced together," and this is true because "all the possibles are not compatible together" (T 201). But if God's actual perfections are all mutually compatible—as surely they must be if God actually exists—and if all possibilities are built up from combinations of this mutually compatible base, where could combinatorial incompatibilities and the resulting non-actual possibilities come from?[11]

Leibniz provides an alternative account of the theistic grounds of modality that avoids these concerns. He claims that God's intellect is the ground of modal truths and modal truth-makers, and this grounding involves non-causal, ontological dependence. Very roughly, a state of affairs is possible because God *thinks* it, as opposed to because God *wills* it, or *can make* it, or actually *has* the relevant features.[12] On Leibniz's intellectualist account, the content of God's ideas, plus

---

10 For more on this dilemma, see Samuel Newlands, "Backing into Spinozism," *Philosophy and Phenomenological Research* 93, no. 3 (2016): 511–537.

11 There is a vast literature on Leibniz's account of the grounds of incompossibility; for a recent summary, see Gregory Brown and Yual Chiek, *Leibniz on Compossibility and Possible Worlds* (Cham: Springer, 2016).

12 For more details on Leibniz's account and the aforementioned alternatives, see Samuel Newlands, "Leibniz and the Ground of Possibility," *Philosophical Review* 122, no. 2 (2013): 155–187.

God's active thinking of those ideas, are the grounds of possibility and necessity:

> It is true that God is not only the source of existences, but also that of essences insofar as they are real, that is, of the source of that which is real in possibility. This is because God's understanding is the realm of eternal truths or that of the ideas on which they depend. (PE 218)

One advantage of Leibniz's intellectualist account over Descartes' volitional account concerns the problem of evil. On Leibniz's account, God's will ranges over possibilities without establishing them. This allows Leibniz to argue that God could not create a better world than ours because, on the hypothesis that God in fact created the best, there just is no better possible world than ours, even with all of its evils. On Descartes' account, God could have created a better world and yet did not, raising hard questions about God's goodness and praiseworthiness.

An advantage of Leibniz's account over Spinoza's version is that the intellectualist account creates a divide between the content of God's ideas and the rest of God's nature. God can think about things that are radically unlike God's own nature. This representational firewall prevents the content of God's ideas from slipping into God's actual, non-representational nature. Most saliently, God can represent possibilities like extension, pain, and moral failure without those features being traceable to God's own nature. On this account, God's creative mind generates truly novel ideas, and God need not think only about God's own nature to ground and generate possibility space.

The cost of this Leibnizian firewall is that it is unclear where all this additional mental content comes from. If God doesn't decide to create it—since God's volitions are downstream from the establishment of possibility—and if the content is not the result of God just thinking about God's own actual nature, what is its source? The only available reply seems to involve a primitively creative intellect. For at least some divine ideas, that's just what God thinks up. To theists with high explanatory demands, accepting primitive divine mental content may be too high a price to pay.[13] But accepting primitive divine intellectual creativity might be worth avoiding the costs of the alternatives. As ever, nothing comes cheaply in metaphysics.

4. Linking the Leibnizian Projects

Leibniz was an especially restless and creative philosopher, constantly developing, retooling, abandoning, and renewing theories. His fertile mind generated an impressive range of modal theories and insights, some of which have decisively shaped subsequent modal theories. As we have seen, however, none of Leibniz's responses to the Necessitarian Argument is beyond challenge. In recent years, some interpreters have even claimed that Leibniz never really intended to reject necessitarianism, after all.[14]

To the extent to which this revised narrative is driven by the sense that Leibniz failed to block the necessitarian distribution answer (and so he must not have wanted to do so in the first place), fresh hope for Leibniz may be on the horizon. As I suggested above, at least some of Leibniz's modal accounts look more promising in light of recent developments in metaphysics that challenge the once dominant possible worlds framework—a framework that, somewhat ironically, Leibniz is often credited with introducing in the first place.

Alternatively, we could try to bolster Leibniz's anti-necessitarian efforts by drawing some of his discrete modal projects into a more coherent package. In particular, we might link Leibniz's rejection of necessitarianism, per se analysis, and intellectualist grounding accounts. As we saw in the previous section, Leibniz argued that possibilities are

---

[13] For some other potential costs, see Samuel Newlands, "Baumgarten's Steps toward Spinozism," *Journal of the History of Philosophy* 60, no. 4 (2022): 609–633.

[14] E.g., see Michael V. Griffin, *Leibniz, God, and Necessity* (Cambridge: Cambridge University Press, 2013).

wholly independent of and prior to all divine volitions. If so, Leibniz wondered, how could God's volition to create a world affect any world's modal status? "For things remain possible, even if God does not choose them. Indeed, even if God does not will something to exist, it is possible for it to exist, since, by its nature, it could exist if God were to will it to exist" (PE 21). This anti-volitional commitment provides the basic impulse for Leibniz's entire per se modal analysis. For if God's volitions do not make a world's existence possible, impossible, or necessary, then how could God's volition to create the best possible world make the actual world's existence necessary and every other possible world's existence impossible? That would imply that divine volitions *can* change a possible world's modal status to necessary or impossible, a capacity of divine volitions that Leibniz steadfastly rejected.

Of course, it is one thing to assert that every possible world's modal status is unaffected by God's willing the best possible world to exist and it is another to show how that is the case. Here we might discern a deeper connection between some of the details of Leibniz's per se analysis and his intellectualist grounding account. The core of Leibiniz's positive grounding thesis is that the nature and structure of possibility is rooted in the intentional structures and contents of the divine intellect. This grounding of modality in intentional entities could in turn explain why modal facts exhibit the more fine-grained conceptual variability that, I suggested in Section 2.1, Leibniz's per se analysis seems to require. That is, his intellectualist grounding account explains why the structure of modal facts mirrors relations among God's ideas, which in turn provides him the concept-sensitive, fine-grained machinery that his per se defense of contingency needs to challenge [3] of the Necessitarian Argument.

This combination still allows Leibniz to deny that God's creation of the world involves a value-neutral act of non-purposive or "blind" causation, but it better explains how and why God's will is informed by God's wisdom and intellect, as his moral necessity analysis claims it must be. By itself, this rich combination still might not wholly vindicate Leibniz's anti-necessitarian project. But at least for those sharing Leibniz's goals, it serves as a fresh reminder why Leibniz's wide-ranging modal thinking is worth our continued attention.

Abbreviations

References to Leibniz's works are cited by page number and abbreviated as follows:

CP   *Confessio Philosophi: Papers concerning the Problem of Evil, 1671–1678*, trans. and ed. Robert C. Sleigh Jr. (New Haven, CT: Yale University Press, 2005).
GR   *Textes inédits*, 2 vols., ed. Gaston Grua (Paris: PUF, 1995).
L   *Philosophical Papers and Letters*, trans. and ed. Leroy E. Loemker (Dordrecht: Kluwer, 1989).
MP   *Philosophical Writings*, trans. Mary Morris and G. H. R. Parkinson (London and Melbourne: Dent, 1973).
PE   *Philosophical Essays*, ed. and trans. Roger Ariew and Daniel Garber (Indianapolis, IN: Hackett, 1989).
T   *Theodicy: Essays on the Goodness of God, the Freedom of Man, and the Origin of Evil*, trans. E. M. Huggard (Chicago: Open Court, 1985).

Reflection

THE INFINITY OF WORLDS IN MODERN KABBALAH

Jonathan Garb

The following teaching is recorded in the name of R. Pinhas Shapiro of Koretz (1726–1791), an associate student of R. Israel Ba'al Shem Tov, the founder of Hasidism:

A resolution to the question found in the *'Etz Hayyim*: "Why God did not create this world earlier." He [R. Pinhas] said to us, that God still creates worlds incessantly, and it is possible that at that time there is a world in which Moses gave the Torah there to Israel, so thus one cannot say why the world was not created earlier, because it was indeed. And later he said to us: "I believe in perfect faith that this is true, so there is no need of [further] resolutions." And on another occasion, he gave several options and resolutions to this, but I do not remember [them].[1]

At least on one occasion, R. Pinhas boldly seeks to render superfluous the suggested solutions to a metaphysical quandary that were offered in the canonical work of modern

---

1 Pinhas Shapiro, *Imrei Pinhas*, 2 vols. ed. E. E. Frankel (Bnei Brak: 2003), 1: 29.

Kabbalah—*[Derekh]'Etz Hayyim*, R. Meir Poppers' editing of the recorded teachings of its central figure, R. Itzhak Luria (1534–1572). R. Pinhas' response, framed as one of the articles of faith (employing the traditional formula "I believe in perfect faith") seems to be that the Hasidic idea of continuous creation requires positing an infinity of worlds, so that the world has always already been created. It is possible to read this text as implying (as one can indeed find in other Hasidic texts) that there is another world somewhere in which Moses gives the Torah. An 18th-century version of Philip Pullman's *His Dark Materials* . . .

Actually, this move is less bold than it seems, as in the *Derekh 'Etz Hayyim* itself we find, shortly after the discussion R. Pinhas addressed, the following statement:

"It is clear and simple that several kinds of worlds were emanated and created and formed and made a thousand thousands and myriad myriads, and all as one are in that place of space [vacated by the primordial withdrawal of the infinite divinity] . . . and each and every world has ten detailed *Sefirot* [potencies], and each and every detailed *Sefira* in each world contains ten details of detailed *Sefirot* . . . without end and number." And shortly after: "Know that in this emanation there are infinite worlds, that shall not be explained here, and we will now begin to explain one detail that contains the entire reality of this space and from which all the worlds extend . . . and this is the aspect of reality of *Adam Qadmon* [the macro-anthropos]."[2]

In other words, the anthropomorphic cosmic entity that includes the entire vastly complex scheme detailed throughout this work is merely "one detail" within the infinity of worlds. The difference between this post-Lurianic, 17th-century text and its later Hasidic

---

2 Meir Poppers, ed., *Derekh 'Etz Hayyim* (Jerusalem: Yerid ha-Sfarim, 2013), pt. 1, fols. 12A, 12B.

parallel is that the former is couched in spatial, cosmological terms and the latter in temporal language, reaching toward historical events, such as the revelation at Sinai. Lest one err in thinking that the profound implications of these passages were overlooked in the subsequent history of Kabbalah, beyond the Hasidic world, one should turn eastward to the most authoritative (yet sadly under-researched) formulation of post-Lurianic Kabbalah, the 18th-century corpus of R. Shalom Shar'abi (1720–1777) of Jerusalem. In one of his *Shemesh* glosses on *Derekh 'Etz Hayyim*, he writes, in temporal terms, that "every day all that was done in the creation of world is performed."[3] In other words, the drama of creation is rendered quotidian. Far from being a one-time event, it is part of an infinite set, as in our opening Hasidic text.

The overall belief system that underpins the profound relativity of creation and of the universe itself is expressed in numerous modern texts that cannot be enumerated here: "Need to know basis." In the language of the major 19th-century Hasidic Kabbalist R. Tzevi Hirsh Eichenstein of Ziditchov (1763–1831): "For every world that you attain in your intellect for purposes of worship, there are a myriad of myriads of worlds that you cannot attain."[4] In other words (or other worlds . . .), the contours of our universe are determined by the human mission, while reality itself is infinite, and thus extends well beyond possible grasp. To conclude: modern Kabbalah breaks out of the enclosed medieval cosmology to a potentially unsettling infinity of universes. This move galvanized the ever-increasing complexity of the kabbalistic system. It also produced a balancing force, that of psychologization, which enabled an acceptance of the epistemological limitations of the human horizon, dictated by the requirements of worship. According to one prominent early 18th-century formulation, that

---

3 Shalom Shar'abi, glosses on Poppers, *Derekh 'Etz Hayyim*, pt. 1, fol. 84B.
4 Tzevi Hirsh Eichenstein, *Sur me-R'a ve Ase Tov* (Bnei Brak: Mosdot Bnei Shloshim, 2011), 61.

of R. Ya'akov Kopel Lipshitz, the anthropomorphic structure (around *Adam Qadmon*) is selected from all of the parallel universes, all known as *Ein-Sof* or infinite, precisely because it fits the contours of human psychology, or "the souls of Israel."[5] The national focus of this phrase indicates a third major characteristic of modern Kabbalah, its move from more universal cosmology to an ethnocentric discourse. In other words, it is precisely the awareness of the vastness of the cosmos, with accompanying cultural anxieties that forces such writers to zoom in on the national collective. Comparatively speaking, such trends parallel the Christocentric focus accompanying the "decentering" effects of the reflection on the infinity of God, as in the writings of Nicholas of Cusa (1401–1464), who has already been compared to Luria.[6]

---

5 Ya'akov Lipshitz, *Sh'arei Gan Eden*, reprint ed. (New York, 1994), 20A.
6 See Karsten Harries, *Infinity and Perspective* (Cambridge, MA: MIT Press, 2011), 185–199.

CHAPTER 6

Hume on Modal Discourse

Thomas Holden

1. Introduction

Humans talk and think in a disciplined way not just about the way the world is, but about the ways it might have been, and the ways it must be. What is such modal talk and thought ultimately about?

In surface appearance our modal language might seem representational, and perhaps to suggest a commitment to a realist metaphysics. There *are* such and such necessities and possibilities, we say. It is a *fact* that there are. And there *would be* such necessities and possibilities whether or not we humans existed. So begins the hunt for an eternal and immutable order of mind-independent modal truth-makers, and for a human faculty that might reveal the mind-independent structures of the modal multiverse.

Hume's science of human nature suggests a different approach. Committed to an imagistic model of mental representation and a concept empiricism that traces all ideas back to impressions, Hume finds the representational content of modal talk and thought systematically elusive. We simply cannot picture modal facts imagistically, nor does the empirical mosaic of impressions present us with materials from which we can frame for ourselves an idea of necessity or possibility. The student of human nature therefore "quit[s] the direct survey" of the metaphysical question regarding the subject matter and supposed truth-makers of modal discourse (T 1.3.6.3). Instead, "beating about . . . the neighbouring fields," he turns his attention to the more tractable question of the genealogy of modal language and thought: the question of what kinds of circumstances actually prompt humans to make modal pronouncements, and of what purpose such talk and thought might serve in our lives (T 1.3.2.13). Eventually Hume arrives at his account of talk about *causal* necessity as a systematic expression of our habit-induced inferential dispositions—as a sign or display of the fact that we can no longer help but expect the one type of event to follow upon the appearance of the other. And similarly, or so I argue, he also arrives at an account of our talk about *absolute* necessity as a systematic expression of our imaginative blocks—as a sign or display of the fact that we find certain propositions inconceivable.

2. Causal Necessity and Absolute Necessity

There is a difference between saying that

> (A1) the shock of the first billiard ball is followed by the motion of the second

and saying that

> (A2) the shock of the first billiard ball is necessarily followed by the motion of the second.

Likewise, there is a difference between saying that

(B1) two times two is four

and saying that

(B2) two times two is necessarily four.

How should we understand this difference?

Hume famously distinguishes the 'causal' necessity at work in A2 from the 'absolute' (or 'metaphysical') necessity at work in B2. He also famously offers us an account of the difference between what is said in the non-modal A1 and the (causally) modal A2.

For Hume, our practice of talking and thinking in terms of causal necessity—of supplementing the kind of assertion we have in A1 with the further pronouncement we have in A2—is a response to the regular patterns of event-types that we encounter in the empirical world. But it is not simply an attempt to represent or describe these empirical regularities. It is also a display of our own habit-induced inferential dispositions—of the fact that, in virtue of our exposure to regular empirical conjunctions of event-types, "we make no longer any scruple of foretelling one [type of event] upon the appearance of the other" (EHU 7.27). Talk and thought about causal necessities expresses these habit-induced anticipatory attitudes, and in this sense, "the necessity or power, which unites causes and effects, lies in the determination of the mind to pass from the one to the other" (T 1.3.14.23). Hume is not plausibly understood as saying that talk about causal necessity *represents* or *describes* our inferential dispositions, for someone talking about the causal powers of billiard balls is not plausibly saying anything about human psychology. But he does hold that such talk systematically *advertises* or *displays* our inferential dispositions—that it puts them on show in such a way that an observer might infer them. In this way Hume presents us with an expressivist account of talk and thought about causal necessity, an account of such talk and thought as displaying (without thereby describing or representing) certain non-representational states of mind—specifically, certain habit-induced inferential and anticipatory dispositions.[1] And in this way he demystifies talk and thought about causal necessity, explaining what A2 adds to A1 in a naturalistic and empiricist-friendly manner, avoiding any commitment to a mind-independent and extra-empirical order of modal properties or facts, or to a human faculty that might trace such invisible and intangible phenomena.[2]

Now consider B1 and B2, our statements about an arithmetical relationship. As with the causal case, the second, modalized statement B2 adds something to the non-modalized B1—but this time, an assertion

---

[1] Hume does also identify "an idea of [causal] necessity," which is copied from "an internal impression" of felt determination accompanying the movement of the mind from the idea of one event-type to an idea of its customary sequel (T 1.3.14.22, 1.3.14.20). But what matters for Hume is the habit-induced movement of thought from one event-type to another, not any feeling that happens to accompany that movement. That is why this feeling does not appear in Hume's two "definitions" of cause, which rather concern merely the observable regularities on the one hand and the mind's habit-induced inferential dispositions on the other (T 1.3.14.35; EHU 7.29). And that is why Hume repeatedly emphasizes the inferential disposition itself (insisting that causal necessity "depends on the inference" from one event to another, "lies in the determination of the mind to pass from the one to the other," and "is the transition arising from the accustom'd union [of event-types]" (T 1.3.6.3, 1.3.14.23; see also EHU 7.27)), rather than any feeling that might accompany such inferences. It may also be why Hume most often equates the impression from which the idea of necessity is copied *not* with a feeling accompanying the inferential disposition (as he apparently does in T 1.3.14.20), but rather the inferential disposition itself—characterizing the "sentiment or impression, from which we form the idea of ... necessary connexion" variously as the "*customary transition of the imagination* of one object to its usual attendant," the "*customary connexion in the thought or imagination* between one object and its usual attendant," and "that *propensity*, which custom produces, to pass from an object to the idea of its usual attendant" (EHU 7.28, 7.30, T 1.3.14.22, emphases added). On this issue, see Peter Millican, "Against the 'New Hume,'" in, ed., *The New Hume Debate*, 2nd ed., ed. Rupert Read and Kenneth A. Richman (London: Routledge, 2007), 224, 249 note 26.

[2] For versions of this expressivist interpretation of Hume on causal necessity, see Jonathan Bennett, *Learning from Six Philosophers: Descartes, Spinoza, Leibniz, Locke, Berkeley, Hume*, 2 vols. (Oxford: Clarendon Press, 2001), 2: 271–274; Simon Blackburn, *Essays in Quasi-Realism* (New York: Oxford University Press, 1993), 94–107; Angela Coventry, *Hume's Theory of Causation* (London: Continuum, 2006); Millican, "Against the 'New Hume,'" 238–239; and Walter Ott, *Causation and the Laws of Nature in Early Modern Philosophy* (Oxford: Oxford University Press, 2009), 203–205, 244. Other commentators resist the expressivist interpretation. See, for instance, P. J. E. Kail, *Projection and Realism in Hume's Philosophy* (Oxford: Oxford University Press, 2007), 77–124, and Galen Strawson, "David Hume: Objects and Power," in *The New Hume Debate*, revised ed., ed. Rupert Read and Kenneth A. Richman (London: Routledge, 2007), 31–51.

of what Hume will call *absolute* necessity, the kind of necessity that attends demonstrable truths and aprioristic "relations of ideas" (EHU 4.1; see also T 1.3.1.1–2). What is it that explains our practice of employing this further language, adding an 'absolute' modal gilding to the bare non-modalized statements of the demonstrable sciences? What does such talk and thought do for us?

Hume is sometimes said to be a realist about absolute necessity, in which case talk and thought about absolute necessity might naturally be regarded as an attempt to describe the mind-independent system of modal phenomena.[3] But there are simply no texts on the realist side of the ledger. And in fact, for Hume, there are fewer things in Heaven and Earth than are dreamt of in the absolute modal realist's philosophy. Although he never presents us with anything like a full-dress account of absolute necessity, the texts that we do have show that Hume regards it as simply a mind-dependent phenomenon and, more specifically, as a manifestation of our sense of the inconceivability of certain propositions by the human mind. This much is strongly confirmed by the texts, or so I argue.[4] Somewhat more speculatively, but developing

---

[3] Commentators who take Hume to be a realist about absolute necessity include John Passmore, *Hume's Intentions* (New York: Basic Books, 1952), 19; Alan Hausman, "Some Counsel on Humean Relations," *Hume Studies* 1 (1975): 58; Kail, *Projection and Realism*, 39; Peter Millican, "Hume's Fork and His Theory of Relations," *Philosophy & Phenomenological Research* 95 (2017): 3–65. Commentators who take Hume to be endorsing some sort of anti-realist, mind-dependent view of absolute necessity include Don Garrett, "Should Hume Have Been a Transcendental Idealist?," in *Kant and the Early Moderns,* ed. Daniel Garber and Béatrice Longuenesse (Princeton, NJ: Princeton University Press, 2008), 193–208; Wayne Waxman, *Kant and the Empiricists* (Oxford: Oxford University Press, 2005), 500–503; and Ott, *Causation and the Laws of Nature*, 235–236.

[4] Notice that this first thesis has a significant consequence for the 'New Hume' debate. According to advocates of the 'New Hume,' Hume holds that there are real mind-independent connections between causes and effects that would license a priori inferences from the one to the other, but also holds that these connections are forever hidden to human inquiry, making such a priori insight into the causal order impossible for minds like ours. (See Kail, *Projection and Realism*, 77–102; Strawson, "David Hume"; and the other papers, pro and con, collected in Read and Richman, *The New Hume Debate*.) If this amounts to the view that Hume holds that there are hidden *absolute necessities* connecting causes and effects (which would seem required in order to license an a priori inference), then notice that even if such a reading could be established, it would not suffice to make Hume a causal realist. On the interpretation that I advance in the current paper, Hume is not a realist about absolute necessity, and so even if he holds that causal regularities are a consequence of hidden absolute necessities, this would not entail realism about causal necessity.

the account along the same expressivist lines that we find in Hume's treatment of causal necessity in order to avoid otherwise obvious objections, I will also argue that the most plausible hypothesis is that Hume regards our talk and thought about absolute necessity not as an attempt to describe or represent the limits of what we can conceive, but as an expression of systematically related non-representational attitudes.[5] I made an initial case for this mind-dependent and expressivist interpretation on an earlier occasion.[6] Here I develop and defend the proposed reading, paying particular attention to its expressivist component, and situating Hume's treatment of 'absolute' modal discourse in the wider context of his philosophy of language.

3. Absolute Necessity and Conceivability

First I summarize the most significant textual evidence that Hume regards absolute necessity as a mind-dependent phenomenon, and, more specifically, as a manifestation of our sense of what is and is not conceivable. We can begin with his famous comparison of causal necessity and absolute necessity in the *Treatise*:

Either we have no idea of [causal] necessity, or [causal] necessity is nothing but that determination of the thought to pass from causes to effects, and from effects to causes, according to their experienced union.

Thus as *the necessity, which makes two times two equal to four, or three angles of a triangle equal to two right ones, lies only in the act of the understanding, by which we consider and compare these ideas*; in

---

[5] On this reading, Hume anticipates the expressivist treatment of metaphysical and/or logical modality that one finds in certain 20th- and 21st-century philosophers, including Wittgenstein, Ryle, and Sellars. For a useful summary of this tradition, see Amie Thomasson, "Non-Descriptivism about Modality: A Brief History and Revival," *Baltic International Yearbook of Cognition, Logic and Communication* 4 (2009): 1–26, and for more recent defenses of the expressivist approach to metaphysical modality, see Thomasson's paper and Blackburn, *Essays in Quasi-Realism*, 52–74.

[6] Thomas Holden, "Hume's Absolute Necessity," *Mind* 123 (2014): 377–413.

like manner the necessity or power, which unites causes and effects, lies in the determination of the mind to pass from the one to the other. (T 1.3.14.22–23, my emphasis)

Absolute necessity "lies in an act of the understanding" in a way that bears analogy with the way that causal necessity "lies in a determination of the mind." So absolute necessity is explicitly to be understood as some sort of manifestation or consequence of psychological processes. But what is the relevant "act of the understanding" in which absolute necessity resides? All the evidence suggests that it is another kind of psychological determination of human thought—not (as with the case of causal necessity) a habit-induced associative determination that makes us anticipate one kind of event upon the appearance of another, but some other psychological operation that makes us relate ideas in some other way when we "consider and compare" the various ideas belonging to demonstrable propositions.

To see this, consider what it is to accept a proposition as a result of demonstrating it for oneself—a case where one does not merely accept that the proposition is demonstrable on someone else's say-so, but where one's assent is produced by working through the demonstration for oneself. Typically in this sort of case we do not merely believe that the demonstrable conclusion is inexorable and inevitable, but that we have grasped this for ourselves. We have, or so we believe, an *understanding* of the conclusion's necessity: we believe that we have *seen for ourselves* that it could not have been otherwise. But what does this sense that we have 'seen' or 'understood' the necessity of a demonstrable proposition amount to?

Here is Hume's account of the nature of beliefs arrived at through demonstration:

> [W]herein consists the difference betwixt believing and disbelieving any proposition? The answer is easy with regard to propositions, that are prov'd by intuition or demonstration. In that case,

the person who assents not only conceives the ideas according to the proposition, but is necessarily determin'd to conceive them in that particular manner, either immediately, or by the interposition of other ideas. Whatever is absurd is unintelligible; nor is it possible for the imagination to conceive any thing contrary to a demonstration. But ... in reasonings from causation, and concerning matters of fact, *this absolute necessity* cannot take place, and the imagination is free to conceive both sides of the question (T 1.3.7.3, emphasis added; see also A 18)

Hume tells us that when we believe a proposition as a result of a demonstration (or an immediate self-evident "intuition," which, simplifying harmlessly, we can hereafter regard as comprehended under 'demonstration') we find ourselves "determin'd to conceive" the relevant ideas in accordance with that proposition, and unable to conceive of "any thing contrary." We become "sensible" that the contradictory proposition is inconceivable, aware that the alternative combination of ideas is quite literally unthinkable (A 18).

Plausibly it is for Hume this *psychological* fact that we are unable to conceive the alternative that explains the determination of thought at work when "we are determin'd by reason to make the transition [from one idea to another]" in demonstrative reasoning (T 1.3.6.4). And notice that, taking Hume's words at face value, T 1.3.7.3 actually identifies absolute necessity with the property possessed by demonstrable propositions of being such that their contradictory is inconceivable. (What else in the passage could his expression "this absolute necessity" refer back to?) Perhaps Hume is simplifying matters somewhat here. But if the understanding of a proposition's absolute necessity that we acquire when we work through a demonstration for ourselves just *is* a matter of our apprehending the inconceivability of the alternative, then our grasp of absolute necessity is some sort of manifestation of what we find conceivable. So I suggest that we read T 1.3.7.3 as implying a genealogical account of what psychological circumstances are actually moving us when we declare that a proposition is absolutely necessary. Plausibly, it is the fact that we find certain propositions inconceivable that stands behind Hume's assertion that absolute necessity "lies only in an act of the understanding" (T 1.3.14.23)—the act of the understanding (I suggest) in which we find ourselves incapable, as a causal-psychological matter, of forming certain combinations of ideas. We might grasp this absolute necessity for ourselves when we find that, try as we might, we just cannot frame for ourselves an idea of two pairs of objects that is not at the same time also an idea of four objects.[7] So the thought is that, while a non-modalized demonstrable proposition such as B1 might (at least for all that has been said here) be true in virtue of objective and mind-independent relations, when we go further and add (as in B2) a modal operator to a bare non-modalized proposition, what we are doing is manifesting our sense of what is conceivable by the human mind—not indeed our sense of what is conceivable by this or that *actual* human mind (since any actual mind may labor under various parochial and in-principle avoidable limitations on its powers of conception),[8] but rather our sense of what is in-principle conceivable by the human mind given its permanent structure and constitution.[9]

This interpretation also explains otherwise surprising features of Hume's modal epistemology. Hume is not usually upbeat about the capacity of the human mind to discern the ultimate metaphysical

---

[7] See T 1.1.7.8 for the contrary case of a false claim about a relation among ideas. Should we mistakenly hazard the false assertion that all triangles have equal internal angles, decisive counterexamples will readily come to mind, and the ideas "of a scalenum and isosceles, which we over-look'd at first, immediately crowd in upon us."

[8] For instance, any actual human mind is unlikely to have been exposed to all possible simple impressions, and hence will lack certain simple ideas altogether. Moreover, any actual human mind will be prone to fatigue and distraction, limiting its combinatorial mental powers in practice. I elaborate on these issues in Holden, "Hume's Absolute Necessity," 30–33.

[9] This idealization is of a piece with Hume's treatment of causal, moral, and aesthetic judgment, where our judgments are similarly subject to correction with reference to a standpoint free from parochial and in-principle avoidable practical constraints (T 3.3.1.15–21, 3.3.3.2; EPM 5.41; E 232, 231; and see Holden, "Hume's Absolute Necessity," 30–31). *Pace* Millican ("Hume's Fork," 42 note 82), there is nothing problematic or unusual in Hume's appealing to an idealized standard in this context.

structure of the mind-independent universe. So it is remarkable that he has not a scintilla of doubt when it comes to our ability to track the extra-empirical phenomena of absolute necessity and possibility. Instead Hume proceeds with perfect confidence both in the *conceivability principle*, according to which conceivability entails absolute possibility, and in the *inconceivability principle*, according to which inconceivability entails absolute impossibility (and hence the absolute necessity of the alternative), in each case blithely taking psychological facts about what humans can or cannot conceive to be a completely reliable (T 1.1.7.6, 1.2.2.8; EHU 4.25) and at least in the case of the conceivability principle, explicitly a "necessar[y]" (T 1.2.4.11) and "undeniable" (T 1.3.6.5) correlate of modal truths. Here Hume simply ignores the possibility (notoriously pressed by Descartes and Bayle) of a disconnect between our clear and distinct conceivings on the one hand and aprioristic necessary truths on the other. This relaxed attitude would be quite puzzling if Hume were a modal realist. Why would he think that psychological facts about what human beings can and cannot conceive must infallibly trace the system of mind-independent modal truths? And what would explain Hume's surprising confidence in this divinatory process?

This puzzle does not arise on the mind-dependent interpretation. If the absolute modal status of propositions just *is* an expression of what humans can and cannot conceive, then there is no gap between facts about conceivability on the one hand and modal properties on the other. Skeptical doubts about the inference from the former to the latter do not arise, and the conceivability principle and the inconceivability principle will indeed be "necessar[y]" and "undeniable." Of course, there may be room for doubt about whether a certain proposition is or is not genuinely conceivable. That is just as it should be. But if a proposition *is* conceivable, then it is absolutely possible, and if it is *not* conceivable, then its contradictory is absolutely necessary.

Not just the basic commitments but the detailed expression of Hume's modal epistemology supports the mind-dependent interpretation. Consider the well-known paragraph in which Hume sets out the principles that govern his modal inferences:

> 'Tis an establish'd maxim in metaphysics, *that whatever the mind clearly conceives includes the idea of possible existence,* or in other words, *that nothing we imagine is absolutely impossible.* We can form the idea of a golden mountain, and from thence conclude that such a mountain may actually exist. We can form no idea of a mountain without a valley, and therefore regard it as impossible. (T 1.2.2.8)

Were we to read Hume as a modal realist, this passage would present two major blunders. First, in the opening sentence Hume seems to conflate two different theses in his successive formulations of the "establish'd maxim." The first italicized formulation makes a claim about *the idea of* possible existence, whereas the second makes a claim about absolute possibility itself. Hume connects these two formulations with the expression "in other words," and apparently regards them as equivalent. But from any realist perspective this is a serious conflation, confusing a thesis about *human thought about possibility* on the one hand with a thesis about *possibility itself* on the other.

The second conflation concerns Hume's examples of the establish'd maxim at work. On the face of it, Hume tells us in the first sentence of T 1.2.2.8 that the conceivability principle is "an establish'd maxim in metaphysics," but says nothing whatsoever about the inconceivability principle. However, when Hume points in the second and third sentences to particular illustrations of modal inferences, he offers us both the case of a conceivable and therefore possible gold mountain, and the case of an inconceivable and therefore impossible mountain without a valley. The movement through these three successive sentences strongly suggests that each of these examples is intended to illustrate and confirm the establish'd maxim announced at the start of the passage. But from any realist point of view, the latter example simply does not belong. If we find that we cannot frame an idea of a mountain without a valley and "therefore" regard a mountain without a valley as impossible, our inference seems to rely on the *inconceivability* principle, not the conceivability principle. Hume appears to have conflated the two principles, which from any realist perspective is a stupefying logical error. After all, even if every state of affairs that we can conceive of is possible, it hardly follows that we can conceive of every possible state of affairs.

We avoid attributing these errors to Hume with the mind-dependent interpretation. First, if Hume regards absolute possibility and impossibility as a systematic expression of what humans can and cannot conceive, his insouciance in shifting between claims about human thought regarding absolute possibility and claims about absolute possibility itself becomes perfectly intelligible. We can see why he might well regard his two formulations of the establish'd maxim as different ways of saying the same thing. Second, we can see why Hume regards the inconceivability principle as the inseparable flipside of the conceivability principle, for each follows immediately from his underlying view that the line between what is absolutely possible and what is absolutely impossible is simply the shadow of what humans can and cannot conceive. Of course, as a matter of logic, the principle that conceivability entails possibility is different from the principle that inconceivability entails impossibility. But once one grants that to be possible just *is* to be conceivable—or, more cautiously and precisely, that any judgment affirming or denying possibility just is some sort of manifestation of the fact that one finds the proposition in question conceivable or inconceivable—the two principles can be seen as amounting to the same 'identification' of conceivability and possibility looked at in two different ways.[10]

---

10 Some commentators deny that Hume accepts the inconceivability principle, seeing in the third sentence of T 1.2.2.8 (quoted above in full) only (i) a "negative example" of the conceivability principle, or (ii) the "contradiction principle" that "if an idea of a thing is contradictory, then that thing is absolutely impossible." See, respectively, Millican, "Hume's Fork," 38, and D. T. Lightner, "Hume on Conceivability and Inconceivability," *Hume Studies* 23 (1997): 116. But these alternative readings are strained. Contra Millican, a case of inferring something's impossibility from our

4. THE EXPRESSIVIST INTERPRETATION

Other passages also help to confirm the hypothesis that Hume views talk and thought about absolute necessity as a systematic manifestation of our imaginative blocks.[11] But, regarding this first interpretative hypothesis as sufficiently secure, I now make the case for the more speculative hypothesis that Hume views talk and thought about absolute necessity not as an attempt to describe or represent our imaginative blocks, but rather as a display of non-representational attitudes or states of mind that track with our beliefs about those blocks. Just as Hume is most plausibly understood as endorsing an expressivist account of causal necessity according to which judgments about causal necessity express inferential dispositions, so he is most plausibly understood as endorsing an expressivist account of absolute necessity according to which judgments about absolute necessity express some other kind of non-representational attitude or state of mind.

Unfortunately, Hume does not tell us the particular non-representational attitude or state of mind that he takes to be expressed by a judgment about absolute necessity, and any specific interpretive proposal here would of course add to our speculative hazard. But it is sufficient to note that there are possible candidates. For instance,

---

inability to frame an idea of it cannot be read as any kind of example ("negative" or otherwise) of the principle that conceivability entails possibility. And contra Lightner, the third sentence of T 1.2.2.8 says nothing whatsoever about the contradictoriness of ideas, and rather explicitly concerns an inference from inconceivability to impossibility—i.e., it illustrates the inconceivability principle, not the contradiction principle. (For more on this issue in T 1.2.2.8, see my "Hume's Absolute Necessity," 17 note 15.) Hume also implies a commitment to the inconceivability principle when he writes that "[nothing is] beyond the power of thought, except what implies an absolute contradiction" (EHU 2.4). Granted, Hume immediately qualifies this claim by asserting that actual human imaginings are limited to combinations of those ideas that happen to have been "afforded us by the senses and experience" (EHU 2.5) (as Millican emphasizes in "Hume's Fork," 38). But this is only a limitation on what any actual mind with its particular parochial experience can conceive. So far as the idealized human mind furnished with all simple ideas that sets the relevant standard for what is and is not conceivable is concerned, what Hume says in EHU 2.4 still stands. EHU 12.15 and DNR 9.6 present further circumstantial evidence that Hume accepts the inconceivability principle. But the decisive and sufficient text for this question is T 1.2.2.8.

11 See T Introduction 5; EHU 4.2, 12.28; DNR 9.6; and for discussion, my "Hume's Absolute Necessity."

perhaps Hume regards judgments about absolute necessity as expressing *prescriptive* attitudes, such that in labeling certain propositions 'absolutely necessary' we are *insisting* that they be treated as a non-negotiable part of our system of beliefs; that in labeling other propositions 'absolutely impossible' we are *ruling out* any attempt to entertain their truth; and that in labeling other propositions 'absolutely possible' we are *allowing* speculation about their truth or falsehood in light of the empirical evidence. To *insist on, rule out,* or *allow speculation about* a proposition is not to describe anything—neither the proposition itself, nor our own sense of its conceivability (even if it is our sense of what is conceivable that controls the particular prescriptions that we issue).[12] Or again, perhaps Hume regards a judgment about absolute necessity as expressing a certain kind of resilience in our confidence in the truth of the proposition at issue (prompted, as it might be, by our sense of the inconceivability of the alternative). But for our purposes the essential point is simply that Hume regards talk about absolute necessity not as representing or describing the limits of the human imagination, but as expressing *some* sort of non-representational attitude or state of mind that tracks in harmonic correspondence with our sense of what is and is not conceivable.

Why favor this expressivist reading over the representationalist alternative? First, because in any typical case, someone making a claim about the absolute modal status of a proposition or state of affairs is not talking about human psychology. So far as its representational content goes, the statement "Two times two is necessarily four" says nothing at all about the human mind. So if Hume holds that talk and thought about absolute modality is a systematic manifestation of our sense of our imaginative blocks, he cannot sensibly hold that such talk and thought reports our beliefs about those blocks. Rather such talk and thought must express some sort of non-representational attitude

---

12 Blackburn, *Essays in Quasi-Realism,* 60.

that co-varies with our beliefs about what is and is not conceivable. The case here is parallel with Hume's treatment of talk and thought about causal necessity, where judgments about the collisions of billiard balls display but do not report our habit-induced inferential dispositions.

Second, consider the constraints that Hume's concept empiricism imposes on his theorizing about causal and absolute modality. When examining the nature of causal necessity, Hume explicitly frames his discussion in terms of his 'copy principle' (as it is usually known), according to which all our ideas are ultimately derived from impressions, i.e., from original perceptions of sensation and reflection (T 1.3.14.1; EHU 7.4–5). If we could form a genuine mental representation of causal necessity answering to the realist's picture of an objective, mind-independent connection linking distinct events together, then (given the copy principle) we ought to be able to point to the originating impressions for this idea. But since we cannot identify any such impressions, Hume concludes that we must look elsewhere for an explanation of this kind of discourse—ultimately, to an understanding of this vocabulary's non-representational function as an expression of our habit-induced inferential dispositions. And here the case of absolute necessity seems to be of a piece with that of causal necessity. Absolute necessity is as empirically elusive as causal necessity: experience no more reveals an impression of the former than it does of the latter. So, treating like cases alike, one would expect Hume to regard talk and thought about absolute necessity as no more representational than talk and thought about causal necessity.

Third, even if we bracket the issue of the empirical etiology of ideas, given Hume's imagistic model of thought as a play of so many mind-pictures, it is difficult to see how we could frame any mental representation of either causal or absolute necessity.[13] What indeed would the *imagistic* difference be between a mental picture of a certain state of

---

13 Elijah Millgram, "Hume on Practical Reasoning," *Iyyun* 46 (1997): 260–261, note 45.

affairs, and a mental picture of that same state of affairs *as necessary*? None that I can imagine. In the causal case, Hume will reply that the difference between thinking of a state of affairs and thinking of that same state of affairs as (causally) necessary is not to be understood in terms of a difference in mental imagery, but rather as involving the superaddition of non-representational inferential or associative dispositions on top of the play of representational images or mind-pictures. And again, if Hume is consistent across the cases, one might expect him to offer a similar sort of answer in the case of absolute necessity as well.

5. In defense of the expressivist interpretation

Two objections are commonly made against the kind of reading that I propose in this paper. The first is an objection to the thesis that Hume regards absolute modality as a manifestation of the workings of human psychology. This thesis might seem to imply that the modal status of propositions is dependent on contingent and potentially mutable facts about the workings of the human mind, and this result is said to be absurd. I have addressed this objection in detail elsewhere.[14] It fails, for while the modal status of propositions rests on a contingent foundation, it rests, immutably, on a *particular* contingent foundation, namely our actual human nature, and Hume at least finds nothing absurd in endorsing just this sort of position in his analogous treatments of the standard of vice and virtue, the standard of taste, and causal modality.

Here I focus on the second objection, which is leveled against the further hypothesis that Hume is an expressivist about absolute modality. The charge here is that the expressivist interpretation lacks appropriate textual support and is perhaps also anachronistic—a case, perhaps, of reading a 20th-century development in the philosophy of

---

14 Holden, "Hume's Absolute Necessity," 22–30.

language back into an 18th-century philosopher. According to Jennifer Marušić,

> there is no evidence that Hume is an expressivist. He says very little about linguistic meaning, in general, and nothing that would suggest that he employs a distinction between expressive and descriptive uses of language.[15]

Marušić is here attacking expressivist readings of Hume on *causal* necessity. But if the point is just, it will equally tell against any expressivist interpretation of Hume on absolute necessity. For Peter Millican, on the other hand, attributing a form of expressivism to Hume in the case of causal necessity "appears relatively plausible." Nevertheless, he resists reading Hume as an expressivist about absolute necessity, suggesting that this "looks suspiciously anachronistic," and that "unlike the parallel move in the case of causal necessity... there is nothing whatever in Hume's texts to support it."[16] So each of these commentators regards the kind of expressivist reading that I advance in this paper as an unsupported interpolation.

I grant that there are no passages that positively confirm the expressivist reading of Hume on absolute modality. But this absence of direct textual support needs to be put in context. Hume never addresses the language and metaphysics of absolute modality as topics in their own right, and the few remarks that do touch on these questions are made in oblique contexts as he works through this or that other issue in his philosophical program. So it is not so surprising that we have no passage that confirms the expressivist reading—or for that matter any passage that confirms the rival representationalist interpretation favored by Millican and Marušić. Any preference for the one reading over the

---

15 Jennifer Smalligan Marušić, "Hume on Projection of Causal Necessity," *Philosophy Compass* 9 (2014): 270.
16 Millican, "Hume's Fork," 42.

other must then be determined by wider systematic considerations, which is why I said that the expressivist interpretation has the status of a speculative hypothesis as we try to make sense of Hume's explicit remarks, including, for instance, his claim that absolute necessity "lies only in an act of the understanding." My case for this hypothesis is an inference to the best explanation—the best explanation of the texts that we do have, in light of the three considerations outlined above: that modal judgments are very plainly not descriptions of the workings of human psychology; that Hume's concept empiricism rules out any representationalist understanding of absolute modality; and that his imagistic model of thought does the same. Mutatis mutandis, each of these three points is widely thought to constrain any appropriately charitable and systematic interpretation of Hume's treatment of causal modality. I concur, and extend the same courtesy to Hume in the case of absolute modality.

But in case it still seems doubtful that expressivism about absolute necessity was a thinkable option for Hume, I now show, contra Marušić, that Hume *does* employ the distinction between descriptive and expressive uses of language in his theorizing, and that he sees that the expressivist mode of explanation might domesticate areas of discourse that otherwise appear involved in untenable metaphysical commitments. Moreover, I also show that Hume's philosophy of language not only can accommodate expressivist interpretations of areas of discourse, but turns on its head the presumption that our words are descriptive until proven otherwise. Contra Millican, there is nothing anachronistic in the suggestion that Hume might regard discourse about absolute necessity simply as an expression of non-representational attitudes or states of mind.

Virtue and vice, aesthetic value, causal necessity: while the interpretation of Hume across each of these areas of discourse is contested, in each case there is a significant body of scholarship that takes him to be advancing some sort of expressivist account. But for a particularly clear example of Hume entertaining a form of expressivism, consider the account of religious speech advocated in the *Dialogues concerning Natural Religion* by the character Philo, the spokesman for a "careless scepticism" that is at least in significant part a reflection of Hume's own views (DNR "Pamphilus to Hermippus" 6). Although undeniably expressivist in character, Philo's treatment of religious speech has not previously been registered as such by commentators on Hume's philosophy of language.

As is well known, Philo comprehensively rejects any attempt to describe the attributes of the first cause of all on the basis of the flimsy evidence available to human reasoners. Yet at the same time, he also insists that we can "justly" ascribe each of the traditional divine perfections to the first cause, and therefore speak of it properly as mind-like, wise, benevolent, and the rest. The trick is that we may talk this way only insofar as we intend to "express our adoration" in words employed purely for their honorific force, not for their usual representational content:

> [T]he original cause of this universe (whatever it be) we call GOD; and piously ascribe to him every species of perfection. . . . But as all perfection is entirely relative, we ought never to imagine, that we comprehend the attributes of this divine being, or to suppose, that his perfections have any analogy or likeness to the perfections of a human creature. Wisdom, thought, design, knowledge; these we justly ascribe to him; because these words are honourable among men, and we have no other language or other conceptions, by which we can express our adoration of him. But let us beware, lest we think, that our ideas anywise correspond to his perfections, or that his attributes have any resemblance to those qualities among men.
> (DNR 2.3; see also 10.27, and compare Demea at 3.13)

If we are speaking as Philo says we ought, our talk about God's attributes will advertise our reverence and awe, but not any attempt to describe the actual nature of this being or principle. Although the words 'wisdom,' 'thought,' 'design,' and 'knowledge' have a descriptive function when used in non-religious contexts, Philo explicitly disclaims so much as an analogical residue of this descriptive content ("any analogy or likeness," "any resemblance to these qualities among men") when applying these words to the incomprehensible first cause of all. When we ascribe attributes to God, the words we utter should not be intended as a description of anything, but simply an expression of our obeisance and adoration. Perhaps one might wonder whether Philo (or Hume himself) sincerely endorses this expressivist account of religious speech, or whether he invokes it simply to provide pious cover from which to launch his attack on descriptive natural theology.[17] But however that question falls out, it is clear that Hume appreciates the distinction between descriptive and expressive uses of language, and that he sees that an expressivist account of an area of discourse might help to explain away the superficial appearance of realist metaphysical commitments.[18]

Finally consider Hume's central linguistic notion of 'signification,' which renders expressivism a perfectly natural approach in certain areas of language. As Walter Ott has plausibly argued, when Hume speaks of our words signifying this thing or that, we should not take the relationship of signification at work to be the contemporary philosopher's semantic notion of *reference*, such that our words necessarily

---

[17] For discussion, see Thomas Holden, "Hume on Religious Language and the Divine Attributes," in *The Humean Mind*, ed. Angela Coventry and Alex Sager (New York: Routledge, 2019), 182–192.

[18] Philo's expressivist treatment of religious speech was most likely modeled on Hobbes' approach in *Elements of Law* and *Leviathan*, or so I argue in Holden, "Hume on Religious Language," 188. Hobbes himself is very clear about the expressivist character of his own theory, insisting that talk about the divine attributes properly serves "not to tell one another what [*God*] *is*, nor to signify our opinion of his nature, but our desire to honour him with such names as we conceive most honourable among ourselves." Thomas Hobbes, *Leviathan*, ed. Noel Malcolm (Oxford: Clarendon Press, 2012), 614; and for discussion, see Thomas Holden, *Hobbes's Philosophy of Religion* (Oxford: Oxford University Press, 2023), 8–26. The case of Hobbes on talk about the divine attributes helps to show that expressivism was not such a rare bird in early modern philosophy. Other examples include George Berkeley on force and grace, *Philosophical Writings*, ed. Desmond M. Clarke (Cambridge: Cambridge University Press), 299–307, and perhaps Locke on meaning more generally: Lewis Powell, "Speaking Your Mind: Expression in Locke's Theory of Language," *Protosociology* 34 (2017): 15–30.

refer to or are *about* the things that they signify.[19] Rather, to 'signify' in Hume's philosophy of language, as in a wider early modern tradition also encompassing Hobbes and Locke, is just to *indicate* a kind of thing in virtue of being reliably correlated with it, such that an observation of the 'sign' supports a reliable inference to the 'signified'—the same kind of signification that is at work when a blush serves as a sign of embarrassment, a fever serves as a sign of illness, or dark clouds serve as a sign of rain.[20] In the linguistic case, the relevant correlations hold between word-types on the one hand and types of ideas or passions in the speaker's mind on the other, so that our words are signs of our own mental states. Exploiting these reliable correlations, we use words to indicate our mental states—to advertise or display them, revealing our passions and our ideas to our audience. But none of this implies that our words necessarily *refer to* or are *about* the things that they signify. For instance, when I say "The door is open," I will be signifying a certain complex idea in my mind, revealing the fact that I have this inner mental state to my audience. But in any typical case I will not thereby be *referring to* or *talking about* the contents of my own mind. Our words—and hence all of our general, classificatory, or predicative thoughts, all of these depending on the use of words (T 1.1.7.7–10)—*signify* (i.e., indicate, advertise, display) but at least typically do not *describe* the speaker's own mental states.

---

19 Ott, *Causation and the Laws of Nature*, 203–205; Walter Ott, "What Can Causal Claims Mean?," *Philosophia* 37 (2009): 468–469; and Walter Ott, "Hume on Meaning," *Hume Studies* 32 (2006): 233–252.

20 On Hobbes, see Robert McIntyre, "Language," in *The Bloomsbury Companion to Hobbes*, ed. Sharon Lloyd (London: Bloomsbury, 2013), 97–98; Arash Abizadeh, "The Absence of Reference in Hobbes' Philosophy of Language," *Philosophers' Imprint* 15 (2015): 1–17; and Thomas Holden, "Hobbes on the Function of Evaluative Speech," *Canadian Journal of Philosophy* 46 (2016): 127. On Locke, see Paul Guyer, "Locke's Philosophy of Language," in *The Cambridge Companion to Locke,* ed. Vere Chappell (Cambridge: Cambridge University Press, 1994), 121–122; E. J. Ashworth, "'Do Words Signify Ideas or Things?' The Scholastic Sources of Locke's Theory of Language," *Journal of the History of Philosophy* 19 (1981): 299–326; Powell, "Speaking Your Mind," 19–21. On Hobbes, Arnauld, Locke, and the Stoic background, see Walter Ott, *Locke's Philosophy of Language* (Cambridge: Cambridge University Press, 2004), 7–33.

Given Hume's core linguistic notion of signification, a wholly expressivist treatment of certain areas of discourse would then be a perfectly straightforward move. For instance, when we say that the shock of the first billiard ball necessitates the motion of the second, we are naturally understood as signifying, i.e., advertising, certain of our mental states. Our utterance will display our complex idea of this encounter between the two balls, and it will also display the fact that we have the appropriate habit-induced inferential disposition—the fact, that is, that "we make no longer any scruple of foretelling [the one kind of event] upon the appearance of the other," which dispositional state is, for Hume, precisely what makes us "call the one object, *Cause*; the other, *Effect*" in the first place (EHU 7.27). However, there is no pressure from Hume's philosophy of language for him to go further and add, most implausibly, that our causal talk *reports* or *describes* the mental states that it displays.[21] Likewise, given this understanding of Hume's philosophy of language, talk about virtue or beauty might naturally be seen as signifying, i.e., advertising, the speaker's sentiments of approbation without thereby reporting or describing them. And likewise, talk about absolute necessity might naturally be seen as signifying, i.e., advertising, the speaker's non-representational attitudes that are prompted by our sense of what is and is not conceivable without thereby reporting or describing those attitudes. There is therefore nothing anachronistic or incongruous in the suggestion that Hume might have entertained an expressivist approach to absolute modality. In fact, it is the contrary interpretive presumption that Hume must be read as a representationalist about modal discourse unless he explicitly says otherwise that is more in danger of anachronism—the anachronism of importing the 21st-century philosopher's emphasis on reference and truth-conditions into a context where the central linguistic notion of signification was understood quite differently.

---

21 Ott, *Causation and the Laws of Nature*, 244, and contrast Barry Stroud, *Hume* (London: Routledge, 1977), 83.

I conclude that the hypothesis that Hume was an expressivist about absolute necessity is significantly more plausible than the representationalist alternative. The evidence here includes Hume's texts affirming a mind-dependent view of absolute necessity together with the unlikelihood that he regarded talk about absolute necessity as describing rather than merely displaying the workings of our own minds. It also includes the constraints on Hume's theorizing that are imposed by his concept empiricism and by his imagistic model of thought. The proposed hypothesis fits seamlessly with Hume's general theory of linguistic signification, as also with his customary genealogical approach to areas of discourse—including causal, moral, aesthetic, and religious discourse—that might otherwise seem burdened with ontologically extravagant and epistemically precarious forms of metaphysical realism.[22]

Abbreviations

DNR David Hume, *Dialogues concerning Natural Religion* (1779), ed. Dorothy Coleman (Cambridge: Cambridge University Press, 2007).

EHU David Hume, *An Enquiry concerning Human Understanding: A Critical Edition* (1748), ed. Tom L. Beauchamp (Oxford: Clarendon Press, 2000).

T David Hume, *A Treatise of Human Nature: A Critical Edition*, vol. 1 (1739–1740), ed. David Fate Norton and Mary J. Norton (Oxford: Clarendon Press, 2007).

---

[22] Thanks to David Braun, Angela Coventry, Sean Greenberg, Lewis Powell, the editors of this volume, and participants in the 2018 conference on the history of necessity at Johns Hopkins University.

CHAPTER 7

Modality in Kant and Hegel

Nicholas F. Stang

1. Introduction

Intuitively, the concepts of possibly, actuality, and necessity belong together. But why? What makes these concepts modal, but not, for instance, the concepts 'inherence,' 'subsistence,' 'causation,' or 'truth' (all of which have been held to be modal concepts by some thinkers)?[1] Aristotle has accounts of potentiality, actuality, necessity, contingency, and a complex theory of the logical relations of statements involving them, but no umbrella term for what these notions all have in common. It was Ammonius who first coined a common term, τρόπος, which

---

1 Rainer Specht, "Modalität," in *Historisches Wörterbuch der Philosophie: Völlig neubearbeitete Ausgabe des "Wörterbuchs der Philosophischen Begriffe" von Rudolf Eisler*, 13 vols., ed. J. Ritter, K. Gründer, and G. Gabriel (Basel: Schwabe, 2007), vol. 6, 9–12.

Boethius then translated as *modus*.² To simplify a complex history, the idea was that possibility, actuality, necessity, and contingency all concern 'ways' or 'manners': they characterize either the logical 'mode' of a proposition's truth (it is possibly, actually, or necessarily true), or the ontological 'mode' of a being (it is possibly, actually, or necessarily existent), or both. In contemporary metaphysics, the 'unity' of the modalities might either be stipulated ('modality' just means whatever has to do with possibility, actuality, or necessity),³ or defined in terms of possible 'worlds': the possible is what is true in some world, the actual is what is true in a world designated as 'actual' (*this* world), and the necessary is what is true in *all* worlds.⁴

Kant and Hegel differ from all these traditional and contemporary views, and from one another, concerning the unity of modality. According to Kant, modal concepts (categories, as we will see) do not describe properties of objects, but instead express the relation of concepts of objects to our capacities for cognition. The role of the modal categories is to express the relation of a concept of an object to the matter and form of our cognitive capacities: possibility applies to concepts that agree with the form of the relevant cognitive capacity; actuality applies to concepts that agree with the matter of the capacity; and necessity applies to concepts that follow from the matter of the capacity given its form. Since our capacity for cognition has two "stems," sensibility and understanding, this generates a distinction between two kinds of modality: logical modality, which expresses the relation of a concept to the form and matter of the understanding *alone*, and real modality, which expresses the relation of a concept to the form

---

2 Albert Menne, "Modalität des Urteils," in Ritter, Gründer, and Gabriel, *Historisches Wörterbuch der Philosophie*, vol. 6, 12–16.

3 Cf. Peter Van Inwagen and Meghan Sullivan, "Metaphysics," in *The Stanford Encyclopedia of Philosophy*, ed. Edward N. Zalta, spring 2020 edition, https://plato.stanford.edu/archives/spr2 020/entries/metaphysics/: "Present-day philosophers retain the Medieval term 'modality' but now it means no more than 'pertaining to possibility and necessity.'"

4 For an exhaustive study of the 'possible worlds' view of modality, see John Divers, *Possible Worlds* (London: Routledge, 2002).

and matter of understanding *and* sensibility. What unifies the modal concepts—what makes each of the modal categories *modal*—is that they all express a manner of relating to our cognitive capacities.

In the *Wissenschaft der Logik* Hegel rejects this Kantian account of the unity of the modalities, holding that modal categories are determinations of objects *just as much as* any other category of Logic.[5] The fundamental source of this disagreement is the difference in the philosophical projects in which Kant's and Hegel's modal theories are embedded. Kant's account of the modal categories is a part of transcendental philosophy, which Kant defines as the inquiry into how a priori cognition of sensibly given objects is possible.[6] Kantian transcendental philosophy is thus based on a pair of distinctions: between cognition and its object, and between sensibility (by which objects are given to us) and understanding (by which they are thought). Hegel's project of a speculative Logic denies both distinctions. The subject and object of Logic are the same, what Hegel calls 'pure thinking.' This means that Hegelian modalities do not express the relation of a concept to a cognitive power *rather* than a determination of an object; they describe *both* the determinations of an object *and* the relation of thought to its object, for in Hegel's Logic these are ultimately the same. In Logic, the object of thinking is—thinking. Nor do Hegel's modalities concern the relation of two separate capacities, for 'pure thinking' is unitary.[7] While there are distinctions among Hegelian modalities, they do not map onto the Kantian distinction between logical and real possibility. What unifies Hegelian modalities instead, I will argue, is that they

---

5 I capitalize Logic to distinguish the Hegelian science from what goes under the name of 'logic.' I do not mean to suggest that Hegelian Logic has nothing to do with logic, or that it is not intimately connected to the very same traditions from which contemporary 'logic' derives. For discussion, see Paul Redding, "The Role of Logic 'Commonly So-Called' in Hegel's *Science of Logic*," *British Journal of the History of Philosophy* 22 (2014): 281–301.

6 B25, A56/B80. See the end of this essay for a list of abbreviations of the works of Kant and Hegel.

7 Is thinking a capacity? Interestingly, Hegel typically uses the term *Vermögen* to describe the views of others (e.g., 18th-century faculty psychology), in contexts that are at least implicitly (if not explicitly) critical; see HW 10:12, 240–241, 245, 257. In his own account of thinking in the *Encyclopedia*, it is not characterized as a capacity or as a faculty (§§465–468, HW 10:283–287).

describe structural moments of the self-development of the 'modes' of what Hegel calls 'the Absolute.'[8]

2. Kant on the Unity of Modality

Both Kant's table of "logical functions of understanding in judgment" (A70/B89) and his table of categories (A80/B106) include as their fourth heading "Modality." What makes the modal functions of judging (problematic, assertoric, and apodictic) and the modal categories (possibility, actuality, necessity) all *modal*? Consider his accounts,

---

[8] The modal theories of Kant and Hegel are the subject of a vast, and growing, secondary literature, much of which I will not have the space to engage with here. Kant's theory of modality has recently been the topic of no fewer than four monographs in English and German: Uygar Abaci, *Kant's Revolutionary Theory of Modality* (Oxford: Oxford University Press, 2019); Giuseppe Motta, *Kants Philosophie der Notwendigkeit* (New York: Peter Lang, 2007) and *Die Postulate des empirischen Denkens überhaupt: Kritik der reinen Vernunft, A 218–235/B 265–287. Ein kritischer Kommentar* (Berlin: De Gruyter, 2012); and Nicholas Stang, *Kant's Modal Metaphysics* (Oxford: Oxford University Press, 2016). For further discussion see Ian Blecher, "Kant on Formal Modality," *Kant-Studien* 104 (2013): 44–62 and "Kant's Principles of Modality," *European Journal of Philosophy* 26 (2018): 932–944; Andrew Chignell, "Real Repugnance and Belief about Things-in-Themselves: A Problem and Kant's Three Solutions," in *Kant's Moral Metaphysics*, ed. J. Krueger and B. Bruxvoort Lipscomb (Berlin: De Gruyter, 2010), 177–209, and "Real Repugnance and Our Ignorance of Things-in-Themselves: A Lockean Problem in Kant and Hegel," *Internationales Jahrbuch des Deutschen Idealismus* 7 (2011): 135–159; and Jessica Leech, "Kant's Modalities of Judgment," *European Journal of Philosophy* 20 (2012): 260–284, "Kant's Material Condition of Real Possibility," in *The Actual and the Possible: Modality and Metaphysics in Modern Philosophy*, ed. M. Sinclair (Oxford: Oxford University Press, 2017), 94–116, and "Judging for Reasons: On Kant and the Modalities of Judgment," in *Kant and the Philosophy of Mind: Perception, Reason, and the Self*, ed. A. Stephenson and A. Gomes (Oxford: Oxford University Press, 2017), 173–188. Nahum Brown alone has written two whole monographs on Hegel's modal theory: *Hegel's Actuality Chapter of the Science of Logic: A Commentary* (Lanham, MD: Lexington Books, 2018) and *Hegel on Possibility: Dialectics, Contradiction, and Motion* (London: Bloomsbury, 2020). For further discussion, see, in addition to Dieter Henrich's classic paper "Hegels Theorie über den Zufall," in *Hegel im Kontext* (Frankfurt am Main: Suhrkamp, 1971), 157–186; John W. Burbidge, "The Necessity of Contingency," in *Hegel's Systematic Contingency* (New York: Palgrave Macmillan, 2007), 16–47; George di Giovanni, "The Category of Contingency in the Hegelian Logic," in *Art and Logic in Hegel's Philosophy*, ed. W. E. Steinkraus (Atlantic Highlands, NJ: Humanities Press, 1980), 179–200; Franz Knappik, "Hegel's Modal Argument against Spinozism: An Interpretation of the Chapter 'Actuality' in the *Science of Logic*," *Hegel Bulletin* 36 (2015): 53–79; Martin Kusch and Juha Manninen, "Hegel on Modalities and Monadology," in *Modern Modalities*, ed. S. Knuuttila (Dordrecht: Kluwer, 1988), 109–177; Karen Ng, "Hegel's Logic of Actuality," *Review of Metaphysics* 63 (2009): 139–172; and Christopher Yeomans, "Hegel's Expressivist Modal Realism," in *The Actual and the Possible: Modality and Metaphysics in Modern Philosophy*, ed. M. Sinclair (Oxford: Oxford University Press, 2017), 227–251.

respectively, of what is distinctive of modal functions in judgment and modal categories:

> The modality of judgments is a quite special function of them, which is distinctive in that it contributes nothing to the content of the judgment (for besides quantity, quality, and relation there is nothing more that constitutes the content of a judgment), but rather concerns only the value of the copula in relation to thinking in general. (A74/B100)[9]

> The categories of modality have this peculiarity: they do not in the least augment the concept to which they are ascribed as a determination of the object, but rather express only the relation to the faculty of cognition. (A219/B266)

If we abstract for the moment from the differences between these two sentences (e.g., judgment vs. concept, thinking vs. cognition) we can discern a common scheme: a modality, whether it is a modal function or a modal concept, (i) involves a capacity for representation (e.g., thinking, cognition) and its content, and (ii) a distinction between that representational content and the mode or manner in which it is represented by that capacity, and (iii) it describes the latter, the mode or manner of representation, rather than the content.[10] To say that something is a modality or is modal is to say that it belongs to the manner or mode of representation, rather than the content of representation. As Kant writes in the "What Real Progress?" essay, "Modality and the

---

9 Quotations from the *Critique of Pure Reason* are taken from Immanuel Kant, *Critique of Pure Reason*, ed. and trans. P. Guyer and A. Wood (Cambridge: Cambridge University Press, 1998), which some modifications by me. All other quotations from Kant are my own translations.

10 Throughout this essay I refer to the other *relatum* of modality as the 'content' of the representational capacity, although Kant himself often refers to it as the 'object' (*Gegenstand*) of the capacity. I prefer my terminology, because the relevant notion of object is very weak, akin roughly to 'content of any representation whatsoever.' In this very minimal sense of object, every concept, even self-contradictory ones, have an 'object' (they have a content); see A290/346. In the terminology developed in Nicholas Stang, "Kant and the Concept of an Object," *European Journal of Philosophy* 29 (2021): 299–322, it corresponds to r-objects, not q-objects.

content of a thing have nothing in common" (AA 20:337). The distinctness (ii) of content and mode of representation means that these can vary independently: one and the same content can be represented in different modes. I can judge problematically, assertorically, or apodictically that p; the very same concept C can be represented as possibly, actually, or necessarily instantiated. From (iii) it follows that the modality in which I represent a content cannot become a representational content itself. To anticipate slightly: we do not judge *that* possibly p (we problematically judge *that p*) and we do not have a concept *of* possible Fs (we have a possibly instantiated concepts *of Fs*).

With respect to (i), Kant is very explicit about the connection of possibility and actuality to capacity (*Vermögen, facultas*), one of the key terms in his whole critical philosophy:

> The inner principle of the possibility of an action is called the capacity [*Vermögen*]. This inner principle of the possibility of an action requires a determining ground by which the action will become actual, and this is force [*Kraft*]. The determining ground to the actuality of an action is thus called force. (V-Met/Schön, AA 28:515)

> Capacity and force must be distinguished from one another. With capacity we represent the possibility of an action; it does not contain the sufficient ground of the action, which is force, but the mere possibility of it. (V-Met/Volckmann, AA 28:434)

This means that possibility is conceptually dependent on capacity: it is a conceptual truth that a capacity is an inner ground of the possibility to act. Likewise, it is a conceptual truth that actuality is the actualization of a capacity, an action, whose sufficient ground is force (*Kraft*). Kant extends this conceptual connection to necessity as well:

> We do not cognize through [possibility, actuality, and necessity] (something in) things, but rather the relation of concepts of things

to the capacity of the mind to posit and cancel. First, the relation to the capacity (possibility); second, to activity [actuality—NS], thirdly, to activity whose opposite is not in our capacity [necessity–NS]. (Refl. 5228, AA 18:126; emphasis by NS)

Necessity describes an action whose opposite is not in our capacity, i.e., is not possible. This means that whenever we talk about a modality we must be able to specify the relevant capacity of representation (*Vorstellungsvermögen*). Modalities describe the relation of contents of representation to the capacity by which we represent them; we can represent one and the same content in different ways, different modalities.[11]

There are other modalities (e.g., contingency), but the basic three are possibility, actuality, and necessity.[12] The most general characterization that can be given of these three modalities is in terms of capacity and act: (1) possibility expresses the relation of a capacity to a content that agrees with the inner principle or 'form' of that capacity, what is representable by that capacity; (2) actuality expresses the relation of a capacity to the matter of that capacity; (3) necessity expresses (*a*) the relation of a capacity to a content whose opposite is unrepresentable by that capacity (absolute necessity), or (*b*) the relation of a capacity to a content whose opposite is unrepresentable by that capacity given some actual object of that capacity (hypothetical necessity). Kant tends to skip over (3.*a*), because it can be defined in terms of (1); consequently, my discussions of necessity will mainly focus on hypothetical necessity.

---

11 The same applies to the modal categories in their guise as 'categories of freedom' in the second *Critique*: they express the relation of an object/content (an end to be willed) to our capacity for practical representation, practical reason. See AA 5:66 and, for critical discussion, Ralf Bader, "Kant and the Categories of Freedom," *British Journal for the History of Philosophy* 17 (2009): 799–820.

12 In the original Table of Categories, the modal categories are listed as pairs: Possibility-Impossibility, Existence-Nonbeing, Necessity-Contingency (A80/B106). At B110 the modal categories, like the categories of relation, have 'correlates,' which the categories of quantity and quality lack. Kant comments: "this difference must have a ground in the nature of the understanding" (B110). Elsewhere, Kant includes 'generation' (*Entsehen*), 'corruption' (*Vergehen*), and 'alteration' (*Veränderung*) as 'predicables' (derivative concepts) of modality (A82/B108).

3. Kant on Logical Modality: Concepts, Judgment

In the previous section we saw Kant's most general characterization of modality: the manner of relation of a representational capacity to a content for that capacity. In this section I will briefly explain how this general characterization applies in the case of *logical* modality, where the understanding is the only representational capacity involved.

Recall Kant's remark about the modality of judgments, quoted in the previous section:

> The modality of judgments is a quite special function of them, which is distinctive in that it contributes nothing to the content of the judgment (for besides quantity, quality, and relation there is nothing more that constitutes the content of a judgment), but rather concerns only the value of the copula in relation to thinking in general. (A74/B100)

I take this to mean that once you have specified the concepts in a judgment and you have specified the judgment's quantity (whether it is universal, particular, or singular), quality (whether it is affirmative, negative, or infinite), and relation (whether it is categorical, hypothetical, or disjunctive) you have fully specified its content. You have fully specified what is being judged, the accusative or 'object' of judgment. But you have not specified the modality of your judgment, the relation of that content to the capacity for judging.

There are three such 'modalities,' or modes in which judgmental content can be related to the capacity of judgment: problematic, assertoric, and apodictic. Kant explains them thus:

> Problematic judgments are those in which one regards the assertion or denial as merely possible (arbitrary). Assertoric judgments are those in which it is considered actual (true). Apodictic judgments are those in which it is seen as necessary. (A74/B101)

This cannot mean that problematic judging is judging *that* it is possible that *p*, or that assertorically judging is judging *that* actually *p*, or that apodictic judging is judging *that* necessarily *p*. That would make the modality of judgment into a feature of the content, which it cannot be. As we have seen, Kant's very idea of modality involves distinguishing between the content and the mode in which it relates to the relevant capacity. Modality cannot become content.

Instantiating our scheme from Section 1: (1) possibility expresses the relation of the capacity for judging to a judgment-content that agrees with the inner law or principle of that capacity, i.e., what is representable by that capacity. Since in logical modality we are considering the understanding purely in isolation from sensibility, this means that this inner law or principle is the Principle of Contradiction. Thus, logically possible judgments are logically non-contradictory judgments, i.e., all judgments except those in which the negation of a mark of some concept is predicated of that concept (e.g., some Fs are not Fs). (2) Actuality expresses the relation of that capacity to what it actually judges. That actuality is a modality means that the difference between judging *p* as actual and judging *p* as merely (logically) possible does not lie in the content of judgment (actually *p* vs. possibly *p*), but the manner or mode in which one and the same content (*p*) is judged (assertorically vs. problematically). (3) Apodictic judgment expresses either (*a*) the relation of the capacity for judgment to a judgment-content whose negation is unrepresentable by that capacity (absolute logical necessity), i.e., judgments whose negations are logically impossible. Thus, apodictic judgment is the mode in which the capacity for judgment relates to *analytic* judgments, judgments whose negation contains a contradiction. Additionally, apodictic judgment expresses (*b*) the relation of the capacity to a judgment-content whose opposite is unrepresentable by that capacity *given* some actual object of that capacity (hypothetical necessity). In inferring *q* as a logical consequence of *p*, one judges assertorically that q, i.e., one represents the judging of $\sim q$ as hypothetically impossible given p.[13]

Kant provides a helpful illustration of the modalities of judgment in the case of syllogistic inference:

> The problematic proposition [*Satz*] is therefore that which only expresses logical possibility (which is not objective), i.e., a free choice to allow such a proposition to count as valid, a merely arbitrary assumption of it in the understanding. The assertoric proposition speaks of logical actuality or truth, as say in a hypothetical syllogism the antecedent in the major premise is problematic, but that in the minor premise assertoric, and indicates that the proposition is already bound to the understanding according to its laws; the apodictic proposition thinks of the assertoric one as determined through these laws of the understanding itself, and as thus asserting *a priori*, and in this way expresses logical necessity. (A74–75/B100)

Kant has in mind here a hypothetical syllogism:

(P1) $p \to q$
(P2) p
(C) $\therefore q$

In P1 one judges p and q problematically, but one assertorically judges *if p then q*. In P2 one assertorically judges that p. In C one does not merely judge assertorically that q, one judges it apodictically, i.e., as the logical consequence of other assertoric judgments, namely P1 and P2.

This example is a good illustration of why the modality of judgment cannot be a feature of the content, and why the three modalities

---

13   Log 9:52–53, 108–109; V-Lo/Pölitz 24:579; V-Lo/Busolt 24:662; V-Lo/Dohna 24:719.

of judgment cannot be reduced to one another. The difference between entertaining p (in P1) and asserting p (in P2) cannot be a difference in content, for otherwise the argument would be invalid. It must be *one and the same content* that is represented problematically (as judge<u>able</u>) in P1 and then asserted in P2. Likewise, apodictically judging that p cannot be judging that *necessarily p*, because *necessarily p* is not a consequence of P1 and P2. The validity of the inference requires that the very same content that is judged problematically in P1 be judged assertorically in C. Apodictic judging must be judging of the very same content that is in the consequent of P1, or else the inference is invalid. Apodictic judging is not, for instance, judging *that* C follows from P1 and P2; that would *also* make the argument invalid. Apodictic judging that q is consciousness of q as a conclusion from premises; it is not the judging of some distinct content (e.g., that q is necessary).[14]

4. Kant on Real Modality

But the understanding is only one of the capacities that make up our capacity for cognition (*Erkenntnisvermögen*). Cognition involves not just concepts and judgments, but sensible (receptive) intuitions that acquaint us with objects and thereby give our concepts, and the judgments connecting them, what Kant calls 'content' (*Inhalt*).[15] Without intuition we can formulate general concepts (F, G), and relate them in judgments (All Fs are G), but we cannot think *de re* of a single object that it fall under a concept (F*a*). To do that, we need an intuition of the object. When we have an intuition of the object, and subsume

---

[14] For critical discussion of the logical functions of modality in judging, see Abaci, *Kant's Revolutionary Theory of Modality*, 145–166; Leech, "Kant's Modalities of Judgment"; and Timothy Rosenkoetter, "A Non-Embarrassing Account of the Modal Functions of Judgment," in *Kant und die Philosophie in Weltbürgerlicher Absicht: Akten des XI. Kant-Kongresses 2010*, ed. Margit Ruffing, Claudio La Rocca, Alfredo Ferrarin, and Stefano Bacin (Berlin: De Gruyter, 2013), 383–442.
[15] A51/B75, A55/B79, A58/B83, A62/B 87, A239/B298.

it under a concept, we have accomplished what Kant calls cognition (*Erkenntnis*). In the empirical case, where either the concept or the intuition is empirical (dependent upon sensory affection), cognition is experience of its object.[16]

Given the general tie between modality and capacity we should expect a new kind of modality defined relative to this more complete capacity, the capacity for cognition. In particular, we would expect a notion of modality according to which (1) possibility expresses the relation of the capacity for cognition to an object that agrees with the inner law or principle of that capacity, what is representable (cognizable) by that capacity (cognizable), i.e., what agrees both with the form of understanding and the form of sensibility; (2) actuality expresses the relation of that capacity to what is given in the matter of sensibility and understanding; and (3) necessity expresses *either* (*a*) the relation of that capacity to a content whose opposite is unrepresentable by that capacity (absolute real necessity), i.e., what cannot be cognized, *or* (*b*) the relation of that capacity to a content whose opposite is unrepresentable by that capacity *given* some actual object of that capacity (hypothetical real necessity).[17]

This expectation is fulfilled when we examine the Postulates of Empirical Thinking, which concern the modal categories:

1. Whatever agrees with the formal conditions of experience (in accordance with intuition and concepts) is possible.
2. That which is connected with the material conditions of experience (of sensation) is actual.
3. That whose connection with the actual is determined in accordance with general conditions of experience is (exists) necessarily. (A218/B265–266)

---

16 B147.
17 This raises the question of whether there should be a modality defined solely in relation to the sensible faculty, but I cannot address that here.

These three principles clearly instantiate the general scheme of modality. Possibility expresses the relation of the capacity for cognition to concepts of objects that agree with the form of sensibility and understanding, i.e., concepts of objects that can be *both* intuited *and* subsumed under concepts. Actuality expresses the relation of that capacity to what is given to it, i.e., the matter of experience. This means that we represent concepts as concepts of actual objects (i.e., as actually instantiated) when these concepts agree, not merely with the form of experience, but with the material content of experience, sensation.[18] Finally, we represent concepts as necessary when their objects follow from other actual objects by principles grounded in the form of cognition itself. As becomes clear in Kant's discussion of the third Postulate, the sole case in which we can apply this concept of real necessity is alterations in substances: given that the causal principle is grounded in the very form of experience itself, actual alterations in substances follow from other actual objects (their causes) by the very form or nature of the understanding itself (expressed in the causal principle).[19] Kant here leaves out a principle specifically for absolute real necessity (that whose non-being is incompatible with the form of cognition itself), but this is the modal status that would apply to the synthetic a priori principles for which Kant has argued up to this point (e.g., the causal principle itself): they are not logically necessary (their negations are compatible with the form of the understanding purely on its own) but their negations are incompatible with the

---

18 Working out the details of Kant's theory of actuality, and how exactly actuality is given through sensation, perception, experience, etc., is a large task. An initial attempt is sketched in Nicholas Stang, "Hermann Cohen and Kant's Concept of Experience," in *Philosophie und Wissenschaft bei Hermann Cohen/Philosophy and Science in Hermann Cohen*, ed. Christian Damböck (Cham: Springer, 2018), 13–40.

19 A227/B280. This raises a complication: it is absolutely really necessary (it is mandated by the form of experience) that there are causal laws, but the particular causal laws are not absolutely really necessary. So it remains unclear what the modal status of particular causal laws is. For more on the modal status of Kantian laws of nature, see Stang, *Kant's Modal Metaphysics*, ch. 8.

form of cognition, hence really impossible. They are absolutely really necessary.[20]

We are now in a position to understand more fully Kant's explanation of what is distinctive of the modal categories:

> The categories of modality have this peculiarity: they do not augment the concept to which they are ascribed in the least, as a determination of the object, but rather express only the relation to the faculty of cognition. If the concept of a thing is already entirely complete, I can still ask about this object whether it is merely possible, or also actual, or, if it is the latter, whether it is also necessary? No further determinations in the object itself are hereby thought; rather, it is only asked: how is the object itself (together with all its determinations) related to the understanding and its empirical use, to the empirical power of judgment, and to reason (in its application to experience)? (A219/B266)

First of all, modal concepts are not concepts that can be predicated of objects. They are properly predicated of our concepts of objects, and they express the relation of those concepts to our capacity for cognition. Just as the modality of judgment does not affect the content of a judgment (its constituent concepts, and its quantity, quality, and relation), neither does the modality of a concept (whether it is possibly, actually, or necessarily instantiated) affect its content. Modal predicates cannot be added as marks to concepts. Just as we do not judge *that p is possible*, but instead problematically judge *that p*, which expresses the possibility of *p*, we do not have the concept 'really possible Fs,' for this would make possibility into a feature of the content of the concept. We

---

20 Kant argues that "if a judgment is thought in strict universality, i.e., in such a way that no exception at all is allowed to be possible, then it can only be known a priori" (B4) and then goes on to argue that we do have knowledge, thus a priori knowledge, of such strict necessities in mathematics, metaphysics, and pure natural science (B5).

simply have the concept F and we represent it as really possibly instantiated by representing it as a concept of an object that agrees with the form of cognition. The role of modal concepts is to express the relation of concepts of objects to our capacity for cognition: whether they are concepts of objects that agree with that form (possibly instantiated concepts), concepts of objects that are given to us in experience (actually instantiated concepts), or concepts of objects that follow from other actually given objects by laws of the understanding (necessarily instantiated concepts).

5. From Kant to Hegel: Modality as Not Merely Subjective

At various points in the *Wissenschaft der Logik* (WL) and the so-called "Encyclopaedia Logic" (EL)[21] Hegel refers to Kant's view that modal categories express the relation of the object to the subject's cognitive capacity, rather than being determinations of objects themselves. For instance, in the EL, Hegel writes:

> It is probably the determination of possibility that enabled Kant to regard it, along with actuality and necessity, as modalities, because these determinations did not in the slightest add to the concept as object but instead express only the relation to the capacity for cognition.* (EL §143 Zu, 8:281–282)[22]

At the point indicated by the asterisk (*) Hegel cites the very passage about the subjectivity of the modal categories we discussed in Section

---

[21] More precisely, Part One of the *Encyclopaedia of Philosophical Sciences in Outline*, titled "The Science of Logic."

[22] Cf. WL (5:80, 387, 6:344). "Anm." (*Anmerkung*) indicates Hegel's own indented remarks on the paragraphs-texts in the 1830 edition; "Zu." (*Zusatz*) indicates material from lecture transcripts included only in posthumous editions. Translations from Hegel are taken from the published translations listed at the end of this volume, with my modifications.

2 (A219/B266).[23] Here, and elsewhere, he takes note of the Kantian doctrine of the subjectivity of the modal categories, but then goes on to reject it.[24] Understanding why Hegel rejects Kant's subjective conception of modality requires understanding his project of a science of Logic, a task to which I now turn. Understanding Hegel's alternative conception of modality will be the task of Section 4.

The science of Logic, the science contained in the EL and presented more comprehensively in the WL itself, is the science of pure thinking.[25] This means that the topic or 'object' of Logic is thinking. Logic is about what thinking, just in virtue of thinking about anything, thinks. It is the science of 'pure' thinking, the content that thought has merely qua thought. The aim of Logic is to unfold, from the very nature of thinking, this 'pure' content of thought. Hegel rejects the Kantian thesis that (pure general) Logic can study only the form of thinking because the content of thinking must be given exogenously by a different capacity (sensibility). He argues, on the contrary, that the pure content of thinking follows from the very nature of thinking itself. Hegel's term for these contents is 'thought-determinations': they are the determinations of the content of thought, i.e., what makes the content of thought the determinate content it is.[26] The most

---

[23] Hegel cites only B266, because, like many German philosophers between Jacobi and Schopenhauer, he knew the *Kritik* only from the B edition. He also seems to have quoted from (imperfect) memory, because the text he attributes to Kant ("indem diese Bestimmungen den Begriff als Objekt nicht im mindesten vermehrten, sondern nur das Verhältnis zum Erkenntnisvermögen ausdrücken") deviates somewhat from the original, "daß [die Kategorien der Modalität] den Begriff, den sie als Prädikat beigefügt werden, als Bestimmung des Objekts nicht im mindesten vermehren, sondern nur das Verhältnis zum Erkenntnisvermögen ausdrücken" (A219/B266).

[24] WL 5:388, 6:345. See also Hegel's discussion of measure (*Maaß*) as a modality in the first edition of the Doctrine of Being, *Wissenschaft der Logik, Erster Band: Die Objektive Logik* (1812), in *Gesammelte Werke*, ed. Rheinisch-Westfälische Akademie der Wissenschaften (Hamburg: Meiner, 1968), vol. 11, 189.

[25] The rest of this section sketches a reading of Hegel's Logic that is articulated more fully in Nicholas Stang, "Determinacy, Contradiction, Movement: Towards a Reading of Hegel's Logic," unpublished manuscript (available on my Academia.edu and PhilPapers pages); some of this material is covered in Stang, "With What Must Transcendental Philosophy Begin? Kant and Hegel on Nothingness and Indeterminacy," in *Kantian Legacies in German Idealism*, ed. G. Gentry (London: Routledge, 2021), 102–134.

[26] EL 8:81 Zu.

indeterminate, and thus least informative, characterization of the content of thinking, what thinking thinks about, is 'being.' Thinking, just in virtue of thinking, thinks about *what is*. The project of the science of Logic is to unfold the more determinate content in thought's thinking of what is, its thinking of being.

The object of the Logic is (the content of) thinking, but thinking is also the subject of the Logic. Logic is an activity of thought. In Logic, thought thinks about itself, and does so purely, without dependence upon sensory experience, historical tradition, divine revelation, etc. This means that the contents of thought uncovered in the Logic, 'thought-determinations,' are also determinations of thought itself. Since Logic uncovers the content of any thought whatsoever, and in Logic thought thinks about itself (it is both the subject and object of Logic), the thought-determinations of Logic apply not only to the 'object' of Logic (what is, being) but also to its 'subject,' thinking itself. Thus, the Logic is the successive unfolding, from the nature of thinking, of the 'object' of thinking (what thinking thinks about), but also of the nature of pure thinking itself. The thought-determinations of the Logic are simultaneously determinations of thinking itself. Just as the least determinate characterization of the content of thinking is that thinking thinks about *what is*, so is the least determinate characterization of thinking itself that it *is*.[27]

Over the course of the Logic, the object of thinking is further determined as determinate being, being-for-itself, quantity, measure, etc. But these are not merely determinations in the content of thought, i.e., determinations of how thinking must think about being. They are determinations of being itself. There is no gap between how Logic must think being, and how being is. To entertain the putative thought that the thought-determinations of Logic do not apply to what there is, or do not apply to it 'as it is in itself,' is to endeavor to think there

---

27 Thanks to Clinton Tolley for pressing me on this point.

might be something to which the thought-determinations of Logic do not apply. But there is no such thought. Trying to entertain skepticism about the metaphysical import of Logic is trying to entertain the putative thought that thinking as such must think with a certain content while also thinking there might be something (perhaps being 'in itself') to which this determination does not apply, i.e., there might be a true thought in which this content does not appear. In other words, it is trying to think simultaneously that thinking must think a certain content, and that some true thought does not have this content. The putative skeptical thought about the metaphysical import of logic is self-contradictory. This is the idea behind Hegel's famous claim that Logic (the science of thinking qua thinking) "coincides" (*fällt zusammen*) with metaphysics (the science of being qua being).[28] Logic, in uncovering the determinate content of thinking (how the content of thinking is structured) as such, also uncovers the determinate content of being as such (how being is structured).

Aside from this 'coincidence' thesis, Hegel's most startling claim is that there is 'movement' in Logic, and this movement works by thought uncovering contradictions and resolving them.[29] On my reading, one (but only one) important 'motor' of this movement is a version of the Spinozistic doctrine *determinatio est negatio*.[30] While

---

28 EL §24, 8:81; cf. WL 5:43.
29 EL §11, 8:55; WL 5:52.
30 From Spinoza's letter of June 2, 1674, to Jarig Jelles. Hegel repeatedly references this Spinozistic doctrine (HW 4:434, 5:121, 8:195, 18:287), even going so far as to say that it is "im ganzen die Spinozistische Idee" (HW 20:164). He quotes the phrase as "omnis determination est negatio" but in the text of Spinoza's letter, there is no *omnis* (as Hegel would have known from the *Opera Omnia*): "Quia ergo figura non aliud, quam determinatio, et determinatio negatio est." See Karolina Hübner, "Spinoza's Thinking Substance and the Necessity of Modes," *Philosophy and Phenomenological Research* 92 (2016): 3–34 for a discussion of the original Spinozistic doctrine and a defense of Spinoza from the classic Hegelian objection that it renders God (who contains no negations) wholly indeterminate (cf. HW 20:165–166). See Yitzhak Y. Melamed, "*Omnis determinatio est negatio*: Determination, Negation, and Self-Negation in Spinoza, Kant, and Hegel," in *Spinoza and German Idealism*, ed. E. Förster and Y. Melamed (Cambridge: Cambridge University Press, 2012), 175–196, for a discussion of the original meaning of this principle, and the different ways it is interpreted by Kant and Hegel.

Spinoza (as Hegel reads him) intended this as the metaphysical claim that all finite beings are ontologically constituted by a negative relation to other finite beings that limit them, Hegel internalizes this principle within the content of thought: all thought-determination (all content of thought) is partly defined by a negation relation to what it is not. In order to think of A as A (in order for A to be in the content of thinking), A must be able to be contrasted with its negation, not-A (not-A must be in the content of thought).[31] I will refer to this contrastive principle of thought as the "Spinoza Principle" (SP).[32]

The Spinoza Principle requires that for each thought content A in the Logic, thought must be able to think its negation, i.e., that not-A must also be a thought content in Logic. But thought merely thinking A and not-A does not generate a contradiction; thinking does not get involved in a contradiction merely by possessing two mutually contradictory concepts. The contradiction results, on my reading, from the fact that when thinking thinks only with the thought-determinations of a particular stage of the Logic, A and not-A are (i) *distinct*, because by SP they are constituted by their negative relationship to one another, but (ii) *identical*, because with the thought-determinations available to thought at that stage in the Logic, A and not-A are the same content.

---

[31] I use 'not' rather than the standard modern symbols for negation (∼, ¬) to indicate that we cannot assume at the outset that the negation required by the SP is sentence or predicate negation, or otherwise assimilable to contemporary models of negation.

[32] The claim that the SP (*omnis determinatio est negatio*) plays such an important role in the Logic, and that it even plays a role in the 'transition' from Being to Nothing, is highly controversial; many Hegel scholars will be tempted to simply reject it out of hand. I cannot fully defend this interpretation here but let me reply to a few of the most pressing objections: (i) *Does this make the SP a presupposition?* No, because Hegel makes clear that a presupposition is something that a skeptic can negate (EL §78 Anm., HW 8:168) and that the 2nd moment (e.g., Nothing) is the skeptical moment of the dialectic (Enc. §81 Anm., HW 8:172), i.e., the negation of the 1st moment. On my interpretation the SP represents neither the 1st nor the 2nd moment, but the form of the movement from the 1st to the 2nd (the so-called 1st negation; see GW 11:376, 12:244). It is not a presupposition (1st moment) but the form of the skeptical moment of dialectic that undermines every such presupposition; (ii) *Does this violate the rules of the Logic, because the SP is only derived later, with the category of determinacy?* No, I argue, because in general certain contents are operative in driving the Logic forward before they are explicitly derived, e.g., the Logic "moves" to resolve contradictions long before the category of contradiction is derived (GW 11:279–283).

The paradigm example of this is the opening of the Logic, where 'pure being' and 'pure nothing' are said to be 'the same' and 'absolutely distinct' (HW 5:83). Hegel introduces 'becoming' to name the contradictory process in which thinking moves from 'pure being' to its negation, 'pure nothing' via the Spinoza Principle, and then vice versa, without finding a non-contradictory way to think their relation. The next thought-determination, 'determinate being' (*Dasein*) is introduced to resolve this contradiction.[33]

This is a sketch of the opening moves of the Logic, but on my reading this is the structure of 'movement' within the Logic quite generally.[34] Thought thinks a content, contrasts it with its negation by SP, finds that it cannot consistently think their negative relation to one another, and resolves this contradiction by introducing further thought contents, which lead to further contradictions, etc. This 'movement' is only resolved by the complete system of thought-contents in the Logic, what Hegel calls the 'Absolute Idea,' but accounting for how the Idea resolves all remaining contradictions lies outside the scope of this essay. Hegel's term for the thought-contents in Logic is thought-determinations, but in what follows, for brevity and clarity I will refer to them sometimes as 'concepts.'[35]

---

33 The second "motor" of the Logic (mentioned above) is the so-called 'negation of the negation' (GW 12:246–247) that generates new thought-contents that resolve the contradictions among previous thought-contents (e.g., Determinate being, *Dasein*). I do not have space here to address adequately what 'negation of the negation' is in Hegel, but I do want to emphasize that talk of "two" motors is misleading, since 1st negation (which I think is governed by a Hegelian version of the SP) and 2nd negation (negation of the negation) are dependent moments of a single, unified dialectical process. For more on Hegelian negation see Dieter Henirch, "Formen der Negation in Hegels Logik," in *Seminar: Dialektik in der Philosophie Hegels*, ed. R.-P. Horstmann (Frankfurt: Suhrkamp, 1978), 213–229; and Christian Martin, *Die Ontologie der Selbstbestimmung: Eine operationale Rekonstruktion von Hegels 'Wissenschaft der Logik'* (Tübingen: Mohr Siebeck), esp. 25–64.

34 Hegel gives an abstract schema that is supposed to apply to movement in the Logic as a whole (GW 12:244–247), but also specifies that each part of the Logic has its own form of movement: transition into another (Being), shining in another (Essence), and self-development (Concept)— EL §161 Anm., HW 8:308). I think this means that the latter two movement-forms can be developed immanently from the movement-form of Being and that, when properly understood, they also realize its abstract structure, but I do not have the space to argue that there.

35 The former expression should not be confused with Hegel's semi-technical term *der Begriff*, the thought-determination to which the third and final book of the Logic is devoted (the Doctrine

From these minimal remarks about the project of a Hegelian speculative Logic we can see that the Kantian subjective conception of modality will have no place there. Hegel builds into the very idea of a science of Logic the rejection of the two dichotomies necessary to sustain the Kantian conception of modality: (i) the distinction between the cognitive subject and its capacities on the one hand, and the object of cognition on the other, and (ii) the distinction between two capacities, sensibility and understanding.

With respect to distinction (i), all thought-determinations in Logic, including modal thought-determinations, are equally objective *and* subjective.[36] They are objective because they are determinations of the object of thought, which, according to Hegel, means *any object whatsoever*.[37] Because Logic 'coincides' with metaphysics, if the thought-determinations of Logic contain modal contents like possibility, actuality, and necessity, then objects as such are modally determinate, i.e., determinate in respect of possibility, actuality, and necessity. But at the same time, because thinking is self-conscious in Logic, these determinations are also determinations of thought, so thinking is determinate in respect of possibility, actuality, and necessity. The objectivity and subjectivity of modal determinations in Hegel's Logic are two sides of one coin: thinking thinks modally, which means it thinks everything modally, including itself. Since Logic coincides with metaphysics, this means everything, including thinking, is modally determinate.

---

of the Concept). Although I think that all thought-determinations in the Logic are concepts in Hegel's own technical sense (and thus the Doctrine of the Concept is the meta-logic of the Logic itself), I will not attempt to defend that claim here.

36 I here mean 'subjective' in Kant's sense (characterizing the subject of cognition, not its object). As we will see, there is a distinctively Hegelian sense of 'subjective' (reflexive), in which some thought-determinations are more explicitly subjective, i.e., reflexive, than others. For more on the 'subjectivity' of Hegel's Subjective Logic, see Robert Pippin, *Hegel's Realm of Shadows: Logic as Metaphysics in the Science of Logic* (Chicago: University of Chicago Press, 2018), 251–259, and Clinton Tolley, "The Subject in Hegel's Absolute Idea," *Hegel Bulletin* 40 (2019): 143–173.

37 Because the putative thought that there are, or might be, objects that cannot be thought about is, according to Hegel, incoherent.

With respect to distinction (ii), Hegel's Logic, unlike Kant's transcendental philosophy, does not concern itself with the interplay of two distinct capacities, but with pure thinking on its own. So nothing like the Kantian conception of the distinction between 'logical' (relation to the form and matter of the understanding alone) and 'real' (relation to the form and matter of both sensibility and understanding) modalities will be available in Hegel's Logic. While Hegel does draw a distinction between 'formal' and 'real' possibility and necessity, it has a very different meaning from the Kantian one.

6. Modes, Modality, and the Absolute

Before we examine Hegel's own account of the unity of the modal concepts, i.e., why modal concepts "belong together," we first need to understand the systematic place of Hegel's discussion of modality in the WL, the "Actuality" chapter of the Doctrine of Essence.[38]

The most important fact about the systematic place of the "Actuality" chapter is that it immediately follows the chapter entitled "The Absolute." Given the systematic structure of the Logic, sketched in the previous section, this means that the thought-determinations used to think the Absolute (e.g., Absolute, attribute, and mode) are still "on the table," still contained within the set of thought-determinations thought is thinking.[39] When possibility, actuality, and necessity are discussed in "Actuality" we are implicitly talking about the possibility, actuality, and necessity of the Absolute and its modes.

---

38 Confusingly, the "Actuality" chapter bears the same title as the larger section of which it is a part. I will refer to them, respectively, as the Actuality section and the Actuality chapter (the second chapter of the Actuality section).

39 This is one potential difference between the EL and the WL, for in the EL the first chapter of Actuality, on the Absolute, is absent. I interpret this to mean that the discussion of modality in EL §§142–149 is not downstream of the totalizing (or absolutizing) movement that occurs in the WL. Whether this is an artifact of the condensed form of the EL, or whether this represents Hegel's considered view (both the 1817 and 1830 EL versions of the Doctrine of Essence are later than the 1813 WL Doctrine of Essence, so a change of mind may not be out of the question), I will not attempt to determine here.

While the term 'Absolute' will naturally put readers in mind of Spinoza and Schelling, Hegel has already made clear in "The Exposition of the Absolute" that the Absolute is the complete system of thought-determinations of the Logic itself:

> In its true presentation, this exposition [of the Absolute—NS] is the preceding whole of the logical movement of the spheres of being and essence, the content of which has not been gathered in from outside as something given and contingent; nor has it been sunk into the abyss of the absolute by a reflection external to it; on the contrary, it has determined itself within it by virtue of its inner necessity, and, as being's own becoming and as the reflection of essence, has returned into the Absolute as into its ground. (WL 6:189)

The exposition of the Absolute is revealed to be thought's exposition of its own content in the Logic. While this may seem like a demetaphysicalized conception of the Absolute, it is very far from that, given that Logic coincides with metaphysics. If the system of thought-determination of the Logic at this point is the Absolute, then its object, being (what is) understood as systematically determinate according to the categories of Logic, is itself the Absolute.

Hegel signals that his discussion of modality in the Actuality chapter relates back to the Absolute in the very first sentence:

> The Absolute is the unity of the inner and outer as *first, being-in-itself* unity [*ansichseiende Einheit*]. The exposition [*Auslegung*] appeared as an external reflection which, for its part, has the immediate as something it has found, but it equally is its movement and the reference connecting it to the absolute and, as such, it leads it back to the latter, determining it as a mere "way and manner." But this "way and manner" is the determination of the Absolute itself, namely its first identity or its mere implicitly existent unity. (WL 6:189)

Hegel's point here is that what originally appeared as thought's external relation to the Absolute, in which thought "reflects" on the Absolute, has revealed itself to be the Absolute's own exposition, because the Absolute is the system of Logical thought-determinations and the Logic is the exposition of those determinations by thought itself. The exposition of the Absolute, in other words, is Logic itself. What thought initially, mistakenly, took itself to simply "find" as "immediately" given are the 'modes' of the Absolute. In a Spinozistic conception of the Absolute, these modes would be the determinate beings that are "in" the one substance, God. On Hegel's transformed 'Logical' conception of the Absolute, these 'modes' are determinate thought-contents, the thought-contents in the Logic itself. But, of course, they are not simply "found"; they arise from the very nature of the Absolute, from the very nature of thinking. The exposition of these modes is not an external reflecting on what is "given," but the self-exposition of thought: thought thinking itself in Logic.[40]

Hegel introduces the modal thought-determinations by talking about the "way and manner" in which the Absolute determinates itself. Hegel is here playing on the etymological connection between

---

[40] Thus, as much as I appreciate his meticulous logical reconstructions of the argument of the Actuality chapter, I fundamentally disagree with the approach of Knappik, "Hegel's Modal Argument." While the critique of Spinoza is never far from Hegel's mind in the entire Actuality section (Absolute, Actuality, Absolute relationship), it cannot be the principal topic because the critique of other systems is never the principal topic of the Logic. The Logic is about thought's necessary self-unfolding, not the criticism of previous doctrines and systems, although Hegel will often devote a remark or brief discussion to such criticism (e.g., the Remark on Spinoza at HW 6:195–199). What's more, the critique of Spinoza Knappik extracts from the Actuality chapter begs the question against Spinoza in at least three places. First, the modal distribution principle Knappik appeals to ($\Box(p \rightarrow q) \rightarrow (\Box p \rightarrow \Box q)$, p. 66) does not apply to the necessity that characterizes the one substance (necessity of its own nature, or per se necessity); it follows from the substance's nature that if it exists it causes m to exist, and it follows from its nature that it exists, but it does not follow from the nature of m that m exists. Second, the substance's complete explanation of the existence of finite modes does not mean explanatory relations among finite modes are "explanatorily idle" (p. 69); it means that those explanatory relations are themselves explained by a larger explanatory story. Finally, the objection that a Spinozistic rationalist is "unable to spell out the connection in virtue of which the explanandum is explained by the explanans" conflates an epistemic and a metaphysical point: the Spinozistic view is that there is such a complete story, even if our finite minds cannot grasp it in its full complexity.

the (originally Scholastic) terms *modalitas* and *modus*: the 'modal' categories concern the way or manner (the mode) in which modes (determinate beings) are posited in the Absolute's 'movement,' i.e., the self-unfolding of the determinations of being/thought contained in the Logic. This means that the modes (that which is to be "modalized," i.e., thought in respect of possibility, actuality, and necessity) are *both* determinations of being *and* thought-determinations, because, in Logic, these are ultimately the same thing. The "modal status" of modes of thought (i.e., their possibility, actuality, and necessity) just is the modal status of the modes of being of which they are the thoughts. Thus, in uncovering how beings are to be modalized (i.e., thought in respect of their possibility, actuality, and necessity) we thereby uncover how thought-contents in the Logic itself are to be modalized (i.e., thought in respect of their possibility, actuality, and necessity). The Actuality chapter is, so to speak, the modal logic for the Logic itself. But, since the Logic coincides with metaphysics, this means it is modal metaphysics as well.[41]

This tells us what is to be modalized. It does not yet tell us what the 'modality' is, i.e., what ways or manners of the self-positing of these modes in and by the Absolute the modalities are. But, once again, if we take seriously the idea that the 'exposition' of the Absolute is the 'exposition' of the thought-determinations of being and essence up to this point, a natural answer applies: the modalities are the "manner" or "way" in which thought-determinations have been posited in the Logic. But what "manners" or "ways" are these? If the Logic is absolute, and thus depends on nothing outside it, then the answer must flow from the very nature of Logic, from the very nature of the development of thought-contents within a science of Logic.

As I briefly indicated in Section 3, the Logic "moves" by uncovering contradictions in thought-determinations or sets of

---

41 Albeit in a very different sense than contemporary modal metaphysics (e.g., David Lewis, Timothy Williamson).

thought-determinations. The canonical form of such a contradiction is that one category is defined by its negative relation to another (e.g., 'pure nothing' is not 'pure being'), but, within a given set of categories (e.g., the pair 'pure being'–'pure nothing'), they are identical in content (e.g., 'pure nothing' and 'pure being' have the same, absolutely empty content). This contradiction is then resolved by introducing further thought-contents (e.g., 'determinate being'), which resolves the prior contradiction. These further thought-contents are later revealed to contain a contradiction, and so on.

Just from this brief sketch we can see the following different ways (modalities) in which determinate thought-contents (modes) can be posited in the Logic (in the Absolute): they can be considered solely in themselves, as containing no internal contradiction; they can be considered as depending on prior thought-contents in the Logic, as depending for their thinkability on that logical context; they can be considered as the result of a transition from one set of thought-contents to another, as being mandated by thought's need to resolve a contradiction; or they can be considered 'absolutely,' i.e., in the context of the whole Logic, in which case they are considered as mandated by the very nature of thought itself. I have expressed these modalities as ways of "considering" these thought-contents but this is not intended in any way as external or "subjective." These ways of consideration correspond exactly to the relations these thought-contents stand in to the rest of the Logic: they relate to themselves, as self-identical; they relate to their immediate logical context, as enabling them; they relate to their immediate logical context, as mandated by it; and they relate to the whole Logic itself, as emerging from the very nature of thinking itself.

7. The 'Actuality' Chapter in the *Wissenschaft der Logik*

In classical Hegelian fashion, the 'Actuality' chapter divides into three sub-sections (A, B, C), the first two of which divide further into three numbered parts (1, 2, 3). In the rest of this section I briefly sketch Hegel's exposition of the modal structure of the Absolute.

A. *Contingency, or formal actuality, possibility, and necessity.* In (1) Hegel gives the first characterization of actuality as "immediate and unreflected." This means that the first manner in which modes can be posited in the Absolute is that they are immediately present. In other words, we can modalize the modes of the Absolute as follows: all of its immediate modes, insofar as they are immediate, are actual. By "immediate modes, insofar as they are immediate" I mean that in thinking modes of the Absolute as actual in this initial sense (what Hegel will call "formal" actuality), we do not need to relate them in thought to (mediate them with) other modes or to the Absolute itself. On the level of the Logic itself, this means that thought-determinations (modes of thought), insofar as they are thought immediately in some part of the Logic, are thought as actual.[42] Now of course, to think any mode of the Absolute (to think any thought-determination in Logic) we must ultimately think it in relation to (mediated by) other modes and to the Absolute itself. But this simply means we cannot think of modes *only* as actual/immediate; we will need other modal concepts to think the manner or way in which they are "in" the Absolute. We need other modal concepts to think of the manner or way in which they are mediated by other modes.

In (2) Hegel defines possibility as "identity with itself or being-in-itself in general" (WL 6:203).[43] This is also a 'modality' because it characterizes the manner in which a mode is posited, rather than being a feature or property of the mode itself: a mode is possible in this initial, formal sense just in case it is internally self-consistent, if it does not violate the principle of contradiction. 'Formal' possibility thus corresponds to what Kant would call 'logical' possibility if we temporarily ignore Kant's definition of logical possibility as agreement with

---

42 In each triad, the first term is immediate; see WL 6:564.
43 Cf. EL §143, 8:281–284.

the form of the capacity of understanding. Since what is immediately posited in the Absolute (any immediately present thought-content) is internally consistent, "what is actual is possible" (WL 6:202).

Three paragraphs after introducing formal possibility Hegel makes the shocking claim that "therefore everything is just as much contradictory and therefore impossible" (WL 6:203).[44] However, this claim needs to be understood within the context of the Logic itself: every finite thought-determination (every mode of the Absolute) is self-contradictory when thought in its finitude, i.e., without thinking it in the context of the complete system of the Logic itself. Hegel is here simply modalizing a very general structural feature of the Logic: every finite thought-determination (every thought-determination other than the Absolute Idea itself) is partly constituted by its relation to its negation, another finite thought-determination: "because it is only one possible [*ein möglicher*], its other and its opposite is equally possible" (WL 6:204).[45] The argument of the WL is that every such finite thought-determination, though in negative relation to its opposite, has contradictory properties (e.g., the intrinsic properties of a being are the essence that explains its extrinsic "shine," but are also not the essence, because they explain nothing). This contradiction is only resolved by the introduction of further thought-contents, i.e., further "movement" within Logic. This is why everything 'possible' (every putatively consistent thought-content) is just as much 'impossible' (generates a contradiction when thought in relation to its determinate negation).[46]

This contradiction must be resolved or sublated (*aufgehoben*) by a new thought-determination:

---

44 Burbidge, "The Necessity of Contingency," 19 reads this as the much weaker claim that every possibility contradicts some other possibility. But the sentence unambiguously states that every possibility contradicts *itself*: "Daher ist alles ebensosehr ein Widersprechendes und daher Unmögliches." Brown, *Hegel's Actuality Chapter,* 10 contains a helpful comparison and discussion of different readings of this sentence.

45 Cf. Knappik, "Hegel's Modal Argument," 57 on "two-sided possibility."

46 The claim, that every possibility is just as much impossible, appears to be lacking in the *Encyclopedia*; see EL §§142–144, 8:279–284.

But this connection, in which the one possible also contains its other, is as such a contradiction that sublates itself. Now, since it is, according to its determination, reflected and, as we have just seen, self-sublatingly reflected, it is also therefore the immediate and it consequently becomes actuality. (WL 6:204)

The new thought-determination, which resolves the contradiction between the first two, is actual in the sense that it is now the immediate content of thought: thought thinks that content and by means of it thinks a consistent relation between the previous two thought-contents. The sublating thought-content is immediate, but mediates the thought of the sublated, contradictory thought-contents.[47]

In (3) Hegel draws out the consequences of this movement among thought-contents (from possibility, to opposing possibility, to thought-content that sublates the contradiction) for the concept of actuality. The actual is no longer thought merely as what is immediately present, but as what is immediately present as opposed to other possibilities: "the actual is determined as *only one possible*" (WL 6:205). The actual is one possibility among others. Hegel's term for this is 'contingency': "what is possible, is actuality in this sense: it has only as much value as contingent [*zufällig*] actuality; it is itself accidental" (WL 6:205).[48] But in order to think of the actual as contingent, as being merely one possible among others, we need to contrast this in thought with a different case: where one possibility is actualized because it has a *ground*. And this requires thinking of a new 'modality,' a new way that modes can be posited in the Absolute (a new way finite thought-determinations can be posited in Logic): they are *necessary*,

---

47 Cf. Knappik, "Hegel's Modal Argument," 58, who reads this passage as making the claim that either the one possibility or its negation is actual (actually, p or $\sim p$), which effectively trivializes Hegel's point here.

48 EL §144, 8:284. I translate *zufällig* as "contingent" to preserve the unity of the modalities. Traditionally, contingency, but not accidentality, is included among the modalities.

i.e., they are actualized by some prior actuality.[49] Every actual finite mode of the Absolute has a ground (cause) in some prior finite mode, and every finite thought-determination in Logic has a ground in a prior set of thought-determinations (those whose self-contradiction generated it).[50]

B. *Relative necessity, or real actuality, possibility, and necessity.* In (1), Hegel further determines the concept of necessity which emerged at the end of section A as 'real' actuality—not merely what is immediately present in the Absolute (so-called formal actuality), but that whose actuality is grounded in some other actuality. Likewise, the thought-determinations of Logic are not merely actual qua immediately present to thought (formally actual); they are actualized, and thus necessitated by, thought's transition from previous thought-determinations. They are what Hegel calls 'really' actual.[51]

This brings with it a new concept of possibility, which in (2) Hegel calls "real" possibility: a mode (finite determination of the Absolute) is 'really' possible when there are (really) actual modes that can bring that mode about. In the Spinozistic case, a mode is 'really' possible when causes sufficient to bring it about exist. In the

---

49 Cf. Stephen Houlgate, "Necessity and Contingency in Hegel's *Science of Logic*," *Owl of Minerva* 27 (1995): 41 for a different account of the initial transition from contingency to necessity in the WL.

50 This is a point where it is crucial to understand the meta-logical function of the Actuality chapter: thought-determinations have grounds because they are embedded in the Logic, they are necessary to resolve contradictions, etc. Otherwise Hegel must be read as simply assuming the PSR (everything has a ground) at this point. Cf. Knappik, "Hegel's Modal Argument," 59. By contrast Houlgate, "Necessity and Contingency," 41 reads the claim that the contingent is grounded as the claim that contingency requires (is grounded in) that one possibility rather than another be actualized.

51 Knappik, "Hegel's Modal Argument," 60 reads real possibility as dealing with "processes in the empirical world" and cites in support of this Hegel's claim that what is really actual is "the thing of many properties, the existing world" (a reference back to the eponymous sections of the Doctrine of Essence). This is in tension with my meta-logical reading of Actuality. I cannot hope to respond adequately on this issue here, but let me just add that I extend my 'meta-logical' reading to *all* sections of the Logic: at every point in the Logic, thought must think about itself and about its object (being) using the very same categories. For instance, in thinking about the 'existing world' thought thinks of its thought as an 'existing' world of thoughts (roughly, as thoughts that appear against a background). Thus, the reference back to previous 'concrete' sections is not in itself incompatible with the meta-logical reading.

Logic, a finite thought-determination is really possible when there are actual thought-determinations that are sufficient to motivate the transition in thought to that thought-determination: "The real possibility of a thing [*einer Sache*] is therefore the existing [*daseiende*] manifold of circumstances that refer to it [*die sich auf sie beziehen*]" (WL 6:209).

Yet again, the introduction of this new concept of possibility requires us to modify our conception of necessity: "When all of the conditions of a thing are completely present, it enters actuality;— the completeness of the conditions is the totality in the content, and the thing itself [*die Sache selbst*] is this content, determined just as much to be actual as possible" (WL 6:210). If a thing (finite mode) is actualized when all of its conditions are present, then there is no such thing as an unactualized real possibility. Everything really possible is actual, which means that the actual is 'really' necessary: there is no condition that could posit its opposite. In terms of the Logic, this means that there is no ground or condition for positing a finite thought-determination that does not appear in the Logic; there is no condition or ground for positing any such alternate thought-determinations, so all thought-determinations of the Logic are really necessary.

In (3), however, Hegel reminds us that the conditions that make things really necessary are still "formally" contingent: their opposites are formally possible (internally consistent). This means that the really necessary is only relatively necessary: necessary given its actual conditions. But these actual conditions are themselves really necessary, which means necessary relative to their conditions, ad infinitum. But in order to think this relation as a relation of relative necessity, we need a concept to contrast it with: absolute necessity. We need to be able to think of determinations as necessitated by something that is not merely one determinate content among others. In terms of the Logic, we need to be able to think of thought-contents as necessitated by something other than merely the particular finite thought-determinations or set of thought-determinations that precede them. Hegel's term for this new modal concept is 'absolute necessity.'[52]

C. *Absolute necessity*. In the third sub-section Hegel abandons the tripartite numbering, but, just as before, discusses in turn absolute actuality, absolute possibility, and absolute necessity. In each case the 'absoluteness' of these modalities indicates that they are non-relative or non-dependent in some sense.

Hegel begins by characterizing the really necessary, which he had described as the relatively necessary in B, as 'absolute' actuality, "actuality that can no longer be otherwise" (WL 6:213). The really necessary is not merely or immediately actual; it is necessarily actual, necessary, that is, conditional on some ground that necessitates its actuality. But at the same time he also describes the absolutely actual as 'absolutely' possible: "this possibility is itself absolute possibility, for it is precisely the possibility of being determined as possibility just as much as actuality. In being this indifference towards itself, it is thereby posited as empty, contingent determination" (WL 6:213). While Hegel's reasoning here is not pellucid, I take his point to be that the absolutely actual is the result of one internally possible series of conditions (maybe even a non-terminating one); if other internally possible series of conditions are possible, each is indifferent to its actuality, i.e., contingent. The internal possibility of the absolutely actual is "indifferent" to its actuality, because it is actualized by something outside it, a ground.

The main topic in section C, though, is absolute *necessity*. The previous concept of necessity, real necessity, was a concept of relative necessity. In order to think this concept as a concept of relative necessity we must contrast it with something non-relative, i.e., with a concept of non-relative or absolute necessity. The really necessary is contingent in itself, because both what is really necessary and its opposite are

---

52 Thus, Hegel's grounds for introducing the concept of absolute necessity is not to prevent a regress, but to provide a determinate contrast (by the *omnis determinatio est negatio* principle) to the concept of real, i.e., relative necessity. Cf. Knappik, "Hegel's Modal Argument," 63.

internally consistent. The really necessary is actual because of some actual ground. So the contrasting concept of absolute necessity would be something whose non-being is not possible in itself, something whose actuality is not explained by some condition external to its possibility.

The alternative is what Hegel calls absolute necessity: "its possibility is its actuality. It is, because it is" (WL 6:215). On the one hand, this is clearly Hegel's reconstruction within the Logic of the modal status of Spinoza's *causa sui*: "by cause of itself I understand that whose essence involves existence, or [*sive*] that whose nature cannot be conceived without existing" (*Ethics* 1d1).[53] This means that the Spinozistic Absolute exists just in virtue of its possibility, its essence. In the Logic, this means that the absolute necessity of the Absolute is not a 'modality' strictly speaking because it does not concern how modes are "in" the Absolute, but how the Absolute itself is actual (it is actual because of what it is, its essence). But applying this thought to the Logic itself, it means that the complete set of thought-determinations in the Logic is absolutely necessary because their actuality follows from their mere thinkability, indeed, from the thinkability of anything whatsoever. If anything is thinkable, if there is any content of thought whatsoever, then all of the thought-determinations of the Logic are thought. That is the argument of Hegel's Logic, taken as a whole. But this means that every finite thought-determination of the Logic (every mode of thought) follows from the mere possibility of any thought whatsoever; each such thought-determination is (actual) because it is (possible, thinkable). Every thought-determination of the Logic is as absolutely necessary as the complete totality of such thought-determinations.[54] Because any one of these thought-determinations,

---

[53] Translation from Benedict Spinoza, *The Collected Works of Spinoza: Volume One*, ed. and trans. Edwin Curley (Princeton, NJ: Princeton University Press, 1985), 408. Cf. Knappik, "Hegel's Modal Argument," 62.

[54] Cf. "the concept of necessity is very difficult, because *it is the Concept itself*" (EL §147, 8:288). In the *Zusatz* Hegel qualifies this: necessity is the Concept in itself (implicitly), while the Concept is the 'truth' of necessity (8:290). See also Hegel's discussion of modality and method at the end of the WL, 6:551.

if thought consistently, sets thought into a movement that will eventuate in the totality of the Logic, and because the totality of the Logic contains them as determinations, the 'modes' and the 'Absolute' are mutually entailing: each of them is absolutely necessary.[55]

8. Conclusion

For Kant, the modal categories are specifically modal because they concern the relation of concepts to our capacity for cognition, rather than properties of the object itself. Because our capacity for cognition has two "stems," understanding and sensibility, this generates a distinction between 'logical' and 'real' modality. Logical modality concerns the relation of concepts to the capacity of understanding alone, while real modality concerns the relation of concepts to both the understanding and sensibility, our complete capacity for cognition. Hegel's Logic draws no such distinction between the subjective capacity for cognition and its object (pure thinking is both the subject and the object of cognition in Logic) and between sensibility and understanding (Logic concerns pure thinking). However, as we have seen, a distinction does arise for Hegel between 'formal' possibility and 'real' possibility, which might be thought to mirror the Kantian distinction insofar as Hegelian formal possibility concerns the internal self-consistency of some thought-content, while Hegelian real possibility concerns whether there is a ground external to that thought-content that could posit it. However, this Hegelian distinction does not map onto the

---

[55] This raises the question of what role, if any, contingency has in Hegel's theory of modality and whether he can account for the intuitive contingency of individuals (e.g., Krug's pen). I have been discussing the modal thought-determinations that apply in Logic itself, i.e., the modal thought-determinations necessary to think about any being whatsoever. When Logic transitions to philosophy of Nature, we must introduce thought-determinations necessary to think something other than thinking itself (other than the 'realm of shadows'), and this requires a new modal thought-determination: the contingent, what is not determined solely by the self-movement of thought, but is partly determined by the material realization of that self-movement. So there will be room for contingency in Nature and Spirit, but not in the Idea. See Henrich, "Hegels Theorie über den Zufall" for a more complete discussion.

Kantian one, for the Hegelian distinction is drawn within Logic and exclusively concerns the thinkability of some content: a formally possible content is intrinsically thinkable, while a really possible content is thinkable in virtue of ("mediated by") some other content. Since this is a distinction in the manner (modality) in which a thought-content is thinkable (immediately, mediated), and thinkability is agreement with the form of pure thinking, the very topic of the Logic itself, this is ultimately within Hegelian 'logical' possibility: what thinking as such can and must think. The 'absoluteness' of Hegelian Logic, its independence of anything that is not Logic, means that there is no place for an exogenous contribution of 'matter' or 'content' to thought, and thus no modality (e.g., Kantian real possibility) defined in terms of that contribution.[56]

Abbreviations

A/B   *Kritik der reinen Vernunft*. Cited by page number in 1st edition (A, AA 4), and 2nd edition (B, AA 4).

AA   *Kants gesammelte Schriften* (vols. 1–29), ed. Berlin-Brandenburg (formerly: Royal Prussian) Academy of Sciences (Berlin: de Gruyter, 1902–). Cited by volume and page number.

EL   *Enzyklopädie der philosophischen Wissenschaften im Grundrisse, Erster Teil: Wissenschaft der Logik*, 3rd ed., 1830. Unless noted otherwise, cited by volume and page number in HW.

GW   *Gesammelte Werke*, ed. Rheinisch-Westfälische Akademie der Wissenschaften (Hamburg: Meiner, 1968). Cited by volume and page number.

---

56 I would like to thank numerous individuals and groups for their feedback, over the course of several years, on the material that became this paper: Charlie Cooper-Simpson, Eckart Förster, Daniel Leblanc, Michaela Manson, Yitzhak Melamed, Dean Moyar, Sam Newlands, Manish Oza, Amogha Sahu, Tad Schmaltz, Clinton Tolley, as well as all the participants in a graduate seminar on Hegel's Logic at Toronto in the fall of 2017, a mini-seminar on Hegel's logic at San Diego in the spring of 2018, and the fall 2019 workshop on modality at Johns Hopkins.

HW	*Hegels Werke in zwanzig Bänden*, ed. E. Moldenhauer and K. M. Michel (Frankfurt a.M.: Suhrkamp, 1986). Cited by volume and page number.
LOG	*Logik, herausgegeben von Gottlob Benjamin Jäsche*. Cited by volume and page number in AA.
REFL.	*Kants handschriftlicher Nachlaß*. Cited by four-digit number and volume and page number in AA.
V-LO/BUSOLT	*Logik Busolt* (AA 24).
V-LO/DOHNA	*Logik Dohna-Wundlacken* (AA 24).
V-LO/PÖLITZ	*Logik Pölitz* (AA 24).
V-MET/SCHÖN	*Metaphysik von Schön* (AA 28).
V-MET/VOLCKMANN	*Metaphysik Volckmann* (AA 28).
WL	*Wissenschaft der Logik: Lehre vom Sein* (1832, 2nd edition, HW 5; 1812, 1st edition, GW 11), *Lehre vom Wesen* (1813, HW 6), *Lehre vom Begriff* (1816, HW 6). Unless noted otherwise, cited by volume and page number in HW.

Reflection

MUSIC AND MODALITY

Domenica G. Romagni

1. Introduction

[E]very art presupposes rules which first lay the foundation by means of which a product that is to be called artistic is first represented as possible. The concept of beautiful art, however, does not allow the judgment concerning the beauty of its product to be derived from any sort of rule that has a concept for its determining ground. . . . Yet since without a preceding rule a product can never be called art, nature in the subject must give the rule to art.[1]

Before we feel an aesthetic emotion for a combination of forms, do we not perceive intellectually the rightness and necessity of the combination?[2]

As the foregoing quotes evidence, discussion of art (and, in particular, fine or beautiful art) is often saturated with modal language. Bell asks us what it is to perceive something as a work of art other than to perceive in it a sort of necessity of form. Kant tells us that, while beauty cannot be determined by a rule

---

1 Immanuel Kant, *Critique of the Power of Judgment*, edited by Paul Guyer, translated by Paul Guyer and Eric Matthews (Cambridge: Cambridge University Press, 2000), 307.
2 Clive Bell, *Art* (New York: Frederick A. Stokes, 1914), 26.

or concept, fine art presupposes or necessitates a rule. However, it is often unclear what this modal talk is supposed to mean. It might be that we should take it as analogical—we perceive the artistic form *as if* it were necessary; a rule is necessary for art, *as it were*. This would mean that, when appreciating fine art as such, we are appreciating a certain kind of regularity or orderliness to the work that perhaps shares some similarities with things like entailments or causal relationships. However, noticing this alone is not entirely helpful in that it does not indicate what kind of similarity is present. In addition, it is unclear how a work of art would be similar to a necessary consequence while not in fact possessing the same kind necessity. In this *Reflection*, my aim will be to discuss this general puzzle in art as it manifests in music. As I will show, the modal talk in the case of music ends up being analogous to other kinds of modality, but not *merely so*. Rather, musical perception turns out to require a robust modal structure in its own right. I will proceed as follows. First, I will briefly outline the relevant modal considerations outside of music. Following this, I will turn to the musical case, using the "Gratias agimus tibi" from Bach's Mass in B Minor to illustrate the operation of modal perception in music.

Before discussing other kinds of modality, it will be useful to make clear what kind of modal talk in music we are concerned with. I have in mind statements to the effect that a musical passage "had to be there" or "couldn't have proceeded differently." For instance, musicologist Jonathan Kramer remarks of a passage from Mozart's G Minor Symphony that it is "locally necessary because of the need to return from a far-flung but structurally inessential motion away from the tonic."[3] We also often hear this kind of talk

---

3 Jonathan Kramer, "Beyond Unity: Toward an Understanding of Musical Postmodernism," in *Concert Music, Rock, and Jazz since 1945: Essays and Analytical Studies*, ed. Elizabeth West Marvin and Richard Hermann (Rochester, NY: University of Rochester Press, 1995), 16. I should note that

applied to a whole piece (e.g., the piece proceeded with a sense of necessity), so I take my discussion to be applicable to both passages of music and whole pieces. In this chapter, I will use the term 'musical necessity' to refer to these cases. The main aim is to understand what these kinds of expressions mean and their relationship to discourse in other modal domains. I will argue that there are similarities between musical necessity and some other kinds of modality, but that musical necessity also requires a robust modal hierarchy in its own right.

2. Different Kinds of Modality

In order to get clear on what is meant by our modal talk in the musical case, it will be helpful to briefly discuss some other kinds of modality. I will begin by ruling out those I believe will not be particularly helpful in our endeavor: logical and metaphysical modality. Regarding the former, it doesn't seem like we are claiming that a musical passage described as 'necessary' must obtain in all counterfactual situations or is somehow logically entailed by the passages that precede it. Another way to put it is to point out that when we describe a musical passage or work as necessary, we are not saying something as strong as "it logically could not have been otherwise." The case with metaphysical necessity is similar—when we characterize a musical passage as 'necessary,' it doesn't seem like we are thinking of a strong sort of metaphysical necessity (i.e., that the particular passage in the piece unfolds the same way in every other metaphysically possible world). In contrast, it seems quite possible that the piece could have unfolded in a number of different

---

this article focuses on the fraught notion of 'unity' in music, which is often seen as related to what I'm calling musical necessity. It should be noted that I am discussing only musical necessity (not unity in music) and am not committed to the idea that either musical necessity or musical unity are essential to aesthetic value.

ways, that the piece might never have been written, or that humans might exist without "music" at all.

However, there are a number of different kinds of necessity that are somewhat weaker than logical or metaphysical necessity. I will focus here on nomological necessity and deontic necessity. Nomological necessity deals with laws of nature—for example, the necessity that attends a statement like "For every action there is an equal and opposite reaction." Deontic modality deals with what is possible or necessary according to certain normative systems. Deontic necessity, then, deals with the kind of necessity that is conveyed by phrases like 'must' or 'ought to.' What is of interest for us is that there are certain features of nomological and deontic necessity that are relevant to understanding musical necessity. These features include the ways in which nomological and deontic necessity (1) relate to rules or rule-like generalizations that impose certain restrictions on how we expect events to unfold, and (2) exhibit a relatively high level of modal force that is nevertheless compatible with the conception that they could have been otherwise.

Let's begin with (1)—that both natural and conventional laws can be understood as rules or rule-like generalizations and, moreover, these rules serve to structure our expectations in certain ways. The rules of natural necessity describe the systems in which the relevant laws hold. Deontic necessity, in contrast, can be expressed as a collection of normative rules that hold in certain domains or situations. Both of these kinds of formulations provide us with modal information—information about what is possible or necessary in the particular system or domain in question, which in turn informs us of what we might expect in a given situation. For instance, when I drop a watermelon off the top of a hundred-story building, I can expect it to fall at a certain rate, accrue a certain amount of velocity, and hit the ground with an explosive impact. My expectations are structured according to my knowledge of natural laws regarding the nature and interaction of gravitation, falling bodies, the physical makeup and structural integrity of fruit and concrete, etc. Similarly, when seated next to a stranger on an airplane, I can expect they might say nothing, say hello, or perhaps ask if I'd like to borrow their magazine. I also expect that they won't spit in my face or try to steal my belongings. These expectations are structured according to my knowledge of rules of politeness, etiquette, or morality.

Let's turn to (2)—both natural laws and deontic norms exhibit a high level of modal force that nevertheless is compatible with the conception that things could have been otherwise. What I have in mind is when we say that some fact P obtains necessarily because of natural law v, the modal force of this statement is high, but consistent with the possibility that the natural laws for our world could have been different, such that v was not included. Another way of putting this view would be that P is necessitated by v in all worlds that include v in their collection of natural laws, where this set of worlds is a proper subset of the set of all metaphysically possible worlds.[4] In the case of deontic norms, when we say that some action O should obtain as a result of norm N, the force of this statement is relatively high but is consistent with the non-occurrence of O, even in contexts where N holds. In both cases, there are possible worlds where the stipulated event doesn't occur.

These are similar to the musical case in that (1) it is generally agreed that many kinds of music (omitting aleatoric music, or music where some element of the composition is intentionally left up to chance) follow conventional rules that govern musical

---

4 The view that nomological necessity is not identical to metaphysical necessity is not universally accepted. For an account opposing this view, see B. Ellis, *Scientific Essentialism* (Cambridge: Cambridge University Press, 2001). For one in favor, see Kit Fine, "The Varieties of Necessity," in *Conceivability and Possibility*, ed. Tamar Szabo Gendler and John Hawthorne (Oxford: Oxford University Press, 2002), 235–260.

expectations,[5] and (2) musical necessity exhibits a high level of modal force that nevertheless is compatible with the conception that things could have been otherwise. Regarding (1), the rules can be more or less general (i.e., "dissonances must resolve" vs. "the tritone in the V7 chord must resolve the fourth scale degree to the third and the seventh to the tonic"), can differ depending on time period and style (i.e., the rules of a Renaissance mass, those of a Hindustani *raga*, etc.), and can be more or less explicit or salient to the listener (i.e., the experience of a music theory specialist vs. a layperson), but have in common the fact that they have a particular domain of operation that, like natural laws or deontic norms, provide modal information. Regarding (2), I mean that musical necessity is weaker than metaphysical necessity but, as I will discuss in the next section, still exhibits some level of modal force.

3. So What Is Musical Necessity?

What can we say to positively characterize musical necessity? First off, musical necessity carries with it a certain amount of modal force. Whenever we perceive a musical work as 'necessary,' there is a sense in which we are saying that it could or should not have been otherwise. While it lacks the kind of force that characterizes something like metaphysical necessity, we can perhaps understand it as operating similarly to deontic necessity. Musical necessity is perceived in the context of certain musical rules or conventions, such that the music is constrained by these rules or conventions and a 'necessary' musical event follows from them. As with deontic necessity, musical necessity is consistent with the fact that the rule-dictated event does not always obtain.

---

[5] I omit aleatoric music not because it is not relevant to the discussion, but because it is a more difficult case whose explanation would require an understanding of the basic framework that I am sketching here and, thus, would take us too far afield. I choose to focus here only on musical systems whose rules are acknowledged and codified in some sense.

However, unlike the rules of a game or of etiquette, there is not a fixed set of rules in music, even when considering a particular style. For instance, etiquette might dictate that there is one permissible way, say, to use a soup spoon (i.e., *the* way one *must* use the soup spoon; otherwise one is considered uncouth). In music, there is hardly ever a single rule that *must* be followed in this way. Rather, there are several rules that prescribe what one may do. Again, though, this is not a limited, exhaustive disjunction. To bring out the contrast, imagine a game setting: one's character might be given the choice that they may either bargain or fight in a certain situation. It is permissible for the player to either bargain or fight, but they *must* do one or the other. In the musical case, the rules are not set in this way. There are a number of rules that a composer or performer may follow in any given circumstance, but the list of permissible actions is not closed.

This point underscores one peculiarity that attends musical necessity. Music follows rules or conventions, but these don't function like other kinds of rules or conventions. If there is a seemingly unlimited collection of permissible actions available to a performer or composer in any given setting, in what sense can we say that they are constrained to follow a rule? Or, to put it slightly differently, how is it that this collection of rules is going to get us anything like a robust, non-trivial sense of 'necessity'? What will help here is to introduce a *ranking* to our set of musical rules or conventions. While there might be an extremely large set of permissible musical outcomes, these will not all be equally ranked. There are certain musical outcomes that will be much more likely than others. What determines this ranking or level of likelihood? The best way of characterizing it would be 'paradigmaticity'— certain musical events are more likely in the sense that they are either cases of paradigm musical rules or are occurrences that are more or less closely related to those rules. For instance, consider paradigm rules for musical cadences (i.e., musical phrase endings).

Many music theorists would agree that the cadence with the highest level of paradigmaticity in the system of western tonal music as practiced roughly between the 17th century and the 19th century is the Perfect Authentic Cadence (PAC).[6] This construction occurs when the penultimate chord of a phrase is a dominant (V) chord in root position and is followed by a tonic (I) chord in root position, where the leading tone in the V chord resolves to the tonic pitch of the I chord, and the tonic pitch is in the top voice of the I chord. There are other permissible ways of ending a phrase (e.g., Half Cadence, Deceptive Cadence, etc.) but these do not rank as high.

With this understanding of musical rules ranked according to paradigmaticity, the most natural thing would be to assume that musical modality would map onto the paradigmaticity ranking as follows: the collection of ranked rules as a whole captures the realm of permissibility or possibility, and the musically 'necessary' passage is the one that instantiates the rule with the highest ranked level of paradigmaticity for that particular musical setting. This would be wrong in a couple of ways, though. First of all, despite the simple toy analysis I gave of a paradigmaticity ranking of cadential forms, determining the particular event with the absolute highest level of paradigmaticity for any given musical state of affairs would very likely be humanly impossible. This is because there are many distinct parameters at play in even the simplest musical case, each of which has its own paradigm rule sets (e.g., melodic considerations, functional harmony, orchestration and arrangement, etc.). Given this, the already complicated task of determining the musical occurrence with the highest level of paradigmaticity according to one parameter would become exponentially more complicated by having to do so for each parameter present, along with then having

---

[6] It should be noted that pardigmaticity is not determined by the rule that is *in fact* most often followed, nor should we assume that there must be, in all cases, a single ruling paradigm.

to devise a higher-order ranking for the paradigmaticity sets of each parameter.

However, the second, more important problem is that this isn't how music works. We don't attempt to calculate the paradigmatically most likely musical event and evaluate a work on whether it succeeds in presenting it. If this were so, music would be very boring and musical criticism would be far more straightforward. This brings us to a final feature of musical modal talk that will be important to note. When we talk about musical necessity, this term is not only meant to be descriptive, as with nomological necessity, or normative, as with deontic necessity, but also evaluative. It is not simply reporting how a musical passage unfolds or should unfold, but also characterizing it as particularly satisfying, successful, or good. Once we note this, it seems clear that a musically 'necessary' passage must be more than a passage possessing the highest level of paradigmaticity. If this were the case, then every PAC would rank as 'necessary.' This is not the case, though—many tepid and banal works of music contain PACs, failing to capture the evaluative element that is connoted by talk of musical necessity. In fact, I think many would agree that a work of music that attempted to follow every paradigm rule of a style very conceivably might be the most boring piece ever written.

What do we do with our conception of rule-ranking according to paradigmaticity, then? If the passage with the highest ranking of paradigmaticity does not match the passage that we would describe as musically necessary, does this mean that our conception of the ranking of musical rules is useless? On the contrary, this ranking is of fundamental importance for understanding our talk of musical necessity. When we perceive a passage as 'necessary,' we are remarking that something is (1) noteworthy, (2) aesthetically satisfying or successful, (3) characterized by a certain strength or permanence (i.e., the character of *having had to be that way*). What satisfies all three of these criteria is a piece that does not always employ musical rules with the highest level of paradigmaticity, but rather picks and chooses from among this hierarchy in such a way that musical events unfold in an unexpected, but nevertheless rule-governed way. With this characterization, I have in mind a kind of musical analogue to Aristotle's conception of a good complex plot in tragedy, which involves a "reversal" and/or "discovery" that, nevertheless, is "in the probable or necessary sequence of events."[7] However, it is important to note that in order to perceive this characteristic of a piece, one must have at least a general, implicit understanding of the pardigmaticity rankings of that musical style, understood as a genuine possibility space. This is because, if they did not, listeners could not form the relevant expectations, which are then confronted in the appropriate way such that surprise is generated, along with rule-conformity still being appreciated.[8]

In order to unpack this characterization of musical necessity, it will be helpful to have an example in mind. Take the "Gratias agimus tibi" from Bach's Mass in B Minor. The movement, written in *stile antico*,[9] opens with the primary subject, a series of half notes rising stepwise, in the bass. This subject is subsequently introduced at the fifth in the tenor voice, the octave in the alto, and the octave plus a fifth in the soprano (Figure 1). The entrance of the alto is particularly striking because, while this entrance is consonant with

---

[7] Aristotle, *Poetics*, 1452a23-24 in Aristotle, *The Complete Works of Aristotle, Vol. 2: The Revised Oxford Translation*, ed. Jonathan Barnes (Princeton: Princeton University Press, 1984), 2324. To continue with the narrative analogue, this might be compared to a scene in a movie in which the characters are put in an improbably extreme and dire situation. This might prompt us to ask of the characters "Wow—how will they get out of *this* one?" Part of what will then be satisfying is seeing how the characters extricate themselves in a way that nevertheless makes sense and, moreover, seems to be connected to earlier details regarding the plot and characters.

[8] For an extensive discussion of musical expectation and surprise, see David Huron, *Sweet Anticipation: Music and the Psychology of Expectation* (Cambridge: MIT Press, 2008). For a contrasting account of musical surprise, see Jenny Judge, "The Surprising Thing about Musical Surprise," *Analysis* 78, no. 2 (2018): 225–234.

[9] A contrapuntal style that emulates 16th-century counterpoint in that its emphasis is on independent melodic lines.

FIGURE 1 Opening to the "Gratias agimus tibi" from Bach's *Mass in B Minor*
Source: J. S. Bach, *Mass in B Minor BWV 232*, Neue Bach-Ausgabe, Serie II, Band I, ed. Friedrich Smend (Kassel: Bärenreiter-Verlag, 1954), 73.

the bass (the alto voice is on a D and the bass is on a G), it creates a dissonance with the tenor, whose C# is a half-step away from the alto and a tritone away from the bass. Bach resolves this harmonic dissonance in a way that is in accordance with the rules in this style—the C# passes stepwise down to a B, forming consonant major third with the bass and minor third with the alto. This resolution is short-lived however, since the tenor voice returns to the C# while the bass G ties over the bar line. This dissonance is then resolved in a more permanent way, with the G resolving down to an F# while the tenor leaps to a D and the alto rises to an F#, just as the soprano begins the fourth entrance of the subject on an A, giving us a consonant triad in first inversion.

There are a couple of noteworthy things about this passage. The first is that the way the dissonance is introduced sets up a resolution where the upper voices are essentially pushed upward.[10] This happens at exactly the same time as the subject is introduced in the highest voice, which continues to rise, as if toward heaven. The second thing to note is what happens when the subject returns later in the piece (Figure 2).

---

10 This is because a tritone is paradigmatically resolved through contrary motion (lines moving in different directions). The bass goes down to an F#, so the upper voice rises.

FIGURE 2 Re-entrance of the primary subject in the "Gratias Animus Tibi" from Bach's Mass in *B Minor*
Source: J. S. Bach, *Mass in B Minor BWV 232*, Neue Bach-Ausgabe, Serie II, Band I, ed. Friedrich Smend (Kassel: Bärenreiter-Verlag, 1954), 75.

Bach slightly changes the pitch content. In the opening, the subject's lowest note in the bass is a D and its highest is a G but in the return of the subject, the range is augmented so that the lowest note is now a B, and the highest note is a D an octave above that. The B in the bass leaps an octave to form a cluster (i.e., a chord composed of pitches separated only by tones or semitones) with the C# in the tenor and the D in the alto. This much more condensed dissonance is followed by a resolution stepwise down in the bass like before, but is then followed by a larger leap upward. The change that Bach makes then essentially causes an even stronger push upward for the primary subject in the upper voices that imitate it. This trend of upward motion continues with each subsequent introduction of the primary theme. The next time it is introduced, it only appears in three voices (beginning with the tenor), but since the tenor begins the theme on the tonic, this forces the soprano line (also introduced on the tonic, an octave above this time) to reach the highest note of the movement yet. Later in the piece, the subject is introduced in a similar way to the beginning, but the trumpets join the voices, taking the subject above the soprano line.

This is of course a very cursory description of just a few elements of a vastly complex piece of music, but even this helps to bring out some points from above. In particular, we should note the modal language that was used in this description—words like 'forces,' 'causes,' etc. If we apply the framework from earlier, what this language amounts to is the application of certain rules from a paradigm-spectrum in a particular musical context. What makes the piece proceed in a way that seems 'necessary' is that Bach's choice of material, in addition to the small changes made with each introduction of the subject, combines with various musical rule-paradigms to culminate in an unforeseen, but nevertheless law-abiding way. All of these elements come together to give the sense that the general upward motion over the course of the movement proceeds 'necessarily.' We are able to perceive the modal force of this because of our understanding of the space of musical possibilities (i.e., musical rules ranked according to paradigmaticity). However, the passage is perceived as particularly noteworthy and satisfying because of the choices that Bach makes in setting up the sequences. At each moment in the piece, we think "Given *these* conditions (i.e., this particular collection of notes at this particular time), the passage *must* proceed like this." What gives force to this *must* is the set of rules ranked according to paradigmaticity, but part of what provides us with the evaluative component of this kind of necessity is the choice of starting conditions and small changes made at any given point.

In conclusion, we can see how musical necessity is analogical. It does not carry with it the force of anything like logical or metaphysical necessity. In many ways, it is different also from nomological or deontic necessity in that it is weaker and is consistent with many more possibilities. The point of connection is that, in a musical setting, we feel some force that seems to connect the series of musical events. I have argued that this force comes from sets of musical rules that, while not limited, are ranked according to paradigmaticity. This allows for composers to make choices and for music to contain an element of surprise, while nevertheless being perceived as 'necessary,' in both a descriptive and an evaluative sense. While this kind of difference renders musical necessity analogous to other kinds of necessity, I argued that it is not *merely* so, in that it requires the listener to consider, at least implicitly, a genuine space of specifically musical possibilities, each of which proceeds according to musical rules. This space enables the listener to evaluate the level of paradigmaticity for any given musical choice on the part of the composer, as well as the ramifications of that choice for how the music is likely to proceed from there.

CHAPTER 8

Modality in 20th-Century Philosophy

Kris McDaniel

1. Introduction

It is hard to overstate how important the topic of modality was for philosophy in the 20th century. Fittingly, a comprehensive discussion of this topic and its role in the development of 20th-century philosophy in a piece this size is impossible, and as such, choices must be made about what to cover. Here is what I plan to do here. First, much of early 20th-century modal theorizing is a response, either direct or indirect, to Kant, and so I begin by outlining some key Kantian claims about modality. Second, I describe two philosophical traditions stemming from this reaction, the phenomenological tradition, with a focus on Husserl and Heidegger, and the analytic tradition, with a focus on Russell and Quine. Next, I turn to the relatively recent history of modality in the analytic tradition, and focus on work by Barcan Marcus on the formula discovered by and named after her, Kripke on the necessary a posteriori and contingent a priori, and Lewis on modal realism.

With this plan in mind, let us turn now to Kant. More specifically, let us turn to those claims about modality made in *The Critique of Pure Reason* that are relevant to the developmental story I am here telling. The central claim is that modal phenomena are not observable. Explicating why Kant holds this will take some doing, and will be the job of the remainder of this section.

Kant distinguishes intuitions and concepts. Both are representations, but they differ in three ways.

First, intuitions are singular representations: they represent a this or a that, rather than many things.[1] Concepts, on the other hand, represent many things but do so in a way that is indifferent to the particularities of what they represent. My concept of redness subsumes many red things under it, such as the stop sign at the end of my street and my giant red dog. But an analysis of my concept of redness—an inspection of its inner constitution—will tell me nothing about the particular street signs or animals that fall under it, because concepts represent things in a *general* way.

Second, intuitions are immediate representations, while concepts are mediate representations.[2] An immediate representation is one that represents an object but not in virtue of some other representation representing an object. In this sense, an intuition can be said to be directly referential. Moreover, when we have an intuition of an object, that object is represented as present to us and, in principle, can be known to be present without inferring its existence from something else. Concepts do not present objects in this way: if you intuit an object, you can in principle know without inference that the object exists, but even if an object falls under a concept, that concept doesn't justify a non-inferential belief in the existence of that object.

---

1 See *The Critique of Pure Reason* A19/B33.
2 *The Critique of Pure Reason* B41.

Finally, intuitions "rest on affections," while concepts do not.[3] (Concepts "rest on functions," but elucidating this claim needn't detain us here.)[4] An affection is a causal relation. In the paradigmatic case, an intuition rests on affection by being caused by the interaction of the object of that intuition with the subject who has that intuition. Moreover, this causal relation grounds the representational relation between an intuition and its object: an intuition represents this object rather than some other object because it is this object that is the cause of its existence. The majority of our intuitions rest on affections in the paradigmatic way; call such intuitions "empirical intuitions." There are two intuitions that do not; these are our intuitions of space and time, which are not caused by causal interactions with space and time. But they rest on affections in a derivative way, by being intuitions of things (space and time) that are themselves forms of empirical intuitions. (Roughly, space is the form of our empirical intuitions of things distinct from thinkers and their thoughts, while time is the form of our empirical intuitions of thinkers and their thoughts.)

We know about the empirical world through intuitions and concepts formed from the data that intuitions provide them.[5] But although our intuitions rest on affections, we do not have intuitions *of* affections. The causal relation induces a particular kind of necessary connection between things, but in general we do not intuit necessary connections, and although we often truly judge that things are necessarily connected, these judgments are not themselves perceptions of necessary connections. In order to understand how we can know that there are necessary connections, we need to go beyond the data provided by intuition and look at the data provided by the faculty of concepts—that is, the faculty that Kant calls the understanding.

---

3 *The Critique of Pure Reason* A19/B33; see also A68/B93.
4 *The Critique of Pure Reason* A68/B93.
5 See Immanuel Kant, *Lectures on Logic*, ed. J. Michael Young (Cambridge: Cambridge University Press, 2004), 248–252 for a discussion of the formation of empirical concepts.

On Kant's view, most but not all of our concepts are derived in some way from experiences we've had. Those non-empirically derived concepts are *pure*, and at their base are twelve categories.[6] Among these categories are the concept of causation as well as the explicitly modal concepts of possibility, necessity, and actuality. For each category, there is a synthetic a priori principle that employs that category. Our knowledge of modality is at root not observational, but conceptual—but nonetheless it is synthetic knowledge rather than analytic.

Moreover, our knowledge of necessary connections is not the result of our discovery of them, since reason has insight only into that which follows a plan of its own making.[7] Necessary connections are imposed by us rather than discovered. The categories, including the modal categories, are generated spontaneously by the understanding, unlike intuitions, which are generated by interactions with other objects.

The ramifications of Kant's theory of our knowledge of modality continued to be felt in the early 20th century. If modal features can't be observed, but we nonetheless have knowledge of them, then Kant's theory seems plausible. Both Husserl and Russell implicitly accept this conditional, but this is because they both deny its antecedent. Husserl argues that we have observational knowledge of modal features, while Russell denies that there really are modal features period, so of course there is no knowledge of them.

2. Husserl

What if modal features are observable? One key claim of Husserl's phenomenological method is that they are: contrary to what Kant claimed, we have intuitions of the essences of things.[8] In general, many kinds of

---

6 There are more than twelve pure concepts since there are concepts that Kant calls "predicables" that are defined in terms of the categories; see *The Critique of Pure Reason* A82/B108.

7 *The Critique of Pure Reason* B: xiii.

8 See Edmund Husserl, *Logical Investigations*, 2 vols., trans. J. N. Findlay (London: Routledge, 2005: Investigations two and three). For commentary, see Dallas Willard, "Wholes, Parts, and

entities are available for observation on Husserl's view. Consider a red ball. This is the sort of thing I can observe. But I can also observe the redness of the ball, and the roundness of the ball. I can see that redness is a color, and roundness is a way of being shaped. But I can see that nothing could have a color without having a shape. And here what I see is a necessary connection between two types of things—a necessary connection that in this case is grounded, both metaphysically and epistemically, in the essence of color itself.

This necessary connection is intuited—it is discovered—rather than imposed by our concepts. We do have a concept of necessary connection, just as we have a concept of redness, but in both cases, these concepts owe their existence to intuitions of their respective objects. Because essences can be intuited, it makes sense to develop an observation-based science of them, and this is the purported science of phenomenology. Moreover, just as there might be some colors that human beings can intuit and others that they cannot, there might be certain essences available to us for inspection while others are not. So, one of the jobs of phenomenology will be to determine which kinds of essences can be intuited by us. Since the relevant scope of the modality "can" is "can in principle by creatures like us," phenomenology presumably will seek to determine which kinds of essences can be intuited by us by attempting to intuit and then describe the essences of things such as intuition, meaning, and human perception broadly construed. Phenomenology is thereby a self-reflective enterprise.

Because both token objects and the types of which they are tokens have essences, and there are systematic correlations between these kinds of essences, there are laws of essences. These laws of essence subsume particular essential connections underneath them. And where there are laws, there is the possibility of a science that takes the discovery

---

the Objectivity of Knowledge," in *Parts and Moments: Studies in Logic and Formal Ontology*, ed. Barry Smith (Munich: Philosophia Verlag, 1982), 385 and Kris McDaniel, "Metaphysics, History, Phenomenology," *Res Philosophica* 91 (2014): 339–365.

of these laws as its task. Phenomenology is the science that studies the essential laws governing the essences of various ways in which objects can be given to us. Other disciplines, such as logic, have different laws as their themes.

Husserl's early investigations focused on articulating our intuitions of the essences of purely logical phenomena, and explaining how our logical concepts where derived from these intuitions.[9] By doing so, he was able to sharply distinguish the logical concepts needed to develop a science of formal logic, whose subject matter consisted of abstract meanings and their inferential relations to each other, from those concepts that are needed to develop various psychological sciences. Husserl also proposed a *formal ontology* akin to formal logic whose theme was the essence of an object as such, regardless of what kind of object it might be.[10] Formal ontology would issue laws governing absolutely all objects, and in the course of doing so, explicate the various ontological categories one needs to characterize objects as such. Among these categories are propositions, properties, relations, parts and wholes, and numbers.

Husserl's later works backslid into a kind of transcendental idealism that his earlier works promised an escape from. His earliest and most prominent students did not follow him here, but rather continued to be *realist phenomenologists*. This group included Adolf Reinach, Roman Ingarden, and Edith Stein, who was Husserl's first research assistant.[11] These realist phenomenologists shared a commitment to a

---

9 See Husserl, *Logical Investigations*, 168 for the demand that logical concepts have their origins in intuitions.
10 See Husserl, *Logical Investigations*, Investigation III.
11 For a representative work of Adolf Reinach, see "On the Theory of Negative Judgment," in *Parts and Moments: Studies in Logic and Formal Ontology*, ed. Barry Smith (Munich: Philosophia Verlag, 1982), 289–386. See also Roman Ingarden, *On the Motives Which Led Husserl to Transcendental Idealism* (Springer, 2012); Edith Stein, *Life in a Jewish Family*, trans. Josephine Koeppel (ICS, 1986): 250; and Edith Stein, *Finite and Eternal Being*, trans. Kurt F. Reinhardt (ISC, 2002). MacIntyre (2006) stresses Stein's commitment to transcendental realism; see also Kris McDaniel, "Edith Stein: *On the Problem of Empathy*," in *Ten Neglected Philosophical Classics*, ed. Eric Schliesser (Oxford University Press, 2014), 195–211.

mind-independent domain of things that have essences that are discoverable by us.[12]

3. Heidegger

Although this is very controversial, I think that the Heidegger of *Being and Time* is also a realist phenomenologist in the sense just elucidated. Here, I will briefly sketch why.

Much of *Being and Time* focuses on a project that Heidegger calls "the existential analytic of Dasein." On the reading of Heidegger I prefer, the fundamental goal of the existential analytic of Dasein is to determine the meaning of Dasein's particular mode of being, *Existenz*.[13] Dasein is the kind of thing that you and I are. A determination of meaning in the sense Heidegger has in mind is at root a determination of real definition: in short, Heidegger wants to know the essence of Existenz. Similarly, the attempt to determine the meaning of being in general is the attempt to discover the real definition—the essence—of being itself.

Heidegger claims that the fundamental essence of Dasein simply is that it exists in the way in which it exists. However, having this mode of being as our essence grounds further derivative essential truths about us, such as that we are essentially embedded in social contexts, that we are finite beings, that we are users of tools, and so on.[14]

Heidegger makes these claims because he thinks that the essence of Dasein is itself given in some way. Heidegger and the Husserl of the

---

12 See Rodney (2021) for an important recent collection on the conflicts between Husserl and his more realist students.

13 I read Heidegger as an *ontological pluralist*, that is, someone committed to modes of being or fundamentally different ways to be. See Kris McDaniel, *The Fragmentation of Being* (Oxford: Oxford University Press, 2017), ch. 1 for a defense of this interpretation and Denis McNamus, "Ontological Pluralism and the *Being and Time* Project," *Journal of the History of Philosophy* 51 (2013): 651–673 for a critical response to it.

14 In McDaniel, *The Fragmentation of Being*, ch. 9, I call the attempt to distill a rich array of essential properties from a mode of being an "articulation" of that mode of being, and use Heidegger's ontology as an illustration of such an attempt.

Logical Investigations differ in *how* they think essences can be given, since Heidegger thinks that there are intentional acts that are more fundamental than the perceptions that Husserl calls "intuitions." These more fundamental acts are pre-cognitive ways of comporting ourselves toward our objects; they are what we do more than what we see.[15]

So far, I've only provided an interpretation in which Heidegger embraces a phenomenological method that demands descriptions of essences that are given to us. But this is not yet sufficient for being a realist phenomenologist. What makes Heidegger a realist phenomenologist is his commitment to a domain of things that are mind-independent, namely those things that are present-at-hand. On the reading of Heidegger I favor, there are at least three different kinds of entities: Daseins, which is what you and I are, ready-to-hand things, which roughly are artifacts or tools like hammers and pencils, and present-at-hand things, which roughly are something like lumps of matter. Each of these three kinds of things exists in a different manner from the others, and each of these three kinds of things have distinctive essences that are given to us. It is part of the essence of present-at-hand things that they can exist independently of Daseins.[16]

4. Russell

While the phenomenological tradition originated with a group of philosophers committed to discoverable real essences, modal phenomena were less congenially received by many philosophers in the analytic tradition. Although early in his career, Russell embraced a Kantian account of modality, he later abandoned it. Instead, he became a

---

15 Steven Galt Crowell, "Heidegger and Husserl: The Matter and Method of Philosophy," in *A Companion to Heidegger*, ed. Hubert Dreyfus and Mark Wrathall (London: Blackwell, 2005), 59–60 notes that, for Heidegger, essential features are revealed in comportments. See also Kris McDaniel, "Heidegger's Metaphysics of Material Beings," *Philosophy and Phenomenological Research* 87 (2013): 332–357.

16 See again McDaniel, "Heidegger's Metaphysics of Material Beings," 346–349.

prominent opponent of genuine modality.[17] This is especially clear in his *Philosophy of Logical Atomism*, which we will focus on here.[18] Some commentators suggest that at this period of his philosophical development, Russell wants to show that all necessity reduces to logical necessity.[19]

By this period, Russell has rejected merely possible entities.[20] So if there are objects with modal features, they must be actual objects. However, according to Russell, properly speaking, ordinary things do not have modal features. Nor, properly speaking, can ordinary things be said to have existence. More surprisingly, not even whole propositions, properly speaking, can be said to be possibly true or necessarily true. Instead, necessity, possibility, and existence are fundamentally properties of propositional functions, rather than of objects or propositions.[21] General existential sentences—such as "dogs exist"—are meaningful. But the analyses of such sentences are always in terms of propositional functions being sometimes true; "dogs exist" is analyzed as "the propositional function *x is a dog* is sometimes true."[22] Particular existential sentences, such as "I exist" or "Charlie exists," are meaningless if they cannot be analyzed in terms of general existential sentences.

---

17 See Bertrand Russell, *An Essay on the Foundations of Geometry* (Cambridge: Cambridge University Press, 1897). For commentary, see Sanford Shieh, *Necessity Lost* (Oxford: Oxford University Press, 2019), 233–234, 241–249, 267–269.

18 Russell had already indicated dissatisfaction with what he regarded as Kant's theory of modality in 1903; see his *Principles of Mathematics* (New York: W. W. Norton, 1996), section 430. In this same section, he also suggests that there is no sense in which a true proposition might have been false. See Shieh, *Necessity Lost*, 274–275 for discussion of this passage.

19 See, for example, George Landini, *Russell* (New York: Routledge, 2011),162, 184, 218. Kevin Klement, "Russell's Logical Atomism," in *The Stanford Encyclopedia of Philosophy*, ed. Edward N. Zalta, Spring 2020 edition, https://plato.stanford.edu/archives/spr2020/entries/logical-atomism/ provides a somewhat skeptical response to this claim. Shieh, *Necessity Lost* extensively discusses Russell's philosophical reasons for his hostility to modality.

20 See, e.g., Bertrand Russell, *The Collected Papers of Bertrand Russell, vol. 7: Theory of Knowledge: The 1913 Manuscript* (London: George Allen and Unwin, 1984), 152.

21 See Bertrand Russell, *The Philosophy of Logical Atomism* (London: Taylor and Francis, 2010), 65–67 and for discussion see Shieh, *Necessity Lost*, 395–400.

22 Although I speak of the analysis of sentences here, strictly speaking for the Russell of this time period, the objects of analysis are facts rather than sentences.

Perhaps we can dispense with modal properties of objects. But the use of sentential operators such as "possibly" and "necessarily" are ubiquitous. Some sense must be made of them. Russell is aware of this, and offers a reductive analysis of them. Recall that fundamentally possibility and necessity are properties of propositional functions. A propositional function is possible if and only if it is sometimes true; a propositional function is necessary if and only if it is always true. According to Russell, our ordinary notion of possibility is to be analyzed in terms of possibility as applied to propositional functions plus an epistemic notion such as ignorance.[23] For example, if I say that it is possible that it will rain tomorrow, the analysis of what I said is something like this: the propositional function *x is raining* is sometimes true, but I do not know that one of those times at which it is true is tomorrow.[24]

Russell's idea here is provocative, but was not developed into a general theory of possibility. What we want is a uniform recipe for analyzing sentences of the form "It is possible that P" into sentences in which no sentential modal operator appears. One might consider an analysis of modality wholly in terms of ignorance. For example, consider this formula: "It is possible that P" means as a matter of analysis "It is not known whether P but P is among some salient class of propositions C such that some member of C is known to be true." However, this analysis of "possibly" as a sentential operator does not appeal to the allegedly more fundamental notion of possibility as a property of propositional functions.

So, let's consider a more complicated formula: "It is possible that P" means as a matter of analysis "It is not known whether P but P contains some constituent, which, when replaced with a variable, yields a propositional function that is sometimes true." This putative account seems in line with Russell's intentions.

---

23 Russell, *The Philosophy of Logical Atomism*, 93–94.
24 Compare with Shieh, *Necessity Lost*, 397–398.

However, it is not an adequate account of possibility. Suppose I do not know that 7 + 5 = 12. I think the sum is 13 rather than 12. Since I know that what is actual is thereby possible, I confidently assert that it is possible that 7 + 5 = 13. It is not known to me that 7 + 5 = 13. (It couldn't be known to me, since knowledge requires true belief.) But it also the case that the proposition that 7 + 5 = 13 contains a constituent—the number 7—which when replaced with a variable x yields the propositional function $x + 5 = 13$. This propositional function is sometimes true in the sense of having at least one true instance, namely the number 8. It follows then that it is possible that 7 + 5 = 13. But it is necessarily false that 7 + 5 = 13.

Counter-examples of this sort are easy to produce.[25] Consequently, it is hard to think that Russell really intends to propose an analysis of possibility per se rather than that of an epistemic phenomenon that will play some but not all of the roles that possibility was thought to have played—that it would have played if only there had been a real phenomenon there, rather than the illusion of one. Accordingly, it is plausible to regard Russell as an eliminativist rather than a reductionist about genuine possibility.

However, Russell also says some things that do not fit well with his remarks about possibility. Russell tells us that each particular, which for Russell are short-lived sense data, "stands alone" and is "completely self-subsistent," and that no particular "logically depends" on the existence of any other particular.[26] Accordingly, for any particular, it is possible that it is the only particular that exists, and for any collection of particulars, it is possible that they are the only particulars that exist. It might be though that here Russell is speaking merely of logical possibility, despite what is suggested in these remarks just mentioned.

---

25 Compare the counter-example produced above with a similar one discussed by Shieh, *Necessity Lost*, 398.
26 Russell, *The Philosophy of Logical Atomism*, 30.

Russell's embryonic hostility to metaphysical necessity would fully develop once adopted by Quine, to whom we turn to next.

5. QUINE

W. V. Quine marks the high water of skepticism about modality in the analytic tradition. His skepticism—perhaps better characterized as outright hostility—has many sources, of which three interconnected ones will be noted here: his ontological system, his rejection of the analytic/synthetic distinction, and his concerns about quantified modal logic and "Aristotelian essentialism."

Quine's preferred "desert landscape" ontology seems inherently inhospitable to modal phenomena. According to this ontology, fundamentally there are only two categories of things: physical objects, which correspond to any matter-filled region of spacetime, and sets constructed out of physical objects. This ontology is thoroughly extensional in the following sense: physical objects are identical if and only if they have the same parts, and sets are identical if and only if they have the same members.[27] There are no possibilities or potentialities; even causal necessity is understood in a Humean fashion: one thing causally necessitates another thing if and only if there is a suitably general regularity that subsumes them both. Moreover, properties and propositions, which are objects typically thought of as bearers of modal properties, are dispensed with completely.

Still, we have an apparently meaningful sentence operator, "necessarily," and could reasonably wonder whether it can preface complete sentences to yield, in some cases, true sentences. If the sentence in question is a logical truth, then yes—Quine would allow us to go this far, but not further.[28] But what about analytic truths, that is, those truths

---

[27] For an overview of Quine's extensionalism, see essay 46 of W. V. Quine, *Confessions of a Confirmed Extensionalist and Other Essays*, ed. Dagfinn Føllesdal and Douglas Quine (Boston: Harvard University Press, 2008), among many of the others in this collection.

[28] See also Quine, *Confessions*, 191.

that can be shown to be equivalent to logical truths by replacing phrases in them with synonymous phrases to yield a logical truth? If there is an analytic/synthetic distinction, then we can make sense of "necessarily," since this expression will be analyzed as "it is analytic that." In short, we can understand necessity only if we can understand analyticity. However, Quine, circa "Two Dogmas of Empiricism," which might be his most widely read article, denies that there is an analytic/synthetic distinction.[29]

Part of Quine's explanation for why there is no analytic/synthetic distinction is ontological: there are no meanings understood as entities that expression can *have*. Since there are no meanings, we can't say that two expressions are synonymous when they have the same meaning.[30]

Instead, we must consider other criteria for synonymy. Perhaps we can say that two expressions are synonymous when they are interchangeable in all sentences without changing the truth values of those sentences. (Ignore the concern that "interchangeable" is itself a modal notion, since with some effort we could dispense with it provided that there are sentence types to quantify over.) But Quine argues that this is not sufficient for synonymy. Whether two expressions are interchangeable is relative to a language. Suppose we begin with a language L just like English except that it lacks any modal expressions—or for that matter, any sentential operators beyond the truth-functional ones. Consider now these two expressions: "has a heart" and "has a kidney." As a matter of fact, every creature with a heart has a kidney. So, these two expressions are substitutable in any sentence in L without changing the truth-values of those sentences. But they are not synonymous expressions in L. In a slightly richer language that has an adverb like

---

29 W. V. Quine, "Two Dogmas of Empiricism," in *From a Logical Point of View* (New York: Harper and Row, 1963), 20–46. Quine was not the first philosopher in the analytic tradition to deny that there are analytic truths. G. E. Moore, "Necessity," *Mind* 9 (1900): 295–296 presents arguments for this conclusion, albeit ones that are both simplistic and unconvincing. See also Shieh, *Necessity Lost*, 371–374 for a discussion of Moore's accounts of analyticity and necessity.
30 See Quine, "Two Dogmas," 22–23, as well as Quine, *Confessions*, 501, 504.

"necessarily," these expressions would not be universally intersubstitutable.[31] So, if we could understand "necessarily," we could then understand when expressions are intersubstitutable without change in truth value, which we could then use to understand "analyticity." But, sadly, we need to first understand "analyticity" in order to understand "necessarily."

Would an appeal to alleged semantical rules help? We are trying to understand analyticity, which at rock-bottom is a relation between a sentence and a language: *a statement S is analytic for language L.* There are artificial languages that have explicit semantic rules, but they are of no help since we are trying to make sense of whether there is a philosophical viable notion of analyticity for natural languages. Still, if a natural language such as English had semantical rules, we could consider this proposal: a statement is analytic for L if and only if it is true according to the semantical rules of L.

But how do we distinguish in a natural language which general statements are semantical rules instead of merely highly general claims about the way the world is? We have no behavioral criteria to guide us. In both cases, we should expect that competent speakers will assent to these statements regardless of whether they are alleged semantical rules. Since we have no clear criterion for what it is to be a semantic rule, we should eschew this notion altogether.[32]

Finally, the Verification Theory of Meaning will not save us. If the Verification Theory of Meaning were true, the meaning of a sentence would consist in the circumstances in which it is confirmed; and we could say that two sentences are synonymous if and only if they are confirmed in exactly the same circumstances. But the Verification Theory of Meaning is true only if individual sentences can be confirmed or disconfirmed in isolation from other sentences in the same language—and this is not the case. Instead, no particular experiences

---

31 See Quine, "Two Dogmas," 27–32.
32 See Quine, "Two Dogmas," section 4.

are linked with any particular statements and empirical confirmation is a matter of whole theories being confirmed or disconfirmed by the totality of experiences.[33] Given this, one cannot draw a distinction between analytic and synthetic sentences: any sentence can be held true, come what may, if we make drastic enough adjustments elsewhere in our theory.

We cannot make sense of analyticity and so we cannot make sense of necessity.

But our situation might actually be worse than that—it might be that even if we could understand analyticity, we still couldn't understand necessity. Suppose that there is an understandable notion of necessity expressed by a sentential operator. Then we should be able to attach this sentential operator to an open sentence and then preface that sentence with a quantifier that binds the variable in that open sentence. (E.g., we should be able to write, "Something is necessarily a dog.") But our doing so commits us to an unintelligible "Aristotelian essentialism" in which things have necessary properties independently of how they are designated. We can't understand this idea, so we really don't understand what necessity is supposed to be even if we grant that we understand analyticity.[34]

6. Barcan Marcus

A large part of the explanation for resurgence of modal metaphysics in the 20th century was the rediscovery of modal logic, and subsequent increasingly sophisticated treatments of this subject matter. Ruth

---

33 See Quine, "Two Dogmas," section 5. See also Quine, *Confessions,* 393, where he suggests a weaker version of this claim.

34 Dagfinn Føllesdal, "Quine on Modality," in *The Cambridge Companion to Quine,* ed. Roger Gibson (Cambridge: Cambridge University Press, 2006), 202 suggests that the first published objection to "quantifying in" appeared in Quine's review of Russell's *An Inquiry into Meaning and Truth:* W. V. Quine, "Review of 'An Inquiry into Meaning and Truth,'" *Journal of Symbolic Logic* 6 (1941): 29–30. Perhaps here Quine was anticipated, albeit embryonically, by Russell; see Landini, *Russell,* 214, who stresses that "quantifying in" is as ill-formed on Russell's view as it is on Quine's.

Barcan Marcus was at the forefront of the development of quantified modal logic—a logic of possibility and necessity that also incorporates the notions of something and everything.[35]

Barcan Marcus also was at the forefront of rehabilitating a notion of essence in modal terms. In one remarkable passage, she provides a sophisticated modal interpretation of what it is for a property to be essential, according to which such properties are necessarily had by what has them but not had by everything, and correspond to "natural" predicates.[36] Moreover, Barcan Marcus argued that genuine identities always hold as a matter of necessity, that is, there is no genuine contingent identity.[37] Genuine identities are sentences that contain proper names understood as "mere tags," that is, as directly referential expressions that lack descriptive content.[38]

As part of her axiomatic treatment of modal logic, Barcan Marcus introduced what has come to be called "the Barcan formula."[39] The Barcan formula is a biconditional that permits permutation of modal operators and quantifiers. In English, we could state the Barcan formula as follows: Necessarily, everything is F if and only if Everything is necessarily F. There is an equivalent statement of the formula in terms of possibility: Possibly, something is F if and only if something is possibly F.

---

35 Dagfinn Føllesdal, "Ruth Marcus, Modal Logic and Rigid Reference," in *Modalities, Identity, Belief, and Moral Dilemmas: Themes from Barcan Marcus*, ed. Michael Frauchiger (Berlin: De Gruyter, 2015), 40 credits Barcan Marcus with being the first philosopher to develop quantified modal logic, followed shortly thereafter by Carnap.

36 See Ruth Barcan Marcus, *Modalities: Philosophical Essays* (Oxford: Oxford University Press, 1993), 57.

37 See Ruth Barcan Marcus, "The Identity of Individuals in a Strict Functional Calculus of Second Order," *Journal of Symbolic Logic* 12 (1947): 12–15 and Barcan Marcus, *Modalities*, 225–226.

38 See Ruth Barcan Marcus and Michael Frauchiger, "Interview with Ruth Barcan Marcus," in *Modalities, Identity, Belief, and Moral Dilemmas: Themes from Barcan Marcus*, ed. Michael Frauchiger (Berlin: De Gruyter, 2015), 159–160.

39 See Ruth Barcan Marcus, "A Functional Calculus of First Order Based on Strict Implication," *Journal of Symbolic Logic* 11 (1946): 1–16 for the first appearance of the Barcan formula, in which it appears as an axiom (axiom 11), rather than as a derived theorem. Strictly speaking, it appears as a schema for axioms, and strictly speaking that which is called "the Barcan formula" (as well as its directions) in what follows contains schema for formulae rather than formulae themselves.

The Barcan formula became the centerpiece of many intriguing metaphysical debates, as will be illustrated below momentarily. As Parsons notes, it is customary to distinguish the two directions of the Barcan formula, a contentious one and uncontentious one, one of which is sometimes (confusingly) called "the Barcan formula" and the other of which is sometimes called "the Converse Barcan formula." But Parsons also notes that it is hard to remember which of them is called which.[40] Accordingly, I will avoid these phrases in what follows.

Since the focus of this chapter is on the metaphysics of modality rather than its logic, I will focus largely on metaphysical interpretations of the Barcan formula rather than explore which logical systems validate it and which do not.[41]

With that said, let us turn now to a discussion of the two directions of the famed Barcan formula, with a focus on its more contentious direction! The relatively uncontentious Barcan formula is this: If necessarily, everything is F, then everything is necessarily F.[42] The contentious formula is its converse: If everything is necessarily F, then necessarily, everything is F. It seems that there are many counter-examples to the contentious formula. Suppose that, as a matter of fact, everything is a material object, and that material objects must be material objects. It doesn't seem to follow—and in fact seems to be false—that there couldn't be non-material objects.

But it also seems that a simple and elegant modal semantics for quantified modal logic validates the contentious formula. On this semantics,

---

40 Terence Parsons, "Ruth Barcan Marcus and the Barcan Formula," in *Modality, Morality, and Belief: Essays in Honor of Ruth Barcan Marcus,* ed. Walter Sinnott-Armstrong, Diana Raffman, and Nicholas Asher (Cambridge: Cambridge University Press, 1995), 4.

41 See Timothy Williamson, *Modal Logic as Metaphysics* (Oxford: Oxford University Press, 2013) for an extended discussion of the Barcan formula.

42 As Daniel Nolan has pointed out to me, even the less contentious direction is not wholly uncontentious, since it seems to imply that if, necessarily, everything exists, then everything necessarily exists.

the modal operators "necessarily" and "possibly" just are universal and existential quantifiers (respectively) that range over worlds. One-place predicates are reinterpreted as two-place predicates that have a reserved slot for a world. So, instead of writing, "Kris is hungry" as "Hk," write "Hka," where this means "Kris is hungry at the actual world." And "Possibly, Kris is hungry" is re-interpreted as "There is a world, w, such that Hkw." Finally, the standard semantics and inference rules for first-order logic are upheld.

With all this held fixed, the contentious version of the Barcan formula follows from the uncontentious version. Begin with the claim: "Necessarily, everything is F," which is interpreted as "For every world w and every object x, Fxw."[43] Perform two instances of universal instantiation with constant symbols not used earlier in the proof to derive "Fab." Now universally generalize in the opposite order, first to derive "For every world w, Faw," and then to derive "For every object x and every world w, Fxw." Finally, retranslate back into the language of necessity and possibility: "Everything is necessarily F." This is the contentious Barcan direction.[44]

There are several metaphysical views that make the contentious Barcan formula true. One of them, however, is distinctive in that it makes it trivial, but at the cost of making all of modal logic trivial: necessitarianism, which is the view that every truth is necessarily true. If every truth is necessarily true, then if everything is F, it is necessary that everything is F and everything is necessarily F. This way of saving the Barcan formula seems rather extreme!

---

[43] An alternative translation is this: "For every world w and every object x, if x exists in w, then Fxw." An informal derivation analogous to the one above goes through on this translation as well. Thanks to Daniel Nolan for discussion here.

[44] What was just presented is an informal "proof" of the Barcan formula that appeals to a possible worlds semantics for modal operators. But there are "direct" proofs stateable solely in the language of first-order quantified modal logic. For an example of one, see, e.g., Christopher Menzel, "The Possibilism-Actualism Debate," in *The Stanford Encyclopedia of Philosophy*, ed. Edward N. Zalta and Uri Nodelman, Spring 2023 edition, https://plato.stanford.edu/archives/spr2023/entries/possibilism-actualism/.

I will focus on ways of making accepting the Barcan formula more palatable. These ways share a common theme: they detach quantification from a thicker notion of existence.

Consider a kind of Meinongian possibilism.[45] On this view, being an object and being a possible object are coextensive, and being actual and existing are coextensive. But not every possible object is actual. Objects that do not exist can nonetheless have properties, some of which they have as a matter of necessity. The quantifiers in the Barcan formula range over all objects, regardless of whether they exist; on this view, to be might be to be the value of a bound variable, but to exist is not. It is unsurprising that the Barcan formula is validated by Meinongian possibilism.

Another view, which perhaps is a notational variant of the first, distinguishes existence from being concrete.[46] The former is expressed by the existential quantifier; the latter is not. The quantifiers in the Barcan formula range over everything whatsoever, and everything whatsoever exists. Moreover, everything whatsoever is a necessary existent, but some things are not necessarily concrete. You and I, tables and teapots, and so on, are merely contingently concrete. But the nonconcrete can have properties as a matter of necessity. Again, it is unsurprising that the contentious Barcan formula is validated by this metaphysics.

Both of the preceding metaphysical systems are inflationary: they save the formula by introducing more things than we antecedently thought there were. And necessitarianism, mentioned earlier, is highly revisionary: it saves the formula by eliminating possibilities that we antecedently thought there were.

---

45 For example, Edward Zalta, *Intensional Logic and the Metaphysics of Intensionality* (Cambridge, MA: MIT Press, 1988). For a critical appraisal, see Christopher Menzel, "Possibilism and Object Theory," *Philosophical Studies* 69 (1993): 195–208.

46 For a development of these views, see Bernard Linsky and Edward N. Zalta, "In Defense of the Simplest Quantified Modal Logic," *Philosophical Perspectives* 8 (1994): 431–458; Bernard Linsky and Edward N. Zalta, "In Defense of the Contingently Nonconcrete," *Philosophical Studies* 84 (1996): 283–294; as well as Timothy Williamson, "Bare Possibilia," *Erkenntnis* 48 (1998): 257–273.

Barcan Marcus' own solution attempts to do neither, but interprets the quantifier in such a way that detaches it from existence while not introducing a wider domain of things that do not exist. Her solution is distinctive also in that it is a *meta-metaphysical* solution rather than a metaphysical solution: rather than introducing a new theory about what things there are, it is a solution based on a theory about what "there are" means.

Barcan Marcus argues that the quantifiers in her formula are *substitutional* quantifiers.[47] According to Marcus, the fundamental notion by which quantifiers are to be understood is truth of a sentence rather than satisfaction of a predicate by an object in a domain. Roughly, a universally quantified sentence is true if and only every sentence that is the result of the following procedure is true: delete the quantifier, and uniformly replace the variable it binds with a name. Similarly, an existentially quantified sentence is true if and only if some sentence that is the result of this same procedure is true. According to Barcan Marcus, a sentence containing a name can be true regardless of whether that name refers to an object.[48]

The "existential" quantifier so understood—that is, "something"—does not carry with it ontological commitment, contra Quine. When I say that something is a winged horse, I don't commit myself to the existence of a winged horse.

Marcus also claims that we can use the notion of reference to introduce "objectual" senses of the quantifiers[49]: these would correspond to inferentially analogous expressions that bind variables that can be substituted only by names that refer to objects. But these objectual

---

47 Ruth Barcan Macus, "Dispensing with Possibilia," *Proceedings and Addresses of the American Philosophical Association* 49 (1975–1976): 46–47. See also Barcan Marcus, *Modalities*, essay 1, and Ruth Barcan Marcus, "Interpreting Quantification," *Inquiry* 5 (1962), especially 257–259.

48 See Williamson, *Modal Logic*, ch. 2.5 for discussion of Barcan Marcus's appeal to substitutional quantification.

49 Barcan Marcus, "Dispensing with Possibilia," 48–49.

quantifiers are not to be used alongside modal operators like "necessarily" on pain of reintroducing the problem the substitutional interpretation hopes to solve.

7. Kripke

Saul Kripke's *Naming and Necessity* defended a number of theses about modality. One central thesis is that three distinctions that had often been conflated are in fact largely independent of each other: the distinctions between what is a priori knowable and what is knowable only via experience, what is necessary and what is contingent, and between what is analytic and what is synthetic.[50] According to Kripke, there are necessary truths that can only be known via experience, and there are contingent truths that can be discovered a priori.

Part of the motivation for this claim is that ordinary proper names, such as "Kris" or "Sam," are what Kripke calls *rigid designators*.[51] A rigid designator is an expression that refers to an object when used outside the context of a modal operator but also refers to the same object when used within the context of a modal operator. Consider the sentence "Kris is hungry." In this sentence, "Kris" refers to Kris. Now consider the sentence "Possibly, Kris is hungry." The same expression "Kris" appears in this sentence, and it continues to refer to Kris even in this sentence that is prefixed with a modal operator. A similar thing is true of sentences that do not contain modal operators but do contain prefixes such as "In world w": in the sentence "In world w, Kris is hungry," "Kris" still refers to Kris. Kripke expresses this idea by saying that a rigid designator refers to the same individual in every possible world.[52]

---

50 See Saul Kripke, *Naming and Necessity* (Boston: Harvard University Press, 1980), 34–40.
51 Kripke, *Naming and Necessity*, 3, 48–49.
52 Kripke, *Naming and Necessity*, 48.

Kripke claims that true identity sentences containing only rigid designators always express propositions that are necessarily true.[53] Suppose that "Hesperus" and "Phosphorus" are both rigid designators and that the sentence "Hesperus is identical with Phosphorus" is true. Then it is necessarily true that Hesperus is identical with Phosphorus. But this necessary truth couldn't be known a priori; instead, it was an empirical astronomical discovery that Hesperus is Phosphorus (and Venus).[54]

Kripke also argues that natural kind terms, such as "tiger" or "water," are rigid designators.[55] Suppose that "the chemical substance H_2O" is also a rigid designator, and that "water is identical with the chemical substance H_2O" expresses a true proposition. If so, this true proposition is a necessarily true proposition. But we couldn't know a priori that water is identical with the chemical substance H_2O. So, here is a second example of a necessary truth that is knowable only via experience.

But didn't it initially seem that water could have turned out to have been something other than H_2O? And if so, is this intuition that water could have turned out to have been something other than H_2O evidence against Kripke's claim that if two things are identical, they are necessarily identical?[56]

Kripke claims that there is a sense in which it could have turned out that water is not H_2O: it is possible that someone could be in the same epistemic situation as myself and used expressions like "water" and "H_2O" in that situation, but in that situation, those expressions do not refer to the things that we refer to when we use "water" and "H_2O." Two people are in the same epistemic situation when their qualitative

---

53 See Kripke, *Naming and Necessity*, 4, 100. The latter page indicates agreement with Barcan Marcus's claim the identity sentences containing names that are "mere tags" express necessary truths.

54 Kripke, *Naming and Necessity*, 101–102, 109.

55 Kripke, *Naming and Necessity*, 5, 125–135. A similar view was defended earlier by Hilary Putnam, "The Meaning of 'Meaning,'" *Minnesota Studies in the Philosophy of Science* 7 (1975): 215–271.

56 Compare with Kripke, *Naming and Necessity*, 141.

experiences feel exactly the same.[57] So, suppose that in our world a scientist is about to test whether water is H_2O but that in another world, someone is in the same epistemic situation. In both cases, they have a clear fluid in a vial in front of them. The fluids and the vials look the same; the liquid tastes and smells the same; the laboratory looks the same; and so on. If each scientist were to describe how things feel to her, each would give the same description as the other. The qualitative experiences of the scientist in our world—which is the same as those of the scientist in the other world—do not settle whether she is in a world in which the stuff in front of her is water (and hence is something that is necessarily H_2O) or whether it is some other stuff with a different chemical makeup. In this sense, it could have turned out that water is not H_2O, even though it is necessarily true that water is H_2O.

Kripke argues against a kind of type materialism on the basis of these considerations.[58] Kripke argues that "pain" is a rigid designator. Suppose that the neural state that correlates with our experience of pain is the state of C-fibers firing. Suppose that "the state of C-fibers firing" is also a rigid designator. Kripke then considers the view, allegedly popular at the time, according to which although pain is identical with the state of C-fibers firing, this identity is merely a contingent identity. This view is false, given that a true identity sentence containing rigid designators expresses a necessary truth. So, either it is necessary that pain is identical with the state of C-fibers firing, or pain is not identical with the state of C-fibers firing. The former disjunct is wildly counter-intuitive, as is demonstrated by the fact that previous defenders of the identity of pain with the state of C-fibers firing agreed that they are only contingently linked. So, we should conclude pain is not identical with the state of C-fibers firing. Since the state of C-fibers firing was the neural state that correlates with pain, but pain is

---

57 See Kripke, *Naming and Necessity*, 104, 141–143.
58 Kripke, *Naming and Necessity*, 144–150.

not identical with C-fibers firing, pain is not identical with any neural state. And more generally, pain is not identical with any physical state.

Might it be true that pain is necessarily identical with the state of C-fibers firing, but it nonetheless could have turned out to be the case that pain was not identical with the state of C-fibers firing—just as water is necessarily identical with H_2O, but it could have turned out to be the case that water was not H_2O? No.[59] It could have turned out to be the case that pain was not identical to C-fibers firing only if there could be someone in a qualitatively identical situation as I am who has an experience that is qualitatively the same as pain but which is not identical with C-fibers firing. But any experience that is qualitatively the same as pain is an experience of pain! And, if pain is necessarily identical with the state of C-fibers firing, then this person is also having their C-fibers fire. So, it's not true that it could have turned out to be the case that pain was not identical with C-fibers firing if in fact it is identical with C-fibers firing. The intuition that pain and the state of C-fibers firing are only contingently associated cannot be reconciled with the claim that pain is identical with the state of C-fibers firing. And so the latter claim is false.

Let us turn to the claim that there are contingent a priori truths. Part of Kripke's argument for their existence turns on the idea that we can introduce a rigid designator and fix its reference with a definite description without its being part of the meaning of that rigid designator that its referent satisfies that definite description. Here is an example to illustrate this idea. Suppose I say, "Let the next person who enters this room be named 'Fred.'" As it turns out, Sally is the next person who enters the room. I have introduced a name, "Fred," that refers to her. But it is not part of the meaning of the name "Fred" that Fred was the next person who entered the room. This is demonstrated by my being able to truthfully say that although Fred was the person

---

[59] Kripke, *Naming and Necessity*, 150–152.

who next entered the room, it could have been someone else who next entered the room. I would not be able to truthfully utter this sentence if it were part of the meaning of "Fred" that Fred was the next person who entered the room.

Suppose now that I have a metal rod in front of me. The metal rod is of a certain length. This length is an abstract property instantiated by the rod. The expression "the length of this metal rod" is not a rigid designator, since the rod could have been longer or shorter, and had it been longer or shorter, the lengths thereby designated in those situations would be different from the length actually instantiated. But we can use this definite description to fix the reference of a rigid designator of that length.[60] For example, we could say, "Let 'one meter' designate the length of this metal rod." Now consider the claim that this metal rod is one meter in length, and suppose that we entertain this claim immediately as we introduce the term "one meter" in the fashion just described. Kripke claims that we do not need empirical evidence to know that this claim is true. We know it a priori.[61] But it is of course a contingent truth that this metal rod is one meter in length. If it were heated sufficiently, it would not be.[62]

Kripke also asserts further modal claims about objects beyond those that can be directly supported via the apparatus of rigid designation and claims about identity. One such claim is the claim human persons, and other biological organisms, have their origins essentially.[63] For example, Sally had to have originated from the sperm-egg pair that generated her. Her parents could have conceived a child via a different sperm-egg pair, but that child couldn't have been Sally. A second such claim is that artifacts have their original material constitution essentially. Suppose that I have a wooden table in front of me, created by

---

60 See Kripke, *Naming and Necessity*, 55.
61 Kripke, *Naming and Necessity*, 56.
62 Kripke, *Naming and Necessity*, 56.
63 Kripke, *Naming and Necessity*, 112–113.

joining four table legs to a wooden table top. It is not possible, according to Kripke, that this very table could have been originally made of ice instead of wood.[64]

8. Lewis

The high-water mark for modal metaphysics in the 20th century is undoubtably Lewis' masterwork, *On the Plurality of Worlds*, which we will focus on here.[65]

Suppose that what there is consists of spatiotemporally related things and sets that have them as members. What room is there for modal properties? How is it that things could have been otherwise if these two kinds of things exhaust what there is? Earlier, I suggested an answer on behalf of Quine: there is no room for modal properties, and it does not make sense to say that things have to be the way that they are or that they could have been different.

However, Lewis provides a simple and elegant answer to these questions without introducing further ontological categories beyond the two that Quine accepted. Instead, Lewis introduces far more tokens of these categories. Lewis' answer is called *modal realism*.

Say that a *world* is a maximal spatiotemporally related whole: if two things are spatiotemporally related to one another, then they are part of the same world.[66] If this world were the only world, things could not have been different than they are. But according to modal realism, this world is not the only world, but rather every way that a world could be is a way that some world is. There are infinitely many worlds, each just as real as every other. Many of them are much like our own, filled with planets and potholders, people and plants, pleasures and pains.

---

64 Kripke, *Naming and Necessity*, 113–114.
65 David Lewis, *On the Plurality of Worlds* (Oxford: Basil Blackwell, 1986).
66 See Lewis, *On the Plurality of Worlds*, 2.

Each world is a spatiotemporal object rather than an object of a new ontological category.

Worlds do not overlap: an object that is a part of one world is a part of that world only.[67] They are spatially, temporally, and causally disconnected from each other.[68]

Only one of these worlds is actual. But being actual is not a special metaphysical status that one world—our world presumably—has but that others lack. Rather, to be actual is simply to be here in the world that I am in. "Actual" is an indexical term, and its function is to pick out the world that the speaker is in, much like "here" picks out the place the speaker is located in.[69] Were I able to speak with someone in another world, I could truthfully say that I am actual, but so could she, in the same sense in which my mom, who lives in Olympia, Washington, can say that she is here while I, who live in South Bend, Indiana, can say that I am here (and she is there). Those things that are not actual are merely possible.

To be possibly true is to be true at some world; to be necessarily true is to be true at all worlds; to be actually true is to be true at the actual world. There is no primitive notion of possibility or necessity.

Just as there are other worlds than this one, there are other sets beyond those built up ultimately from denizens of our world. For any things that aren't sets, regardless of which world they belong to, there is a set that has exactly those things as members. These sets are not mere oddities or byproducts of Lewis' theory, but rather are the bases for reductions of other putative ontological categories. A property, such as the property of being a dog, is just a set of its actual and possible instances—in this case, it is the set of all the dogs, possible or actual.[70] A proposition is a special kind of property: it is a property

---

67 Lewis, *On the Plurality of Worlds*, 198–209.
68 Lewis, *On the Plurality of Worlds*, 69–80.
69 Lewis, *On the Plurality of Worlds*, 92–93.
70 Lewis, *On the Plurality of Worlds*, 50.

of whole worlds.[71] A proposition just is the set of worlds at which it is true; for example, the proposition that there are dogs is the set whose elements are all and only those possible worlds that have at least one dog as a part.

As noted earlier, each object is a part of exactly one world. How then can it be true that an object could have been different? A *counterpart* of a thing is something similar to that thing in contextually determined relevant respects, which can include similarity of origin. And a thing could have been a certain way if and only if it has a counterpart that is that way.[72] I could have been handsome although I am not, but not by virtue of being a part of a different possible world and being handsome there. Instead, I have a counterpart who can get a date; he's really handsome and in great shape, albeit in a world far from actuality.

Some worlds are closer to the actual world than others. This relation of closeness is itself a relation of similarity. Some worlds are more similar to the actual world than others; those that are more similar are closer to us than those that are not. This notion of similarity does theoretical work as well. Counterfactuals—sentences of the form "If P had been the case, then Q would have been the case"—are analyzed in terms of closeness between worlds. Roughly, a counterfactual is true if and only if the closest world in which P is true is also a world in which Q is true.[73]

Note how many analyses and reductions are doable given this simple base.[74] But what for Lewis is an analysis? One reason why this question matters is for the sake of clarity of what Lewis seeks. Lewis wants an analysis of modality; he is not primarily looking for truth-makers for

---

71 Lewis, *On the Plurality of Worlds*, 53.
72 This theory is called "counterpart theory." See Lewis, *On the Plurality of Worlds*, ch. 4 for an extensive defense of counterpart theory.
73 See Lewis, *On the Plurality of Worlds*, 20–24, as well as David Lewis, *Counterfactuals* (Oxford: Blackwell, 1973).
74 In Lewis, *On the Plurality of Worlds* there are also analyses offered of *intrinsicality, supervenience, verisimilitude*, and many others.

true modal claims, and he is certainly not looking for their grounds—the notion of grounding so prominent today would be decisively rejected by him.[75]

However, surprisingly, Lewis doesn't explicitly explain what analyses are supposed to be at this stage of his philosophical development. There are passages in Lewis in which he indicates sympathy for the project of conceptual analysis, which if done well yields a body of non-obvious analytic truths.[76] Plausibly, the analysis of counterfactual conditionals in terms of possible worlds is an example of a non-obvious conceptual truth. But what about the analysis of possibilities in terms of concrete possible worlds? Such an analysis is not something that can be discerned simply by ordinary language analysis, for no analysis of possibility in terms of truth at a concrete world would be revealed by an investigation of "what ordinary people mean"—but it is also very hard to see how the analysis of possibilities in terms of concrete possible worlds could even be a non-obvious conceptual truth.

Nor is the analysis of possibilities in terms of concrete possible worlds an articulation of the structure of modal facts understood as that which makes modal propositions true—for Lewis denies that there are any facts so construed.[77] What about propositions? On Lewis' seemingly preferred and most straightforward account of propositions, propositions are merely sets of worlds and hence have no articulatable structure to discern.[78]

---

75 See David Lewis, *Philosophical Letters of David K. Lewis*, vol. 1: *Causation, Modality, Ontology*, ed. Helen Beebee and A. R. J. Fisher (Oxford: Oxford University Press, 2020), 71, 575 for expressions of qualms about notions of priority. Fraser MacBride and Frederique Jannsen-Lauret, "Why Lewis Would Have Rejected Grounding," in *Perspectives on the Philosophy of David K. Lewis*, ed. Helen Beebee and A. R. J. Fisher (Oxford University Press, 2022) persuasively explain why Lewis would have rejected grounding.

76 See Lewis (1989: 129). See MacBride and Jannsen-Lauret, "Why Lewis Would Have Rejected Grounding," 71–73 for discussion of Lewis on non-obvious conceptual truths.

77 See David Lewis, "Forget about the 'Correspondence Theory of Truth,'" *Analysis* 61 (2001): 275–280. Lewis will happily endorse facts construed as true propositions. See also MacBride and Jannsen-Lauret, "Why Lewis Would Have Rejected Grounding," 79–83 for discussion of Lewis's rejection of facts understood as truth-makers.

78 See Lewis, *On the Plurality of Worlds*, 53–55.

Let me offer another Lewisian answer to the question of what, metaphysically speaking, an analysis is: it is a property identification between a property expressed via an ordinary language predicate and a property expressed in a metaphysically regimented language.[79] A metaphysically regimented language is one in which every undefined predicate stands for what Lewis calls *perfectly natural* properties and relations, which for Lewis are those properties and relations that collectively provide a minimal supervenience base for every other property and relation, and which account for objective similarity between things, and which typically figure in fundamental laws of nature.[80] In this regimented language, all other predicates are explicitly defined in terms of the undefined predicates. In Lewis's regimented language, there will most likely be undefined predicates for parthood or spatiotemporal distance, but the predicates for modal properties will be explicitly defined. In this way, an analysis of a phenomenon thereby shows not only that the phenomenon is not fundamental, but it also shows how close to being fundamental it is.

We noted that modal realism makes possible a variety of analyses. This fact is largely why we should believe modal realism, according to Lewis. We should believe it not because we have an intellectual insight into its truth, or because we have at hand an indispensability argument that tells us that we must believe it, but rather because it is a serviceable view: we should believe in modal realism because our theoretical life is easier if modal realism is true.[81] The project of offering analyses presupposes the accuracy of our pre-theoretical modal beliefs, but these beliefs are not justified by intuitions of modal entities, whether they be possible objects, properties, or facts, but rather because in general, our antecedent pre-theoretical beliefs are to be maintained and

---

79 Compare with Lewis, "Forget about the 'Correspondence Theory of Truth,'" 61.
80 See Lewis, *On the Plurality of Worlds*, 60–69.
81 See Lewis, *On the Plurality of Worlds*, vii, 3–5.

respected to the extent that there are no countervailing pressures to reject them. Despite Lewis's return to the grand metaphysical theorizing of an earlier time, his meta-philosophy is largely part of the pragmatic tradition so characteristic of early 20th-century American philosophy.[82]

---

82 I thank Daniel Nolan and Ross Cameron for helpful comments on earlier versions of this paper.

Reflection

VACUISM AND THE STRANGENESS OF IMPOSSIBILITY

Rohan French

Consider the following two sentences:

1. If Sally were to square the circle, we would be surprised.
2. If Sally were to square the circle, we would not be surprised.

These two sentences are both examples of counterfactual conditionals with impossible antecedents (henceforth 'counterpossible conditionals'). According to the orthodox semantics for counterfactuals due to Lewis and Stalnaker,[1] among others, what is required for a sentence like (1) to be true is for the most similar possible worlds to the actual world in which the antecedent is true (in this case, worlds in which Sally squared the circle), to be worlds in which the consequent is true (in this case, worlds in which we are surprised). According to these theories, because the antecedents of (1) and (2) are impossible, and thus true at no possible worlds, sentences (1) and (2) both come out vacuously true, as in all the possible worlds in which their antecedent is true (i.e., none of them), their consequent is also true.

---

[1] David Lewis, *Counterfactuals* (Oxford: Blackwell, 1973); Robert C. Stalnaker, "A Theory of Conditionals," in *Studies in Logical Theory*, ed. N. Rescher (Oxford: Blackwell, 1968), 98–112.

These are *vacuist* theories of counterpossible conditionals—theories according to which all counterpossibles are vacuously true.

Surely (1) is true and (2) is false, though! After all, if Sally had squared the circle she would have done something which is mathematically impossible, which is surely cause for surprise if anything is! According to *nonvacuist* theories of counterpossibles, conditionals like (1) and (2) have non-trivial truth conditions. Typically this is achieved by enriching the orthodox semantics by considering not only the most similar possible worlds where the antecedent is true, but instead considering the most similar possible *and impossible* worlds where the antecedent is true (as in Nolan, for example).[2] So in this case the nonvacuist will say that (1) is true because the most similar worlds, in this case impossible worlds, where Sally squares the circle, are worlds where we are surprised, and (2) is false because in these most similar worlds in which Sally squares the circle it is not the case that we are not surprised.

By incorporating possible as well as impossible worlds into their semantics nonvacuist theories are able to express a range of fine-grained distinctions between impossibilities, and it is this which allows them to count (1) as true and (2) as false. This results in nonvacuist logics invalidating a range of valid-seeming inferences involving counterfactuals, depriving them of the most natural way of explaining the felt correctness of these inferences by having them come out logically valid like the vacuist can. As a result vacuists have charged nonvacuists with being committed to a counterfactual logic which is too weak, and that as a result they are unable to explain why those inferences are good inferences.[3] For example, one of the most basic inference patterns involving counterfactuals involves the drawing out of deductive consequences in the scope

---

2 Daniel Nolan, "Impossible Worlds: A Modest Approach," *Notre Dame Journal of Formal Logic* 38 (1997): 535–572.

3 Cf. Timothy Williamson, *The Philosophy of Philosophy* (Oxford: Oxford University Press, 2007), 174.

of counterfactual suppositions. This pattern is captured by the rule CLOSURE below—informally, if A has B as a deductive consequence then for any sentence C, 'If it were that C, then it would be that A' has 'If it were that C, then it would be that B' as a deductive consequence. By classical logic "$2 + 2 = 4$ and it's not the case that $2 + 2 = 4$" has anything as a deductive consequence (this is the truth-functional inference principle *ex falso quodlibet*), and so 'we would not be surprised' as a consequence, and so, writing X for our sentence "$2 + 2 = 4$ and it is not the case that $2 + 2 = 4$," CLOSURE then gives us that 'If it were that X, then it would be that X' has 'If it were that X, then we would not be surprised' as a deductive consequence. But it's highly plausible that 'If it were that X, then it would be that X' is an instance of a theorem of counterfactual logic even by nonvacuist lights, while 'If it were that X, then we would not be surprised' seems to fall afoul of similar issues to (2). So plausibly nonvacuists will need to give up principles like CLOSURE. Given that most of our use of counterfactuals does not involve counterpossibles on the face of it this seems to be a great cost to the nonvacuist.

How should the nonvacuist react to this situation? The common reaction is to put forward principles that 'tame' impossibility.[4] For example, the nonvacuist will point out that we only explicitly consider impossible situations when they are explicitly called for. So, for example, when I evaluate non-counterpossible conditionals like 'If Kangaroos were to not have tails, then they would fall over,' I don't consider situations in which Kangaroos are inconsistent objects which both have and don't have tails. This line of thought

---

[4] The suggestion offered here is a further elaboration of the general point made in section 3.1 of F. Berto, R. French, G. Priest, and D. Ripley, "Williamson on Counterpossibles," *Journal of Philosophical Logic* 47 (2018): 693–713 and section 12.3 of F. Berto and M. Jago, *Impossible Worlds* (Oxford: Oxford University Press, 2013), the present argument making more explicit the manner in which we are able to recover the inferences validated by vacuist theories. See also E. D. Mares, "Who's Afraid of Impossible Worlds?," *Notre Dame Journal of Formal Logic* 38 (1997): 516–526, Theorem 6.3 of which is especially relevant.

motivates a constraint on similarity called in Nolan "The Strangeness of Impossibility":[5]

Strangeness of Impossibility: Possible worlds are more similar to the actual world than any impossible world is to the actual world.

Adapting the semantics given above, this means that to determine whether a conditional like 'If Kangaroos were to not have tails, then they would fall over' is true we consider the most similar worlds to the actual world, both possible and impossible, where the antecedent is true (i.e., worlds where Kangaroos don't have tails) and see whether the consequent is true there (i.e., whether there are worlds where Kangaroos fall over). On the (quite reasonable) assumption that it is metaphysically possible that Kangaroos don't have tails, the Strangeness of Impossibility tells us that the most similar worlds to the actual world where this is true must be possible worlds. This seems to point the way toward an account of how it is that the inferences which nonvacuists regard as strictly speaking invalid are nonetheless rationally compelling. What I will show here is a very clear and precise way in which this happens at the level of logic, allowing us to largely bypass contentious issues concerning the correct formal semantics for counterfactuals. In particular we will show how a very simple and natural nonvacuist logic can, in a certain sense, mimic a natural minimal vacuist logic modeled on the favored minimal logic for counterfactuals given in the appendix of Williamson's *The Philosophy of Philosophy*.

***

---

[5] Nolan notes that he is "hesitant to endorse" ("Impossible Worlds," 566) the Strangeness of Impossibility in light of potential counterexamples to the principle (see 551, 569). D. Vander Laan, "Counterpossibles and Similarity," in *Lewisian Themes: The Philosophy of David K. Lewis*, ed. F. Jackson and G. Priest (Oxford: Oxford University Press, 2004), 271 also gives another notable potential counterexample. We think that reasoning broadly along the lines given in Berto and Jago (Impossible Worlds, 274) can defuse all of these putative counterexamples, though, and so we dwell on them no further, instead expanding on the positive case for the Strangeness of Impossibility.

Our formal language $\mathcal{L}$ will consist of denumerably many sentential variables $p_1, p_2, p_3, \ldots$, along with the unary connective '$\neg$' (negation), '$\Diamond$' (possibility), '$\Box$' (necessity), and the binary connectives '$\rightarrow$' (the material conditional), and '$>$' (the counterfactual conditional). The connectives $\wedge, \vee,$ and $\leftrightarrow$ are taken as defined out of these in the usual way. Throughout we will use uppercase Roman letters as schematic variables over arbitrary formulas of the language. We will consider as our prototypical vacuist counterfactual logic a slight variant on Williamson's minimal counterfactual logic, defined as follows, letting $\vdash_{\text{Vac}}$ indicate theoremhood in our vacuist logic.[6]

K   If A is theorem of the modal logic K, then $\vdash_{\text{Vac}} A$

MODUS PONENS   If $\vdash_{\text{Vac}} A$ and $\vdash_{\text{Vac}} A \rightarrow B$, then $\vdash_{\text{Vac}} B$

NECESSITATION   If $\vdash_{\text{Vac}} A$, then $\vdash_{\text{Vac}} \Box A$

IDENTITY $\vdash_{\text{Vac}} A > A$

VACUITY $\vdash_{\text{Vac}} \Box B \rightarrow (A > B)$

CLOSURE   If $\vdash_{\text{Vac}} (B_1 \wedge \ldots \wedge B_n) \rightarrow A$, then
$$\vdash_{\text{Vac}} (C > B_1 \wedge \ldots \wedge C > B_n) \rightarrow (C > A)$$

EQUIVALENCE   If $\vdash_{\text{Vac}} C \leftrightarrow C^*$, then $\vdash_{\text{Vac}} (C > A) \leftrightarrow (C^* > A)$

To see that this is a vacuist logic for counterfactuals, we will show that $\vdash_{\text{Vac}} \neg \Diamond A \rightarrow (A > B)$—that it is a logical truth of Vac that all impossible propositions entail all counterfactuals with that proposition as their antecedent, regardless of their consequent.

---

[6] In what follows we presume some familiarity with classical truth-functional logic and propositional modal logic. For more on modal logic the interested reader should consult the excellent B. Chellas, *Modal Logic: An Introduction* (Cambridge: Cambridge University Press, 1980) and G. Hughes and M. J. Cresswell, *A New Introduction to Modal Logic* (London: Routledge, 1996). Note that Appendix 1 of Williamson, *The Philosophy of Philosophy* is concerned with investigating the definition of the modal operators in terms of the counterfactual conditional, and so in place of our VACUITY he has $(\neg A > A) \rightarrow (A > B)$, where $(\neg A > A)$ is one of his candidate definitions of '$\Box$' in terms of '$>$'.

(1) $\neg \Diamond A \to \Box(A \to B)$ K

(2) $\Box(A \to B) \to (A > (A \to B))$ VACUITY

(3) $\neg \Diamond A \to (A > (A \to B))$ 1,2, K, MODUS PONENS

(4) $((A \to B) \land A) \to B$ K

(5) $((A > (A \to B)) \land (A > A)) \to (A > B)$ 4, CLOSURE

(6) $(A > (A \to B)) \to (A > B)$ 5, IDENTITY, K, MODUS PONENS

(7) $\neg \Diamond A \to (A > B)$ 3,6, K, MODUS PONENS

***

As we saw above, if we assume the Strangeness of Impossibility principles, such as CLOSURE and EQUIVALENCE, have a number of instances which are safe for the nonvacuist, namely those instances where the antecedents of counterfactuals involved are possible—the Strangeness of Impossibility having as a consequence that in such cases we only need to consider possible worlds and so in such special cases things will proceed just as the vacuist claims they should in all cases. This motivates the following rules, where $\vdash_{\text{NVac}}$ indicates theoremhood in the Strangeness of Impossibility endorsing nonvacuist's logic:

- $\Diamond$-CLOSURE: If $\vdash_{\text{NVac}} (B_1 \land \ldots \land B_n) \to A$, then
  $$\vdash_{\text{NVac}} \Diamond C \to ((C > B_1 \land \ldots \land C > B_n) \to (C > A))$$

- $\Diamond$-EQUIVALENCE: If $\vdash_{\text{NVac}} C \leftrightarrow C^*$, then
  $$\vdash_{\text{NVac}} \Diamond C \to ((C > A) \leftrightarrow (C^* > A))$$

Furthermore, the sentence characteristic of the Strangeness of Impossibility itself corresponds to the safe version of VACUITY:

- SIC: $\vdash_{\text{NVac}} \Diamond A \to (\Box B \to (A > B))$

Note that it is this principle which semantically corresponds (in the sense of van Benthem)[7] to the Strangeness of Impossibility (as was pointed out in French et al.)[8] and not the principle $(A > B) \rightarrow (\Diamond A \rightarrow \Diamond B)$ as was claimed in Williamson,[9] and strongly implied in Berto et al.[10]

Combining these with the parts of Vac which are unobjectionable to the nonvacuist we get the logic $\vdash_{NVac}$, which is defined as follows:

K — If A is theorem of the modal logic K, then $\vdash_{NVac} A$

MODUS PONENS — If $\vdash_{NVac} A$ and $\vdash_{NVac} A \rightarrow B$, then $\vdash_{NVac} B$

NECESSITATION — If $\vdash_{NVac} A$, then $\vdash_{NVac} \Box A$

IDENTITY — $\vdash_{NVac} A > A$

SIC — $\vdash_{NVac} \Diamond A \rightarrow (\Box B \rightarrow (A > B))$

$\Diamond$-CLOSURE — If $\vdash_{NVac} (B_1 \wedge \ldots \wedge B_n) \rightarrow A$, then

$\vdash_{NVac} \Diamond C \rightarrow ((C > B_1 \wedge \ldots \wedge C > B_n) \rightarrow (C > A))$

$\Diamond$-EQUIVALENCE — If $\vdash_{NVac} C \leftrightarrow C'$, then $\vdash_{NVac} \Diamond C \rightarrow ((C > A) \leftrightarrow (C' > A))$

Importantly NVac does not validate $\neg \Diamond A \rightarrow (A > B)$. To see this we can use a toy model from French et al.[11] which consists of only two worlds, a possible world x and a single impossible

---

7 J. van Benthem, "Correspondence Theory," In *Handbook of Philosophical Logic*, ed. D. Gabbay and F. Guenthner, Synthese Library, vol. 165 (Dordrecht: Springer, 1984), 167–247.

8 R. French, P. Girard, and D. Ripley, "Classical Counterpossibles," *Review of Symbolic Logic* 15 (2022): 265.

9 Timothy Williamson, "Counterpossibles in Semantics and Metaphysics," *Argumenta* 2 (2017): 200.

10 Berto et al., "Williamson on Counterpossibles," 667. In the setting of Nolan, "Impossible Worlds," which Williamson explicitly mentions, this principle corresponds not to the Strangeness of Impossibility, but to what Nolan calls *The Lesser Strangeness of Impossibility*, which informally states that "no impossible world is less distant than any possible world" (566).

11 French, Girard, and Ripley, "Classical Counterpossibles," 268.

world y where, approximately speaking, the most similar world to our possible world is that possible world itself, and so for a counterfactual $A > B$ with a possible antecedent (i.e. one where A is true at our sole possible world x) to be true at x we must have B true at x also. Our logic NVac is essentially the logic dubbed Successful-Quasi-Vacuism in French et al., restricted to the present language,[12] and as a result every theorem of $\vdash_{\text{NVac}}$ is true at x in the model for Successful-Quasi-Vacuism given there. As noted there $\neg \Diamond A \rightarrow (A > B)$ can be made false in such a model, for suppose A is true at our impossible world only, and B is true nowhere. Then we have $\neg \Diamond A$ true at x, but $A > B$ false, as the nearest A-world (our impossible world y) fails to be a B-world. So as $\neg \Diamond A \rightarrow (A > B)$ is not true in that model at x, while every theorem of $\vdash_{\text{NVac}}$ is, it follows that $\neg \Diamond A \rightarrow (A > B)$ is not a theorem of $\vdash_{\text{NVac}}$—the logic $\vdash_{\text{NVac}}$ is properly nonvacuist.

One thing which is important to note at this point, which we will need to appeal to in a moment, is the fact that $\vdash_{\text{NVac}} \subseteq \vdash_{\text{Vac}}$, as all the axioms of NVac are either axioms of Vac or the truth-functional weakenings of axioms of Vac, and anything which follows from theorems of NVac by ◊-CLOSURE or ◊-EQUIVALENCE also follows from CLOSURE or EQUIVALENCE along with truth-functional reasoning in K.

***

Recall now the motivating idea behind the Strangeness of Impossibility, namely that we only consider impossibilities when evaluating counterfactuals when impossibilities are explicitly involved. If they accept the Strangeness of Impossibility, and consequently a logic like NVac, the nonvacuist is in a position to understand vacuist talk as being correct, but about a subtly

---

12 The rules ◊-CLOSURE and ◊-EQUIVALENCE are not covered there, but are easily seen to preserve truth at x in that model.

different subject matter—the nonvacuist is able to agree with the vacuist if they reinterpret their talk of counterfactual conditionals as talk of counterfactual conditionals conditional on the possibility of their antecedent. So, for example, the nonvacuist can understand the vacuists' (by their lights, incorrect) claim that (2) is true, as the (by their lights, correct) claim that (3) is true:[13]

> 3. Either it is impossible for Sally to square the circle, or if Sally were to square the circle, we would not be surprised.

Put more formally we are able to translate between vacuist theories and appropriate SIC-endorsing nonvacuist theories using the following translation t which maps formulas of $\mathcal{L}$ to formulas of $\mathcal{L}$.

$$t(p) = p$$
$$t(\neg A) = \neg t(A)$$
$$t(A \to B) = t(A) \to t(B)$$
$$t(\Diamond A) = \Diamond t(A)$$
$$t(\Box A) = \Box t(A)$$
$$t(A > B) = \Diamond t(A) \to (t(A) > t(B))$$

It is easy to show by induction on length of derivations that if $\vdash_{\text{Vac}} A$ then $\vdash_{\text{NVac}} t(A)$. For the basis case the only interesting cases

---

[13] The argument pursued here is reminiscent of one used by Nathan Salmon, "The Logic of What Might Have Been," *Philosophical Review* 98 (1989): 3–34 in the course of arguing against the correctness of the modal logic S5 as the correct logic for metaphysical necessity. Salmon argues that the strongest acceptable logic for metaphysical necessity is the weak modal logic KT, and that philosophers advocating for S5 conflate 'possibility' and 'necessity' with 'actual possibility' and 'actual necessity'. This is made precise by Timothy Williamson, "Iterated Attitudes," *Proceedings of the British Academy* 95 (1998): 98f. in the form of the following translation result: A is a theorem of S5 then its translation $\tau(A)$ is a theorem of the logic KT@S (KT enriched with a rigidifying actuality operator '@') where $\tau(\Diamond A) = @\Diamond \tau(A)$, and similarly for $\Box$.

are when A is an instance of IDENTITY or VACUITY, in which case we have $\vdash_{\text{NVac}} t(A)$ by IDENTITY and truth-functional reasoning in K, or SIC and truth-functional reasoning in K respectively. For the induction step, suppose that for formulas B with derivations of length $< n$ in $\vdash_{\text{Vac}}$ we have $\vdash_{\text{NVac}} t(B)$, and suppose (for example) that the next inference applied is CLOSURE. Then we have $\vdash_{\text{Vac}} (B_1 \wedge \ldots \wedge B_n) \to A$ and so by our induction hypothesis $\vdash_{\text{NVac}} t((B_1 \wedge \ldots \wedge B_n) \to A)$, i.e. $\vdash_{\text{NVac}} (t(B_1) \wedge \ldots \wedge t(B_n)) \to t(A)$. Then by $\Diamond$-CLOSURE we have

$$\vdash_{\text{NVac}} \Diamond t(C) \to ((t(C) > t(B_1) \wedge \ldots \wedge t(C) > t(B_n)) \to (t(C) > t(A)))$$

But truth-functional logic, and hence K, contains all instances of the formula $A \to (B \to C) \to ((A \to B) \to (A \to C))$, and so K and Modus Ponens applied to the above yields:

$$\vdash_{\text{NVac}} \Diamond t(C) \to (t(C) > t(B_1) \wedge \ldots \wedge t(C) > t(B_n))$$
$$\to \Diamond t(C) \to (t(C) > t(A)).$$

Making use of the truth-functional tautology $(A \to (B \wedge C)) \leftrightarrow ((A \to B) \wedge (A \to C))$ and Modus Ponens applied to the above then gives:

$$\vdash_{\text{NVac}} (\Diamond t(C) \to (t(C) > t(B_1)) \wedge \ldots \wedge \Diamond t(C) \to (t(C) > t(B_n)))$$
$$\to (\Diamond t(C) \to (t(C) > t(A))),$$

which is to say, $\vdash_{\text{NVac}} t((C > B_1 \wedge \ldots \wedge C > B_n) \to (C > A))$.

Moreover, the theorems of Vac are *precisely* the theorems of NVac of the form $t(\cdot)$. To see this first note that we can prove by induction on the complexity of A that $\vdash_{\text{Vac}} A \leftrightarrow t(A)$. For the case where A is of the form $B > C$. we make use of the fact that $\vdash_{\text{Vac}} (\Diamond A \rightarrow (A > B)) \rightarrow (A > B)$, this following from the provability of $\neg \Diamond A \rightarrow (A > B)$ (shown above) and the truth-functional tautology $(\neg A \rightarrow C) \rightarrow ((A \rightarrow C) \rightarrow C)$, the other direction of the equivalence being a truth-functional tautology. Now, suppose that $\vdash_{\text{NVac}} t(A)$. Then as $\vdash_{\text{NVac}} \subseteq \vdash_{\text{Vac}}$ we also have $\vdash_{\text{Vac}} t(A)$ and so by truth-functional reasoning and the fact that $\vdash_{\text{Vac}} A \leftrightarrow t(A)$ we have $\vdash_{\text{Vac}} A$ as desired.

***

Accepting the Strangeness of Impossibility allows the nonvacuist to reply to the complaint that they cannot explain the correctness of inferences involving counterfactuals. Whenever the vacuist claims that a given inference is valid the nonvacuist translation of that inference will also be valid. In many contexts that will amount to that inference being truth-preserving if it's clear in that context that the antecedents of the conditionals are possible. This is, I think, the clearest positive argument in favor of the Strangeness of Impossibility.

CHAPTER 9

Modality and Essence in Contemporary Metaphysics

Kathrin Koslicki

1. INTRODUCTION

Essentialists hold that at least a certain range of entities can be meaningfully said to have natures, essences, or essential features independently of how these entities are described, conceptualized, or otherwise placed with respect to our specifically human interests, purposes, or activities. For quite some time, it was common among contemporary metaphysicians to regard essence as a modal notion: an essential truth, on this conception, is a modal truth of a certain kind (viz., one that is both necessary and *de re*, i.e., about a certain entity); and an essential property is a feature an entity has necessarily, if it is to exist. The essential truths, according to this approach, are thus a subset of the necessary truths; and the essential properties of entities are included among their necessary properties.

All this changed, however, with Kit Fine's pioneering work on essence in the 1990s. In this body of work, Fine mounts a sizable attack on the modal conception of essence and advances an alternative non-modal approach which brings us closer again to an older Aristotelian notion of essence. According to Fine, a statement of the essence is a non-modal truth which gives a *real definition* of an entity or a plurality of entities; that is, it specifies *what it is to be* the entity or entities in question in a special definitional sense. The *de re* necessary truths, on this approach, are thought to follow in some way from the essential truths; and *de re* necessary features of objects, traditionally known as the "propria" or "necessary accidents," similarly are conceived of as in some way derivative from the essential features of objects. Thus, the explanatory direction, according to Fine, is reversed: rather than *being explained by* modality, the non-modalist holds that essence *explains* modality.

This chapter begins, in Section 2, with a brief summary of Fine's challenge to the modal account, which centers on a series of frequently discussed alleged counterexamples. Section 3 considers a recent attempt by "sparse modalists" like Sam Cowling and Nathan Wildman to respond to Fine's counterexamples by adding a sparseness constraint to the "bare" modal account of essence. Section 4 examines whether, and how, Fine's definitional approach can avoid his own counterexamples to the modal approach to essence. Section 5 concludes this chapter with some final thoughts concerning the theoretical roles ascribed to essence by modalists and non-modalists.

2. Fine's Counterexamples to the Modal Account of Essence

In his seminal paper, "Essence and Modality," Kit Fine distinguishes two types of approaches to essence. According to the first, essence is conceived of "on the model of definition," and in particular *real* (or *objectual*) definition, as opposed to *nominal* (or *verbal*) definition. The definitional approach, as Fine describes it, holds that:

> [J]ust as we may define a word, or say what it means, so we may define an object, or say what it is. The concept of essence has then [been] taken to reside in the "real" or objectual cases of definition, as opposed to the "nominal" or verbal cases.[1]

Thus, according to the definitional approach, the essence of an entity "resides" in its real definition and to define an entity (i.e., to state its essence) is to say what it is.

According to the second approach, essence is conceived of in modal terms. This approach, as Fine puts it, supposes that

> the notion of necessity may relate either to propositions or to objects—that not only may a proposition be said to be necessary, but also an object may be said to be necessarily a certain way. The concept of essence has then been located in the "de re," as opposed to the "de dicto," cases of modal attribution.[2]

According to the modal account, to state the essence of an entity is to say what holds of the entity necessarily. As Fine points out, the modal account can be formulated in different ways, unconditionally or conditionally, and even the conditional modal account has different variants, depending on whether the necessity of a property is relativized to the existence or the identity of its bearer. According to the unconditional modal account, to state the essence of an entity is to say what holds of the entity necessarily simpliciter. According to the conditional modal account, to state the essence of an entity is to say what holds of the entity necessarily, if it is to exist or if it is to be identical to that very

---

[1] Kit Fine, "Essence and Modality," *Philosophical Perspectives* 8 (1994): 2.
[2] Fine, "Essence and Modality," 2.

entity. Assuming, as Fine does, that the modal approach conceives of essences in terms of properties (or collections thereof), we arrive at the following characterization of a property's being essential to an entity, where (M) states the unconditional modal characterization, while (ME) and (MI) state the conditional modal characterization, relativized to existence and identity, respectively:

(M) A property F is essential to an entity x iff necessarily x has F.
(ME) A property F is essential to an entity x iff necessarily, if x exists, x has F.
(MI) A property F is essential to an entity x iff necessarily, if x= x, x has F.

Since the differences between these formulations will not concern us here, I will typically have in mind the existentially relativized variant of the modal account in what follows, since this formulation is most commonly adopted in the literature. Given (ME), and assuming that the essence of an entity can be identified with the collection of its essential properties, we can state the modal account of essence as follows:

(MAE) E is the essence of an entity x iff E is the collection of properties x has necessarily, if x exists.[3]

As is well-known, Fine goes on to adopt the definitional conception of essence and urges us to resist the contemporary assimilation of essence to modality:

My point,rather, is that the notion of essence which is of central importance to the metaphysics of identity is not to be understood in

---

[3] It is not necessary, however, that the modal account of essence be formulated in terms of properties; for instead of saying that a property F is essential to an entity, x, we can also say that x is essentially F, where "F" is being used predicatively.

modal terms or even to be regarded as extensionally equivalent to a modal notion. The one notion is, if I am right, a highly refined version of the other; it is like a sieve which performs a similar function but with a much finer mesh.[4]

The arguments Fine presents are by now quite familiar and feature a number of alleged counterexamples which are intended to call into question the sufficiency of the modal account of essence, while leaving intact its necessity, which Fine accepts. In particular, so Fine argues, the modal account of essence incorrectly classifies the following properties as essential to a particular entity, viz., Socrates, when intuitively (in Fine's view) they should not be so classified:

(i) the property of being a member of Socrates' singleton set;
(ii) the property of being distinct from the Eiffel Tower (or from any other entity whose nature is disconnected from Socrates' nature);
(iii) the property of being such that there are infinitely many prime numbers (where any other necessary truth may be substituted for "there are infinitely many prime numbers");
(iv) the property of being such that the Eiffel Tower is spatiotemporally continuous (where any other essential truth concerning an entity whose nature is disconnected from Socrates' nature may be substituted for "the Eiffel Tower is spatiotemporally continuous"); and
(v) the property of existing.

In each case, the property in question holds of Socrates necessarily, assuming that Socrates exists, but it is implausible to think (so Fine reasons) that the property in question has any bearing on what Socrates

---

4 Fine, "Essence and Modality," 3.

is, i.e., his essence or nature. After running through a series of proposed fixes to the modal account, Fine concludes that it is unlikely that a modified formulation of the modal account could be found which would avoid his alleged counterexamples. For, in Fine's view, the modal account suffers from an underlying difficulty which is fundamental, namely its inability to reflect the sensitivity of essentialist claims to the source of their truth or falsity, viz., the identity of the entity or entities whose nature or essence is under consideration.[5]

3. Responses to Fine's Counterexamples: Sparse Modalism

Nevertheless, Fine's discussion has spawned a considerable literature which attempts to develop precisely the strategy whose chances of success Fine estimated to be low: the strategy of formulating modified versions of the modal account which are designed specifically to avoid Fine's counterexamples. In this vein, for example, Sam Cowling and Nathan Wildman have put forward versions of modalism which supplement (MAE) with a sparseness constraint on properties, while David Denby proposes to amend (MAE) with an intrinsicality constraint on properties. Below, I briefly consider the sparse modalist response and argue, with Fine, that the strategy of adding a "patch" to (MAE) that is designed specifically to avoid the alleged counterexamples cited in (i)–(v) is unlikely to succeed.[6]

---

[5] Concerning his use of the terms "essence," "identity," and "nature," Fine writes: "In general, I shall use the terms 'essence' and 'identity' (and sometimes 'nature' as well) to convey the same underlying idea." Kit Fine, "Senses of Essence," in *Modality, Morality, and Belief: Essays in Honor of Ruth Barcan Marcus*, ed. Walter Sinnott-Armstrong, Diana Raffman, and Nicholas Asher (New York: Cambridge University Press, 1995), 69, n. 2. Regarding his use of the term "definition," Fine remarks: "definitions, either nominal or real, might plausibly be taken to correspond to statements of essence." Kit Fine, "Unified Foundations for Essence and Ground," *Journal of the American Philosophical Association* 1, no. 2 (Summer 2015): 308.

[6] Sam Cowling, "The Modal View of Essence," *Canadian Journal of Philosophy* 43 (2013): 248–266; Nathan Wildman, "Modality, Sparsity, and Essence," *Philosophical Quarterly* 63, no. 253 (October 2013): 760–782, "How (Not) to Be a Modalist about Essence," in *Reality Making*, ed. Mark Jago

In "The Modal View of Essence," Sam Cowling formulates the following two-pronged response to Fine's challenges on behalf of the modalist. Concerning (v), the property of existing, Cowling holds that modalists should recognize a distinction between necessary existence and essential existence: necessary existence can only be ascribed to entities, such as God or, possibly, numbers, which exist in all possible worlds if they exist at all, whereas essential existence can be ascribed to entities, such as Socrates, which exist in only some but not all worlds. Even though we may initially find it surprising to attribute essential existence to a contingent being like Socrates, so Cowling argues, all that is needed to overcome this reaction is some retraining on our part: for, given (ME), to say of Socrates that he has the property of existing essentially amounts to nothing more than to say of Socrates that he necessarily exists, if he exists, which of course sounds quite unobjectionable in its triviality.[7] Therefore, so Cowling reasons, the property of existing, when properly interpreted, does not present modalists with a genuine counterexample to their account.

Concerning the properties cited in (i)–(iv), however, Cowling recommends a different strategy. With respect to these cases, which in his view do genuinely make trouble for the unmodified modal account,

---

(Oxford: Oxford University Press, 2016), 177–196, and "Against the Reduction of Modality to Essence," *Synthese* 198 (Suppl 6) (2021): 1455–1471; and David Denby, "Essence and Intrinsicality," in *Companion to Intrinsic Properties*, ed. R. Francescotti (Berlin: De Gruyter, 2014), 87–109. For other modalist responses, see, for example, Gaétan Bovey, "Essence, Modality, and Intrinsicality," *Synthese* 198 (2021): 7715–7737; Berit Brogaard and Joe Salerno, "A Counterfactual Account of Essence," ed. Jon Williamson, *The Reasoner* 1 (2007): 4–5 and "Remarks on Counterpossibles," *Synthese* 190 (2013): 639–660; Fabrice Correia, "(Finean) Essence and (Priorean) Modality," *Dialectica* 61 (2007): 63–84; Michael della Rocca, "Essentialism: Part 1," *Philosophical Books* 37 (1996): 1–20 and "Essentialism: Part 2," *Philosophical Books* 37 (1996): 81–89; Thiago Xavier de Melo, "Essence and Naturalness," *Philosophical Quarterly* 69/276 (2019): 534–554; Jonathan Livingstone-Banks, "In Defence of Modal Essentialism," *Inquiry* 60 (2017): 816–838; and Edward Zalta, "Essence and Modality," *Mind* 115 (2006): 659–693. For critical discussion, see, for example, Kit Fine, "Response to Fabrice Correia," *Dialectica* 61 (2007): 85–88; Alexander Skiles, "Essence in Abundance" *Canadian Journal of Philosophy* 45 (2015): 100–112; Alessandro Torza, "Speaking of Essence," *Philosophical Quarterly* 65 (2015): 754–771; and Justin Zylstra, "Essence, Necessity, and Definition," *Philosophical Studies* 176 (2019): 339–350.

7 Cowling, "The Modal View," 250.

Cowling advocates supplementing (MAE) with a sparseness constraint on properties. As a defender of the modal account, Cowling takes the essential properties of an entity to be just those properties the entity has necessarily, if it exists; or (using the possible worlds construal of the modal account, as Cowling does) those properties the entity has in every possible world in which it exists. In addition, however, Cowling adopts a conception of an entity's *nature* that is distinct from the entity's merely modal *essence*. According to his "Sparse Essence View of Natures" (SEN), a property, F, is part of the nature of an entity, x, just in case F is instantiated by x in every world in which x exists; and F is a sparse property.[8] (SEN) thus identifies an entity's nature with the intersection of its essential (i.e., necessary) and sparse properties. Although Cowling himself does not give a positive account of sparseness, he characterizes the sparse properties at least roughly as those which "figure into the causal-nomic joints of the world and ground relations of resemblance between things"; in contrast, he takes the merely abundant properties to be those which "play no significant role in the workings of nature; they are shared by gerrymandered collections of things."[9] As for the particulars of how to understand the notion of sparseness, Cowling holds that "several views are available, none of which we are forced to settle on here."[10] He cites the notion of naturalness advanced by David Lewis in "New Work for a Theory of Universals" and *On the Plurality of Worlds* and the conception of sparseness proposed by Jonathan Schaffer in "Two Conceptions of Sparse Properties" as possible contenders for approaches to sparseness which could be substituted into (SEN).

As Cowling himself notes, however, the strength and plausibility of (SEN) as a response to Fine's challenges to (MAE) depends crucially on the details of how a particular account of sparseness is developed. Suppose, for example, that sparseness is construed in terms

---

8 Cowling, "The Modal View," 258.
9 Cowling, "The Modal View," 255.
10 Cowling, "The Modal View," 258.

of a Lewisian understanding of perfect naturalness and the sparse properties are the perfectly natural properties that are instantiated by entities belonging to the inventory of fundamental physics. Given such a conception of sparseness, (SEN) classifies the properties in (i)–(iv) as merely abundant, but only at the cost of denying that macroscopic entities like Socrates have natures at all. A conception of sparseness which privileges the microphysical, thus, does not yield the result that the property of being human, say, belongs to Socrates' nature, while the properties in (i)–(iv) do not. As it stands, therefore, it is unclear how, in the absence of a suitable account of sparseness, (SEN) actually yields the benefits Cowling claims for his account:

> SEN delivers plausible answers to what-questions that square with the cases considered in Fine's challenge for the modal view of essence. For Fine, membership properties like being a member of singleton Socrates are not suitable answers to what-questions. According to SEN, these properties fall outside the nature of Socrates, since being a member of singleton Socrates is not a sparse property. The same goes for other properties of Socrates like being distinct from Aristotle, being such that Aristotle is essentially human, and being such that 2+2=4. Since these properties are essential but not sparse, none of them figure into Socrates' nature so Fine's challenge is handily avoided.[11]

Even if a more liberal conception of sparseness, such as that suggested by Jonathan Schaffer, is substituted into (SEN), Cowling's account still does not seem to deliver the sought-after classifications. According to Schaffer, sparse properties can be "drawn from all the levels of nature— they are those invoked in the scientific understanding of the world";[12]

---

11 Cowling, "The Modal View," 259.
12 Jonathan Schaffer, "Two Conceptions of Sparse Properties," *Pacific Philosophical Quarterly* 85 (2004): 92.

these properties, on Schaffer's construal, satisfy the following constraints: "(1) Similarity: sparse properties ground objective similarities; (2) Causality: sparse properties carve out causal powers";[13] and "(3') Primacy: sparse properties serve as the ontological basis for linguistic truths."[14] Using Schaffer's broader conception of sparseness, Cowling's account will continue to exclude large swaths of entities from having natures, if these entities fail to satisfy (1)–(3'): e.g., abstract entities (such as numbers or sets), logical operations (such as conjunction or disjunction), as well as arguably the members of many social kinds, e.g., artifacts.[15] Thus, even with Schaffer's broader conception of sparseness, (SEN) is still unable to capture the following sort of asymmetry: that it is *not* part of Socrates' nature to instantiate the property of being a member of Socrates' singleton set, while it *is* part of the nature of Socrates' singleton set to instantiate the property of having Socrates as its sole member. But the recognition of precisely such asymmetries is of course a crucial component of Fine's challenges to (MAE). Contrary to what Cowling's remarks above seem to imply, Fine does not hold that membership properties *tout court* are unsuitable to figure in real definitions; rather, when the entities under consideration are sets (e.g., Socrates' singleton set), then membership properties (e.g., the property of having Socrates as its sole member) are exactly what we would expect to find in an appropriate answer to a definitional "what is it?" question.

The account proposed by Nathan Wildman in "Modality, Sparsity, and Essence" is in broad outline similar to Cowling's. Like Cowling, Wildman proposes to amend (MAE) by adding a sparseness constraint on properties: according to Wildman's "sparse property modalism" (SPM), a property, F, is essential to an entity, x, if and only if (i) necessarily, x has F, if x exists; and (ii) F is a sparse property.[16] Like Cowling,

---

13 Schaffer, "Two Conceptions," 94.
14 Schaffer, "Two Conceptions," 100.
15 Cowling, "The Modal View," 265, nn. 29 and 30.
16 Wildman, "Modality," 765.

Wildman as well cites David Lewis and Jonathan Schaffer, when introducing the distinction between sparse and abundant properties, but notes that (SPM) as such is compatible with different approaches to sparseness: "sparse modalism does not actually fix the sparse or modal facts; instead, it merely generates essentialist results from a sparseness conception and modal facts pairing."[17] Along the way, however, Wildman offers a variety of interesting choices not yet canvassed above to modalists wishing to formulate responses to Fine's alleged counterexamples. How a particular version of (SPM) proceeds will depend, for example, on whether the framework in question views existence as a property; and, if so, whether it is a property that everything has or a property that distinguishes the existent from the non-existent entities; whether entities can be said to have properties at worlds at which they do not exist; whether relational properties in general are viewed as abundant, even if their underlying relations are sometimes classified as sparse; and so forth. For reasons of space, although there is much to discuss in Wildman's defense of (SPM), I will focus in particular on his treatment of (i), the set-theoretic property of being a member of Socrates' singleton set, which turns out to be especially tricky for sparse modalists.

In responding to Fine's challenges, Wildman reaches the conclusion that, in all but one case, with the right conception of sparseness and supplementary apparatus in hand, modalists need not regard the properties in question as sparse and hence essential to the entity in question, viz., Socrates. The sole exception is (i), the set-theoretic property of being a member of Socrates' singleton set. In this case, Wildman proposes a different strategy: here, he argues that modalists should, so to speak, "bite the bullet" and accept that, contrary to initial appearances, the property in question *is* in fact essential to Socrates (or, rather, the underlying relation of *being a member of* is one that Socrates essentially

---

[17] Wildman, "Modality," 766.

bears to his singleton set). To counteract the initial implausibility of this result, Wildman offers a diagnosis of what might have led to our intuitive judgment in the first place that it is *not* part of Socrates' nature to be a member of Socrates' singleton set, while it *is* part of the nature of Socrates' singleton set to have Socrates as its sole member. The root cause of this apparent asymmetry in our plausibility judgments, in Wildman's view, is that we have taken the metaphors of "building" or "constructing" too seriously, and have thereby been misled into thinking that a set in some way "metaphysically depends on" its members or that its members are somehow "metaphysically prior to" the set. In fact, however, so Wildman argues, according to one widely accepted conception of sets (viz., the Platonic iterative conception of sets), when given an appropriately minimalist interpretation, such locutions as "building," "construction," "dependence," or "priority" can be read merely as a metaphorical shorthand for designating where in the set-theoretic hierarchy a given set or its members are located. In this way, Wildman takes himself not only to have explained what brought about our intuitive judgments concerning (i) in the first place, but also to have provided reasons for living comfortably with the result that, contrary to initial appearances, it *is* in fact essential to Socrates after all to be the sole member of his singleton set.

I want to highlight two features in particular in Wildman's treatment of (i) which are of special importance given our present concerns. First, in order to reach the conclusion that, contrary to initial appearances, Socrates in fact essentially bears the membership relation to his singleton set, Wildman, unsurprisingly, finds himself forced to give up any proclaimed neutrality and commit to a particular stance concerning the sparseness (or abundance) of the set-theoretic relation, *being a member of*. As noted above, sparse modalism, as such, is a general position which fixes essentialist facts, only once a particular conception of sparseness is substituted into (SPM). Second, in order to reach an assessment concerning the sparseness or abundance of the membership relation, Wildman is required to engage directly with the metaphysical question of what sets are: for it is only when the sparse modalist settles on a particular approach to the metaphysics of sets, so Wildman notes, that the membership relation can be classified as sparse or abundant, according to (SPM).

How, then, does Wildman arrive at the determination that, given the Platonic iterative conception of sets under the minimal interpretation, the membership relation should be classified as sparse, and not abundant? The following passage is revealing in this connection:

> Now, given the sparse/abundant distinction, it seems that a necessary condition for metaphysical significance is sparseness—in other words, abundant properties cannot bear, in the metaphysically significant sense of the phrase, upon what an object is. Suppose that an abundant property P is metaphysically significant to an actually existing object o, such that P plays a part in determining what o is. Because P is metaphysically significant to o, any attempt to characterise the actual world without citing P would not fully determine what o is and would therefore be incomplete. As such, P is required to characterise things completely and without redundancy. And, since the sparse properties are those properties which characterise things completely and without redundancy, P must then be sparse. This, however, contradicts the initial assumption regarding P's abundance. So either P is not metaphysically significant or P is a sparse property, which is logically equivalent to the claim that being sparse is a necessary condition for being metaphysically significant.[18]

In Wildman's view, a property is "metaphysically significant" to an entity when this property plays a role in determining what it is to be the entity in question: in other words, the "metaphysically significant" properties, according to Wildman, are just those properties which

---

18 Wildman, "Modality," 764.

would be classified as *essential* to an entity, according to Fine's definitional account, viz., those properties that have a bearing on what the entity in question is, in the "metaphysically significant sense." The "metaphysically significant" properties instantiated by an entity are, so Wildman reasons, sparse (i.e., sparseness is a necessary condition for a property that is instantiated by an entity to count as "metaphysically significant" to that entity), because the sparse properties are needed to characterize the actual world "completely and without redundancy." As he puts it elsewhere, using the familiar metaphor, the sparse properties are those which "carve nature at the joints."[19] When the entities under consideration are sets, then membership facts must be included in a complete and non-redundant characterization of the actual world: "because sets are taken to be sui generis entities of which membership is the primary characterising relation, membership seems to be a sparse relation."[20]

It is thus to be expected that, when we attempt to give a "complete and non-redundant" characterization of what it is to be Socrates' singleton set (i.e., when, in Wildman's terms, we specify those properties and relations that are "metaphysically significant," in the relevant sense, to Socrates' singleton set), we find ourselves appealing to membership facts; and, for this reason, it makes sense that, when the entities at issue are sets, the membership relation is classified as sparse. But *Socrates* is not a set, even though (as long as the conception of sets at issue is an impure one) he appears as one of the ur-elements at the bottom level of the infinite set-theoretic hierarchy from which the remaining sets are, so to speak, "built up." What happens when, instead of engaging with the question of what is "metaphysically significant" to Socrates' singleton set, we ask what sorts of properties and relations are "metaphysically significant" to Socrates? Suppose, for the sake of the argument, that an accurate answer to the question

---

[19] Wildman, "Modality," 768.
[20] Wildman, "Modality," 776.

of what it is to be Socrates includes the fact that he is a human being. Then, in order to determine what properties and relations are "metaphysically significant" to Socrates, sparse modalists would need to engage with the metaphysical question of what it is to be a human being, and only then could they take a stand on what the "genuinely characterising" sparse properties and relations are concerning human beings which would need to be included in a "complete and non-redundant characterisation of the actual world." But whatever these properties or relations might be—whether they concern the evolutionary origin of the biological species, *homo sapiens*; language-use; consciousness; agency, morality, free will, or what have you—we can be quite sure (and this is of course precisely Fine's point regarding (i)) that a "complete and non-redundant characterisation" of that component of the actual world which concerns human beings in particular will not single out the set-theoretic membership relation as a "primary characterising relation" governing members of the kind, human being. Thus, Wildman's account incorrectly predicts a certain *clash* between different ways of settling the question of which properties and relations are to be classified as "genuinely characterising," and hence as "metaphysically significant" to different sorts of entities. Because membership is a "genuinely characterising relation" for sets, and Socrates is, as we would like to say, only *accidentally* swept up in the set-theoretic hierarchy by being a member of some sets without himself being a set, Wildman's account incorrectly predicts that being a member of Socrates' singleton set is partially indicative of what it is to be Socrates. But other components of a "complete and non-redundant characterisation of the actual world" single out different properties and relations as "genuinely characterising" for entities like Socrates (e.g., properties or relations involving evolutionary lineages or speciation events, language-use, consciousness, agency, morality, free will, or what have you): if we take our lead from these accounts, then being a member of Socrates' singleton set will play no part in a characterization of what it is to be Socrates.

What seems to have gone wrong here is that Wildman's sparse modalist response to Fine's challenges has perhaps focused too much on the specific details of Fine's counterexamples and, in the course of doing so, lost sight of the underlying deficiency which Fine's objections to the modal account are meant to bring out: namely the inability of the modal account (modified or not) to reflect the *source-sensitivity* of modal truths to the identity of the entity or entities whose nature or essence is under consideration. In formulating his "patch," Wildman's sparse modalism attempts to use source-*insensitive* notions like sparseness and abundance to do the work that ultimately can only be done by a source-*sensitive* notion like Fine's non-modal conception of essence or Wildman's own notion of "metaphysical significance." In order to avoid competing classifications of what does or does not count as "metaphysically significant" to a particular entity, Wildman's account in effect would need to make room for the possibility that the sparseness or abundance of a particular property or relation can be *relativized* to particular entities or types of entities which instantiate the property or relation at issue, thus permitting us to say, for example, that the membership relation is "genuinely characterising" or "metaphysically significant" when it comes to entities like Socrates' singleton set, but not when it comes to entities like Socrates which are members of sets without themselves being sets, even though the membership relation holds of the pair, Socrates and Socrates' singleton set, and it does so necessarily. But once we find ourselves having to *relativize* the sparseness or abundance of a property or relation to particular entities or types of entities instantiating the property or relation, we might as well avoid the detour through sparse modalism altogether and opt directly for an explicitly source-sensitive account of essence like Fine's definitional approach.

Finally, the strategy by means of which Wildman reaches a determination concerning the sparseness or abundance of a particular property or relation also raises circularity worries. As noted above, in trying to determine whether a particular property or relation should be classified as sparse or abundant, Wildman seems to appeal to what in effect amounts to independently accessed essentialist information, viz., in this case, an answer to the question of what sets are in the "metaphysically significant," i.e., definitional, sense. But if essentialist input must be fed into (SPM), in order for this account to yield a determination concerning the sparseness or abundance of a particular property or relation, then we wonder of course whether sparse modalism is able to deliver essentiality judgments, as advertised, based purely on modal facts together with an allegedly independently given classification of properties and relations as sparse or abundant.[21]

4. Fine's Definitional Approach to Essence

This brings us to our next question: how exactly does it follow on Fine's own definitional approach to essence that the properties in (i)–(v) are *not* essential to Socrates? Fine's approach proceeds differently from sparse modalism in evaluating the question of whether it is essential to an entity, a, to instantiate a property, F, or to stand in a relation, R, to an entity, b. In particular, given that essentialist claims are treated as source-sensitive, Fine's framework at least in principle has the resources to make room for the possibility that a's bearing R to b might be essential to a, but not to b (or vice versa), even in cases in which

---

[21] The account of naturalness given by Thiago Xavier de Melo in "Essence and Naturalness" promises to address at least some of the objections raised here against sparse modalism by offering a notion of naturalness that is relativized both to kinds and (in the case of relations) to slots. Thus, according to de Melo, we can say, for example, that the relation, being a member of, which holds between Socrates and Socrates' singleton set, is natural relative to the kind, set, and relative to the slot occupied by Socrates' singleton set, but not relative to the kind, human being, and the slot occupied by Socrates. It is doubtful, however, that a relativized account of naturalness along the lines developed by de Melo can in fact yield a classification of properties and relations as either essential or non-essential to an entity without at least implicitly appealing to facts about the essences of those entities of which the properties or relations in question hold. Moreover, the resulting account of naturalness seems so far removed from the original motivations driving the Lewisian notion of naturalness, as yielding an independently given classification of properties and relations, that we may wonder whether de Melo's relativized notion still exhibits the other theoretical benefits that were supposed to be associated with the idea of naturalness. A relativized notion of intrinsicality is developed in Gaétan Bovey, "Essence, Modality, and Intrinsicality."

the fact that Rab holds necessarily. Unlike sparse modalism, Fine's approach does not assume that the question of how a particular property or relation is to be classified should be settled first, before it can be determined whether it is essential to an entity to instantiate the property or relation. Rather, Fine's definitional approach instructs us to look directly to the nature or essence of the entity or entities under consideration to answer the question at hand, without the detour through an allegedly independently given classification of properties and relations. Thus, to determine whether, on Fine's definitional approach, it is essential to Socrates to instantiate the properties cited in (i)–(v), we would need to inspect Socrates' real definition and determine whether these properties figure in a statement of his essence. But what *is* Socrates' essence, in Fine's view? And can we be confident that the supposedly "extraneous" material cited in (i)–(v) does not in fact figure in a statement of Socrates' essence?[22]

We can begin to see how a proponent of Fine's definitional approach might answer these questions by noting first, in a negative fashion, what we should *not* expect to find in a real definition or statement of Socrates' essence. First, as a contingently existing concrete particular object, facts concerning Socrates' existence or non-existence will not figure in his essence: given that Socrates exists at some times and in some worlds, but not others, his existence or non-existence is not determined by his nature alone, but rather depends on specific circumstances that can be expected to vary from one time to another and from one world to another.[23] Second, given that Fine understands

---

[22] The notion of essence at issue here must be construed as Fine's narrow notion of "constitutive" essence and not as the more expansive notion of "consequential" essence, which is closed under logical consequence. For the distinction between constitutive essence and consequential essence, see, for example, Kit Fine, "Ontological Dependence," *Proceedings of the Aristotelian Society* 95 (1995): 276–280. For critical discussion, see, for example, Kathrin Koslicki, "Varieties of Ontological Dependence," in *Metaphysical Grounding: Understanding the Structure of Reality*, ed. Fabrice Correia and Benjamin Schnieder (Cambridge: Cambridge University Press, 2012), 191–195.

[23] Kit Fine, "Necessity and Non-Existence," in *Modality and Tense* (Oxford: Clarendon Press, 2005), 348–349.

essence non-modally, Socrates' real definition should not be expected to make reference to facts concerning what is necessary or possible for a being like Socrates; for, according to Fine, Socrates' modal profile should "flow from" his essence and it would therefore be inappropriate for a statement of Socrates' essence to refer to his modal features: "one should not appeal to an object's modal features in stating what the object is, since they could not then be seen to flow from what it is."[24] (As we will see shortly, given the conception of essence advanced in Fine's "Necessity and Non-Existence," what goes for Socrates' modal profile also goes for his temporal profile in a particular world.) Third, since Socrates, in Fine's view, is a substance and therefore may plausibly be taken to be ontologically independent, we should not expect objects numerically distinct and disjoint from Socrates to figure in his essence or real definition: for an entity, x, is ontologically dependent on an entity, y, just in case y is a constituent in x's constitutive essence; and "a substance may be taken to be anything that does not depend upon anything else or, at least, upon anything other than its parts."[25] Thus, as a contingently existing ontologically independent concrete particular object, Socrates' real definition should not be expected to make reference to his existence or non-existence; his temporal-modal profile; or to objects numerically distinct and disjoint from Socrates.

But what can be said, in a more positive fashion, about what *is* to be included in a real definition or statement of Socrates' essence? When we inspect Fine's earlier and more recent writings on essence, we can extract at least the following *partial* answer to this question: the essence of a contingently existing ontologically independent concrete particular object like Socrates can be partially specified by subsuming

---

[24] Fine, "Necessity," 348.
[25] Fine, "Ontological Dependence," 269–270. If it turns out that it is part of Socrates' essence to have had a certain causal origin, then Socrates would, in that respect, not be completely ontologically independent of all entities numerically distinct and disjoint from himself. Socrates' ontological dependence on his causal origin would thus undermine his status as a substance.

the object in question under a "substance-sortal,"[26] to which Fine variously refers, more often than not, as "man" and, occasionally, as "person." When Fine classifies Socrates as a man, I take it that he does not have in mind Socrates' sex or gender, since presumably the possibility should be left open that Socrates might have self-identified as a woman or undergone a sex-change operation. Fine also cautions us to keep in mind that this example is chosen for illustrative purposes only; thus, anyone who has "substantive doubts about whether it is of the nature of Socrates to be a man" should keep in mind that "person" can be substituted for "man," and that "Felix" and "cat" can be substituted for "Socrates" and "man."[27] Exactly what is involved in Fine's classification of Socrates as a man, however, is a tricky question and we should be careful not to jump to any unwarranted conclusions as to what else might be built into Fine's subsumption of Socrates under the "substance-sortal" "man." For one thing, Fine assumes that "man" is itself a defined term, in the sense that an answer to the further question of what it is to be a man is at least in principle available: "The only plausible non-modal definition of 'man' is one that classifies the object under a sort; to be a man is to be an F (where this is the sort) differentiated in such and such a way."[28] Although the details of this further definition are not completely specified, Fine at least entertains the possibility that it is in the nature of men that they are "fleshy animals,"[29] where the combination of "fleshy" and "animal" should be construed in a "non-predicational" way.[30] (More on this below.)

In addition, Fine's subsumption of Socrates under the "substance-sortal" "man" should be read in light of his distinction between "worldly" and "unworldly" sentences:

---

26 Fine, "Necessity," 346.
27 Fine, "Necessity," 328.
28 Fine, "Necessity," 348.
29 Fine, "Necessity," 348.
30 Fine, "Necessity," n. 27.

> [T]he transcendental essence of an object constitutes a kind of skeletal "core" from which the rest of the essence can be derived. We therefore arrive at the view that the identity of an object is independent of how things turn out, not just in the relatively trivial sense that the self-identity of the object is independent of how things turn out and not just in the relatively trivial sense that the identity of the object is something that will hold of necessity. Rather it is the core essential features of the object that will be independent of how things turn out and they will be independent in the sense of holding *regardless* of the circumstances, not *whatever* the circumstances. The objects enter the world with their identity predetermined, as it were; and there is nothing in how things are that can have any bearing on what they are.[31]

As the passage just cited brings out, Fine construes a statement like "Socrates is a man," in which a contingently existing ontologically independent concrete particular object is subsumed under a "substance-sortal," as an "unworldly" or "transcendental truth," which holds *regardless* of the circumstances that obtain in a particular world or at a particular time. Such objects, as Fine puts it, "enter the world with their identity predetermined, as it were";[32] and what they are, in the definitional sense, is thus "subject to the vicissitudes neither of the world nor of time."[33]

In the case of some entities, Fine holds that a *full* specification of their essence can be given in "transcendental" terms, namely when the real definition in question makes reference only to sortal classifications and to what Fine calls "formal relations," e.g., the relation between a set and its members, between an aggregate and its parts, or between a proposition and its constituents.[34] For example, the essence

---

31 Fine, "Necessity," 348–349.
32 Fine, "Necessity," 348–349.
33 Fine, "Necessity," 341.
34 Fine, "Necessity," 344–345.

of an ontologically dependent abstract entity like Socrates' singleton set can be fully specified in "transcendental" terms, in Fine's view, first, by subsuming the entity in question under the relevant sort (viz., set) and, second, by specifying its members (viz., Socrates). The resulting real definition, "Socrates' singleton set is a set whose sole member is Socrates," accomplishes two tasks: first, it *classifies* the entity in question by stating the kind, viz., set, to which it belongs; second, it *differentiates* this particular set from all the other sets by mentioning its members, viz., Socrates. Both tasks, in this case, can be accomplished in purely "transcendental" terms, since neither the sortal classification nor the appeal to the membership relation requires reference to particular circumstances that can be expected to vary from one time or world to another.[35]

But a full specification of the essence of an entity in purely "transcendental" terms is not always possible. In the case of a contingently existing ontologically independent concrete particular object like Socrates, the "transcendental" specification of the essence is only partial and accomplishes only the first *classificatory* task, but not the second *differentiating* task: the sortal truth, "Socrates is a man," classifies Socrates by stating what kind of object he is; but it does not differentiate Socrates from all the other members of the same kind.[36]

Fine's more recent work, in which he explores the connections between essence and ground, provides further elucidation on how to construe statements of the essence. Thus, Fine's project in "Unified Foundations for Essence and Ground" and "Identity Criteria and Ground," for example, is to formulate a unified treatment of essence and ground, which views each notion as contributing its own proprietary type of metaphysical explanation. The key to seeing how statements of essence and statements of ground can be brought into a common framework, according to Fine, is to take notice, first, of the

---

35 Fine, "Necessity," 348.
36 Fine, "Necessity," 348–349.

fact that both notions involve an element of *genericity*, which Fine analyzes by appeal to his earlier theory of arbitrary objects as presented in *Reasoning with Arbitrary Objects*. Second, Fine proposes that statements of ground and statements of essence should be regarded as aiming at a single explanandum, but from two different directions, so to speak, with statements of ground contributing "constitutively *sufficient*" conditions and statements of essence contributing "constitutively *necessary*" conditions for the explanandum in question. Here, the notions of "constitutively necessary" and "constitutively sufficient" conditions are not to be regarded as mere converses of each other, since both are "determinative" in nature.[37] Thus, in light of these developments, the partial "transcendental" specification of Socrates' essence given by the sortal truth, "Socrates is a man," can be read as stating a "constitutively *necessary*" condition that must be met by an *arbitrary* individual, x, if x is to be identical to Socrates.

With these various components of Fine's definitional approach to essence in place, we can now return to our original question and ask whether the partial "transcendental" specification of Socrates' essence at which we have arrived so far is sufficient to establish that the properties cited in (i)–(v) are *not* essential to Socrates. One might expect that, strictly speaking, only a *full* specification of Socrates' essence can put to rest conclusively any lingering doubts we may have as to whether the "extraneous" material mentioned in (i)–(v) does not somehow make its way into Socrates' real definition. Since, according to Fine, "the transcendental essence of an object constitutes a kind of skeletal 'core' from which the rest of the essence can be derived,"[38] a fully expanded specification of Socrates' essence would need to include not only the "transcendental" sortal truth, "Socrates is a man," but also whatever else can be derived from the "constitutively necessary" condition, "x is a man," that is contained within it. As I will suggest in a

---

37 Fine, "Unified Foundations," 306–307.
38 Fine, "Necessity," 348.

moment, however, Fine may be able to offer us a substitute, in lieu of a fully expanded statement of Socrates' essence, by means of which the challenge at hand can be put to rest at least by approximation.

How, then, would a partially specified statement of Socrates' essence be expanded beyond its "transcendental" "skeletal 'core'"? A natural place to look for further instructions is Fine's neo-Aristotelian theory of embodiment as presented in "Things and Their Parts," an early formulation of which can be found in the theory of "qua-objects" in "Acts, Events and Things."[39] I will not explore Fine's mereology and hylomorphism in detail here.[40] For present purposes, it will suffice to focus only on how these independently developed aspects of Fine's broader metaphysical framework can contribute to specific questions of essence, in this case by appeal to a theory that is designed to "give an adequate account of the identity of... material things in general,"[41] including their existence, part-whole structure, location in space and time, as well as their modal and non-modal character.

According to the theory of embodiment, developed in "Things and Their Parts," concrete particular objects are analyzed either as "rigid embodiments" or as "variable embodiments," depending on whether these objects have their material parts timelessly or in a temporary way. A ham sandwich, for example, may be regarded as a rigid embodiment, <a, b, c, ... /R>, where a, b, and c are themselves objects (and hence subject to the theory of embodiment), viz., the material parts (two slices of bread and a slice of ham) which timelessly compose the

---

39 See also Kit Fine, "A Puzzle concerning Matter and Form," in *Unity, Identity and Explanation in Aristotle's Metaphysics*, ed. T. Scaltsas, D. Charles, and M. L. Gill (Oxford: Clarendon Press, 1994), 13–40; "Compounds and Aggregates," *Noûs* 28 (1994): 137–158; "A Counter-Example to Locke's Thesis," *The Monist* 83 (2000): 357–361; "The Non-Identity of a Material Thing and its Matter," *Mind* 112 (2003): 195–234; "Coincidence and Form," *Proceedings of the Aristotelian Society*, suppl. 82 (2008): 101–118; and "Towards a Theory of Part," *Journal of Philosophy* 107 (2010): 559–589.

40 For further details, see Kathrin Koslicki, "Towards a Neo-Aristotelian Mereology," *Dialectica* 61 (2007): 127–159; and *The Structure of Objects* (Oxford: Oxford University Press, 2018), especially chapter 4.

41 Kit Fine, "Acts, Events and Things," in *Proceedings of the 6th International Wittgenstein Symposium* (Vienna: Hölder-Pichler-Tempsky, 1982), 100.

ham sandwich; R is the relation of betweenness; and '/' denotes the sui generis composition relation of rigid embodiment. A variable embodiment, /F/, embodies a principle of variable embodiment, F, which selects a series of "manifestations," f_t, at those times, t, at which the variable embodiment, /F/, exists. The principle, F, of a variable embodiment, /F/, is described by Fine as any "suitable" function from times to objects.[42] For example, a river may be viewed as a variable embodiment, /F/, whose principle of variable embodiment, F, selects at each time, t, at which the river exists, a manifestation, f_t, viz., the particular quantity of water which constitutes the river at t. Depending on the case at hand, the manifestation, f_t, selected by a principle of variable embodiment, F, at a time, t, at which the variable embodiment, /F/, exists may itself be a rigid embodiment or a variable embodiment, resulting in a potential hierarchical arrangement of rigid and variable embodiments. Although the theory of embodiment describes two irreducibly distinct composition relations, viz., rigid embodiment and variable embodiment, an implicit understanding of these primitive notions, as well as their interconnections, in Fine's view, can be derived from a series of postulates which specify conditions for an embodiment's existence, location, identity, part-whole structure, as well as its modal and non-modal character.

Following this exceedingly brief excursion into Fine's theory of embodiment, we can now expand on the previously given statement of the "transcendental" "skeletal 'core'" of Socrates' essence as follows. As a composite concrete particular object capable of persisting through changes with respect to his material parts, it is part of Socrates' nature to be identical to a variable embodiment, /S/, whose principle of variable embodiment, S, selects at each time, t, at which Socrates exists a manifestation, s_t. Perhaps (though this is not necessary) we may think of the manifestation, s_t, selected by Socrates' principle of variable

---

42 Kit Fine, "Things and Their Parts," *Midwest Studies in Philosophy* 23 (1999): 69.

embodiment, S, at each time, t, at which Socrates exists, as rigid embodiments of the form, <a, b, c, . . . /H>, whose objectual components, a, b, c, . . . , are the "fleshy animal" parts that are characteristically associated with a being like Socrates (e.g., a torso, a head, arms, legs, a heart, eyes, and the like) and whose relation, H, reflects the characteristically human arrangement that must be exhibited by these material parts that compose Socrates at each time at which he exists. Socrates' characteristically human "fleshy animal" parts, a, b, c, . . . , in turn, may themselves be regarded as variable embodiments, i.e., concrete particular objects whose material parts may vary over time, thus resulting in a hierarchical arrangement of variable and rigid embodiments. Given the various postulates governing rigid and variable embodiments, the characterization of Socrates as a variable embodiment just stated also serves to determine conditions for Socrates' existence, location in space and time, part-whole structure, as well as his modal and non-modal character. (For further details as to how such a proposed "derivation" might work, the reader is referred to Fine's "Coincidence and Form," where the theory of embodiment is invoked in formulating a response to the so-called Grounding Problem, i.e., the problem of what grounds the modal and non-modal differences between numerically distinct spatiotemporally coincident objects, such as an alloy statue and the piece of alloy constituting it.)

We can now combine the "transcendental" sortal classification of Socrates as a man with the "non-transcendental" characterization of Socrates as a variable embodiment as follows: in order for an arbitrary individual, x, to be identical to Socrates, it is "constitutively necessary" for x to be a man, where this condition requires x to be a variable embodiment whose principle of variable embodiment (following our assumptions above) selects at each time at which x exists a rigid embodiment composed of some characteristically human "fleshy animal" parts, arranged in a characteristically human manner. Presumably, the specification of Socrates' essence just given is still not complete, if (as seems reasonable) we may assume that at least some of the terms that would occur in it, if all the details that are currently still left open were to be filled in, are themselves defined (e.g., "animal," "heart," etc.).[43] Suppose, however, that these further definitions—if they were to be spelled out—appeal only to material that is already covered either by Fine's "transcendental" conception of essence or by his theory of embodiment. Then, even in the absence of a fully expanded statement of Socrates' essence, Fine may nevertheless argue that enough has been said to show how the challenge at hand can be met, at least by approximation. For by inspecting the *methods* by which new material can be introduced into an existing definition, it can be established that only material that is of the same *type* as the material we have already encountered (viz., in this case, "transcendental" sortal classifications, "formal" relations or terms designating the various principles or components of rigid or variable embodiments) can make its way into a real definition that is expanded beyond its "transcendental" "skeletal 'core.'" Moreover, new material can only enter into an existing definition if it can be, so to speak, "pulled out" of a statement of the essence of an entity that is already mentioned in the original specification of the essence to begin with, e.g., by way of a specification of what it is to be an animal or a heart, say.[44] (Of course, if an existing definition can be expanded by other means besides those already discussed, then it would still need to be demonstrated that these additional methods are no less "conservative" than the methods we have already encountered.) In this

---

43 If the "worldly" terms that would be mentioned in a fully expanded specification of Socrates' essence are not understood predicatively, then perhaps the contrast drawn here between sets (whose essence can be specified fully in "transcendental" terms) and persons (whose essence can be specified only by appeal to both "worldly" and "unworldly" material) is not as pronounced as indicated. The predicates "is a sphere" and "is spherical," for example, can be understood both in a "worldly" manner (viz., when we say of an object that it has a certain spherical shape) and in an "unworldly" manner (viz., when we say of an object that it belongs to a certain kind, namely the geometrical kind, sphere).

44 The formal analogue in Fine's logic of essence of the method described here informally is the principle of "Chaining," which states that "if the objects $y_1, y_2, \ldots$ are 'linked' by dependence to the objects $x_1, x_2, \ldots$, then any proposition true in virtue of the linking objects $y_1, y_2, \ldots$ is also true in virtue of the linked objects $x_1, x_2, \ldots$." Kit Fine, "The Logic of Essence," *Journal of Philosophical Logic* 24 (1995): 249.

way, then, the definitionalist may claim that, even in the absence of a fully specified statement of Socrates' essence, we can rest assured that the properties in (i)–(v) turn out *not* to be essential to Socrates, since no opening has been provided by means of which "extraneous" material disconnected from Socrates' nature could make its way into a fully expanded specification of Socrates' essence, if such a specification could ever be given.[45]

As we observed earlier in the case of sparse modalism as well, in order to determine the status of the properties in (i)–(v) within Fine's system, one must appeal not only to material that is drawn from the definitional approach to essence itself, but also to certain "first-order" metaphysical doctrines, in this case Fine's theory of embodiment. For as a contingently existing ontologically independent composite concrete particular object capable of persisting through changes with respect to his material parts, the particular entity under consideration, viz., Socrates, is analyzed by Fine as a variable embodiment and therefore falls under those aspects of Fine's broader metaphysical framework which are meant to give an account of the identity of material things in general, including their existence, part-whole structure, spatiotemporal location, and character. But this feature is of course not

---

45 Is it possible, in Fine's view, to arrive at "constitutively *sufficient*" conditions for an arbitrary individual's identity with Socrates? As Fine states in the following passage, he allows for the possibility that a "reductive" definition, i.e., a definition which specifies both "constitutively necessary" and "constitutively sufficient" conditions, is not available in all cases: "But a statement may lack a sufficient condition though still admitting of some (though not all) necessary conditions. That x is a man, for example, may be constitutively necessary for x to be Socrates (i.e., Socrates may be essentially a man) even though there is no constitutively sufficient condition for x to be Socrates, or truth may be constitutively necessary for knowledge even though there may be no constitutively sufficient condition for knowledge of which truth is a part. Similarly, x being a man may imply all necessary conditions for x to be Socrates without itself being a sufficient condition for x to be Socrates" (Fine, "Unified Foundations," 307). Whether a "constitutively sufficient" condition can be given in the particular case of an arbitrary individual's identity with Socrates in part depends on whether an appeal to Socrates' causal origins is built into a specification of Socrates' essence and, if so, whether such an appeal in fact provides a "constitutively sufficient" condition for an arbitrary individual's identity with Socrates. I argue against the sufficiency of sameness of original matter for crossworld identity in my *Form, Matter, Substance* (Oxford: Oxford University Press, 2018), 89–103; see also Kathrin Koslicki, "Essence and Identity," in *Metaphysics, Meaning and Modality: Themes from Kit Fine*, ed. Mircea Dumitru (Oxford: Oxford University Press, 2020), 113–140.

unique to the two approaches to essence we have considered; rather, we would expect that *any* approach to essence requires a certain amount of "out-sourcing" in order to settle specific questions of essence, viz., a direct engagement with the metaphysics of the particular type of entity under consideration. Unlike sparse modalism, however, Fine's definitional approach to essence is specifically set up in such a way that "first-order" metaphysical information concerning the nature of the entity or entities under consideration can enter into a statement of its essence in a non-circular fashion. Given the source-sensitivity of Fine's approach, fine-grained mechanisms are available, in this framework, to allow for the possibility of scenarios in which an entity, a's, standing in a relation R to an entity, b, might be essential to a, but not b (or vice versa), even when the fact that Rab obtains necessarily. In order to determine whether such a scenario obtains in a particular case, however, one must take a stand on metaphysical questions that are not exclusively settled by the theory of essence itself, but require direct engagement with broader metaphysical questions concerning the identity of the entities under consideration.

5. Concluding Thoughts: The Theoretical Roles of Essences

This chapter has focused on the question of whether and how Kit Fine's well-known challenges to the modal account of essence can be adequately addressed by modified modal approaches, in particular Sam Cowling's and Nathan Wildman's sparse modalism, as well as by Fine's own definitional approach to essence. An important topic which has so far stayed in the background, however, concerns the theoretical roles that are ascribed to essences or definitions, i.e., statements of the essence, by modalists and non-modalists. Our preceding discussion highlighted three contenders for such theoretical roles in particular: that of (a) explaining modality (see Section 1, "Introduction"); (b) classifying an entity by specifying the kind to which it belongs; and (c) differentiating an entity from other entities belonging to the same kind (see Section 4, "Fine's Definitional Approach to Essence"). As a proponent of a non-modal approach, Fine accepts (a) as being among the primary responsibilities of essences or their linguistic/propositional counterparts, viz., definitions. And although Finean definitions also in general seem to satisfy (b), the same cannot be said for (c): definitions, for Fine, may be, but "need not... be individuating."[46]

The question of which theoretical roles should be ascribed to essences or definitions, however, is itself controversial; and the controversy in this case, at least to some extent, crosscuts the dispute between modalists and non-modalists. For while modalists and non-modalists of course take opposing positions concerning (a), these theorists can agree or disagree with one another on whether the explanatory work done by essences or definitions includes one or both of (b) and (c), independently of their particular take on the connection between essence and modality.[47] And the three theoretical roles emphasized so far certainly do not exhaust the range of possible job descriptions that have been proposed for essences or definitions in one context or another. Aristotle, in *Met.* Z. 17 and *Met.* H.6, for example, points to the form or essence of a matter-form compound not only as the cause of its being what it is, but also as (d) its principle of unity. Moreover, as Paul Teller puts it, an Aristotelian essence is also expected to yield (e) "a unifying causal and scientific explanation of an entity's other properties."[48] The theoretical roles cited in (a)–(e) are by no means intended as a complete list of possible explanatory responsibilities associated with essences or definitions; but they do give us an indication of the

---

46 Fine, "Ontological Dependence," 275.

47 For an argument in favor of individual forms on the grounds that the essences of concrete particular objects should satisfy (c) and serve as principles of crossworld identification, see my *Form, Matter, Substance*, 89–103; see also Koslicki, "Essence and Identity."

48 Paul Teller, "Essential Properties: Some Problems and Conjectures," *Journal of Philosophy* 72, no. 9 (May 8, 1975): 248. To account for the role of essence in giving causal scientific explanation of the non-fundamental properties of an entity in Fine's framework would require an appeal to his distinction between metaphysical and natural necessity as drawn in "The Varieties of Necessity."

multitude and diversity of options which arise in this context. It is only by developing a clearer grasp of the explanatory work that is done by essences or definitions that we can in turn also arrive at a more fine-tuned understanding of what sort of material we should expect to find in the specification of an entity's essence or definition.[49]

---

49 I am grateful to Kit Fine for taking the time to comment on a draft of this chapter. I hope to have incorporated his recommendations accurately. I would also like to acknowledge the Canada Research Chairs program as well as the Social Sciences and Humanities Research Council of Canada for its support of the project "The Essence of Anti-Essentialism."

Reflection

CLARICE LISPECTOR—WRITING OF NECESSITY

Paula Marchesini

The great difficulty for Clarice Lispector's narrators and characters is that of accepting the actual world as the one and only legitimate source of necessity. A source which, actual as it may be, is forever out of reach. Fully realized and, for this very reason, impossible. So we find Lóri, the protagonist of *An Apprenticeship or the Book of Pleasures*, sitting motionless at the poolside, yearning to take in the overwhelming actuality of trees, elements, colors, and people: "All of it was absolutely impossible, that was why Lóri knew she saw it."[1] And in *Besieged City*, the sharpness of daytime in São Geraldo—with its concrete roads, statues, and an orchestra of clocks announcing the present—makes Lucrécia scream: "What actuality!... what actuality!"[2] In the Brazilian writer's masterpiece, *The Passion According to G.H.*, we come upon her most concise expression for the necessity and concomitant

---

1 Clarice Lispector, *Uma Aprendizagem ou o Livro dos Prazeres* [An Apprenticeship or the Book of Pleasures] (Rio de Janeiro: Rocco, 1969), 72. Translations are mine throughout, unless otherwise noted.
2 Clarice Lispector, *A Cidade Sitiada* [The Besieged City] (Rio de Janeiro: Rocco, 1949), 40.

impossibility of the actual world: "my unreachable actuality is my lost paradise."[3]

In Lispector's writings, actuality is more than simply realized possibility. It is pure, unjustifiable necessity. We only know that it must be because it is. Living requires crossing over from impossible to actual without ever touching the muddy waters of the merely possible. The possible comes later, from the refusal to accept the actual, the desperate attempt to escape its scorching light.[4] For Lispector, possibility is so efficacious in its purpose of delaying contact with the actual and providing shelter from ruthless immediacy, that humans never cease to crystallize the merely possible into endless forms of false necessity.

To understand Lispector's notion of what counts as genuinely necessary and how it is grounded in the actual world, it is useful first to examine three deceptive forms of necessity that her creations painstakingly reject. These are practical necessity, which rules social life; divine necessity, which rules religious life; and abstract necessity, which rules mathematics, logic, and science.

The first kind of deceitful necessity Lispector refutes in her work appears when the sort of practical information that allows for human society, which is at bottom contingent, is accepted as absolute truth. Pondering about what is truly necessary at every turn would take an infinite amount of time. In order to keep the social wheels turning, we must settle for a host of names and entities that allow us to engage with reality and that are only effective to the extent they are placed beyond question.

---

[3] Clarice Lispector, *A Paixão Segundo G.H.* [The Passion According to G.H.] (Rio de Janeiro: Rocco, 1964), 150. Lispector was born in Chechelnik, in Ukraine, in 1920. The Lispectors were Jewish and escaped to Recife, in northeastern Brazil, when the writer was two years old, to flee the wave of pogroms that swept over Ukraine following the First World War. For more on Lispector's life, her Jewish roots, her family's tragedy, and her pledge to Brazil, see Benjamin Moser, *Why This World: A Biography of Clarice Lispector* (New York: Oxford University Press, 2009).

[4] See, for instance, Lispector, *Paixão*, 148.

In Lispector's writings, "becoming human"[5] requires just this acceptance of the contingent as necessary: "Ah, could it be that we were originally not human? And that, out of practical necessity, we became human?"[6] To partake in "humanized life,"[7] one must embrace one's given name, one's age, occupation, social status, and other biographical data as one's essence, in place of dealing directly with one's nameless existence. One must adhere to commonplace opinions about things—about what goes on in the news, what counts as right or wrong, what makes a good dancer or a fine theater play—so as to spare oneself the impossible task of accounting for every subtlety of actual experience.[8] One must have recognizable things to say in a conversation, involving "facts and particulars,"[9] to avoid being startled into silence by the mysterious encounter with another human being. In Lispector's work, the particulars that compose one's "human assemblage"[10] and that make up the bulk of human conversation are not factual in the least. They pose as necessary but are mere possibility, dangerous fictions meant to block contact with what is actually the case, which is too complex to form a basis for action.

Another way of escaping the actual, which leads to the second kind of false necessity countered by Lispector, is turning to the idea of a God and appealing to a divine realm that might explain and justify what we observe. God and the perfect kingdom religions save for an afterlife are easier to fathom than the actual world, because they have the advantage of not being now: "I believed in

---

5 See Lispector, *Paixão*, 119.

6 Lispector, *Paixão*, 119.

7 See Lispector, *Paixão*, 12.

8 See Lispector, *Cidade Sitiada*, 122–123, 127; *Paixão*, 21.

9 Clarice Lispector, *Um Sopro de Vida: Pulsações* [A Breath of Life: Pulsations] (Rio de Janeiro: Rocco, 1978), 42, passage translated by Moser, *Why This World*, 4. Lispector's aversion to "facts and particulars" is one of the most important themes in her work. Perhaps its most in-depth exploration appears in *A Hora da Estrela* [The Hour of the Star] (Rio de Janeiro: Rocco, 1977), 13–24.

10 Lispector, *Paixão*, 11.

what exists so little that I postponed actuality to a promise and to a future."[11] Additionally, the pristine interior of a soul is less troublesome than the living entrails of ever-hungry creatures who are guided not by some soulful variety of necessity but by relentless physical need. The idea of perfect love is less frightening than the reproductive indifference that allowed for the development of life on earth, an indifference to which lovers might confess if they did not follow the unquestioned norm of embellishing what they feel. For Lispector, turning to "the God of the religions"[12] for the ultimate source of necessity requires admitting that what must be the case conflicts with what already is. Yet whatever it is that must be the case, it must match the "evidence of vision."[13] The real purpose of a God who contradicts the actual world, by performing miracles, for instance, is that of providing relief from the already indecipherable reality before us: "What I used to call miracle was really a desire for discontinuity and interruption, the desire for an anomaly: I called miracle precisely the moment when the real continuous miracle of the process was interrupted."[14] This is what G.H. discovers in *The Passion*, when she understands that her "insides"[15] are made of the same gooey paste she sees pouring out of a cockroach and that her neutral matter dictates a necessity more forceful than divine, since it is "today and now and right now."[16] This living necessity is not discovered intellectually as an afterthought, but is experienced in the flesh as immediate and brutal need, like the visceral hunger Lóri feels for Ulisses in *An Apprenticeship*, which surpasses her desire for divine justification or even an afterlife: "The hunger for living, my God. To what point

---

11 Lispector, *Paixão*, 146.
12 Moser, *Why This World*, 112.
13 Lispector, *Paixão*, 108.
14 Lispector, *Paixão*, 169.
15 Lispector, *Paixão*, 61.
16 Clarice Lispector, *Água Viva* [Living Water] (Rio de Janeiro: Rocco, 1973), 35.

she went in the misery of necessity: she would exchange an eternity of after death for the eternity of while she was alive."[17]

The third type of false necessity that Lispector discredits, which follows the same pattern of creating a shield of possibilities against the force of the actual, supports the kind of theoretical abstraction found in mathematics, logic, and science. Such abstract endeavors provide an escape route via the promise of a simple and elegant foundation for the real, as well as the soothing prospect of total comprehension. The problem, for Lispector, is that the exact sciences are too exact to account for the complexity of the world. Whoever seeks the perfect abstract formulation to produce or explain what is already the case has to deal with the embarrassment of having to "transform the growth of the wheat into numbers."[18] There is always one more variable to add, one last exception to consider, and meanwhile the wheat is growing. This is the frustration Martim, a statistician, experiences in *The Apple in the Dark*, which leads him to abandon his quest for immaculate precision before reality: "'I don't know how to deduce! My deductions were wrong!' . . . 'Not even the little bird fit my explanation, much less me!'"[19] And in *A Breath of Life*, the "Author" declares himself "specialized in physics"[20] but refrains from using "technical vocabulary"[21] to account for his experiences, choosing literature instead. In Lispector's writings, the kind of naive rigor sought in mathematics, logic, and science makes them inaccurate instruments to accomplish their own aims. The logic that rules actuality exceeds any exact formulation. Lispector calls it an "obscure logic,"[22] "secret

---

17 Lispector, *Uma Aprendizagem*, 143. See also *Paixão*, 74.
18 Clarice Lispector, *A Maçã no Escuro* [The Apple in the Dark] (Rio de Janeiro: Rocco, 1974), 170.
19 Lispector, *Maçã no Escuro*, 218.
20 Lispector, *Sopro de Vida*, 78.
21 Lispector, *Sopro de Vida*, 78.
22 Lispector, *Maçã no Escuro*, 91.

logic,"[23] or "impalpable logic,"[24] an erratic ordering that makes life coherent, but only as much as a dream.[25] One can go along with the dream without comprehending it by making peace with the imprecise yet strangely predictable stream of impressions that constitutes one's only authentic encounter with the real.[26]

What, then, counts as genuine necessity for Lispector? In short, whatever it is that sustains actuality, since the actual world is the only thing that is always the case. Perhaps the most characteristic feature of Lispector's literary project is the decision to never give this nucleus of the actual a definitive name. Throughout her novels and short stories, she offers a host of candidate names for it: "the thing itself," "Nature," "The Mystery," "the mystery of the impersonal," "the nothing," "the neutral," "the unsayable," "the unfinished," "the everything," "the great potency of potentiality," "the fourth dimension of the instant-now," "the it," "that," "Simptar," "Force of what Exists," "the Unknown," and "the Ah" are some examples.[27] Lispector's G.H. calls it "the God,"[28] opposing it to the Christian God throughout *The Passion*. Whatever it is, it forms the wild heart of the actual world, a "secret"[29] to which we must allude without naming and which the ideas sustaining human

---

23 Lispector, *Maçã no Escuro*, 330.

24 Lispector, *Maçã no Escuro*, 330.

25 Lispector, *Sopro de Vida*, 76.

26 The concept of "impression" is of the utmost importance in Lispector's work and evokes this imprecision that is nonetheless strangely predictable. Lispector alternates the term with "sensation" and "thought-sensation." See Clarice Lispector, *Outros Escritos* [Other Writings], edited by Teresa Montero and Lícia Manzo (Rio de Janeiro: Rocco, 2005), 139; Clarice Lispector, *Perto do Coração Selvagem* [Near to the Wild Heart] (Rio de Janeiro: Rocco, 1944), 21–22, 194; *Sopro de Vida*, 20; Moser, *Why This World*, 54.

27 See, respectively: Lispector, *Paixão*, 85, 52, 23; *Água Viva*, 30; *Paixão*, 60, 84, 176; *Água Viva*, 27; *Perto do Coração Selvagem*, 66; *Água Viva*, 27, 9, 30; *Maçã no Escuro*, 176; *Água Viva*, 45, 75; *Sopro de Vida*, 130, 140. Many of these terms and expressions point to Lispector's most important defining influences, particularly Jewish thought and mysticism and the philosophy of Spinoza. For more on this, see Moser, *Why This World*, 12–24, 109–112, 118, 122–123, 161, 220, 227, 268, 379, 390.

28 Lispector, *Paixão*, 83.

29 Lispector, *Cidade Sitiada*, 69; *Paixão*, 35; *Água Viva*, 65.

society, religion, and the exact sciences always miss with their rigid definitions.

What we know about the "secret" is that it *is* and it is *now*. What we know about the truth is that it "happens": "Whoever does not believe that the truth happens should look at a chicken walking by force of the unknown. 'In fact truth has been happening a lot.' "[30] Most important, the way to approach this secretive necessity is not "knowing," but "being." We are it. Our faces and bodies understand it even if we ourselves do not, since they exist according to its rule.[31] We ourselves only understand without understanding how, a feeling Lispector's Virgínia calls "subcomprehension"[32] in *The Chandelier*, the "indecipherable clarity"[33] that characterizes our contact with the essence of the real.

Finally, whatever it is that is genuinely necessary for Lispector, it is also what fuels her writing. Literature, for her and her creations, is the most precise available tool for dealing with necessity. It alone can mirror, with precision, the strange logic that governs the actual world. The writer mirrors reality effectively by devising plots, characters, and linguistic means that are not arbitrary but rather necessary in the same obscure way as what they are summoned to reflect. Writing of necessity requires a skill similar to that employed when one arranges flowers in a vase: a mix of fatality and chance.[34] For Lispector, writers are those "chosen by the fatality of chance,"[35] free only "to go without hindrance toward the fatal,"[36] taking on subcomprehension as their preferred method.

---

30 Lispector, *Maçã no Escuro*, 310.
31 Lispector, *Maçã no Escuro*, 303.
32 Clarice Lispector, *O Lustre* [The Chandelier] (Rio de Janeiro: Rocco, 1946), 54, 146.
33 Lispector, *O Lustre*, 54.
34 Lispector, *Água Viva*, 69.
35 Lispector, *Água Viva*, 69.
36 Lispector, *Maçã no Escuro*, 324.

Literature, like all other ways of accounting for reality, must ultimately fail for Lispector. But the failure of literature is unique: it is not the failure of giving up on an unreachable actuality to choose the safer track of the merely possible. Literature fails only to the extent that the necessary truth sustaining the actual world is itself beyond our grasp. Literature has the advantage of never reaching for shields of possibility, of dealing directly with "the impossible."[37] For this reason, its failure provides a successful point of contact with what the writer longs for: "My spectacular and continuous failure proves that its contrary exists: success. Even if success is not given to me, I take satisfaction in knowing of its existence."[38]

For Lispector, this assurance through failure is the best that humans can do. One of her most important premises is that what is genuinely necessary must be beyond our reach. Any alleged necessary truth that can be known by us is smaller than what we already are. And if it is smaller than what is, then it is mere possibility. Necessity must be as out of reach to us as we—who are embodied necessity—are to ourselves:

Perhaps no force could ever achieve more than extend to the maximum the length of a man's arm—and then fail to reach that which, with one more impulse, the final and impossible one, would fill one's hand with life. For a man's arm has a precise length. And there is something we will never know. There is something we will never know, you feel that, don't you?[39]

---

37 Lispector, *Água Viva*, 72.
38 Lispector, *Sopro de Vida*, 74. See also *Maçã no Escuro*, 173.
39 Lispector, *Maçã no Escuro*, 306.

Bibliography

Literature before 1900

Abarbanel, Yitzhak. *Perush ha-Torah* [Hebrew: *Commentary on the Pentateuch*]. Venice, 1579.

Alan of Lille. *Regulae caelestis iuris.* Edited by N. M. Häring. *Archives doctrinale et littéraire du moyen âge* 78 (1981): 97–226.

Albert the Great. *Liber I Perihermeneias.* Vol. 1 of *Opera omnia.* Edited by August Borgnet. Paris: Vivès, 1890.

Anonymous. *De obligationibus.* Edited by Romuald Green, in "The Logical Treatise 'De obligationibus': An Introduction with Critical Texts of William of Sherwood (?) and Walter Burley." PhD diss., University of Louvain, 1963.

Anonymus Aurelianensis. *"Anonymus Aurelianensis III" in Aristotelis* Analytica priora. Critical edition. Introduction, notes, and indexes by Christina Thomsen Thörnqvist. Leiden: Brill, 2015.

Aquinas, Thomas. *Summa theologiae.* Edited by Pietro Caramello. Turin: Marietti, 1948–1950.

Aquinas, Thomas. *Summa contra gentiles.* Edited by Ceslas Pera, Pietro Marc, and Pietro Caramello. Turin: Marietti, 1961–1967.

Aquinas, Thomas. *In Aristotelis libros De caelo et mundo, De generatione et corruptione, Meteorologicorum exposition.* Edited by Raymundo M. Spiazzi. Turin: Marietti, 1952.

Aquinas, Thomas. *In Aristotelis libros Peri hermeneias et Posteriorum analyticorum exposition.* Edited by Raymundo M. Spiazzi. Turin: Marietti, 1964.

Aquinas, Thomas. *In duodecim libros Aristotelis Metaphysicorum expositio.* Edited by Marie-Raymond Cathala and Raymundo M. Spiazzi. Turin: Marietti, 1971.

Aquinas, Thomas. *In octo libros Physicorum Aristotelis exposition*. Edited by Mariani Maggiòlo. Turin: Marietti, 1965.

Aristotele. *Peri Hermeneias*. 3rd edition. Edited by H. Weidemann. Berlin: de Gruyter, 2014.

Aristotle. *The Complete Works of Aristotle*. Edited by Jonathan Barnes. Princeton, NJ: Princeton University Press, 1984.

Augustine. *Confessions*. Translated by E. B. Pusey. Chicago: Henry Regnery, 1948.

Averroes. *Aristotelis Opera cum Averrois commentariis*. Venice, 1562. Reprinted, Frankfurt am Main: Minerva, 1962.

Averroes. *Qestions in* Physics. Translated by Helen T. Goldstein. Dordrecht: Kluwer, 1991.

Bach, J. S. *Messe h-Moll*. Edited by Friedrich Smend. Kassel: Bärenreiter Verlag, 1954. Plate BA 5001.

Berkeley, George. *Philosophical Writings*. Edited by Desmond M. Clarke. Cambridge: Cambridge University Press, 2008.

Boethius. *Commentarii in librum Aristotelis Peri hermeneias I–II*. Edited by Carl Meiser. Leipzig: Teubner, 1877–1880.

Boethius. *Consolatio Philosophiae*. Edited by Ludwig Bieler. Corpus Christianorum Series Latina 94. Turnhout: Brepols, 1957.

Campanella, Tommaso. *Compendio di Filosofia della Natura (Physiologiæ Compendium)*. Latin text edited by Germana Ernst. Italian translation by Paolo Ponzio. Milan: Rusconi, 1999.

Campanella, Tommaso. *Epilogo Magno*. Edited by Carmelo Ottaviano. Rome: Reale Accademia d'Italia, 1939.

Campanella, Tommaso. *Selected Philosophical Poems*. Translated by Sherry Roush. Chicago: University of Chicago Press, 2011.

Crescas, Hasdai. *Light of the Lord*. Translated by Roslyn Weiss. Oxford: Oxford University Press, 2018.

Crescas, Hasdai. *Or ha-Shem* [Hebrew: *Light of the Lord*]. Edited by Rabbi Shlomo Fisher. Jerusalem: Ramot, 1990.

Curley, Edwin. *Spinoza's Metaphysics: An Essay in Interpretation*. Cambridge, MA: Harvard University Press, 1969.

De Rijk, L. M. *Logica Modernorum. A Contribution to the History of Early Terminist Logic I: On Twelfth Century Theories of Fallacy, II.1–2: The Origin and Early Development of the Theory of Supposition*. Assen: van Gorcum, 1962/1967.

Descartes, René. *Oeuvres de Descartes*. 12 vols. Edited by Charles Adam and Paul Tannery. Paris: J. Vrin, 1964–1976.

Descartes, René. *The Philosophical Writings of Descartes*. 3 vols. Translated by John Cottingham, Robert Stoothoff, and Dugald Murdoch. Cambridge: Cambridge University Press, 1985–1992.

Eichenstein, Tzevi Hirsh. *Sur me-R'a ve Ase Tov*. Bnei Brak: Mosdot Bnei Shloshim, 2011.

Gersonides. *The Logic of Gersonides: A Translation of Sefer ha-Heqqesh ha-Yashar The Book of the Correct Syllogism*. Introduction, commentary, and analytical glossary by Charles H. Manekin. Dordrecht: Kluwer, 1992.

Gersonides. *Milhamot ha-Shem*. Riva di Trento, 1560.

Gersonides. *The Wars of the Lord*. 3 vols. Translated by Seymour Feldman. Philadelphia, PA: Jewish Publication Society, 1984–1999.

Hegel, G. W. F. *Encyclopedia of Philosophical Sciences in Outline. First Part: Science of Logic*. Translated and edited by D. Dahlstrom and K. Brinkmann. Cambridge: Cambridge University Press, 2010.

Hegel, G. W. F. *Science of Logic*. Translated and edited by G. di Giovanni. Cambridge: Cambridge University Press, 2010.

Hegel, G. W. F. *Wissenschaft der Logik. Erster Band: Die Objektive Logik* (1812). In Hegel, *Gesammelte Werke*, edited by Rheinisch-Westfälische Akademie der Wissenschaften, vol. 11. Hamburg: Meiner, 1968.

Henrich, D. "Hegels Theorie über den Zufall." In *Hegel im Kontext*, 157–186. Frankfurt am Main: Suhrkamp, 2003.

Hobbes, Thomas. *Leviathan*. Edited by Noel Malcolm. Oxford: Clarendon Press, 2012.

Houlgate, S. "Necessity and Contingency in Hegel's *Science of Logic*." *Owl of Minerva* 27 (1995): 37–49.

Hume, David. *Dialogues concerning Natural Religion* (1779). Edited by Dorothy Coleman. Cambridge: Cambridge University Press, 2007.

Hume, David. *An Enquiry concerning Human Understanding: A Critical Edition*. Edited by Tom L. Beauchamp. Oxford: Clarendon Press, 2000.

Hume, David. *A Treatise of Human Nature: A Critical Edition*. Vol. 1. Edited by David Fate Norton and Mary J. Norton. Oxford: Clarendon Press, 2007.

John Buridan. *Quaestiones super libros* De generatione et corruptione *Aristotelis*. Edited by Michiel Sreijver, Paul Backer, and Johannes Thiessen. Leiden: Brill, 2010.

John Buridan. *Quaestiones super octo Physicorum libros Aristotelis*. Paris, 1509.

John Buridan. *Tractatus de consequentiis*. Edited by H. Hubien. Louvain: Publications Universitaires, 1976.

John Buridan. *Treatise on Consequences*. Translated by Stephen Read. New York: Fordham University Press, 2015.

John Duns Scotus. *Contingency and Freedom: Lectura I.39*. Introduction, translation and commentary by Antoine Vos, Henry Veldhuis, Aline Looman-Graaskamp, Eef Dekker, and Nico den Bok. Dordrecht: Kluwer, 1994.

John Duns Scotus. *Opera omnia*. Edited by Commissio Scotistica. Vatican City: Typis Polyglottis Vaticanis, 1950– .

John Duns Scotus. *Quaestiones super libros Metaphysicorum Aristotelis libri VI–IX*. Edited by Robert Andrews. St. Bonaventure: Franciscan Institute, St. Bonaventure University, 1997.

John Duns Scotus. *Tractatus de primo principio/Abhandlung über das erste Prinzip*. Edited with translation and notes by Wolfgang Kluxen. Darmstadt: Wissenschaftliche Buchgesellschaft, 1974.

John of Jandun. *In libros Aristotelis De caelo et mundo quae extant quaestiones*. Venice, 1552.

John of Jandun. *Quaestiones in duodecim libros Metaphysicae*. Venice, 1525.

Kant, Immanuel. *Critique of Pure Reason*. Edited and translated by P. Guyer and A. Wood. Cambridge: Cambridge University Press, 1998.

Kant, Immanuel. *Critique of the Power of Judgment*. Edited by Paul Guyer. Translated by Paul Guyer and Eric Matthews. Cambridge: Cambridge University Press, 2000.

Kant, Immanuel. *Lectures on Logic*. Edited by J. Michael Young. Cambridge: Cambridge University Press, 2004.

Lambert of Auxerre (?). *Logica*. Edited by F. Alessio. Florence: La Nuova Italia Editrice, 1971.

Leibniz, G. W. *Confessio Philosophi: Papers concerning the Problem of Evil, 1671–1678*. Translated and edited by Robert C. Sleigh Jr. New Haven, CT: Yale University Press, 2005.

Leibniz, G. W. *Essais de Théodicée*. Vol. 6 of *Die philosophischen Schriften*. Edited by C. I. Gerhardt. Berlin, 1885.

Leibniz, G. W. *The Labyrinth of the Continuum: Writings on the Continuum Problem, 1672–1686*. Translated and edited by Richard T. W. Arthur. New Haven, CT: Yale University Press, 2001.

Leibniz, G. W. *Philosophical Essays*. Edited and translated by Roger Ariew and Daniel Garber. Indianapolis, IN: Hackett, 1989.

Leibniz, G. W. *Philosophical Papers and Letters*. Translated and edited by Leroy E. Loemker. Dordrecht: Kluwer, 1989.

Leibniz, G. W. *Sämtliche Schriften und Briefe*. Deutsche Akademie der Wissenschaften. Multiple volumes in 7 series. Berlin: Akademie Verlag, 1923–.

Leibniz, G. W. *Textes inédits*. 2 vols. Edited by Gaston Grua. Paris: PUF, 1995.

Leibniz, G. W. *Theodicy: Essays on the Goodness of God, the Freedom of Man, and the Origin of Evil*. Translated by E. M. Huggard. Chicago: Open Court, 1985.

Lipshitz, Ya'akov. *Sh'arei Gan Eden*. Reprint ed. New York: 1994.

Locke, John. *An Essay concerning Human Understanding*. Edited by P. H. Nidditch. Oxford: Clarendon Press, 1975.

Maimonides, Moses. *Guide of the Perplexed*. 2 vols. Translated by Shlomo Pines. Chicago: University of Chicago Press, 1963.

Maimonides, Moses. *A Maimonides Reader*. Edited by I. Twersky. Springfield, NJ: Behrman House, 1972.

Malebranche, Nicholas. *Search after Truth*. Translated and edited by Thomas Lennon and Paul Olscamp. Cambridge: Cambridge University Press, 1997.

Peter, Abelard. *Dialectica*. Edited by L. M. de Rijk. Assen: Van Gorcum, 1956.

Peter Abelard. *Glossae super Perihermeneias*. Edited by Klaus Jacobi and Christian Strub. Corpus Christianorum Continuatio Mediaevalis 206. Turnhout: Brepols, 2010.

Peter Lombard. *Sententiae in IV libris distinctae, I–II*. Grottaferrata: Editiones Collegii S. Bonaventurae ad Claras Aquas, 1971.

Peter of Poitiers. *Sententiae I*. Edited by Philip S. Moore and Marthe Dulong. Notre Dame, IN: University of Notre Dame Press, 1961.

Peter of Spain. *Tractatus called afterwards Summule logicales*. Edited by L. M. de Rijk. Assen: Van Gorcum, 1972.

Poppers, Meir, ed. *Derekh 'Etz Hayyim*. Jerusalem: Yerid ha-Sfarim, 2013.

Richard, Sophista. *Abstractiones*. Edited by Mary Sirridge and Sten Ebbesen with E. J. Ashworth. Auctores Britannici Medii Aevi 25. Oxford: Oxford University Press for the British Academy, 2016.

Robert Grosseteste. *De libero arbitrio* in Neil Lewis, "The First Recension of Robert Grosseteste's *De libero arbitrio*." *Mediaeval Studies* 53 (1991): 1–88.

Robert Kilwardby. *Notule libri Priorum*. 2 vols. Edited by Paul Thom and John Scott. Auctores Britannici Medii Aevi 23. Oxford: Oxford University Press for the British Academy, 2016.

Roger Bacon. *Summulae dialecticae*. Edited by Alain de Libera. *Archives de␣h'histoire doctrinale et littéraire du moyen âge* 53 (1986): 139–289; 54 (1987): 171–278.

Shapiro, Pinhas. *Imrei Pinhas*. 2 vols. Edited by E. E. Frankel. Bnei Brak: Zol Sefer Press, 2003.

Siger of Brabant. *Quaestiones in Metaphysicam*. Edited by William Dunphy. Louvain-la-Neuve: Éditions de l'Institut Supérieur de Philosophie, 1981.

Spinoza, Benedict. *The Collected Works of Spinoza*. 2 vols. Edited and translated by Edwin Curley. Princeton, NJ: Princeton University Press, 1985/2016.

Spinoza, Benedict. *The Vatican Manuscript of Spinoza's Ethics*. Edited by Leen Spruit and Pina Totaro. Leiden: Brill, 2011.

Spinoza, Benedict. *Opera*. 4 vols. Edited by Carl Gebhardt. Heidelberg: Carl Winter, 1925.

Suárez, Francisco. *On Efficient Causality: Metaphysical Disputations 17, 18, and 19*. Translated by Alfred Freddoso. New Haven, CT: Yale University Press, 1994.

William of Ockham. *Summa logicae*. Edited by Philotheus Boehner, Gideon Gál, and Stephen Brown. Guillelmi de Ockham Opera philosophica I. St. Bonaventure: Franciscan Institute of St. Bonaventure University, 1974.

William of Sherwood. *Introductiones in logicam*. Edited by Hartmut Brandt and Christoph Kann. Hamburg: Meiner, 1995.

William of Sherwood. *Introduction to Logic*. Translated with an introduction and notes by Norman Kretzmann. Minneapolis: University of Minnesota Press, 1966.

Literature since 1900

Abaci, Uygar. *Kant's Revolutionary Theory of Modality*. Oxford: Oxford University Press, 2019.

Abizadeh, Arash. "The Absence of Reference in Hobbes's Philosophy of Language." *Philosopher's Imprint* 15 (2015): 1–17.

Altmann, Alexander. "The Religion of the Thinkers." In *Religion in a Religious Age,* edited by S. D. Goitein, 35–45. Cambridge, MA: Association for Jewish Studies, 1974.

Anstey, Peter. *John Locke on Natural Philosophy*. Oxford: Oxford University Press, 2011.

Anstey, Peter. "Locke and the Problem of Necessity in Early Modern Philosophy." In *Logical Modalities from Aristotle to Carnap: The Story of Necessity*, edited by Max Cresswell, Edwin Mares, and Adriane Rini, 174–193. Cambridge: Cambridge University Press, 2016.

Ashworth, E. J. "'Do Words Signify Ideas or Things?' The Scholastic Sources of Locke's Theory of Language." *Journal of the History of Philosophy* 19 (1981): 299–326.

Bader, Ralf. "Kant and the Categories of Freedom." *British Journal for the History of Philosophy* 17 (2009): 799–820.

Barcan Marcus, Ruth. "Dispensing with Possibilia." *Proceedings and Addresses of the American Philosophical Association* 49 (1975–1976): 39–51.

Barcan Marcus, Ruth. "A Functional Calculus of First Order Based on Strict Implication." *Journal of Symbolic Logic* 11 (1946): 1–16.

Barcan Marcus, Ruth. "The Identity of Individuals in a Strict Functional Calculus of Second Order." *Journal of Symbolic Logic* 12 (1947): 12–15.

Barcan Marcus, Ruth. "Interpreting Quantification." *Inquiry* 5 (1962): 252–259.

Barcan Marcus, Ruth. *Modalities: Philosophical Essays*. New York: Oxford University Press, 1993.

Barcan Marcus, Ruth, and Michael Frauchiger. "Interview with Ruth Barcan Marcus." In *Modalities, Identity, Belief, and Moral Dilemmas: Themes from Barcan Marcus*, edited by Michael Frauchiger, 147–166. Berlin: De Gruyter: 2015.

Barnes, Jonathan. *Truth, etc.: Six Lectures on Ancient Logic*. Oxford: Clarendon Press, 2007.

Becker, Albrecht. *Die Aristotelische Theorie der Möglichkeitsschlüsse*. Berlin: Junker und Dünnhaupt, 1933.

Beebee, Helen. *Hume on Causation*. New York: Routledge, 2006.

Bell, Clive. *Art*. New York: Frederick A. Stokes, 1914.

Belo, Catarina. *Chance and Determinism in Avicenna and Averroes*. Leiden: Brill. 2007.

Bennett, Jonathan. *Learning from Six Philosophers: Descartes, Spinoza, Leibniz, Locke, Berkeley, Hume*. 2 vols. Oxford: Clarendon Press, 2001.

Bennett, Jonathan. *A Study of Spinoza's Ethics*. Indianapolis, IN: Hackett, 1984.

Berto, Francesco, R. French, G. Priest, and D. Ripley. "Williamson on Counterpossibles." *Journal of Philosophical Logic* 47 (2018): 693–713.

Berto, Francesco, and Mark Jago. *Impossible Worlds*. Oxford: Oxford University Press, 2013.

Blackburn, Simon. *Essays in Quasi-Realism*. New York: Oxford University Press, 1993.

Blecher, Ian. "Kant on Formal Modality." *Kant-Studien* 104 (2013): 44–62.

Blecher, Ian. "Kant's Principles of Modality." *European Journal of Philosophy* 26 (2018): 932–944.

Bobzien, Susanne. "Chrysippus' Modal Logic and Its Relation to Philo and Diodorus." In *Dialektiker und Stoiker: Zur Logik der Stoa und ihrer Vorläufer*, edited by K. Döring and T. Ebert, 63–84. Stuttgart: Franz Steiner Verlag, 1993.

Bobzien, Susanne. *Determinism and Freedom in Stoic Philosophy*. Oxford: Oxford University Press, 1998.

Bobzien, Susanne. "Logic: The 'Megarics' and the Stoics." In *The Cambridge History of Hellenistic Philosophy*, edited by K. Algra, Jonathan Barnes, and Jaap Mansfeld, 83–157. Cambridge: Cambridge University Press, 1999.

Bovey, Gaétan. "Essence, Modality, and Intrinsicality." *Synthese* 198 (2021): 7715–7737.

Brenner, H. "Eine vollständige Formalisierung der aristotelischen Notwendigkeitssyllogistik." In *Beiträge zum Satz vom Widerspruch und zur Aristotelischen Prädikationstheorie*, edited by N. Öffenberger and M. Skarica, 333–356. Hildesheim: Olms, 2000.

Brogaard, Berit, and Joe Salerno. "A Counterfactual Account of Essence." Edited by Jon Williamson. *The Reasoner* 1, no. 4 (2007): 4–5.

Brogaard, Berit, and Joe Salerno. "Remarks on Counterpossibles." *Synthese* 190 (2013): 639–660.
Brown, Gregory, and Yual Chiek. *Leibniz on Compossibility and Possible Worlds*. Cham, Switzerland: Springer, 2016.
Brown, Nahum. *Hegel on Possibility: Dialectics, Contradiction, and Motion*. London: Bloomsbury, 2020.
Brown, Nahum. *Hegel's Actuality Chapter of the Science of Logic: A Commentary*. Lanham, MD: Lexington Books, 2018.
Burbidge, John W. "The Necessity of Contingency." In *Hegel's Systematic Contingency*, 16–47. New York: Palgrave Macmillan, 2007.
Chappell, Vere, ed. *The Cambridge Companion to Locke*. Cambridge: Cambridge University Press, 1994.
Chellas, Brian. *Modal Logic: An Introduction*. Cambridge: Cambridge University Press, 1980.
Cerbone, David. "Composition and Constitution: Heidegger's Hammer." *Philosophical Topics* 27 (1999): 309–329.
Chignell, Andrew. "Real Repugnance and Belief about Things-in-Themselves: A Problem and Kant's Three Solutions." In *Kant's Moral Metaphysics,* edited by J. Krueger and B. Bruxvoort Lipscomb, 177–209. Berlin: Walter DeGruyter, 2010.
Chignell, Andrew. "Real Repugnance and Our Ignorance of Things-in-Themselves: A Lockean Problem in Kant and Hegel." *Internationales Jahrbuch des Deutschen Idealismus* 7 (2011): 135–159.
Cooper, John. "Hypothetical Necessity and Natural Teleology." In *Philosophical Issues in Aristotle's Biology,* edited by A. Gotthelf and J. G. Lennox, 243–274. Cambridge: Cambridge University Press, 1987.
Cornford, F. M. *Plato's Cosmology: The* Timaeus *of Plato*. London: Routledge, 1935.
Correia, Fabrice. "(Finean) Essence and (Priorean) Modality." *Dialectica* 61 (2007): 63–84.
Coventry, Angela. *Hume's Theory of Causation*. London: Continuum, 2006.
Coventry, Angela, and Alex Sager, eds. *The Humean Mind*. New York: Routledge, 2019.
Cowling, Sam. "The Modal View of Essence." *Canadian Journal of Philosophy* 43 (2013): 248–266.
Crivelli, Paolo. *Aristotle on Truth*. Cambridge: Cambridge University Press, 2004.
Crivelli, Paolo. "Truth in *Metaphysics* E 4." *Oxford Studies in Ancient Philosophy* 48 (2015): 167–225.
Crowell, Steven Galt. "Heidegger and Husserl: The Matter and Method of Philosophy." In *A Companion to Heidegger*, edited by Hubert Dreyfus and Mark Wrathall, 49–64. London: Blackwell, 2005.

Curley, Edwin, and Gregory Walski, "Spinoza's Necessitarianism Reconsidered."
In *New Essays on the Rationalists*, edited by Rocco Gennaro and Charles and
Huenemann, 241–262. New York: Oxford University Press, 1999.
Della Rocca, Michael. "Essentialism: Part 1." *Philosophical Books* 37 (1996): 1–20.
Della Rocca, Michael. "Essentialism: Part 2." *Philosophical Books* 37 (1996): 81–89.
Della Rocca, Michael. "If a Body Meets a Body: Descartes on Body-Body
Causation." In *New Essays on the Rationalists*, edited by Rocco Gennaro and
Charles Huenemann, 48–81. Oxford: Oxford University Press, 1999.
De Melo, Thiago Xavier. "Essence and Naturalness." *Philosophical Quarterly* 69
(2019): 534–554.
Denby, David A. "Essence and Intrinsicality." In *Companion to Intrinsic Properties*,
edited by R. Francescotti, 87–109. Berlin: De Gruyter, 2014.
de Rijk, L. M. "Some Thirteenth Century Tracts on the Game of Obligation I–II."
Vivarium 12 (1974): 94–123; 13 (1975): 22–54.
Diewald, Gabriele, and Elena Smirnova. "Paradigmaticity and Obligatoriness of
Grammatical Categories." *Acta Linguistica Hafniensia* 42 (2010): 1–10.
Di Giovanni, George. "The Category of Contingency in the Hegelian Logic." In
Art and Logic in Hegel's Philosophy, edited by W. E. Steinkraus, 179–200. Atlantic
Highlands, NJ: Humanities Press, 1980.
Divers, John. *Possible Worlds*. London: Routledge, 2002.
Ellis, Brian. *Scientific Essentialism*. Cambridge: Cambridge University Press, 2001.
Ernst, Germana. *Tommaso Campanella: The Book and the Body of Nature*.
Translated by David L. Marshall. Dordrecht: Springer, 2010.
Ernst, Germana, and Guido Giglioni, eds. *Il linguaggio dei cieli: Astri e simboli nel
Rinascimento*. Rome: Carocci, 2012.
Fine, Kit. "Acts, Events and Things." In *Proceedings of the 6th International
Wittgenstein Symposium*, 97–105. Vienna: Hölder-Pichler-Tempsky, 1982.
Fine, Kit. "Aristotle's Megarian Manoeuvres." *Mind* 120 (2011): 993–1034.
Fine, Kit. "Coincidence and Form." *Proceedings of the Aristotelian Society*, suppl. 82
(2008): 101–118.
Fine, Kit. "Compounds and Aggregates." *Noûs* 28 (1994): 137–158.
Fine, Kit. "A Counter-Example to Locke's Thesis." *The Monist* 83 (2000): 357–361.
Fine, Kit. "Essence and Modality." *Philosophical Perspectives* 8 (1994): 1–16.
Fine, Kit. "Identity Criteria and Ground." *Philosophical Studies* 173 (2016): 1–19.
Fine, Kit. "The Logic of Essence." *Journal of Philosophical Logic* 24 (1995):
241–273.
Fine, Kit. "Necessity and Non-Existence." In *Modality and Tense*, 321–354. Oxford:
Clarendon Press, 2005.

Fine, Kit. "The Non-Identity of a Material Thing and Its Matter." *Mind* 112 (2003): 195–234.

Fine, Kit. "Ontological Dependence." *Proceedings of the Aristotelian Society* 95 (1995): 269–290.

Fine, Kit. "A Puzzle concerning Matter and Form." In *Unity, Identity and Explanation in Aristotle's Metaphysics*, edited by T. Scaltsas, D. Charles, and M. L. Gill, 13–40. Oxford: Clarendon Press, 1994.

Fine, Kit. *Reasoning with Arbitrary Objects*. Oxford: Blackwell, 1985.

Fine, Kit. "Response to Fabrice Correia." *Dialectica* 61 (2007): 85–88.

Fine, Kit. "Senses of Essence." In *Modality, Morality, and Belief: Essays in Honor of Ruth Barcan Marcus*, edited by Walter Sinnott-Armstrong, Diana Raffman, and Nicholas Asher, 53–73. New York: Cambridge University Press, 1995.

Fine, Kit. "Things and Their Parts." *Midwest Studies in Philosophy* 23 (1999): 61–74.

Fine, Kit. "Towards a Theory of Part." *Journal of Philosophy* 107 (2010): 559–589.

Fine, Kit. "Unified Foundations for Essence and Ground." *Journal of the American Philosophical Association* 1, no. 2 (Summer 2015): 296–311.

Fine, Kit. "The Varieties of Necessity." In *Conceivability and Possibility*, edited by Tamar Szabo Gendler and John Hawthorne, 235–260. Oxford: Oxford University Press, 2002.

Fisher, A. R. J. "Causal and Logical Necessity in Malebranche's Occasionalism." *Canadian Journal of Philosophy* 41 (2011): 523–548.

Føllesdal, Dagfinn. "Quine on Modality." In *The Cambridge Companion to Quine*, edited by Roger Gibson, 200–213. Cambridge: Cambridge University Press, 2006.

Føllesdal, Dagfinn. "Ruth Marcus, Modal Logic and Rigid Reference." In *Modalities, Identity, Belief, and Moral Dilemmas: Themes from Barcan Marcus*, edited by Michael Frauchiger, 39–50. Berlin: De Gruyter, 2015.

Fortenbaugh, W. W., Pamela Huby, Robert Sharples, and Dimitri Gutas. *Theophrastus of Eresus: Sources for His Life, Writings, Thought and Influence*: Part One. Leiden: Brill, 1992.

French, R., P. Girard, and D. Ripley. "Classical Counterpossibles." *Review of Symbolic Logic* 15 (2022): 259–257.

Frost, Gloria "Thomas Bradwardine on God and the Foundations of Modality." *British Journal for the History of Philosophy* 22 (2014): 655–679.

Garber, Daniel. "How God Causes Motion: Descartes, Divine Sustenance, and Occasionalism." *Journal of Philosophy* 84 (1987): 567–580.

Garber, Daniel, and Béatrice Longuenesse, eds. *Kant and the Early Moderns*. Princeton, NJ: Princeton University Press, 2008.

Garrett, Don. *Nature and Necessity in Spinoza's Philosophy*. New York: Oxford University Press, 2018.

Garrett, Don. "Should Hume Have Been a Transcendental Idealist?" In *Kant and the Early Moderns*, edited by Daniel Garber and Béatrice Longuenesse, 193–208. Princeton, NJ: Princeton University Press, 2008.

Gaskin, Richard. *The Sea Battle and the Master Argument*. Berlin: de Gruyter, 1995.

Gelber, Hester. *It Could Have Been Otherwise: Contingency and Necessity in Dominican Theology at Oxford 1300–1350*. Leiden: Brill, 2004.

Glazier, Martin. "Essentialist Explanation." *Philosophical Studies* 174 (2017): 2871–2889.

Griffin, Michael V. *Leibniz, God, and Necessity*. Cambridge: Cambridge University Press 2013.

Griffin, Nicholas. *Russell's Idealist Apprenticeship*. Cambridge: Cambridge University Press, 1991.

Gueroult, Martial, *Spinoza II: L'âme*. Paris: Aubier-Montaigne, 1974.

Guyer, Paul. "Locke's Philosophy of Language." In *The Cambridge Companion to Locke*, edited by Vere Chappell, 115–145. Cambridge: Cambridge University Press, 1994.

Harries, Karsten. *Infinity and Perspective*. Cambridge, MA: MIT Press, 2011.

Harvey, Warren Zev. "Maimonides' Interpretation of Genesis 3:22" [Hebrew]. *Da'at* 12 (1984): 15–22.

Harvey, Warren Zev. *Physics and Metaphysics in Hasdai Crescas*. Amsterdam: J. C. Gieben, 1998.

Hattab, Helen. "Concurrence or Divergence? Reconciling Descartes's Physics with His Metaphysics." *Journal of the History of Philosophy* 45 (2007): 49–78.

Hausman, Alan. "Some Counsel on Humean Relations." *Hume Studies* 1 (1975): 48–65.

Heidegger, Martin. *Being and Time*. Translated by John Macquarrie and Edward Robinson. New York: Harper and Brothers, 1962.

Hintikka, Jaakko. *Time and Necessity: Studies in Aristotle's Theory of Modality*. Oxford: Oxford University Press, 1973.

Hoffmann, Tobias. *Creatura intellecta: Die Ideen und Possibilien bei Duns Scotus mit Ausblick auf Franz von Mayronis, Poncius und Mastrius*. Münster: Aschendorff, 2002.

Hoffmann, Tobias. "Duns Scotus on the Origin of the Possibles in the Divine Intellect." In *Philosophical Debates at Paris in the Early Fourteenth Century*, edited by Stephen Brown, Thomas Dewender, and Theo Kobusch, 359–379. Leiden: Brill, 2009.

Holden, Thomas. "Hobbes on the Function of Evaluative Speech." *Canadian Journal of Philosophy* 46 (2016): 123–144.

Holden, Thomas. *Hobbes's Philosophy of Religion*. Oxford: Oxford University Press, 2023.

Holden, Thomas. "Hume on Religious Language and the Divine Attributes." In *The Humean Mind*, edited by Angela Coventry and Alex Sager, 182–192. New York: Routledge, 2019.

Holden, Thomas. "Hume's Absolute Necessity." *Mind* 123 (2014): 377–413.

Holopainen, Toivo. *Dialectic and Theology in the Eleventh Century*. Leiden: Brill, 1996.

Honnefelder, Ludger. *Scientia transcendens: Die formale Bestimmung der Seiendheit und Realität in der Metaphysik des Mittelalters und der Neuzeit*. Hamburg: Meiner, 1990.

Hübner, Karolina. "Spinoza's Thinking Substance and the Necessity of Modes." *Philosophy and Phenomenological Research* 92 (2016): 3–34.

Hughes, George E. "The Modal Logic of John Buridan." In *Atti del Convegno internazionale di storia della logica: Le teorie delle modalità*, edited by Giovanna Corsi, Corrado Mangione, and Massimo Mugnai, 93–111. Bologna: CLUEB, 1989.

Hughes, George, and M. J. Cresswell. *A New Introduction to Modal Logic*. London: Routledge, 1996.

Huron, David. *Sweet Anticipation: Music and the Psychology of Expectation*. Cambridge: MIT Press, 2008.

Husserl, Edmund. *Logical Investigations*. 2 vols. Translated by J. N. Findlay. London: Routledge, 2005.

Imlay, Robert. "Hume on Intuitive and Demonstrative Inference." *Hume Studies* 1 (1975): 31–47.

Ingarden, Roman. *On the Motives Which Led Husserl to Transcendental Idealism*. Dordrecht: Springer, 2012.

Iwakuma, Yokio, and Sten Ebbesen. "Logico-Theological Schools from the Second Half of the 12th Century: A List of Sources." *Vivarium* 30 (1992): 173–215.

Johnston, Spencer. "Essentialism, Nominalism, and Modality: The Modal Theories of Robert Kilwardby and John Buridan." PhD diss., University of St. Andrews, 2015.

Judge, Jenny. "The Surprising Thing About Musical Surprise." *Analysis* 78, no. 2 (2018): 225–234.

Kail, P. J. E. *Projection and Realism in Hume's Philosophy*. Oxford: Oxford University Press, 2007.

Karger, Elizabeth. "John Buridan's Theory of the Logical Relations between General Modal Formulae." In *Aristotle's* Peri *Hermeneias in the Latin Middle Ages*, edited by Henk Braakhuis and C. Kneepkens, 429–444 Haren: Ingenium, 2003.

Kaufman, Dan. "Descartes's Creation Doctrine and Modality." *Australasian Journal of Philosophy* 80 (2002): 24–41.

Kemp Smith, Norman. *The Philosophy of David Hume*. London: Macmillan, 1941.

Kirchhoff, Raina. *Die Syncategoremata des Wilhelm von Sherwood: Kommentierung und historische Einordnung*. Leiden: Brill, 2008.

Kirk, G. S. *Heraclitus: The Cosmic Fragments*. Cambridge: Cambridge University Press, 1962.

Klement, Kevin. "Russell's Logical Atomism." In *The Stanford Encyclopedia of Philosophy*, edited by Edward N. Zalta. Spring 2020 edition. https://plato.stanford.edu/archives/spr2020/entries/logical-atomism/.

Knappik, Franz. "Hegel's Modal Argument against Spinozism: An Interpretation of the Chapter 'Actuality' in the *Science of Logic*." *Hegel Bulletin* 36 (2015): 53–79.

Kneale, William, and Martha, Kneale. *The Development of Logic*. Oxford: Clarendon Press, 1962.

Knuuttila, Simo. "Anselm on Modality." In *The Cambridge Companion to Anselm*, edited by Brian Davies and Brian Leftow, 111–131. Cambridge: Cambridge University Press, 2004.

Knuuttila, Simo. "Duns Scotus and the Foundations of Logical Modalities." In *John Duns Scotus: Metaphysics and Ethics*, edited by Ludger Honnefelder, Rega Wood, and Mechthild Dreyer, 127–143. Leiden: Brill, 1996.

Knuuttila, Simo. "Medieval Commentators on Future Contingents in *De nterpretation 9*." *Vivarium* 48 (2010): 75–95.

Knuuttila, Simo. "Medieval Modal Theories and Modal Logic." In *Handbook of the History of Logic*. Vol. 2: *Medieval and Renaissance Logic*, edited by Dov M. Gabbay and John Woods, 505–578. Amsterdam: Elsevier, 2008.

Knuuttila, Simo. "Medieval Theories of Modality." In *The Stanford Encyclopedia of Philosophy*, edited by Edward N. Zalta. Summer 2021 edition. https://plato.stanford.edu/archives/sum2021/entries/modality-medieval/.

Knuuttila, Simo. *Modalities in Medieval Philosophy*. London: Routledge, 1993.

Knuuttila, Simo. "Necessities in Buridan's Natural Philosophy." In *The Metaphysics and Natural Philosophy of John Buridan*, edited by Johannes Thiessen and Jack Zupko, 65–76. Leiden: Brill, 2001.

Knuuttila, Simo. "Time and Creation in Augustine." In *The Cambridge Companion to Augustine*, edited by David Vincent Meconi and Eleonore Stump, 81–97. Cambridge: Cambridge University Press, 2014.

Knuuttila, Simo. "Time and Modality in Scholasticism." In *Reforging the Great Chain of Being: Studies in the History of modal Ideas*, edited by Simo Knuuttila, 163–258. Dordrecht: Kluwer, 2010.

Knuuttila, Simo, and Taneli Kukkonen. "Thought Experiment and Indirect Proof in Averroes, Aquinas, and Buridan." In *Thought Experiments: Methodological and Historical Perspectives,* edited by Katerina Ierodiakonou and Sophie Roux, 83–99. Leiden: Brill, 2011.

Koistinen, Olli. "Spinoza's Modal Theory." In *Blackwell Companion to Spinoza,* edited by Yitzhak Y. Melamed, 222–230. Hoboken, NJ: Blackwell, 2021.

Koslicki, Kathrin. "Essence and Identity." In *Metaphysics, Meaning and Modality: Themes from Kit Fine,* edited by Mircea Dumitru, 113–140. Oxford: Oxford University Press, 2020.

Koslicki, Kathrin. *Form, Matter, Substance.* Oxford: Oxford University Press, 2018.

Koslicki, Kathrin. *The Structure of Objects.* Oxford: Oxford University Press, 2008.

Koslicki, Kathrin. "Towards a Neo-Aristotelian Mereology." *Dialectica* 61 (2007): 127–159.

Koslicki, Kathrin. "Varieties of Ontological Dependence." In *Metaphysical Grounding: Understanding the Structure of Reality,* edited by Fabrice Correia and Benjamin Schnieder, 186–213. Cambridge: Cambridge University Press, 2012.

Kramer, Jonathan. "Beyond Unity: Toward an Understanding of Musical Postmodernism." In *Concert Music, Rock, and Jazz since 1945: Essays and Analytical Studies,* edited by Elizabeth West Marvin and Richard Hermann, 11–33. Rochester, NY: University of Rochester Press, 1995.

Kripke, Saul. *Naming and Necessity.* Boston: Harvard University Press, 1980.

Kukkonen, Taneli. "Possible Worlds in the *Tahâfut al-falâsifa:* Al-Ghazâli on Creation and Contingency." *Journal of the History of Philosophy* 38 (2000): 479–502.

Kulstad, Mark A. "Leibniz, Spinoza and Tschirnhaus: Metaphysics à Trois: 1675–1676." In *Spinoza: Metaphysical Themes,* edited by O. Koistinen and J. Biro, 182–209. Oxford: Oxford University Press, 2003.

Kusch, Martin, and Juha, Manninen. "Hegel on Modalities and Monadology." In *Modern Modalities,* edited by S. Knuuttila, 109–177. Dordrecht: Kluwer, 1988.

Lagerlund, Henrik. *Modal Syllogistics in the Middle Ages.* Leiden: Brill, 2000.

Lambertini, Roberto. "Jandun's Question-Commentary on Aristotle's Metaphysics." In *A Companion to the Latin Medieval Commentaries on Aristotle's* Metaphysics, edited by Fabrizio Amerini and Gabrielle Galluzzo, 385–411. Leiden: Brill, 2014.

Landini, Gregory. *Russell.* New York: Routledge, 2011.

Lear, Jonathan. *Aristotle and Logical Theory.* Cambridge: Cambridge University Press, 1980.

Lee, Sukjae. "Necessary Connections and Continuous Creation: Malebranche's Two Arguments for Occasionalism." *Journal of the History of Philosophy* 46 (2008): 539–565.

Leech, Jessica. "Judging for Reasons: On Kant and the Modalities of Judgment." In *Kant and the Philosophy of Mind: Perception, Reason, and the Self*, edited by A. Stephenson and A. Gomes, 173–188. Oxford: Oxford University Press, 2017.

Leech, Jessica. "Kant's Material Condition of Real Possibility." In *The Actual and the Possible: Modality and Metaphysics in Modern Philosophy*, edited by M. Sinclair, 94–116. Oxford: Oxford University Press, 2017.

Leech, Jessica. "Kant's Modalities of Judgment." *European Journal of Philosophy* 20 (2012): 260–284.

Lewis, David. *Counterfactuals*. Oxford: Blackwell, 1973.

Lewis, David. "Forget about the 'Correspondence Theory of Truth.'" *Analysis* 61 (2001): 275–280.

Lewis, David. "New Work for a Theory of Universals." *Australasian Journal of Philosophy* 61 (1983): 343–377.

Lewis, David. *On the Plurality of Worlds*. Oxford: Basil Blackwell, 1986.

Lewis, David. "Dispositional Theories of Value." *Proceedings of the Aristotelian Society* Supplementary Volume 63 (1989): 113–137.

Lewis, David. *Philosophical Letters of David K. Lewis*. Vol. 1: *Causation, Modality, Ontology*. Edited by Helen Beebee and A. R. J. Fisher. Oxford: Oxford University Press, 2020.

Lightner, D. T. "Hume on Conceivability and Inconceivability." *Hume Studies* 23 (1997): 113–132.

Linsky, Bernard, and Edward N. Zalta. "In Defense of the Contingently Nonconcrete." *Philosophical Studies* 84 (1996): 283–294.

Linsky, Bernard, and Edward N. Zalta. "In Defense of the Simplest Quantified Modal Logic." *Philosophical Perspectives* 8 (1994): 431–458.

Lispector, Clarice. *A Cidade Sitiada* [The Besieged City]. Rio de Janeiro: Rocco, 1949.

Lispector, Clarice. *Água Viva* [Living Water]. Rio de Janeiro: Rocco, 1973.

Lispector, Clarice. *A Hora da Estrela* [The Hour of the Star]. Rio de Janeiro: Rocco, 1977.

Lispector, Clarice. *A Maçã no Escuro* [The Apple in the Dark]. Rio de Janeiro: Rocco, 1974.

Lispector, Clarice. *A Paixão Segundo G.H.* [The Passion According to G.H.]. Rio de Janeiro: Rocco, 1964.

Lispector, Clarice. *O Lustre* [The Chandelier]. Rio de Janeiro: Rocco, 1946.

Lispector, Clarice. *Perto do Coração Selvagem* [Near to the Wild Heart]. Rio de Janeiro: Rocco, 1944.

Lispector, Clarice. *Todos Os Contos* [The Complete Stories]. Edited by Benjamin Moser. Rio de Janeiro: Rocco, 2016.

Lispector, Clarice. *Uma Aprendizagem ou o Livro dos Prazeres* [An Apprenticeship or the Book of Pleasures]. Rio de Janeiro: Rocco, 1969.

Lispector, Clarice. *Um Sopro de Vida: Pulsações* [A Breath of Life: Pulsations]. Rio de Janeiro: Rocco, 1978.

Lispector, Clarice, . *Outros Escritos* [Other Writings]. Edited by Teresa Montero and Lícia Manzo. Rio de Janeiro: Rocco, 2005.

Livingstone-Banks, Jonathan. "In Defence of Modal Essentialism." *Inquiry* 60 (2017): 816–838.

Loeb, Louis. *Stability and Justification in Hume's Treatise*. New York: Oxford University Press, 2002.

Lorenz, Hendrik. "Understanding, Knowledge, and Inquiry in Aristotle," in *The Routledge Companion to Ancient Philosophy*, edited by J. Warren and F. Sheffield, 290–303. New York: Routledge, 2014.

Lloyd, Sharon, ed. *The Bloomsbury Companion to Hobbes*. London: Bloomsbury, 2013.

MacBride, Fraser, and Frederique Jannsen-Lauret. "Why Lewis Would Have Rejected Grounding." In *Perspectives on the Philosophy of David K. Lewis*, edited by Helen Beebee and A. R. J. Fisher, 66–91. Oxford: Oxford University Press, 2022.

MacIntyre, Alasdair. *Edith Stein: A Philosophical Prologue 1913–1922*. Lanham, MD: Rowman and Littlefield, 2006.

Maier, Anneliese. *Die Vorläufer Galileis im 14. Jahrhundert*. Rome: Edizoni di Storia e Letteratura, 1949.

Malink, Marko. "Aristotle on One-Sided Possibility." In *Logical Modalities from Aristotle to Carnap: The Story of Necessity*, edited by M. Cresswell, E. Mares, and A. Rini, 29–49. New York: Cambridge University Press, 2016.

Malink, Marko. *Aristotle's Modal Syllogistic*. Cambridge, MA: Harvard University Press, 2013.

Malink, Marko, and Jacob, Rosen. "Proof by Assumption of the Possible in *Prior Analytics* 1.15." *Mind* 122 (2013): 953–986.

Mares, E. D. "Who's Afraid of Impossible Worlds?" *Notre Dame Journal of Formal Logic* 38 (1997): 516–526.

Martin, Chistopher J. "Abaelard on Modality: Some Possibilities and Some Puzzles." In *Potentialität und Possibilität: Modalaussagen in der Geschichte der Metaphysik,* edited by Thomas Buchheim, Corneille Kneepkens, and Kuno Lorenz, 97–122..Stuttgart-Bad Canstatt: Frommann-Holzboog, 2001.

Marušić, Jennifer Smalligan. "Hume on Projection of Causal Necessity." *Philosophy Compass* 9 (2014): 263–273.

McDaniel, Kris. "Edith Stein: *On the Problem of Empathy.*" In *Ten Neglected Philosophical Classics*, edited by Eric Schliesser, 195–221. New York: Oxford University Press, 2014.

McDaniel, Kris. *The Fragmentation of Being.* Oxford: Oxford University Press, 2017.

McDaniel, Kris. "Heidegger's Metaphysics of Material Beings." *Philosophy and Phenomenological Research* 87 (2013): 332–357.

McDaniel, Kris. "Metaphysics, History, Phenomenology." *Res Philosophica* 91 (2014): 339–365.

McDonough, Jeffrey K., and Zeynep Soysal. "Leibniz's Formal Theory of Contingency." *Logical Analysis and History of Philosophy* 21, no. 1 (2018): 17–43.

McIntyre, Robert. "Language." In *The Bloomsbury Companion to Hobbes*, edited by Sharon Lloyd, 95–99. London: Bloomsbury, 2013.

McKirahan, R. D. *Principles and Proofs: Aristotle's Theory of Demonstrative Science.* Princeton, NJ: Princeton University Press, 1992.

McNamus, Denis. "Ontological Pluralism and the *Being and Time* Project." *Journal of the History of Philosophy* 51 (2013): 651–673.

Melamed, Yitzhak Y. "Eternity in Early Modern Philosophy." In *Eternity: A History,* edited by Yitzhak Y. Melamed, 129–167. Oxford: Oxford University Press, 2016.

Melamed, Yitzhak Y. "Hasdai Crescas and Spinoza on Actual Infinity and the Infinity of God's Attributes." In *Spinoza and Jewish Philosophy,* edited by Steven Nadler, 204–215. Cambridge: Cambridge University Press, 2014.

Melamed, Yitzhak Y. "'*Omnis determinatio est negatio*'—Determination, Negation and Self-Negation in Spinoza, Kant, and Hegel." in *Spinoza and German Idealism,* edited by Eckart Förster and Yitzhak Melamed, 175–196. Cambridge: Cambridge University Press, 2012.

Melamed, Yitzhak Y. "Spinoza, Althusser, and the Question of Humanism." In Spinoza issue of *Crisis & Critique* 8 (2021): 170–177.

Melamed, Yitzhak Y. "Spinoza's Deification of Existence." *Oxford Studies in Early Modern Philosophy* 6 (2012): 75–104.

Melamed, Yitzhak Y. *Spinoza's Metaphysics: Substance and Thought.* New York: Oxford University Press, 2013.

Melamed, Yitzhak Y. "Spinoza, Tschirnhaus et Leibniz: Qu'est un monde?" In *Spinoza/Leibniz: Rencontres, controverses, réceptions,* edited by Pierre-François Moreau, Raphaële Andrault, and Mogens Laerke, 85–95. Paris: Presses universitaires de Paris, 2014.

Menne, A. "Modalität (des Urteils)." In *Historisches Wörterbuch der Philosophie: Völlig neubearbeitete Ausgabe des "Wörterbuchs der Philosophischen Begriffe" von*

Rudolf Eisler, 13 vols., edited by J. Ritter, K. Gründer, and G. Gabriel, vol. 6, 12–16. Basel: Schwabe Verlag, 2007.

Menzel, Christopher. "The Possibilism-Actualism Debate." In *The Stanford Encyclopedia of Philosophy*, edited by Edward N. Zalta and Uri Nodelman. Spring 2023 edition.https://plato.stanford.edu/archives/spr2023/entries/possibilism-actualism/.

Menzel, Christopher. "Possibilism and Object Theory." *Philosophical Studies* 69 (1993): 195–208.

Millican, Peter. "Against the 'New Hume.'" In *The New Hume Debate*, 2nd edition, edited by Rupert Read and Kenneth A. Richman, 211–252. London: Routledge, 2007.

Millican, Peter. "Hume, Causal Realism, and Causal Science." *Mind* 118 (2009): 647–712.

Millican, Peter. "Hume's Fork and His Theory of Relations." *Philosophy & Phenomenological Research* 95 (2017): 3–65.

Millgram, Elijah. "Hume on Practical Reasoning." *Iyyun* 46 (1997): 235–265.

Modrak, D. K. W. *Aristotle's Theory of Language and Meaning*. Cambridge: Cambridge University Press, 2001.

Mondadori, Fabrizio. "The Independence of the Possible according to Duns Sctous." In *Duns Scot à Paris, 1302–2002*, edited by Olivier Boulnois, Elizabeth Karger, Jean-Luc Solère, and Gérard Sondag, 313–374. Turnhout: Brepols, 2004.

Moore, G. E. "Necessity." *Mind* 9 (1900): 289–304.

Moser, Benjamin. *Why This World: A Biography of Clarice Lispector*. New York: Oxford University Press, 2009.

Motta, G. *Die Postulate des empirischen Denkens überhaupt: Kritik der reinen Vernunft, A 218–235/B 265–287. Ein kritischer Kommentar*. Berlin: De Gruyter, 2012.

Motta, Giuseppe. *Kants Philosophie der Notwendigkeit*. New York: Peter Lang, 2007.

Nadler, Steven. "Malebranche on Causation." In *The Cambridge Companion to Malebranche*, edited by Steven Nadler, 112–138. Cambridge: Cambridge University Press, 2000.

Nadler, Steven. "'No Necessary Connection': The Medieval Roots of the Occasionalist Roots of Hume." *The Monist* 79, no. 3 (1996): 448–466.

Newlands, Samuel. "Backing into Spinozism." *Philosophy and Phenomenological Research* 93, no. 3 (2016): 511–537.

Newlands, Samuel. "The Harmony of Spinoza and Leibniz." *Philosophy and Phenomenological Research* 81, no. 1 (2010): 64–104.

Newlands, Samuel. "Leibniz and the Ground of Possibility." *Philosophical Review* 122, no. 2 (2013): 155–187.

Newlands, Samuel. *Reconceiving Spinoza*. Oxford: Oxford University Press, 2018.

Newlands, Samuel. "Spinoza's Modal Metaphysics." In *The Stanford Encyclopedia of Philosophy*, edited by Edward N. Zalta. Fall 2018 edition. https://plato.stanford.edu/archives/fall2018/entries/spinoza-modal/.

Newlands, Samuel. "Baumgarten's Steps toward Spinozism." *Journal of the History of Philosophy* 60, no. 4 (2022): 609–633.

Newman, Lex. "Locke on Knowledge." In *The Cambridge Companion to Locke's "Essay concerning Human Understanding,"* edited by Lex Newman, 313–351. Cambridge: Cambridge University Press, 2007.

Ng, Karen. "Hegel's Logic of Actuality." *Review of Metaphysics* 63 (2009): 139–172.

Nolan, Daniel. "Impossible Worlds: A Modest Approach." *Notre Dame Journal of Formal Logic* 38 (1997): 535–572.

Normore, Calvin. "Duns Scotus's Modal Theory." In *The Cambridge Companion to Duns Scotus*, edited by Thomas Williams, 129–160. Cambridge: Cambridge University Press, 2003,.

Ott, Walter. *Causation and Laws of Nature in Early Modern Philosophy*. Oxford: Oxford University Press, 2009.

Ott, Walter. "Hume on Meaning." *Hume Studies* 32 (2006): 233–252.

Ott, Walter. *Locke's Philosophy of Language*. Cambridge: Cambridge University Press, 2004.

Ott, Walter. "What Can Causal Claims Mean?" *Philosophia* 37 (2009): 459–470.

Owen, David. "Locke on Real Essence." *History of Philosophy Quarterly* 8 (1991): 105–118.

Parker, Rodney. *The Idealism-Realism Debate among Edmund Husserl's Early Followers and Critics*. Cham: Springer, 2021.

Parsons, Terence. "Ruth Barcan Marcus and the Barcan Formula." In *Modality, Morality, and Belief: Essays in Honor of Ruth Barcan Marcus*, edited by Walter Sinnott-Armstrong, Diana Raffman, and Nicholas Asher, 3–12. Cambridge: Cambridge University Press, 1995.

Pasnau, Robert. *Metaphysical Themes, 1274–1671*. Oxford: Oxford University Press, 2011.

Passmore, John. *Hume's Intentions*. New York: Basic Books, 1952.

Patterson, Richard. *Aristotle's Modal Logic: Essence and Entailment in the Organon*. Cambridge: Cambridge University Press, 1995.

Penner, Sydney. "Free and Rational: Suárez on the Will." *Archiv für Geschichte der Philosophie* 95, no. 1 (2013): 1–35.

Penner, Sydney. "Suárez (and Malebranche) on Necessary Causes." Unpublished manuscript, 2018.
Phemister, Pauline. "Real Essence in Particular." *Locke Studies* 25 (1990): 27–55.
Pines, Shlomo. "Notes on Maimonides' Views concerning Human Will." *Scripta Hierosolymitana* 6 (1960): 195–198.
Pippin, Robert. *Hegel's Realm of Shadows: Logic as Metaphysics in the Science of Logic*. Chicago: University of Chicago Press, 2018.
Posti, Mikko. "Divine Providence in Medieval Philosophical Theology, 1250–1350." PhD diss., University of Helsinki, 2017.
Powell, Lewis. "Speaking Your Mind: Expression in Locke's Theory of Language." *Protosociology* 34 (2017): 15–30.
Prior, A. N. "Diodoran Modalities." *Philosophical Quarterly* 5 (1955): 205–213.
Putnam, Hilary. "The Meaning of 'Meaning.'" *Minnesota Studies in the Philosophy of Science* 7 (1975): 215–271.
Quine, W. V. *Confessions of a Confirmed Extensionalist and Other Essays*. Edited by Dagfinn Føllesdal and Douglas Quine. Boston: Harvard University Press, 2008.
Quine, W. V. "Reference and Modality." In *From a Logical Point of View*, 2nd edition, 139–159. New York: Harper and Row, 1961.
Quine, W. V. "Review of 'An Inquiry into Meaning and Truth.'" *Journal of Symbolic Logic* 6 (1941): 29–30.
Quine, W. V. "Two Dogmas of Empiricism." In *From a Logical Point of View*, 20–46. Harper, 1963.
Read, Rupert, and Kenneth A. Richman, eds. *The New Hume Debate*. Revised edition. London: Routledge, 2007.
Redding, Paul. "The Role of Logic 'Commonly So-Called' in Hegel's *Science of Logic*." *British Journal of the History of Philosophy* 22 (2014): 281–301.
Reinach, Adolf. "On the Theory of Negative Judgment." In *Parts and Moments: Studies in Logic and Formal Ontology*, edited by Barry Smith. Munich: Philosophia Verlag, 1982.
Ritter, J., K. Gründer, and G. Gabriel, eds. *Historisches Wörterbuch der Philosophie: Völlig neubearbeitete Ausgabe des "Wörterbuchs der Philosophischen Begriffe" von Rudolf Eisler*. 13 vols. Basel: Schwabe Verlag, 2007.
Robinson, Lewis. *Kommentar zu Spinozas Ethik*. Leipzig: Meiner Verlag, 1928.
Rodney K. B. Parker. *The Idealism-Realism Debate among Edmund Husserl's Early Followers and Critics*. Cham, Switzerland: Springer Publishing, 2009.
Rodriguez-Pereyra, Gonzalo. "Descartes's Substance Dualism and His Independence Conception of Substance." *Journal of the History of Philosophy* 46, no. 1 (2008): 69–89.

Rosen, Jacob, and Marko Malink. "A Method of Modal Proof in Aristotle." *Oxford Studies in Ancient Philosophy* 42 (2012): 179–261.

Rosenkoetter, Timothy. "Non-Embarrassing Account of the Modal Functions of Judgment." In *Kant und die Philosophie in Weltbürgerlicher Absicht: Akten des Xi. Kant-Kongresses 2010,* edited by Margit Ruffing, Claudio La Rocca, Alfredo Ferrarin, and Stefano Bacin, 383–442. De Gruyter, 2013.

Russell, Bertrand. *The Collected Papers of Bertrand Russell.* Vol. 7: *Theory of Knowledge: The 1913 Manuscript.* George Allen and Unwin, 1984.

Russell, Bertrand. *An Essay on the Foundations of Geometry.* Cambridge: Cambridge University Press, 1897.

Russell, Bertrand. *The Philosophy of Logical Atomism.* Taylor and Francis, 2010.

Russell, Bertrand. *The Principles of Mathematics.* New York: W. W. Norton, 1996.

Salmon, Nathan. "The Logic of What Might Have Been." *Philosophical Review* 98 (1989): 3–34.

Schaffer, Jonathan. "Two Conceptions of Sparse Properties." *Pacific Philosophical Quarterly* 85 (2004): 92–102.

Schechtman, Anat. "Substance and Independence in Descartes." *Philosophical Review* 125, no. 2 (2016): 155–204.

Schmaltz, Tad. "From Causes to Laws." In *The Oxford Handbook of Philosophy in Early Modern Europe,* edited by Desmond Clarke and Catherine Wilson, 32–50. Oxford: Oxford University Press, 2011.

Shieh, Sanford. *Necessity Lost.* Oxford: Oxford University Press, 2019.

Skiles, Alexander. "Essence in Abundance." *Canadian Journal of Philosophy* 45 (2015): 100–112.

Sleigh, Robert C. *Leibniz and Arnauld.* New Haven, CT: Yale University Press, 1990.

Sorabji, R. *Necessity, Cause and Blame: Perspectives on Aristotle's Theory.* London: Duckworth, 1980.

Sowaal, Alice. "Cartesian Bodies." *Canadian Journal of Philosophy* 34, no. 2 (June 2004): 217–240.

Specht, R. "Modalität." In *Historisches Wörterbuch der Philosophie: Völlig neubearbeitete Ausgabe des "Wörterbuchs der Philosophischen Begriffe" von Rudolf Eisler,* 13 vols., edited by J. Ritter, K. Gründer, and G. Gabriel, vol. 6, 9–12. Basel: Schwabe Verlag, 2007.

Spruit, Joke. "Thirteenth-Century Discussions on Modal Terms." *Vivarium* 32 (1994): 196–226.

Stalnaker, Robert C. "A Theory of Conditionals." In *Studies in Logical Theory,* edited by N. Rescher, 98–112. Oxford: Blackwell, 1968.

Stang, Nicholas F. "Determinacy, Contradiction, Movement: Towards a Reading of Hegel's Logic." Unpublished manuscript, 2023.

Stang, Nicholas F. "Hermann Cohen and Kant's Concept of Experience." In *Philosophie und Wissenschaft bei Hermann Cohen/Philosophy and Science in Hermann Cohen,* edited by Christian Damböck, 13–40. Cham: Springer Verlag, 2018.

Stang, Nicholas F. "Kant and the Concept of an Object." *European Journal of Philosophy* 29 (2021): 299–322.

Stang, Nicholas F. *Kant's Modal Metaphysics.* Oxford: Oxford University Press, 2016.

Stang, Nicholas F. "With What Must Transcendental Philosophy Begin? Kant and Hegel on Nothingness and Indeterminacy." In *Kantian Legacies in German Idealism,* edited by G. Gentry, 102–134. London: Routledge, 2021.

Stein, Edith. *Finite and Eternal Being.* Translated by Kurt F. Reinhardt. Washington, DC: ISC, 2002.

Stein, Edith. *Life in a Jewish Family.* Translated by Josephine Koeppel. Washington, DC: ICS, 1986.

Strawson, Galen. "David Hume: Objects and Power." In *The New Hume Debate,* revised edition, edited by Rupert Read and Kenneth A. Richman, 31–51. London: Routledge, 2007.

Strawson, Galen. *The Secret Connexion.* Oxford: Clarendon Press, 1989.

Street, Tony, and Nadja Germann. "Arabic and Islamic Philosophy of Language and Logic." In *The Stanford Encyclopedia of Philosophy,* edited by Edward N. Zalta. Spring 2021 edition. https://plato.stanford.edu/archives/spr2021/entries/arabic-islamic-language/.

Striker, Gisela. *Aristotle's Prior Analytics: Book 1.* Oxford: Clarendon Press, 2009.

Striker, Gisela. "Modal vs. Assertoric Syllogistic." *Ancient Philosophy* 14 (1994): 39–51.

Stroud, Barry. *Hume.* London: Routledge, 1977.

Sylla, Edith D. "*Ideo quasi mendicare oportet intellectum humanum*: The Role of Theology in John Buridan's Natural Philosophy." In *The Metaphysics and Natural Philosophy of John Buridan,* edited by Johannes Thiessen and Jack Zupko, 221–245. Leiden: Brill, 2001.

Teller, Paul. "Essential Properties: Some Problems and Conjectures." *Journal of Philosophy* 72, no. 9 (May 8, 1975): 233–248.

Thom, Paul. *Logic and Ontology in the Syllogistic of Robert Kilwardby.* Leiden: Brill, 2007.

Thom, Paul. *Medieval Modal Systems: Problems and Concepts.* Aldershot: Ashgate, 2003.

Thomasson, Amie. "Non-Descriptivism about Modality: A Brief History and Revival." *Baltic International Yearbook of Cognition, Logic and Communication* 4 (2009): 1–26.

Tolley, Clinton. "The Subject in Hegel's Absolute Idea." *Hegel Bulletin* 40 (2019): 143–173.

Torza, Alessandro. "Speaking of Essence." *Philosophical Quarterly* 65 (2015): 754–771.

Touati, Charles. *La pensée philosophique et théologique de gersonide*. Paris: Édition de minuit, 1973.

Uckelman, Sarah. "Modalities in Medieval Logic." PhD diss., University of Amsterdam, 2009.

van Benthem, J. "Correspondence Theory." In *Handbook of Philosophical Logic*, edited by D. Gabbay. and F. Guenthner, 167–247. Synthese Library, vol. 165. Dordrecht: Springer, 1984.

Vander Laan, David. "Counterpossibles and Similarity." In *Lewisian Themes: The Philosophy of David K. Lewis*, edited by F. Jackson and G. Priest, 258–275. Oxford: Oxford University Press, 2004.

Van Inwagen, Peter, and Meghan, Sullivan. "Metaphysics." In *The Stanford Encyclopedia of Philosophy,* edited by Edward N. Zalta. Spring 2020 edition. https://plato.stanford.edu/archives/spr2020/entries/metaphysics/.

van Rijen, Jeroen. *Aspects of Aristotle's Logic of Modalities*. Dordrecht: Kluwer, 1989.

Walsh, Julie. "Malebranche, Freedom, and the Divided Mind." In *The Battle of Gods and Giants Redux*, edited by Patricia Easton, 194–216. Leiden: Brill, 2015.

Waterlow, Sarah. *Passage and Possibility: A Study of Aristotle's Modal Concepts*. Oxford: Oxford University Press, 1982.

Waxman, Wayne. *Kant and the Empiricists*. Oxford: Oxford University Press, 2005.

Weidemann, Hermann. (2014), *Aristoteles: Peri Hermeneias*, 3rd edn., Berlin: de Gruyter.

Weidemann, H. "Das sogenannte Meisterargument des Diodoros Kronos und der Aristotelische Möglichkeitsbegriff." *Archiv für Geschichte der Philosophie* 69 (1987): 18–53.

Wildman, Nathan. "Against the Reduction of Modality to Essence." *Synthese* 198 (2018): 1455–1471.

Wildman, Nathan. "How (Not) to Be a Modalist about Essence." In *Reality Making*, edited by Mark Jago, 177–196. Oxford: Oxford University Press, 2016.

Wildman, Nathan. "Modality, Sparsity, and Essence." *Philosophical Quarterly* 63, no. 253 (October 2013): 760–782.

Willard, Dallas. "Wholes, Parts, and the Objectivity of Knowledge." In *Parts and Moments: Studies in Logic and Formal Ontology*, edited by Barry Smith, 379–400. Munich: Philosophia Verlag, 1982.

Williamson, Timothy. "Bare Possibilia." *Erkenntnis* 48 (1998): 257–273.

Williamson, Timothy. "Counterpossibles in Semantics and Metaphysics." *Argumenta* 2 (2017): 195–226.

Williamson, Timothy. "Iterated Attitudes." *Proceedings of the British Academy* 95 (1998): 85–133.

Williamson, Timothy. *Modal Logic as Metaphysics*. Oxford: Oxford University Press, 2013.

Williamson, Timothy. *The Philosophy of Philosophy*. Oxford: Oxford University Press, 2007.

Wright, John P. *The Sceptical Realism of David Hume*. Minneapolis: University of Minnesota Press, 1983.

Yablo, Stephen. "Is Conceivability a Guide to Possibility?" *Philosophy and Phenomenological Research* 53 (1993): 1–42.

Yeomans, Christopher. "Hegel's Expressivist Modal Realism." In *The Actual and the Possible: Modality and Metaphysics in Modern Philosophy*, edited by M. Sinclair, 117–135. Oxford: Oxford University Press, 2017.

Yonover, Jason M. "Nietzsche and Spinoza." In *Blackwell Companion to Spinoza*, edited by Yitzhak Y. Melamed, 527–537. Hoboken, NJ: Blackwell, 2011.

Yrjönsuuri, Mikko. "Duties, Rules and Interpretations in Obligational Disputations." In *Medieval Formal Logic: Obligations, Insolubles and Consequences,* edited by Mikko Yrjöönsuuri, 3–34. Dordrecht: Kluwer, 2001.

Zalta, Edward. "Essence and Modality." *Mind* 115 (2006): 659–693.

Zalta, Edward. *Intensional Logic and the Metaphysics of Intensionality*. Cambridge, MA: MIT Press, 1988.

Zylstra, Justin. "Essence, Necessity, and Definition." *Philosophical Studies* 176 (2019): 339–350.

Index

For the benefit of digital users, indexed terms that span two pages (e.g., 52–53) may, on occasion, appear on only one of those pages.

Abarbanel, Yitzhak, 91
Abelard, Peter, 32, 34–35, 48–49
accident
    inseparable, 40–41
    necessary, 264
action, 12, 57–58, 73, 75, 89, 137
    necessary, 134, 177
    possible/permissible, 176, 213, 295–96
actuality, xxiv–xxv, 6–7, 38–39, 43, 44–46, 53, 108, 120, 171–77, 179–80, 182, 183–84, 185, 191–204, 224, 248, 260–61, 294–301
    actualization, 40, 176
adynaton, 4
aesthetics, 155–56, 165–66, 170, 207, 209–10
aeternitas. See eternity
aition, 18
Alexander of Aphrodisias, 22–23, 24, 25, 28, 87–88, 268
al-Ghazali, 31, 48, 114
anagkê and *anagkaion*, 1–3
    anagkê ex hypotheseôs, 3–4

analyticity, 232–35
Anaximander, 1–2
Anselm of Centerbury, 47–48
Aquinas, Thomas, 35–37, 39–41, 43–48, 50–51, 52–53, 138
Aristotle and Aristotelianism
    Categories, 18, 32
    De caelo, 8, 9, 11, 38–39, 40–41, 42–45, 47–48
    De interpretatione, 5–6, 11–13, 23–24, 32, 33–37
    essentialism, 232, 235
    Metaphysics, 2–3, 4, 6–7, 8, 26, 35–37, 43–46
    Posterior Analytics, 17–18, 20–21, 46–47
    Prior Analytics, 4–5, 7, 8, 13–17
Augustine, 47–48, 112–13, 114
Averroes, 35, 40–48, 52–53
Avicenna, 35, 45, 48, 89

Barcan-Marcus, Ruth, 221–22, 235–41, 242, 267–68

Boethius, 23–24, 32, 34–40, 43–47, 49, 108, 171–72
Buridan, John, 34–35, 40–41, 49, 52–54

Campanella, Tommaso, 55, 56
causation
   causal agent, 69–70
   causal necessity, 148–49, 150–51, 152–53, 154, 160, 161–62, 164, 165–66, 232
   causal powers, 150–51
   causal relation, 71–72, 73–74, 75, 207–8, 223
   causa sui, 203–4
   efficient, 133, 138
chimaera, 93
Chrysippus, 6–7, 27–30
cognition, 111–12, 173–74
   capacity of, xxi–xxii, 172–73, 181–82, 183–84, 204–5
conceivability, xviii, 152–53, 155–57, 160–61, 196, 203–5, 211
   principle, 156–57, 158–59
concept empiricism, 162
consistency
   formal, 124, 134
   self-, 204–5
contingency
   epistemic (E-), 93–94, 95–96, 97, 98, 99, 100, 102, 103–4
   real (TC-), 89, 95–96, 98, 99, 103–4, 108–9, 110–12
   genuine, 299–300
contradiction
   involvement of, 38–39, 93, 94–95, 97–98, 101, 124–25, 189–90
   principle of, 179–80, 197–98
cosmology, xviii, 1–2, 55–57, 146–47
counterfactual, 114, 209–10
   alternative, 37, 48–49
   logic of, 252–54, 255–56
   possibility, 27–28
   propositions, 52–53, 248, 249, 252–54, 255, 259–60, 262
counterpart, 248, 291–92

Crescas, Hasdai, xx, 86–87, 89, 90–92
Curley, Edwin, 85–86, 102–3, 104–5, 106–7, 109–11, 203–4

Dasein, 189–90, 227–28
Democritus, 1–2
demonstration
   inductive, 260–62
dependence
   mind dependence, 152–53, 157–58, 159, 170
Descartes, René, xx, 63–69, 92–93, 103–4, 116, 138, 140, 150–51, 156–57
determinism, 47–48, 85–86, 102–3, 104–5
Diodorus, Cronus, 6–7, 23, 24
   master argument, 12–13, 25, 26, 27–29
dispositions, 44–45, 150–51
   inferential, 148–49, 150–51, 160, 161–62, 169
divinity. *See* God
Dynamis and *dynaton*, 4–5, 6–7

eliminativism, 82–83, 231
energeia, 6–7
Epictetus, 25
Erkenntnis. *See* cognition
esse
   intelligibile, 50–51
   possibile, 50–51
essence
   anti-essentialism, 128–29, 292–93
   essentialism, xxiii, 53–54, 128–29, 211, 232, 235, 268, 292–93
   essential properties, 66, 67–68, 73–74, 75, 227, 263, 266, 269–70, 292–93
   essential truth, 227, 263–64, 267
   modal, 269–70
eternity, 99–100, 113, 140, 148, 226–27
Eudemus of Rhodes, 22, 23
expressivism, 164–68

fate and fatalism, xix, 11, 12–13, 27–28, 58, 59–60, 90, 170
Fine, Kit, xxii, 264, 267–74, 275–82, 284–93
finite modes, 102–4, 105–6, 107–8, 109, 110–12, 194

freedom, 27–30, 45, 47–48, 72–73, 85–86, 87–88, 91–92, 143, 177

Garrett, Don, 152–53
Gersonides, 88
Gilbert of Poitiers, 48–49
God
  action of, 132–34, 137
  attribute of, 91–92, 107–8, 133, 136, 166–67
  essence of, 97, 113–14
  existence of, 90–92, 101, 120, 135
  freedom of, 47–48
  intellect of, 50–51, 125, 139–40
  knowledge of, 88
  omnipotence of, 55, 56
  omniscience of, 48
  power of, 47–48, 138
  providence of, 48, 59–60
  volition of, 125, 138, 140–42
  will of, 59–60, 68, 70, 125–26, 128, 136, 138, 140, 142–43
  wisdom of, 60, 136, 137, 142–43
Grosseteste, Robert, 38–39, 48
grounding and ground, xx–xxi, xxiii–xxiv, 18–19, 20–21, 73–74, 119, 199–200, 284–85, 287–88
  in actuality, 200, 202–3
  in causation, 223
  in essence, 61–62, 68–69, 72, 73–74, 75, 79, 81, 82, 83–84, 224–25
  in God, 68, 125, 137–41
  ultimate, 119

harmony of things, 123
Hasidism, 144–45
Hebrew Bible, 90
Hegel, Georg Wilhelm Friedrich, 185–96, 204–5
  the Spinoza principle, 189–90
Heidegger, Martin, xxii, 221–22, 227–28
Heraclitus, 1–2
"Hesperus is Phosphorus," 242
Hobbes, Thomas, 166–68

Hume, David, xxi–xxii, 70
  An Enquiry concerning Human Understanding, 150–53, 162, 169
  Dialogues concerning Natural Religion, 165–66, 170
Husserl, Edmund, 224–27

idealism
  reductive, 139
identity, 197–98, 243–44, 245–46, 278, 283, 286–87, 290–91
  formal, 130
  genuine, 236, 242
imagination, x, 52–53, 111–12, 150–51, 154–61
impossibility, 4, 41, 43, 93–94, 156–57, 159, 252–62
incompossibility, 50, 139
inconceivability principle. *See* conceivability
independence, 51–52, 63, 64, 65, 204–5
infinity, 9, 51–52, 91–92, 96, 129–30, 131, 144–47
  infinite analysis, 121, 129–32
  infinite modes, 107–8, 109
intelligibility. *See* conceivability
intuition, 26, 127, 154–55, 181–82, 222–26, 227–28, 242, 244, 250–51
invariance, 31, 45–46, 48, 52–53

John of Jandun, 42–43, 47–48, 52–53
judgment, 160–62, 174–76, 207, 223, 273–74, 278–79
  Kant on, 178–81
  moral, 164–65

Kabbalah, 144–47
Kant, Immanuel, 174–92, 197–98, 204–5, 207–8, 221–22, 223–24
  Vermögen, 173–74, 176, 177
Kilwardby, Robert, 35, 40–41, 53–54
Koistinen, Olli, 106, 114
Kripke, Saul, 114, 128–29, 241–46

Laërtius, Diogenes, 1–2, 29
language
  modal, 148–49, 207–8, 218–19

Leibniz, Gottfried, 97–98, 114, 118–43
Lewis, David, 194–95, 221–22, 246–51, 252–53, 254–55, 269–71, 272–73
Lispector, Clarice, 294–301
Locke, John, 77–84, 167–68
logic
   deontic, 54
   epistemic, 54
   obligations, 38, 50, 52–53

Maimonides, Moses, 44–45, 87–88
Malebranche, Nicholas, 69–77
   "No Necessary Connection" argument, 70
Marušić Smalligan, Jennifer, 163–65
materialism, 243–44
"matter of propositions," 39
meaning. *See* semantics
Megarians, 23–27
metaphysics
   metaphysical explanation, 284–85
   metaphysical necessity (*see* necessity: metaphysical)
   metaphysical possibility (*see* possibility: metaphysical)
Millican, Peter, 155–56, 159, 164–65
modality
   analysis of, 119, 124, 125, 131, 230, 248–49
   de dicto, xxiii, 15–17, 33, 113, 265
   deontic, 210
   de re, xxiii, 15–17, 33, 113, 181–82, 263, 264, 265
   divided vs. compound, 33, 34–37, 53–54
   grounds of, 119, 139–40
   intentional, 47–53
   logical, xxi–xxii, 152–53, 172–73, 178, 179–80, 204–5
   modal consequences, 53
   modal distribution, xix, 119, 124, 135, 136, 194
   modal essence, 269–70
   modal features, xxiii–xxiv, 224–25, 229, 280–81
   modal judgment, 164–65
   modal profile, 64–66, 67–69, 70, 280–81
   modal realism, 152–53, 173–74, 221–22, 246–47, 250–51
   modal semantics (*see* semantics: modal)
   modal syllogistic, 13–17, 22, 34, 35, 40–41, 54
   modal truth (*see* truth: modal)
   modal truthmaker, 119
   statistic, 106, 108–9, 114–16

natural laws, 210–12
necessary connection, 62, 68, 71, 72–74, 75, 77, 78, 79, 80, 81, 223, 224–25
necessitarianism, xxi, 59–60, 85–87, 91–92, 126–27, 129
   strict, 86, 102–3, 104–5, 109–10, 115
   the necessitarian argument, 120–22, 128–32, 134, 136, 141, 142
necessity
   absolute, 3, 133–34, 148–57, 160–70, 177, 201–4
   abstract, 295
   causal, 148–49, 150–51, 152–53, 154, 160, 161–62, 164, 165–66, 232
   deontic, 207, 210–11, 212, 215
   deductive (*necessitas consequentis*), 3
   divine, 295
   free, 85–86
   genuine, 299–300
   hypothetical (*ex hypothesi*), 123, 124, 125–26, 127
   logical, 179–80
   metaphysical, 71–72, 133–34, 135, 137, 150, 209–12, 219–20, 232, 259–60
   moral, 121, 133–34, 135–37, 142–43
   musical, 208–9, 210–17, 219–20
   natural, 1–2, 210–11, 292–93
   nomological, 71–72, 210, 211, 215
   per accidens, 40–41
   per se, 40–41, 90–91, 123, 194
   practical, 295–96
Newlands, Samuel, 110–12
nominales, 49

obligation. *See* logic: obligation
occasionalism, 63, 69–70, 71–72, 74

Ockham, William of, 53–54
ontology, 232
  formal, 226–27
  modal, 93–94
order of nature (ordo naturae), 93, 103–7, 108–11, 114–15

Parmenides, 1–2
Peripatetics. *See* Aristotle and Aristotelianism
per se analysis, 121, 124, 125, 128–29, 141–42
phenomenology, 225–26
  phenomenological method, 224–25, 228
  realist, 226–27, 228
Philo of Megara, 23–25, 28–30, 165–67
Pinhas Shapiro of Koretz, 144
Plato and Platonism, 2, 24–25, 273–74
Porphyry, 32
possibilism, 238, 239
possible/possibility
  absolute, 47–48, 50–51, 156–57, 159, 202
  logical, 49–52, 180, 197–98, 231
  metaphysical, 134, 209–10, 211, 255
  partial, 44–45
  space, 140, 215–16
  unrealized, 37–39, 40–41, 44–45
possible worlds, xvii–xviii, xxiv–xxv, 50–51, 71, 102–3, 108, 109–10, 114, 209–10, 211, 253–55, 257, 258–59, 260
  Kripke on, 241
  Leibniz on, 118, 120, 124–26, 131, 134, 137, 140, 141–42
  Lewis on, 247–49, 252–53
potency, 47–48, 299–300
  active, 44–45
  unrealized, 44–45
potentiality, xxiv–xxv, 44–45, 171–72, 299–300
pre-Socratics, 1–2
principle of contradiction, 179–80, 197–98
principle of sufficient reason (PSR), 91–92, 101, 103, 199–200
providence. *See* God: providence of

quantifiers, 34–35, 235, 236, 237–38, 239, 240–41
Quine, W. V., 128–29, 232–35

reason
  divine, 133, 134, 136
  non-axiological, 133–34
  regularity, 59, 207–8, 232
Renaissance, 35–37, 55, 108, 211–12
representation
  immediate, 222
  mediate, 222
  relation of, 223
repugnance, 40, 49–52, 173–74
rigid designator, 241–42, 243–45
Russell, Bertrand, 228–32

Scotus, Duns, xix–xx, xxi, 31, 42, 49–53
semantics
  modal, 14, 42, 43, 47–49, 114, 128–29, 237–38
sensibility, xxi–xxii, 172–74, 179–80, 182, 183–84, 186–87, 191, 192, 204–5
set-theory, 276–77
Siger of Brabant, 45–46
simplicity, 55–56
sparse modalism, 268–79
Spinoza, Benedict, 92–116, 133–34, 139, 140, 188–90
  Cogitata Metaphysica, 92–93, 96, 116
  contingens reale, 95
  determinatio est negatio, 188–89, 201–2
  Ethics, 96, 97–98, 101, 103, 104–5, 106–7, 108–9, 116
  Opera Posthuma, 85–86
  Theological Political Treatise, 117
  Treatise on the Emendation of the Intellect, 94, 117
Stoics, xix, 27–28, 29–30, 45, 167–68
Suárez, Francisco, 72
substance, 183–84, 188–89, 194, 242, 280–81, 288–90, 292–93
synthetic *a priori,* 183–84, 224

Theophrastus, 22, 23
thinkability. *See* conceivability
thought-determinations, 186–91, 192, 194–96, 197, 198, 199–202, 203–4
time, 11–13, 283
　present time, 35–41, 106
transcendent, 177, 186–87, 192, 226–27, 283–90
　philosophy, 173–74
　specification, 284–86
truth
　analytic, 232–33, 249
　essential, 227, 263, 264, 267
　logical, 232–33, 256
　modal, xxiv–xxv, 119, 138, 139–40, 156–57, 263, 278
　non-modal, 264
　truth-maker, 119, 138, 139–40, 148–49, 248–49

unity, 55–57, 171–74, 192, 193, 199–200, 208–9, 286, 292–93

vacuism, 252–62
　non-vacuism, 253–55, 257, 258–60, 262
　quasi-vacuism, 258–59

Walski, Gregory, 102–3
Wildman, Nathan, 264, 268, 272–79